The Hierarchies of Slavery in Santos, Brazil, 1822–1888

The Hierarchies of Slavery in Santos, Brazil, 1822–1888

Ian Read

STANFORD UNIVERSITY PRESS
STANFORD, CALIFORNIA

Stanford University Press
Stanford, California

This book has been published with the assistance of Soka University of America.

Printed in the United States of America on acid-free, archival-quality paper

Library of Congress Cataloging-in-Publication Data
Read, Ian (Ian William Olivo), 1976- author.
The hierarchies of slavery in Santos, Brazil, 1822-1888 / Ian Read.
pages cm
Includes bibliographical references and index.
ISBN 978-0-8047-7414-7 (alk. paper)
1. Slaves--Brazil--Santos (São Paulo)--Social conditions--19th century.
2. Slaveholders--Brazil--Santos (São Paulo)--Social conditions--19th century.
3. Slavery--Social aspects--Brazil--Santos (São Paulo)--History--19th century.
4. Social status--Brazil--Santos (São Paulo)--History--19th century. 5. Santos (São Paulo, Brazil)--Social conditions--19th century. I. Title.
HT1129.S265R43 2012
306.3'62098161--dc23 2011040195

Typeset by Bruce Lundquist in 10/12 Sabon

For Elysia & Luciana
(*Per sentes ad astra*)

Contents

List of Tables

List of Figures

Acknowledgments

Many people deserve my gratitude in helping me research and write this book. Margaret Chowning, Zephyr Frank, Mark Granovetter, John Padgett, William Taylor, and John Wirth were most influential at the earliest stages. To Zephyr, in particular, I owe much.

I worked in Brazil for more than two years on this book, but thankfully I rarely felt alone. Without the enormously helpful staff and amazingly well-organized archives in Santos and São Paulo, I would have found far less than I did. Special gratitude goes to Rita Cerqueira and Roberto Tavares at the Fundação Arquivo e Memória de Santos. I hope they remain victorious in their campaigns against the silverfish, firebrats, and all other formidable challenges of archival work in the tropics. Early drafts of *Unequally Bound* were scrutinized by Roderick and Jean Barman, Stanley Engerman, Herbert Klein, Linda Lewin, Aldo Musacchio, Richard Roberts, Lisa Sibley, and two helpful anonymous readers. This group gave me lengthy comments to ponder and act upon. Now that their suggestions are integrated into nearly every page and paragraph, there is additional evidence that books like this are never solitary projects. I alone, however, am responsible for any mistakes.

Historical research, especially of a country that was often more than six thousand miles away, is not cheap. I owe much to the financial support provided by the Division of Social Sciences at the University of Chicago, and from three programs at Stanford University: the Center for Latin American Studies, the Social Sciences History Institute, and, especially, the School of Humanities and Sciences. The Department of Education provided a Foreign Language Areas Studies grant and a much needed Fulbright grant. Finally, my final year of studies was supported by generous funding from the Mrs. Giles Whiting Foundation.

I continued to work on this project part-time as I began two years of adjunct teaching at the University of Puget Sound and the University of California, Berkeley. Many colleagues at these two institutions helped me survive the juggling act that rookie academics face in their first few years out of graduate school. Since then, I am happy to have found a new community of supportive colleagues at my position in Latin American Studies at the Soka University of America. It is heartening to work with Sarah England, Ted Lowe, Lisa MacLeod, James Spady, Michael Weiner, and the many others who make such a tiny university remarkably cosmopolitan.

At Stanford University Press, Norris Pope, Sarah Crane Newman, and Mariana Raykov were always kind, professional, and accommodating. Mary Barbosa ran the manuscript through a fine-tooth comb, correcting many of my mistakes.

I would be in no place such as this without the loving and encouraging community of family and friends. In what is becoming the typical American family, we are scattered to the four winds but use every excuse and technology to maintain our bonds. For my parents and old friends in Chicago, my aunts and grandmother in Wisconsin, my brother and cousins in Georgia, my brother in New Hampshire, and my large, extended Italian American family in Northern California, my love. When my two daughters are old enough to read this book, I hope they realize the significance of not turning a blind eye to all that degrades and dehumanizes. Finally, it is largely owing to the grace of my wife, Chanelle, that I find myself in a career that motivates and a family that sustains the most important kind of expression.

Abbreviations

AESP	Arquivo do Estado de São Paulo (State of São Paulo Archive)
ANB	Arquivo Nacional do Brasil (National Archive of Brazil)
ASCMS	Arquivo da Santa Casa de Misericórdia de Santos (Santos Santa Casa de Misericórdia Archive)
BN	Fundação Biblioteca Nacional do Brasil (National Library of Brazil Foundation)
CCS	Coleção Costa e Silva (Costa e Silva Collection)
CDS	Curia Diocesana de Santos (Santos Diocese Curia)
FAMS	Fundação Arquivo e Memória de Santos (Foundation of the Archive and Memory of Santos)
FSS	Forum de São Sebastião (São Sebastião Forum)
HS	Hemeroteca de Santos (Santos Newspaper Archive)
MPCSP	Museu da Polícia Civil de São Paulo (São Paulo Civil Police Museum)
PCNS	Primero Cartório de Notas de Santos (First Notary Office of Santos)
SCNS	Segundo Cartório de Notas de Santos (Second Notary Office of Santos)

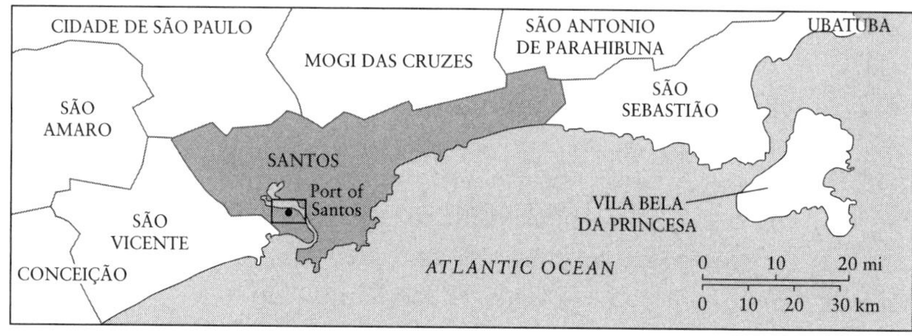

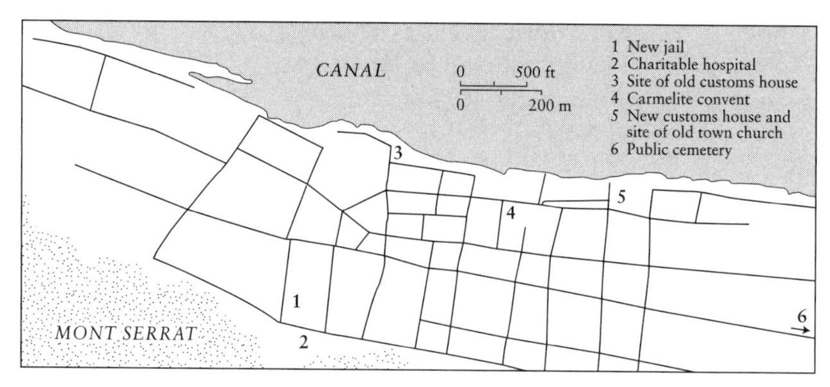

FIGURE 0.1

The Port of Santos Within Its Municipality and the Province of São Paulo

The Hierarchies of Slavery in Santos, Brazil, 1822–1888

Introduction

This book looks at slaves and masters in Santos, São Paulo, a sliver-shaped coastal township in southeastern Brazil. The period of study begins with Brazil's independence (1822), and ends when slavery was abolished (1888). I present evidence of differing slaves' conditions of life and work, their treatment, and most important, the causes for this variation. Some slaves may have been privileged relative to other slaves (and even relative to some free poor), but slaves belonged to the "most disadvantaged element in society" because they lacked basic citizenry and property-holding rights and were socially degraded by their categorization as chattel.[1] Nevertheless, the brutality that was endemic to slavery was not shared equally among slaves; this book seeks to explain why. Fundamentally, I argue that owners' status impacted on the options available to their slaves.[2] Slaves owned by masters with greater social and economic prestige stood a better chance of living healthier lives, working in relatively safer jobs, surrounding themselves with family and community, and even finding pathways out of slavery. For most other slaves, these paths remained unjustly blocked.

Many other historians have presented slaves as living in a hierarchical world, but few have collected information on how and to what degree changes in owner status affected the lives of slaves. For example, historians studying slave families in Brazil and the economics and demography of slavery have found that slaves lived and worked in a great range of environments.[3] As enslaved farmers twisted tobacco on small Bahian farms, trammers pushed wagons through the subterranean tunnels of Mineiro (Minas Gerais) gold mines, and palanquin-bearers hefted gilded carriages over the cobblestone streets of Rio de Janeiro, Brazilian slaves navigated their restrictive worlds in numerous ways. Furthermore, contemporary observers and the first historians of slavery never doubted that conditions varied, even widely so, but this was generally attributed to the different treatment slaves received and the places they lived.[4]

Today, scholars place nearly as much weight on the choices slaves made as they do on the behavior of their masters. It is now common to assert that bondspeople took steps semi-independently to form families or communities, to save for their manumission letters, or to resist some wish of authority. In fact, some slaves were able to profoundly change their lives, even though power within the master-slave relationship could hardly have been more unequal. This commonly accepted idea of limited autonomy does not conflict with the fact that masters treated their slaves in different ways, and while treatment could be indifferent, kind, or cruel depending on the character of a master or mistress, it also varied generally between groups of owners, depending on their status. Drawing inspiration from Eugene Genovese, "treatment" was the degree of freedom of choice, security, and access to legal pathways out of slavery given to slaves or their descendents. Day-to-day living conditions such as food, clothing, housing, and conditions of labor mattered enormously, but a small number of lucky slaves moved from bondage to nearly complete citizenship and lived full lives within sustaining communities.[5] The majority survived against awful odds.

Since the 1960s, historians of slavery have increasingly avoided the word *treatment* because it can give a misleading impression that slaves ultimately lacked agency.[6] Many scholars of slavery have questioned the idea that slaves' autonomy and decision making were always tempered by their owners' actions and preferences. Today the master-slave relationship is often seen as one of negotiation, albeit with vastly unequal terms.[7] For every ounce of agency that slaves had, masters had a pound, and the actions that owners directed at their slaves should be recognized as they were. Still, we need not deny that slaves had a minimal degree of autonomy of behavior in order to view *treatment* as the set of actions taken by masters toward their slaves.

In multiple ways, the life conditions that Santista (Santos) slaves faced were comparable to bondspeople in other parts of Brazil. Santos was a modestly sized coastal township with a port city connected to international trade, but it was not the center of commerce or political rule. Santista slaves were mostly traded locally and in small numbers, as they appear to have been elsewhere.[8] Marriage was closed to slaves except to those owned by mostly wealthy masters, yet childbirth was likely, irrespective of owner background or holding size.[9] Bondspeople were disproportionately targeted by the police for minor offenses, although physical punishments directed at slaves were removed from the town's legal code after 1850.[10] While the social environment presented risks, it was the physical environment where Santista slaves confronted their worst fears. In this they were not alone. Slaves throughout Brazil suffered terribly from and were killed by diseases such as tuberculosis, smallpox, and neonatal tetanus. If they were not killed by disease or injury, a small but fairly steady stream of slaves escaped bondage through manumission. As elsewhere in Brazil, it was mostly child and female slaves who received manumission letters that contained no burdensome stipulations.[11] Skilled working-age males, on the other hand, were the most likely to run away, just like their fugitive counterparts in Rio de Janeiro, Minas Gerais, and Pernambuco.[12] When emancipation approached in the mid-1880s, the Imperial government created an Emancipation Fund to hasten a gradual abolition process. Yet most of the funds were directed toward the wealthiest slave owners.[13] Santos was no different in the types of bondspeople chosen to be freed with this public money. There were other experiences that Santista slaves shared with most Brazilian slaves, but these examples suggest that the principal finding of this book—that slavery in Santos was sufficiently hierarchical such that opportunities for slaves were open or closed depending on owner position and treatment—existed within the larger system of slavery in Brazil.

Like all Brazilian townships, Santos also had characteristics that made it and the slaves who resided there unique. Climate, geography, and port commerce gave Santos much of its individuality. Its tropical climate was suitable for a particular set of agricultural goods that were often at the heart of slave toil in the region. Weather patterns differ along the Paulista (São Paulo) coast from those of the larger southeastern region, which included the provinces of São Paulo, Rio de Janeiro, and Minas Gerais. Coffee and cotton never became important crops in the township, while some common local products such as rice, ocean fish and seafood, and tropical fruits were rarely or never gathered beyond the coastal mountains. Geography also helped distinguish Santos in another way: it gave the township one of the only viable ports for a province roughly the size of New York and Pennsylvania combined. The port reaped the benefits as more and more transatlantic ships embarked carrying coffee and cotton, and manufactured goods arrived. The township was also close enough to both Rio de Janeiro and the city of São Paulo and big enough for some of its politicians to achieve prominence in the Imperial government.[14] Equal to its role as a coffee port, Santos was also an important immigrant's port. Its harbor was one of the main entry points for European and Asian men and families looking for work and new lives in the Americas during the late nineteenth and early twentieth centuries. Most of these immigrants merely passed through Santos, but thousands remained. Today, a large immigrants' hospice, now abandoned and in ruins, stands testament to their passage.[15] The European or Asian "colonists," as they were usually called, did not arrive in large numbers until the last few years of slavery in the 1880s, but those who stayed and worked in the city played a role in the abolition and Republican movements.

Many immigrants disembarked at Santos but rushed to escape fatal risks from "fevers." The biggest danger came from a set of infectious diseases confined to the coast that made the town infamous from the 1870s until the 1900s. Santos became so notorious for disease and epidemics that it was referred to as the "cemetery of the world," although it is yet to be proven whether health was worse there than in other Brazilian port cities. Much of the trouble was caused by the tiny *Aedis aegypti* mosquito, a common carrier of yellow fever, which thrived in Santos but died in the colder weather in and beyond the narrow band of coastal mountains.[16] Contemporaries drew numerous comparisons between the (allegedly) disease-ridden coast afflicted with yellow fever and the healthy highlands. Indeed, travelers and immigrants often rushed the arduous journey from boat, up and over the mountains, and into the highlands during epidemic years, yet the port's "unsanitary" conditions took the brunt of the blame when these individuals or families became sick and died en route.

An immigrant who arrived in Santos before 1880 and hurried from boat to train typically would have encountered slaves. Most bondspeople living in the township of Santos resided in the port city and should thus be classified as "urban slaves." Historians and contemporaries of slavery have traditionally drawn a sharp distinction between slaves who worked in cities and those who labored on farms. City slaves, especially *negros de ganho* (slaves for hire), are now generally perceived to have had much more autonomy than field slaves.[17] Analysis of these separate categories of bondspeople is rooted in earlier slave studies that focused on the typical plantation slave and the anomalous big-city slave. Recent research has shown, however, that the lives of slaves who labored for small landholders were more comparable to those of their free working-class neighbors than to the lives of large-plantation slaves, while bondspeople in Brazil's largest and richest cities such as Rio de Janeiro or Salvador lived in ways vastly different from slaves beyond these city limits.[18]

As Santos grew from a small town into a midsized city during the nineteenth century, it maintained connections to local agriculture despite the port's eventual prominence. For this reason, the lives of its enslaved residents do not comfortably fit into the urban-rural dichotomy that has long marked slave studies. For example, the town's only defined edge was its waterfront, while its broad backsides blurred into fairly populated semicircles of town homes and country houses, and blurred again into a zone of farms, fields, brush, and marsh. Townspeople often owned one home in town and another in the country, and their slaves moved between the two. Slave owners often rented out their slaves to households on the outskirts of town for tending small fields, feeding livestock, and performing a multitude of rural tasks. In these settings, Santos slaves may have had much in common with the majority of Brazilian slaves in hundreds of small- to moderately sized towns and villages in Brazil, who lived and worked in country settings but maintained urban connections. The few large cities such as Rio de Janeiro or Salvador would have struck Santista slaves (and most Brazilian slaves) with awe and bewilderment. Research is only beginning to look closely at this semiurban population. If Santos is representative, the line between urban and rural slaves may blur when the conditions of life and work display characteristics of both categories.

Santos shares an island with São Vicente, one of the oldest European settled towns in the Americas. Here, the first Portuguese explorers and colonists in Brazil built their homes and dug fields in the sixteenth century. In fact, this small part of the Brazilian coast was one of the first regions in the Americas to adopt slave labor as an engine to produce a commodity (sugar) for global markets. Although its economy turned inward after the seventeenth century, Santos and its neighboring townships remained far more dedicated to slavery than other parts of the captaincy or province until the middle part of the nineteenth century.[19] Only by the end of that century could some imaginative residents or visitors foresee the commanding position that Santos would attain in the national and world economy. Today Santos is home to about half a million residents and is one of the busiest ports in the world, serving as the entrepôt for nearly all of the agricultural and manufactured goods of Brazil's industrial powerhouse, the state of São Paulo. Santos, therefore, played a role in global affairs in the sixteenth century and again in the mid- to late nineteenth century, and in both instances depended heavily on African- and Brazilian-born slaves. Despite the importance of this section of the long Paulista coast and the slave labor that dominated the economy, no history of slave life in this region has yet been compiled.[20]

Long after the early colonial sugar boom but before Santos took its strong commercial and maritime position, the town's population was relatively small and production was minor. During the first few decades after independence, the persistence of colonial social and political structures was more noticeable than the town's slow transformation. After 1849, as coffee surpassed sugar as São Paulo's most exported good, the British began construction of a provincial railroad, terrible new epidemics struck the coast, and thousands of European immigrants landed dockside at the town, all conspiring to move Santos away from its long colonial era and toward its contemporary form as an international port and cosmopolitan city. To follow the quickening pace of these trends, this book relies on social and economic maps that track the changing boundaries of wealth, status, and slaveholding. Maps such as these create demographic profiles of slave-owning and non-slave-owning households in both the urban parts of the port city and rural areas of the township. In order to understand when and why major opportunities opened for some slaves but not for others, the first part of this book investigates wealth and material conditions of households, neighborhoods, and farming communities. Additionally, information on owner and slave occupations, familial connections, and a myriad of overlapping social ties creates a picture of a diverse city undergoing significant changes, including an evolution and adaptation of institutions linked to the slave system.

The second part of this book continues to focus on changing social and demographic trends while emphasizing slaves' life conditions and treatment. Here I present evidence that these trends diverged significantly between groups of bondspeople, principally in the degree to which the different groups were able to avoid sale outside of their families and communities, create or re-create families, work in relatively safe jobs, and avoid punishment for behavior authorities deemed criminal. Owners' social position and their treatment of their slaves also influenced slaves' ability to remain healthy; avoid risk of disease, injury, and violence; and receive effective medical care. Finally, social hierarchy also influenced the pathways slaves had to freedom, via either manumission or flight, and, after death, how their remains were handled by owners, friends, and family.

By connecting the behavior of slaves with a systematic analysis of their social conditions I am attempting to find a middle ground between two diverging modes of interpreting and understanding slavery. In the last three decades, as some historians have searched for ways Brazilian slaves found their own voices and carved out a culturally or socially independent space within an oppressive society, other historians have turned to the structural aspects of slavery, usually through quantitative methods and an emphasis on demographic or economic history. Following Stanley Stein's masterful *Vassouras: A Brazilian Coffee County, 1850–1890*, originally published in 1957, some of this research on slavery has also become quite regionalized.[21] I cannot claim to be the first to attempt to bridge what might be characterized as a divide between slaves' actions and the social or economic groups to which they belonged. One successful strategy has been to painstakingly re-create a biography of a slave or a freed slave and his or her family in order to witness the decisions these individuals made within a number of changing structural constraints. Sandra Lauderdale Graham's *Caetano Says No* or Zephyr Frank's *Dutra's World* center on a slave and freeman, respectively, while Nancy Pricilla

Naro, in *A Slave's Place, a Master's World*, used judicial court cases to look at the decisions slaves and their owners made within rural Rio de Janeiro. Brazilian historians have also integrated the intimate experiences of slaves with the changing setting of the economy and society.[22]

Because slaves in Brazil and most other places left so few written narratives, scholars have turned to the many boxes of dusty *processos-crime* (judicial records) to discover the actions of slaves in specific situations and their ability to be autonomous actors. Two other sources—*mapas* (census records) and *testamentos* and *inventarios* (inheritance records)—have also been scrutinized, principally by those interested in the structural side of slavery. Inheritance records often provide meticulous descriptions of households and material culture as well as the occasional contentious passage regarding the bequeathing of slaves and goods to heirs. They also allow historians to look at the important relationship between slaveholding and general wealth holding, with recognizable limits. Census records, especially from São Paulo and Minas Gerais, were often made in such detail that household production, race, age and civil status can be followed in pursuit of important trends. More and more years of these census *mapas* have come under close examination, sometimes in combination with one or two other sources that permit cross-listing of the names of slaves and their owners.[23]

Historians' use of these sources has produced several important new discoveries about Brazilian slavery:

- Sizes of slaveholdings varied enormously, with small numbers often the norm for the purposes of food and commodity production for household and local market.[24]
- Brazilian households were more commonly organized around a nuclear family than an extended family, or headed by a lone individual with or without slaves.[25]
- Slaves were able to form and maintain families under certain conditions and within particular areas.[26]
- The large and populous province of Minas Gerais was not in economic decline after its eighteenth-century gold boom; rather, it had a dynamic economy and was likely one of the few places in Brazil where the slave population experienced natural increases.[27]
- Prior to the coffee boom, the growing African slave labor force in São Paulo accompanied its economic expansion.[28]
- The increasing purchase price of slaves dampened economic mobility for many people during the second half of the nineteenth century.[29]

These findings have challenged the idea that Brazilian society was typically composed of large, extended families that held the majority of slaves on sugar or coffee plantations. Historians have also questioned the idea that slaves were not allowed or were unwilling to create families, and have challenged commonly held beliefs regarding the regional histories of Minas Gerais and São Paulo. By doing so, these studies have altered our understanding of the history of slavery in Brazil and of the history of Brazil as a colony and nation.

Some of these demographic and economic histories noticeably return to a pre-1960s model of scholarship that relied on slavery to describe other trends, such as economic growth.[30] Three important unpublished dissertations—by Robert Slenes (Stanford University, 1976), Pedro Carvalho de Mello (University of Chicago, 1977), and Roberto B. Martins (Vanderbilt University, 1980)—have been credited with a new phase of economic and demographic reanalysis of Brazilian history. These dissertations were important for prompting a number of debates, especially over the nature of the Mineiro economy in the nineteenth century. At the same time, Gilberto Freyre's heavy emphasis on plantation slavery has continued to be questioned, as scholars reexamine the consequences of slavery for the national narrative of Brazil.

Historians have also developed a useful set of tools for examining slavery in Santos. Many of the sources used for this book center much more on slaveholders than slaves. In these sources, I have attempted to find the composition of the larger society, how slave owners were socially positioned, and what those positions meant for the lives and work of the individuals they owned. Residents of Santos, like other Brazilians, lived in a society that was largely rural, deeply unequal in wealth and power, and permeated by the institution of slavery until 1888. Wealthy Brazilians owned hundreds of African- and native-born slaves, held a great deal of property, and grew a range of products sold locally and across the world, in sharp contrast to the many small families squatting on nearby land and the beggars who owned little more than a rope belt, threadbare shirt, pants, and sandals. The poorest free people in society lived highly uncertain lives and were often the first to suffer during times of hardship. They performed what jobs they could, migrated often, lived shorter lives, and held a less steady position in society than did the bondspeople of owners with means. Between the barons and the beggars were the vast majority of Brazilians, those who had sufficient but not abundant resources to endure a year of bad harvests, the death of one or more family member, price increases of basic necessities, and other ill luck.[31]

Considering this wide spectrum, what were the factors that separated groups of people from one another and created differences in wealth, slaveholding, and power? In other words, what stratified society? This is a question often brought up by social scientists and historians for vastly different societies and periods of time and considered by sociologists to be a topic worthy of its own disciplinary field.[32] Looking at how other scholars have approached class, status, and mobility is one way to explain how I use *stratification* in this book.

Generally, sociologists hold that people are capable of categorizing themselves while being categorized by others into social and economic levels, based on perceived differences related to occupation, race, sex, or wealth. It was on this issue that Max Weber famously disagreed with Karl Marx, since he did not believe class struggle was at the heart of all social conflict. Instead, Weber argued that society is a constantly shifting arena, where individuals' status and accepted claim to a specific style of life, combine (or clash) with their defined roles within society, their range of opportunities that stem from material possessions, and their personal chances within the competitive market.[33] Considering the great amount of work done by historians of slavery to show that oppressed peoples often possessed a voice and some degree of power to influence their situations, this Weberian vision of society is arguably more compatible than the Marxist position, although most historians eschew any one-size-fits-all theoretical framework. On the other hand, we must continue to make assumptions about how people are positioned, and constantly adjust those assumptions for any society we examine carefully. Indeed, Latin American Studies has a long tradition of viewing society in terms of social divisions and organization, although the term *social mobility* is used more frequently than *social stratification*.[34] Sociologists rightfully consider the former to be an action that occurs within the organization of the latter.

When it comes to the social ranks of nineteenth-century Brazilian society, there is little doubt that deep inequalities existed, but historians do not always agree how this inequality was structured. Many historians regard civil condition—freedom or slavery—as the most important indicator.[35] Analyses that utilize income brackets correspond with this division because slaves were often the lowest income-earning group. Furthermore, bondspeople could not legally pass property to heirs, thus this categorization scheme places slaves below the free poor in their potential for holding wealth. Considering the extent and depth of poverty among free people, a few historians have questioned the notion that slaves were always at the bottom of the social pyramid. For Mary Karasch, the urban society of Rio de Janeiro had a "top layer" of "white Brazilians and a few *pardos* from elite families," a "middle layer" of "immigrants, white Brazilians and free people of color," and the "lowest layer" that was a "mixed group." Whether one was free or enslaved was "important but not the sole determinant of a person's place in society."[36] Residential location and type of work may have been better indicators of social standing than civil status or income among certain occupational groups.[37]

In this book I draw inspiration from the sociologists who have done much work on stratification and from historians who recognize that income alone is insufficient to explain hierarchy. In the Weberian tradition, I hold status and material possessions to be closely related, and this position frames the connections made in this book between the life experiences of slaves and the wealth and status of their owners. Historical studies are always constrained by their sources, however, and this one is no different. Thus, when sources did not support these connections, I used different demographic groups that are also viable categories for comparing life conditions and treatment. A richer, more complex picture emerges when groups of slaveholders based on occupation, race, or title are not always placed together within the overarching and diminutive categories of class.

Just as a historian who identifies "classes" or "ranks" must choose somewhat arbitrary dividing lines, there is also a degree of subjectivity to finding the order of a society by social, status, or demographic groups. I believe the only way around this problem is to find and use categories used by slaveholders and slaves themselves. For example, one way of looking at the different opportunities available to slaves is to examine occupational groups. The slaves tending sugarcane fields or rice paddies led very different lives than those who regularly washed their neighbors' laundry in town. Or, as another example, *pardos* may not have always felt solidarity with each other, but their midtone skin color and perceived social position was an often-used and important identifying feature, and people often acted differently toward them because of this characteristic. The racial or social categories Brazilians used offer another way of comparing life conditions and treatment.[38]

There is another body of literature that frequently highlighted the hierarchies within slavery. Europeans and Americans who traveled to Brazil in the nineteenth century frequently observed hierarchies based on types of owners, the treatment of slaves, the work they performed, and the resources they displayed. Some observers claimed that treatment varied between the provinces to the degree that slaves in the southern provinces were so notoriously abused that slave owners in the north would threaten their slaves with sale southward if they misbehaved.[39] Other travelers observed that jobs on the sugar plantations and gold mines were worse than those on most coffee *fazendas* (plantations or farms). They observed differences in treatment according to the type of owner: Brazilians were supposedly better masters than the Portuguese, men were better than women, clergy were better than government officials, and slaves and former slaves were "more oppressive overseers and slave-drivers than whites."[40] Many of these accounts were impressionistic and their hierarchies are questionable, but more important is the fact that many travelers observed slaves living and working in a diverse range of conditions and wrote in diaries and published books asserting that they had witnessed slaves treated with inhumane cruelty as well as with emotion and care.

Work was another variable that travelers used to categorize slaves. Slaves who lived in cities and had urban occupations or independently earned a wage for their owners or for themselves and their families could slowly and strenuously improve their position in Brazilian society. City slaves were often characterized as having an easier life, but some thought the enslaved stevedores worked harder than all other slaves.[41] Some travelers wrote that *negros de ganho* (slaves for hire) had a great deal of autonomy, but their conditions depended on their ability to save and willingness to spend. Finally, domestic servants often appeared to be better housed, clothed, and fed than slaves who worked on the street, but they displayed fewer freedoms of action compared to the *negros de ganho*.[42]

Travelers were sometimes shocked to see certain slaves and free blacks in finery and jewelry. Thomas Ewbank, an American traveler, wrote in 1856 while in Rio de Janeiro, "I have passed black ladies in silk and jewelry, with male slaves in livery behind them. Today one rode past in her carriage, accompanied by a liveried footman and a coachman."[43] When C.S. Stewart visited Rio in 1852 he observed that "two black African women, richly and fashionably attired, came sauntering along with the most conscious air of high-bred self-possession. They were followed by black female slaves, also in full dress, carrying a black baby three or four months old, and decked out in all the finery of an aristocratic heir."[44] For Americans unaccustomed to seeing blacks in elegant clothing, these slaves and free people of color exposed their deep racial prejudices.[45]

Opulence such as this was mostly limited to the few big cities in Brazil, especially Rio de Janeiro, but in these places the richly attired slaves could confound distinctions of race and class, especially as material conditions improved for many slaves during the second half of the nineteenth century. Addressing the Brazilian Parliament in 1871, Perdigão Malheiro, a nineteenth-century Brazilian lawyer who wrote an influential book on slave law, said "today it is very common to see slaves better dressed than any of us, and judging by them no one could tell who is a slave, and their masters condone this and even grant them other favors."[46] Rita, a Bahian slave who escaped her master in Rio de Janeiro in 1855, was described as wearing a dress that was secured by buttons made of white gold. Similarly, Helena, who also fled her *Carioca* (Rio de Janeiro) master in 1865, carried rosettes of gold and precious stone. Neither description indicated that these were stolen goods. Slaves such as Helena and Rita may have been limited to a city like Rio de Janeiro, although travelers also reported numerous luxuries available to the large landowners far from Brazil's big cities, some who were even compared to feudal lords.[47]

Just as slaves who wore finery were noticed by visitors to Brazil, privileged, skilled, high-status, and educated slaves and *libertos* (freed slaves) have received the attention of historians. Karasch reported that the dozens of jobs held by slaves in Rio de Janeiro included supervisors, goldsmiths, chambermaids, and the "white slaves" that carried the emperor on his outings. Julio César da Silva Pereira discovered a slave named José Alves who was given the "pompous" title of *1º cirugião da Real Fazenda e Paço de Santa Cruz* (1st Surgeon of the Royal Plantation and Town of Santa Cruz), a position that gave him authority over hundreds of other bondspeople on what was a huge and formerly Jesuit-run farming operation in Rio de Janeiro province.[48] Emília Viotta da Costa cited an advertisement for a slave that spoke French in addition to Portuguese. Sandra Lauderdale Graham described an African who could sign his name in a petition for a work license, while his sponsor "barely managed to scratch out his name and, moreover, referred to the African respectfully as 'senhor' (master)." Likewise, Zephyr Frank told the story of Antonio Dutra, a barber and musician who amassed a considerable fortune for his day, despite being African-born and a former slave.[49] Nancy Priscilla Naro discussed a judicial case of a slave named Eufrasia whose owner "showered" her with attention, "sending her dresses and taking her with him to 'public sports events and entertainment.'"[50] In the unusual case cited by Naro, Eufrasia might have been called an *escravo de estimação* by her neighbors, a term used in 1922 by Alberto Sousa in his account of the slaves who inhabited some of the fanciest houses in Brazil and sometimes slept in the same rooms as their owners. *Estimação* means "esteemed" or "prized" and is sometimes coupled with *animal* in Portuguese to refer to a favorite pet, such as a poodle. Naro reported that Eufrasia's owner treated her brutally in the end, but some skilled slaves had a bit of bargaining power. Stanley Stein quoted an owner who complained that he had to sell his skilled slave because he refused to work for him.[51]

Autonomy and knowledge may have been equally important as a slave's place within the community or his or her price on the market.[52] For example, domestic servants are typically seen to have had less autonomy than those working on the streets, especially compared to the *negros de ganho*, but autonomy among servants most likely depended on the type of household and job. According to a manual on slaveholding written by a *fazendeiro* (plantation or farm owner), slaves would sometimes purposely do a task poorly if asked to perform a job they considered outside of their accepted occupation.[53] Conversely, small households often had one or two slaves who performed a wide range of jobs. Slaves who worked outside the home may have been less likely to be under constant supervision, but Katia Mattoso claims that at times domestic servants became so intimate and closely connected to their masters or mistresses that occasionally "it became difficult to tell who dominated."[54]

In sum, slaves that were unusually situated within society have not gone unnoticed, nor have slaves who suffered great abuses and cruelties. Despite the common recognition that slaves varied in their position and options, no one has undertaken a systematic search for variance stemming from owners' status. In Santos, and likely elsewhere, the social order within society (including conventional material markers but also extending to social and cultural positions) and the conditions that slaves endured were related. Recognition of this fact brings renewed attention to the older idea of treatment and pushes us to make the case that the ways owners acted toward their slaves should be taken into account as much as the ways slaves acted toward (or independently of) their masters.

In pursuit of these arguments I employ a new methodology. Historians have only begun to find connections between primary sources through large databases of slave and owner names, demographic information, and the unique historical data contained in each type of source, but rarely are more than two or three types of documents used in this manner. Because archivists in Santos preserved and organized an exceptional array of material, and because this was not a large city like Rio de Janeiro or Salvador, more than twenty historical sources from the nineteenth century could be combined and matched according to the names of slaves and slave owners. More than two thousand unique slave owners and three hundred slaves were identified in two or more sources. Out of nearly twelve thousand slaves, approximately five thousand were men, women, and children owned by masters who appeared in multiple sources. Despite the nuances and complexities of these data, the vast majority of cross-referenced names in the database open many new ways of investigating Brazilian slavery. For example, two primary sources on slave trading, *escripturas de compra e venda* (bills of sales) and *meia-sizas* (tax records), rarely give information about the former slave owner beyond his or her name. As a consequence, a number of questions regarding the slave trade have gone largely unanswered, such as the position and character of owners that typically purchased slaves. By combining information from these sources with census records and almanacs, we can determine the birthplace, race, and occupation of more than half of the township residents who bought and sold slaves. Similar linkages were found between historical documents that related to slaves' manumission strategies, family formation, work, crime and punishment, health, burial, and flight from slavery. Each of these topics is important standing alone, but the primary purpose of this broad cross-referencing technique is to fit these discussions into a unifying narrative by identifying social patterns that constrained or opened slave choices. The cross-referencing methodology employed by this study, including its challenges and limitations, and the array of sources used, are described in the Appendix.

A broad range of life conditions and treatment are connected to the categories of a hierarchical society in a novel way. Few other histories of slavery have so actively sought the names of owners and slaves in sources; rather, they have relied on finding the broader, but important, demographic or economic trends. In fact, this is the first research of slavery that systematically gathers information on owner status and compares this information with the life conditions and treatment of slaves based on a wide range of topics. It is also the first slave system to be investigated using network analysis methods.

This book is divided into two parts. The first part ("Masters and Their Slaves") includes Chapters One through Three. It contains descriptions of a changing society and the economy in Santos, transformations that became more noticeable and hurried after 1850. Society is best portrayed as "interdependently stratified," that is, containing innumerable personal connections that cut through and across social and economic groups divided into ranks. To make this case, hundreds of marriage records and a number of other sources were analyzed that give network data. Networks were by no means clustered by neighborhood, yet each of the neighborhoods in the city and the countryside were unique in multiple ways. Owners and their slaves shared many attributes within neighborhoods, also true for the limited opportunities slaves had and for the treatment that they received.

In Chapter Two, I track some of the broader demographic, economic, and material changes that occurred during the century. The economy and society of the township largely revolved around the local production of goods, most of which was for local consumption. Some of the township councilmen who regulated the laws, collected taxes, and worked to increase trade and their businesses were from families that owned large plantations. These families typically owned one or two country estates, several pieces of property in town, and between twenty and eighty slaves, who mostly tilled, cut cane, distilled *cachaça* (sugarcane rum), or planted rice or cassava. After 1850, a new class of men inserted itself into positions of power that previously had been reserved for planters. These newcomers made money in other ways, often by buying, storing, and selling coffee, sugar, and cotton to overseas markets. This merchant class sometimes bought rural property and built country homes, but they were more likely to buy town homes for themselves and tenements for their workers. Some spent a considerable amount of time in São Paulo, preferring a lengthy railroad commute over tracks laid by the British in 1869 to the hot and humid climate of the lowland coast of Santos. Even though they took their profits as service middlemen rather than producers, they relied nearly as much as the old elite on slave labor. Their slaves were less commonly farmers; instead, they worked as stevedores, wagon drivers, and warehouse workers.

In the third chapter, I describe the township's slave markets, its principal participants, market "nexuses," and markets as "gateways" for slaves into a hierarchical world. This story mostly takes place in the 1860s, when detailed historical sources are available. More of the town's elite were working in export commerce rather than regional agricultural production and these men looked to buy and sell particular slaves. Some were certainly pleased to have connections to men like Captain Gregorio Innocencio de Freitas, who largely traded slaves who were suitable for hauling bags of coffee.[55] Other townspeople looked for enslaved domestic servants and sought another prominent slave trader who had carved out a different but equally specialized niche.

The second part ("Slaves and Their Masters"), Chapters Four through Seven, situates slave life conditions and their treatment into the changing social and economic picture presented in the first part of the book. Chapter Four looks at family, work, crime, and punishment of slaves of Santos. By the midpoint of the century, both slave prices and coffee export profits were rising, and the new commercial elite often handled their slaves carefully. In fact, they chose to send them to the hospital for medicine and the jail for whipping, rather than perform medical services and punishment within their home as families had done for centuries. The fifth chapter turns to the public and private medical care of slaves, the afflictions from which they suffered and died, and how slaves and free people faced similar disease environments and risks with a few important exceptions such as yellow fever and tuberculosis. It includes a discussion of the dangers slaves faced in a city that was more and more densely populated and where many jobs were opening within an expanding service-oriented economy. Chapter Six details the history of slave manumission and flight, the two pathways to freedom open for a limited number of bondspeople. In the seventh chapter, I return to the slaveholders and freed slaves in a description and history of the abolition movement. In that final, substantive chapter, I explore how a city that had been more dedicated to slavery than most other places in southeastern Brazil could declare itself "free of slavery" two years before the "golden proclamation" ended official slavery in 1888. The Conclusion presents a summary of findings and a discussion of how stratification within the institution of slavery may have influenced its perception and perpetuation.

PART I

Masters and Their Slaves

CHAPTER ONE

Neighborhoods and Inequality

Perched on the northern banks of the Ilha de São Vicente, Santos faces the deep, protected inlet and the southern edge of the Paulista mainland. The old town and original port occupied a narrow stretch of land along a canal that ran behind the island. Along the muddy banks, colonial residents constructed modest wooden docks and stone dockside warehouses to service the entering ships (Figure 1.1). The backside of the city was near the base of several tall hills that, to the eyes of entering ship passengers, painted a dark green and lush tropical backdrop to the white-washed city walls. One important hill, called São Jerŏnimo, had in the colonial days helped provide a natural defense against other ambitious European colonial powers and raiding pirates.[1] São Jerŏnimo hill was crowned by a small Catholic church and a regular pilgrimage climbed its many steep steps. The hill and city faced the jumble of oceanic vessels, coastwise schooners, and dugout canoes as well as the narrow inlet and miles of unpopulated lands. The Santos floodplains were "variegated with lagoons and marshes and crisscrossed by innumerable rivers, straits, and canals, the pattern of which is perpetually lured by a pearly vapor."[2] There were days when it would clear and the mountains on the horizon could come into view. Ship passengers might even catch a glimpse of the highway, which cut through the Atlantic rain forest on a meandering and sometimes treacherous route to the city of São Paulo.

By the nineteenth century, another bumpy and often washed-out dirt road stretched to the southeast, skirting the hills before running due south to the island's ocean beach. It transected Rua Direita, a street that was the backbone of town. Direita connected the army barracks in the east, the center of town, and several small roads ending at the private docks. To the west, a fishing neighborhood called Valongo was linked to the city by a small single road. The mostly Santos-born "Quarteleiros" (barrack residents) and mostly Portuguese fishermen, or "Valongueiros"

FIGURE 1.1
The Port of Santos
SOURCE: Benedito Calixto, Praia e Rampa do Consulado—Porto de Santos, FAMS.

(Valongo residents) were rivals.[3] Between these two neighborhoods were the wealthiest areas of the city, including an important intersection called Four Corners. This affluent neighborhood counted those who lived or owned a house on Rua Direita (Straight or Main Street), Travessa da Alfândega (Customs House Lane), Rua Santo Antonio (Saint Anthony Street), Rua da Praia (Waterfront Street), and Rua da Graça (Grace Street). In 1822 the men who lived on these five roads governed five thousand people in the city and hundreds more scattered throughout the big coastal township. They also regulated the European and South and North American ships as they entered or left port, sometimes with African slaves, and did business with the foreign slave traders coming from Rio de Janeiro and other parts of the Empire.

A SLAVE SOCIETY

Slavery permeated the social structure of the town, but the distribution of slaveholders within society was quite uneven. Santos was certainly a slave society; the organization of owners and slaves had deep roots in the physical space of the town, and particular streets and neighborhoods had very high levels of slaveholding. Yet other neighborhoods had almost no slaves at all. During the first years of the Empire the biggest slave owners lived in the center of town or in its western half, but small- to midsized slaveholders could be found in nearly all of the town's neighborhoods. Some of the largest slave owners lived in the Four Corners neighborhood. Nearly all the households in Four Corners and Dockside neighborhoods had one or more slaves, and several had more than twenty. On a long stretch of Rua Josefina, however, there were thirty-eight homes and shops in a row where not one person owned a slave.[4]

Households also varied substantially in terms of slaveholding sizes, and any simple division of small and large slaveholders does not accurately portray the range of numbers. Data at the street level gives a picture of the variety and connects slaveholding size to other variables of wealth.[5] Table 1.1 shows a list of town streets in 1822 and organizes them according to the number of slaves per household. The streets with the fewest slaves were Beco do Inferno (Hell's Alley) in the center of town, and Rua Itororó (Fountain Road) and Rua Josefina on the edges of town. Beco do Inferno was not on the town's periphery nor was it the poorest in property wealth. This tight alley had a high number of small shopkeepers and artisans but few slaves; it was positioned meters from the houses of the biggest slave owners. For example, Rua da Praia and Rua da Alfândega, two streets that intersected at the corner of the Customs House, composed the two portions of a neighborhood with the most slaves per household. Later in this chapter a fuller picture of the Four Corners neighborhood will be detailed by following one of its wealthiest families, the Machados, who owned a house with balconies overlooking all four streets.

During the first half of the century, the average number of slaves per household in town was low—less than three. The average rises to seven if the households without slaves are excluded. When wealth is gauged purely by slaveholding, as contemporaries often did, Santos was a fairly poor town compared to other parts of Brazil. Distribution, moreover, was uneven. The majority of streets had fewer than three slaves per owner on average; Travessa da Alfândega, on the other hand, averaged about twenty-six slaves per household. The most densely populated streets exceeded the town average slightly, but by far had the most slaves in absolute numbers. For example, the thickly populated Rua Direita created a prominent band of mostly small- to midsized holdings that spread along the town's main thoroughfare.[6]

The degree of slaveholding was related to the balance of sex and racial groups among the free population in these streets. Households were more likely to be headed by a female of color on streets with low levels of slaveholding, while white male heads of households dominated the large slaveholding families. On Travessa da Alfândega, there were six

TABLE 1.1

Characteristics of Santos Streets, 1822

	Population	Households	Slaves	Slaves/ Household	Free and Slave Women (percent)	Whites (percent)	Free Pardos (percent)	Free Blacks (percent)
Beco do Inferno	33	14	2	0.1	61	45	45	10
Rua do Itororó	35	12	2	0.2	55	15	45	39
Rua Josefina	82	36	9	0.3	59	15	78	7
Rua de São Bento	129	35	9	0.3	56	18	61	21
Travessa do Carmo	28	7	2	0.3	62	42	46	12
Rua do Valongo	168	34	16	0.5	53	69	28	3
Rua do Rosario	210	59	39	0.7	60	43	39	17
Travessa do Parto	40	11	8	0.7	50	6	88	6
Rua Áurea	200	50	38	0.8	62	49	48	4
Rua de Santa Catarina	176	43	37	0.9	55	35	64	1
Travessa do Banca de Peixe	33	8	10	1.3	48	65	30	4
Rua do Campo	290	57	81	1.4	66	39	52	10
Rua dos Quarteis	303	52	120	2.3	57	54	45	5
Rua Meridional	140	24	74	3.1	58	52	39	14
Rua Septentrional	169	21	99	4.7	50	76	14	10
Rua Antonina	140	18	93	5.2	51	77	19	4
Rua de Santo Antonio	585	59	354	6.0	59	42	50	7
Rua Direita	657	58	404	7.0	58	72	24	4
Rua de Graça	62	5	41	8.2	67	67	33	0
Rua da Praia	256	18	205	11.4	33	91	3	6
Travessa da Alfăndega	191	6	155	25.8	58	100	0	0
Total	3,927	627	1,798		(N=2,213)	(N=2,227)	(N=1,439)	(N=276)

SOURCE: Nominal lists, 1822, AESP.

households and a total of 155 slaves, owned by three white men and three white women. This street was unique in having an even number of male and female slaveholders, whereas most homes on the large slaveholding streets were headed by men. In the middle spectrum of slaveholding, there were more people of color among the slave owners. One street that fits this definition, Rua de Santo Antonio, had an average of six slaves per household. The census takers who surveyed this block in 1822 found that nearly three out of every five households were headed by a man or woman of color. Between 1817 and 1830, moreover, an increasing number of these individuals of color were slaveholders.[7] The race or color of the free population on several town roads with small to medium slaveholders was not balanced and tipped toward one racial/color group or another. Streets with high numbers of a particular racial group transected to form a few small neighborhoods that attracted and reinforced these racial patterns at a scale slightly larger than one street alone. Rua Santo Antonio, with its many medium-sized slaveholdings and people of color, intersected with Rua de São Bento, a road with far fewer slaves but where whites composed less than a quarter of the street's free population.[8]

The men and women found in the census and tax records had spatial locations that gave clues to their social position. Patterns pertaining to slave owning, property wealth, and demographics can be visualized on a map of the town using computational tools that depict and track changes in urban geography.[9] As we can see, property wealth, like slaveholding, also varied greatly from one part of the town to another. In Figure 1.2, the wealthiest residents, in terms of urban property, appear on the top map. These men and women owned the most expensive property in town, as registered by tax collectors in 1839.[10] These were the largest and fanciest houses in town. They usually had two floors with balconies, as well as colorful hand-painted ceramic tile on their façades. The ground floor was often taken up by a general goods store, a workshop, or a stable. The occupants lived on the second floor, above the customers, mud, and domesticated animals that often entered and exited the large front doors below. Warehouses filled with coffee, cotton, or sugar were interspersed among these relatively expensive buildings. Most of this property was in the middle of town, particularly along Rua Direita, a block away from a handful of private dockside warehouses.

Areas of valuable property only partially overlapped the two neighborhoods with large slaveholding or high property values. The bottom map of Figure 1.2 shows the locations of owners who owned twenty or more slaves in 1822. Seven of these individuals owned plantations in the township, but businessmen, military officers, and high government officials such as the treasurer of the Customs House also counted among

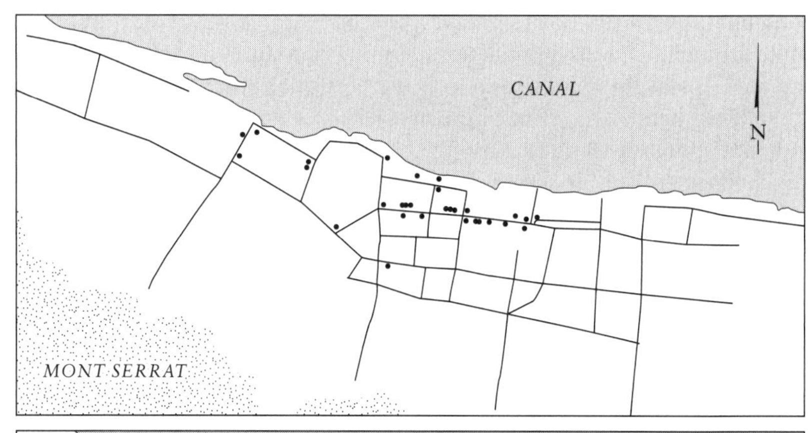

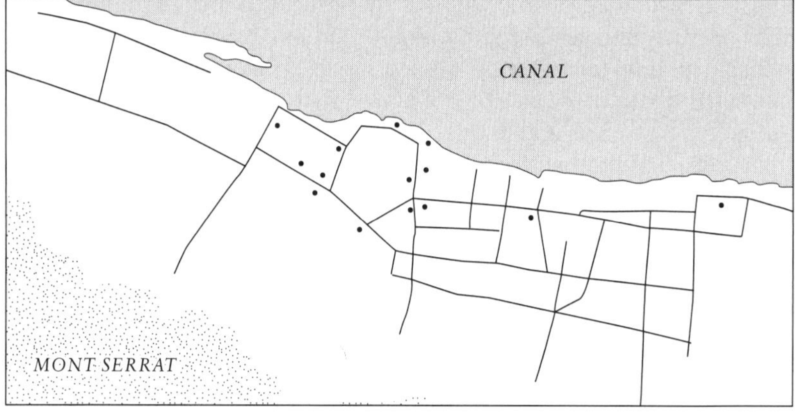

FIGURE 1.2

Location of High-Value Property, 1839 (top), and Large Slaveholders, 1822 (bottom)

SOURCES: Urban property tax rolls, 1834–35; nominal lists, 1822, AESP.

them. These townsmen lived in houses mostly on or near the polygon of streets formed by Rua Antonina, Rua de Santo Antonio, Rua da Praia, and Travessa da Alfândega. Most of the expensive buildings were located on Rua Direita, although only one large slaveholder resided on this street. This confirms similar claims made by historians who, after comparing wealth-holding inheritance records, found that property and wealth in slaves were rarely well-aligned.[11]

On the other end of the wealth-holding spectrum, the social order and physical composition of Santos are also marked by diversity. The least valuable properties were unevenly scattered throughout town. Noticeable pockets existed on the edges of the port town, particularly in the south where Santos was expanding. Although low-income property was more concentrated than the single-slave-owner residences, slaveholding and property holding did not evenly match. In 1822, seventy-one single-slave owners lived in Santos in the town's small neighborhoods and on every street. Single-slave owners were remarkably distributed; some lived in or near buildings listed in the bottom fifth of the tax list, while others owned houses that were among the highest priced. On Rua do Itororó there was a row of seven houses, each estimated to have an annual rental income of twelve *mil-réis* per year.[12] This was considerably inexpensive; the city average was six times higher, and the most expensive building thirty-three times higher. These seven neighboring houses were owned by Francisco Manuel Maco, who rented them to some of the town's poorest residents.[13] No similar cluster of single-slave owners existed elsewhere in town.

NEIGHBORHOODS

Santistas may have separated the Valongeiros from the Quartaleiros, but they generally did not call the sections of their town *bairros* (neighborhoods). Nonetheless, urban microareas were distinguished from each other by a number of characteristics that included the size and appearance of houses and the types of families and individuals that lived within these houses. In addition, households within neighborhoods had a degree of diversity, but most appeared similar demographically. We can begin to put a face on these claims by exploring and comparing the families of Luis Pereira Machado and Maria das Chagas.[14] Machado's family lived in the center of the town, one block from the Customs House and main dockside warehouses, in a corner house of the Four Corners neighborhood. He was a wealthy man, especially in Santos, but would have been considered moderately prosperous by the much higher standards of Rio de Janeiro. He owned numerous slaves and large amounts of property and had influence within township politics. Chagas and her husband lived only three blocks from Machado's house, but they were a world away in social position. Chagas lived on a street that partially blended into the fields and country behind her house. These two neighborhoods differed in the overall wealth, slave ownership, race, sex, and age of their occupants. Their slaves also differed from one another in their demographic profile and occupations, supporting the idea of hierarchical slavery.

Luis Pereira Machado

Luis Pereira Machado's house was at the center and helped define the Four Corners neighborhood. It occupied, in fact, one of the four corners overlooking the intersection of three busy streets and one alleyway: Rua Direita, Rua Antonina, Travessa da Alfândega, and Beco do Inferno. Many residents of these roads were involved in large commercial activities, agriculture, or small business, and it was certainly convenient that the Customs House, where all the province's goods officially entered and exited, was located a short walk away at the end the Travessa da Alfândega. Most of the town's wealthiest residents (at least in terms of slave wealth) lived on one of these three streets (Alfândega, Direita, or Antonina), yet there were noticeable differences between the three. The town's large- to medium-sized planters were concentrated on the end of Rua Direita and on Travessa da Alfândega, while Rua Antonina held mostly medium-sized planters.[15] Beco do Inferno, the narrow, dark alleyway that opened across from Travessa da Alfândega, was probably a tight squeeze for two passing mule carts and was one of the poorest areas in town. Beco do Inferno's residents performed services for the rich residents of the other streets, but were probably visited primarily by their slaves or free servants.

Machado owned a large house with balconies that overlooked the Four Corners. According to a painting by Benedito Calixto (Figure 1.3, Machado's house is front left), his house had a corner oriel supported by a corbel on the second floor, a rare display of wealth for any small town in Brazil. Adjacent balconies afforded Machado a view of the busiest part of the town and would have brought to his ear the numerous sharp sounds of the iron-reinforced wagon wheels on cobblestone, slaves rolling barrels of water or wine, and vendors hawking their wares.[16] Even more important than *seeing*, perhaps, was being *seen*: Machado's house would have caught the view of anyone walking on Rua Direita, Rua Santo Antonio, or Beco do Inferno.

Machado was born in a small town near the northern Portuguese city of Braga. How and when he moved to Brazil and established his fortune is unknown, but he did marry into one of the most prominent Santista families. His wife's father had been born in Santos but studied law at the University of Coimbra in Portugal and held important religious positions in the province. Machado's wife, Quiteria Ferreira Bueno, gave birth to twin daughters in 1787, and the girls grew up in Four Corners and lived there after their parents died. Maria Luiza was officially in charge of the property while her twin sister Luiza Maria is noted as an "additional" member of the family. Neither woman married. They were both active in the church, participated in charity, and were still alive

FIGURE 1.3
The Four Corners Neighborhood
SOURCE: Benedito Calixto, *Cuatro Cantos*, FAMS.

when the epidemics worsened after the middle of the century. Because of their religiosity and charity during the town's terrible bouts with yellow fever and smallpox, Machado's old place was called the "House of the Blessed," even when it was destroyed to make way for a bank in the twentieth century.[17]

Machado may have been involved in a number of business pursuits but his main source of income was the maintenance of a plantation on a part of Santos called by its Tupi-Guarani name, Piassaguera.[18] The plantation was so large that one could not cross the township without passing through Machado's land, which fronted the coast with a width of about four miles and extended from the beach to the mountains for eight miles. On a small portion of this expansive territory he grew rice, cassava, and some coffee, in addition to maintaining a distillery. His slaves carried bundles of sugarcane to the distillery buildings, and they exited with tin *pipas* (funnels) of potent *aguardente* (a rum-style spirit made from sugarcane). The city census in 1817 lists Machado with seventy-two slaves, but a rural property survey completed the next year shows that only thirty of his slaves worked and lived at Piassaguera.[19] A handful of these slaves tended to his house at Four Corners, but the rest must have been rented out in town and to other farms in the township.

Between 1817, when the census taker enumerated Machado's family, and 1825 when he died, Machado's household shrank slightly. It appears that he either sold some of his slaves or did not replace those who had died. By the last year of his life he had ten fewer slaves than a decade earlier. The estimated worth of his property upon his death was more than twenty *contos* (about seventeen thousand dollars today), and when adjusted to 1850 prices, this amount nearly exceeded the total value of the other 121 inheritance records used in this study.[20] The inventory of Machado's inheritance records shows that besides the four houses or buildings on his plantation, he was also the owner of five houses in town. The long list of possessions left for his heirs also included a set of silver cutlery, five intricate metal buckles, one pair of spurs, a clock made of silver and turtle shell, eight large canoes of native woods, and a sugar mill powered by a water wheel that provided the energy to make his spirits. His will and inventory also make evident his family's strong religious ties. Besides religious iconography made of wood and brass featuring Christ and Saint Anthony, he also owned an oratory with two folding wooden doors that rested on a *jacaranda* table protecting his collection of religious objects. All of these items were first passed on to his wife, Quiteria, and then to his two twin daughters.[21]

Machado died at an old age for his day—eighty years. He and his wife, who were white, had neighbors of similar means and appearances that created his immediate community. In this case, if the heart of Four Corners is defined as all of the residents who lived five or six doors down from this important intersection in all four directions, then the small neighborhood displays a degree of demographic homogeneity that is not replicated at a much larger scale. Occupations did vary—residing in the neighborhood were eleven businessmen, four plantation owners, two salesmen or vendors (*vive de sua venda*), one seamstress, one ironsmith, and one ship caulker—but other characteristics did not. Household sizes were generally large and half the residents owned five or more slaves. According to the 1834 property tax, Four Corners was an expensive neighborhood, with annual rents of about 168 percent the average value for the town. This was one of the wealthier neighborhoods in the city, both in terms of slave ownership and property wealth during the first half of the nineteenth century. Nearly all of its households were headed by white men or women involved in business or agriculture; on average they tended to be older and often married.[22] Their slaves also shared characteristics: (1) Black slaves were the majority; (2) male slaves outnumbered female slaves; (3) marriage was infrequent but much higher than other parts of town; and (4) children made up a good portion of Four Corners' slaves.[23]

The census records tell a little about Machado's slaves, servants, and employees. Many of his female slaves served as domestic servants or were rented out. Considering this arrangement, Machado must have had considerable knowledge of the domestic life of many smaller, poorer families in the town. Of course this had to be a two-way street: Machado's family squabbles or financial disputes probably reached the curious ears of the families who rented his slaves.

Francisca Maria das Chagas

Only a short walk away from Four Corners was a different neighborhood in form and function. When one of Machado's slaves set out on an errand that took her directly south, the shortest route would have been through the Inferno Alley south to its end at Rua Áurea (Golden Street). Turning left, she would have passed the backside of the Misericórdia Hospital and Church, crossed a small stream called Ribeiro do Carmo (Carmelite Brook), and neared another street called Travessa do Carmo (Carmelite Lane). At this intersection, Machado's slave might have tried to avoid the wagon wheel puddles by edging near the thick wooden door of Francisca Maria das Chagas, the thirteenth house from the start of the block.[24] These houses were not pressed together as they were at Four Corners or Beco do Inferno. Instead, many of these humble constructions stood independently, separated by soggy ground and shrubby yards. The walk would have taken five minutes or so, yet the slave would have had a glimpse of the developed fields and the swampy land through which Carmelite Brook made its way to the dock area and ocean inlet. The houses and buildings were much smaller and modest, without fancy ornamentation or second floors. Foot traffic and port activity was also less noticeable, as this area was neither between the port and businesses nor on a major thoroughfare leading out of town. We can see some of these attributes and the differences between Rua Áurea and the Four Corners neighborhood by looking at a photograph taken by Militão Azevedo (Figure 1.4) in 1864. In the five decades that passed between the time of this photograph and the time Chagas briefly lived in this neighborhood, urban development filled in many of the empty lots, some property owners built second floors, and the city installed a set of ornamental gas lamps. We know nothing about the woman holding the child in this old photograph, but she might have been a seamstress like Chagas.

Chagas did not live in this neighborhood for very long, and in this respect she was like most of her neighbors who led transient lives. After moving down the street in 1818, Chagas left the neighborhood for good. Only one man with his wife, Benedito Ignacio, lived continuously in the

FIGURE 1.4
Francisca Maria das Chagas's Neighborhood, 1864
SOURCE: Militão Augusto Azevedo, FAMS.

same house on this street between 1817 and 1828. Turnover was so rapid that nearly half of Chagas's neighbors in 1818 were new compared to the year before.[25] That same year, she moved into another house in the neighborhood. Chagas lived on Rua Áurea for a few more years with her neighbor Joanna Antonia and Joanna's eleven-year-old daughter, Gertrudes, six doors down from her previous home. It is unknown why Francisca and Antonia opted to move in together, but they may have found solidarity in that they were both young widows in the midpoint of their childbearing age. The move also shows that despite the rapid turnover in this neighborhood, there existed a network of relations among the many women who presumably lent help and care to one another.

The residents who lived at the intersection of Rua Áurea, Travessa do Carmo, and Rua do Itororó led vastly more modest lives than the wealthier families of Machado's neighborhood. But like Four Corners, the eighteen households that made up Chagas's immediate neighborhood were markedly similar to each other in their local context. Even more than Four Corners, the Áurea neighborhood shows a significant concentration of occupation groups. Within a homogeneous area that extended over portions of three streets, three-quarters of the heads of households were women like Chagas, who worked as a seamstress and did her sewing and hemming without employees or slaves. Six other seamstresses lived in her immediate area; like Chagas, most were single, white, and in their late twenties or early thirties.[26] The five men in the neighborhood were older and included two cobblers, a dry goods store owner, a vendor (*vendas* or "sales"), and an ironsmith. Benedito Ignacio, the same man who remained in the neighborhood after all his neighbors had moved, was also the only black head of household on this part of Rua Áurea.[27]

Household sizes were fairly small and usually did not list more than four people, including slaves.[28] Most of the eighteen households in this neighborhood give the name of one or two *agregados* (household members or dependents), but others listed none. Only five families owned slaves, a much different arrangement than in Four Corners, which averaged nearly eighteen slaves per household. Chagas and her neighbors may have rented slaves, some perhaps from the Machado family, but there are few sources that give specific details on this practice.[29] The eleven slaves owned by Chagas's neighbors were nearly equally divided by sex, all were black, and, in the eyes of the town and church, all were single. Only in the 1830 census records does a married slave appear in the neighborhood. These slaves were also younger than the town average: six were under twenty, and not one was over forty-five. Adolescent slaves cost less, and the poorer residents of Chagas's neighborhood could probably more easily afford them. The female slaves must have assisted with the sewing, laundering, and other trades that brought this neighborhood its small income.[30] These characteristics of slaveholding and of the slaves themselves differ greatly from households found near Machado's house and contribute greatly to the boundaries of function and identity of this neighborhood.

After Chagas moved the second time in 1818, the neighborhood began to lose its strong dedication to the seamstress trade. The number of female-headed households declined from three-quarters to one-half in 1828. Fewer women who listed sewing, hemming, and laundering as occupations resided there. They were replaced by families with different occupations, such as Francisco Ramalho's family. Ramalho, who moved in 1825, served in the town militia; Paulino José helped guard the arsenal; and Luiz José was a goldsmith. By 1828, more of the residents were married (40 percent), and they were younger than the generation of previous neighbors. Finally, whites became a minority within this microarea as *pardo* head of households came to represent 60 percent of all households by 1825. Benedito Ignacio and his wife must have done a reasonable business curling horseshoes and smoothing irons since they remained the only black household in the neighborhood.[31]

The records do not tell where Chagas moved after 1818, but she died in 1838. Between her move and her death, Chagas married Manoel Maximiano Guedes and took his last name as her own. Shortly after her will was completed, a dispute arose over her estate involving the family she had left behind in the northeastern Brazilian province of Pernambuco. The items under dispute included pieces of furniture such as two metal washbasins, two desks, three tables, and six wicker chairs; kitchen appliances such as an iron kettle, a stewing pan with a long handle, a breadboard, and a single mug; and a number of tools such as a trivet, an ax, and a scythe. Since there are no slaves or real estate listed in the inventory, the overall value of her property was low.[32] The property Chagas named in her will gives clues as to her condition of life. She was on the poor side but not the poorest; much of her estate was probably accumulated after she married.

The Rua Áurea neighborhood that Chagas lived in was vastly unlike the intersection of streets in Four Corners considered home to Luis Pereira Machado and his family, despite their proximity. The lives of the slave owners and their slaves differed. For instance, the Áurea neighborhood was characterized by a high degree of mobility. Many of the residents lived in female-headed households with few or no slaves. The details of the lives of Machado and Chagas serve to illustrate that neighborhoods attracted particular residents based on the level of property rents, the cost of living, and other characteristics that were amenable to particular racial or occupation groups. Neighborhoods altered slowly as the demographic and occupational profiles of their residents changed and the city expanded.

NETWORKS

Santistas such as Machado and Chagas, but also country folk in the distant parts of the township, were organized into discernable groups of wealth, status, and race bound by natural or constructed topography. Slaves and owners lived in different material worlds within these neighborhoods, and these worlds opened or restricted opportunities for work, family, and health. The Four Corners neighborhood where Machado's balcony looked over the most prosperous streets in town or the Rua Áurea neighborhood where Francisca Maria das Chagas neighbored seamstresses like herself were part of seven distinctive neighborhoods in town. Two were wealthy, two middling, and three poor. These neighborhoods are mapped in Figure 1.5, and in Table 1.2 we can find their defining characteristics. Most had one or several town institutions at their centers, and these institutions, with their multiple functions and functionaries, added to the identity of the neighborhood. For example, it is no surprise that the neighborhood with the army barracks also housed many

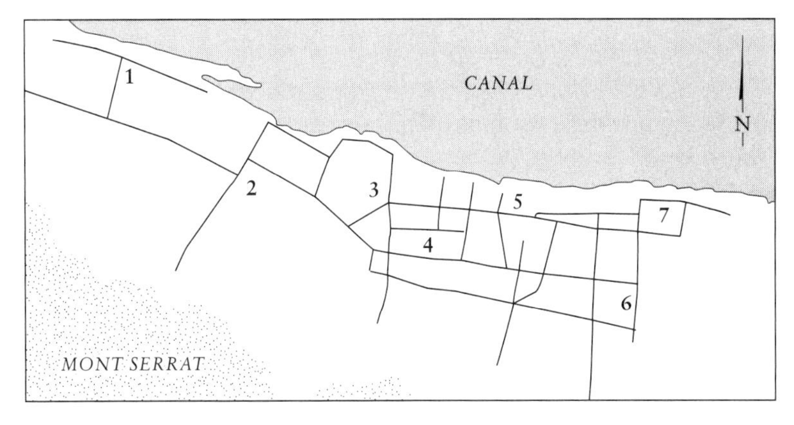

FIGURE 1.5

Santos Neighborhoods (numbers designate approximate center of neighborhood, key in Table 1.2)

TABLE 1.2

Characteristics of Santos Neighborhoods in the Nineteenth Century

Map Number	Neighborhood	Streets	Institutions & Landmarks	Rental Values*	Slaves per Household
1	Valongo	Valongo	Fish Market	34	.5
2	Rua São Bento	Rosario Itororó São Bento	São Bento Convent Itororó Fountain Saint Anthony Church	46	.5
3	Customs House at Four Corners	Álfandega & Antonina Direita (west) Santo Antonio	Old Customs House Saint Anthony Church Consular Offices	136	7.6
4	Rua Áurea and the southern outskirts	Áurea Carmo & Campo	Santos Charity Hospital	67	1.1
5	Dockside	Direita Inferno Santa Catarina Banca de Peixe Carmo Meridional (west) Septentrional (west)	Marina arsenal (colonial) Fish market Commissioner docks (after 1850) Jail Carmelite Convent Pelourinho New Customs House	102	3.6
6	Rua Josefina and the SE outskirts	Josefina (south) Áurea (east)		42	.5
7	Barracks	Quarteis Josefina (north) Meridional (east) Septentrional (east)	Army barracks Army clinic	55	2.3

*Figures illustrate the tax of the rental value of property in 1839.

of the town's soldiers, or that the neighborhood with the old Customs House was home to many influential merchants.

Many aspects of wealth, demographic makeup, occupation, and status corresponded to give these neighborhoods their form and identity. An individual who wished to buy a house in a wealthy neighborhood would have encountered larger families, many more slaves per owner, and fewer free people of color than in other parts of the town and township. This was not a hard-fast rule, of course, and a degree of slippage between the categories was always detectable. Mixture was especially evident in the middle of the hierarchical spectrum, such as in the Rua Áurea neighborhood, where all kinds of people of moderate means lived in rich diversity. In such middling neighborhoods, men and women often headed households with similar frequency; free colored residents lived in interspersed homes with whites, and residents performed a variety of jobs. A black seamstress with one slave might live next to a white male shopkeeper with five slaves. Surrounding these two houses were families without any slaves as well as a few with ten or fifteen.

Why is the neighborhood a useful unit of analysis? Particular owners, such as coffee merchants, petty merchants, army officers, big landowners, seamstresses, and many other occupational groups were concentrated in certain neighborhoods in Santos and other Brazilian towns and cities. Predominantly male, female, white, *pardo*, rich, middling, and poor slaveholders also grouped into neighborhoods where they identified with the neighbors they resembled. Geography provides perhaps the most useful category to connect the life conditions and treatment of slaves to the status of their owners. This is because "high" and "low" status was a shifting composite of wealth, occupation, and education. Neighborhoods captured status and the variance of its components, and this fact will be illustrated with many examples in the following chapters, taken from slaves' families, work, punishment, health and healthcare, manumission, and flight.

After the town became a city in 1839, and as the city grew and prospered with the coffee and import trade, the many long-standing ties based on family, friendship, patronage, and duty began to alter and, in some cases, weaken. In 1886, one almanac writer reflected on three decades of change that was thrusting Santos toward the twentieth century and its place as Brazil's busiest port. Compared to the indifference and hustle of the 1880s, the writer noted that Santos had a much "stronger spirit of sociability" during the middle part of the century. "Ten or twelve" important and interrelated Portuguese families ruled over town life while the rest of the townsfolk included a few foreigners and many "commoners" (*arraia miuda*). The "privileged few" enjoyed the common pastime of "frequent excursions throughout the city on foot," but unlike most, avoided muddy dress hems and damp pant cuffs by riding in elegantly curtained sedan chairs. These vehicles, hefted on the calloused shoulders of two or more slaves (the writer leaves it to the reader to imagine who did the hefting), were "tasteless baubles of . . . birth and position." Back then, and despite society's ostentatious differences, "everyone knew each other, got along well with one another, and visited often."[33]

When this account was published, many of Santos's longtime residents probably agreed that the township had once seemed more sociable and personal. More people knew their neighbors previously, and the strong ties that linked the various strata of society gave the city a degree of cohesion in the colonial days. With the arrival of coffee, the waves of European immigrants, and internally traded slaves after 1850, the city expanded too rapidly to keep track of all of the new neighbors, pedestrians, trolley car riders, and hawkers. These strangers took their chances with unfamiliarity, disease, and often injurious occupations in the hope that they would save a small bit of money for themselves and their families by working one of the new jobs in the port town.

The "spirit of sociability" that the almanac writer mentioned was difficult to describe because it derived from a series of relationships, on the one hand, between people of similar wealth, status, and race that drew strength from birthright familiarity, shared custom, and social parity, and, on the other hand, between poor and rich, slave and master, boss and employee, and client and patron that drew strength from dependence, duty, honor, and reverence. The first set of relationships defined class and status in a little-questioned design; the second cut sharply against the grain of class and material culture. One could only begin to know the contours of his or her set of personal relationships and had to imagine the nearly infinite succession of social ties that stretched like fabric through the city and, in a larger patchwork tapestry, expanded into the township, province, nation, and Atlantic world.

So far, we have begun to explore the physical space of the town, but a social space also existed that only roughly conformed to the city's geography. Within Santos, thousands of men and women wed in churches and chapels during the nineteenth century, usually inviting their relatives and other witnesses to legitimize the union in the name of the church and God. Figure 1.6 uses a computer program to exemplify a kinship network. In this network, each bride, groom, and witness is represented by a node, while lines represent family or marriage connections.[34] Several nodes are given a different color, addressed below.

The network in Figure 1.6 depicts a good portion of the 1,380 marriages registered by various Catholic officials between 1812 and 1870 in

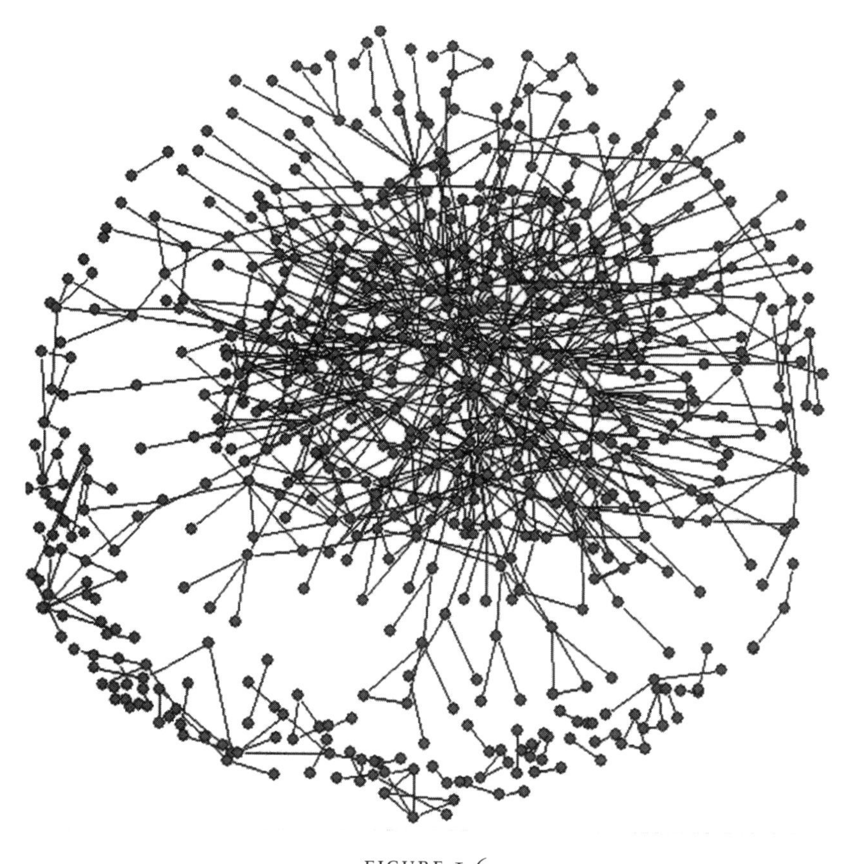

FIGURE 1.6
Santos Marriage Network, 1812–1870
SOURCE: Marriage records, 1812–1870, CCS, FAMS.

the southern half of Santos Township.[35] It captures part of a much bigger and even more interconnected kinship network that existed during the nineteenth century and shows that, despite the uniqueness of the various neighborhoods in Santos, the network of families stretched across these geographical units. The network includes only the men and women who were clearly identified in other sources and who did not have short common names. This means that out of four individuals who married or participated in a Santos wedding (recorded by the regional curia), only one is represented by the graph. Despite its limitations, the figure gives a sense of how exceedingly interconnected social life was for most Santos residents, especially because few ties were more important than those called upon to perform the rituals of a Catholic wedding.

The network as rendered here has several obvious limitations. It is too large and dense to permit labeling and thus does not indicate who the most connected individuals were or what marriages made important bridges between clusters of families. The network also excludes the small group of slaves who were married in a Santos church or chapel but recorded in separate curate books. Many slaves as well as free people formed families but never married, and this is perhaps the biggest limitation to the diagram, because *amazias* (long-term consensual unions) were more numerous in Brazil than unions recognized by the church.[36] Thousands of Santistas entered into lifelong unions with their partners and had children, grandchildren, and extended kin without ever formally recognizing their relationship before a priest. Many people did not have the means or money for a religious ceremony, were unable to perform all of the required catechistic obligations, or perhaps wished to conduct their lives outside the reach of church and government officials, even if it meant their children were labeled "illegitimate." But the point of the diagram is to show the high degree of a single category of connections and to suggest that many other kinds of connections overlapped and wove the fabric of social life even tighter. If *amazias* had been coded, along with the hundreds of mostly poor residents whose names were too common to be identifiable, the network would not have a fragmented nature with sparsely connected nodes. Probably the opposite would occur.

By focusing on only a portion of the network above (Figure 1.7), people of varying status were interconnected despite ostentatious claims to position, and these interconnections pulled people together across the

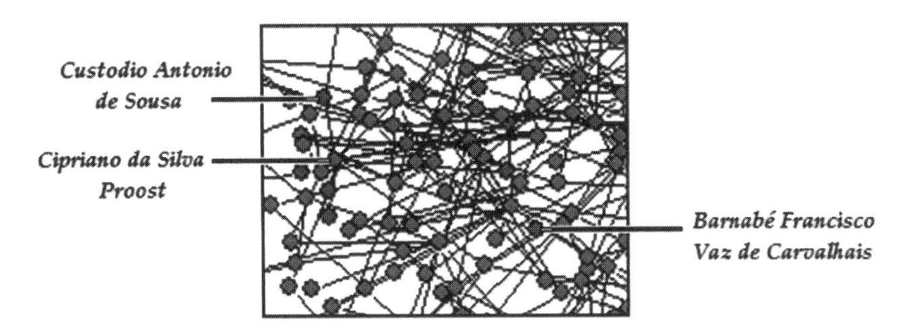

FIGURE 1.7

A Portion of the Santos Marriage Network, 1817–1870

SOURCE: Marriage records, 1812–1870, CCS, FAMS.

different various small city neighborhoods. In this portion I have identified several notes. Small circles refer to Sargeant Major Cypriano da Silva Proost, his children, and a few other kinship connections. One of his daughters, Delfinca Umbélia da Silva Proost, married a Portuguese immigrant named Custodio Antonio de Sousa in 1825. This couple owned an apothecary on Rua Direita run by their slave, Joaquim, who worked as a druggist. Joaquim mixed powders, crushed plants and roots, prepared remedies, set broken bones, and applied leeches to extract tainted blood. Cypriano da Silva Proost also served as one of two witnesses for the wedding of Barnabé Francisco Vaz de Carvalhais, who had a number of official functions in Santos but was famous in the city as a Commander of the Order of Christ (Comandador da Ordem de Cristo). This Portuguese military order was old and distinguished and included some of the most notable early Portuguese voyagers. Proost, Sousa, and Carvalhais were all Portuguese but took Brazil as their adopted country. In fact, Sousa was known for saying that he was "a Brazilian from Porto."[37]

Beyond these connections to kin and close friends, Proost was linked to people in other ways. He knew townsfolk through his import and export business; he dealt with numerous regular customers over the years; he owned many houses in town and had a good number of neighbors; he most likely joked and drank with other army officers and served on the board of at least one brotherhood, charitable organization, and perhaps even a close-knit secret organization such as the Masons. Like most prominent townsmen, Proost had numerous friends and acquaintances who overlapped in multiple ways.

Santos's "spirit of sociability" that existed at this time can be further exemplified with its myriad of overlapping connections, such as in Figure 1.8. The people in this network share the occupation or characteristic labeled near each edge. Several of these connections, especially between Proost and José Ricardo Wright, may be too distant to be pertinent, but other ties connecting these men prevailed, and soon we will learn about an unlikely woman who linked all of these men together in more intimate ways.

The small community of people connected in various ways to Proost included men in neighboring homes, families, wedding parties, the township government, the military, and religious or philanthropic organizations. These were mostly horizontal ties, and these men probably considered one another to share a similar place in the community and society. Some were Portuguese, others Santista, but many owned multiple properties and participated in the organizations that regulated politics and the economy of the town. Some were connected to merchants in Europe, the United States, or the capital cities of São Paulo and Brazil.

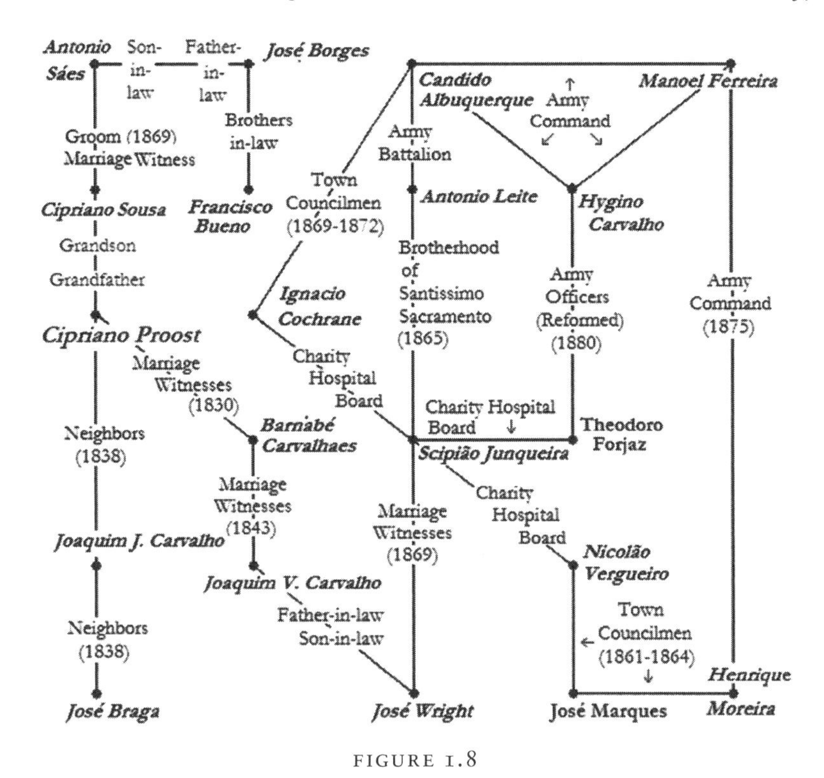

FIGURE 1.8

A Portion of Cypriano da Silva Proost's Social Network

NOTE: For most, only first and last names are included.
SOURCES: Urban property tax rolls, 1834–1835, AESP; marriage records, vol. 1, CCS, FAMS; Sobrinho, *Noutros Tempos*, 524.

Others provided local leadership for the Catholic Church or the town's prestigious charities.

It may come as a surprise, then, that a good number of these same men had a single "taproot" connection that sunk below the strata of their class and position. Six men shared a vertical connection to a former slave and black woman named Thereza de Jesus Januaria. The nature of these connections is best explained in her own words, in the will and testament she composed shortly before her death in 1879:

I, Thereza de Jesus Januaria, finding myself in perfect health and in use of all my intellectual faculties, have resolved to compose my Testament in the following form:

I was born in Angola and my parents have died, according to information that I have received from [the northeastern province of] Pernambuco. I was the slave of Cypriano da Silva Prost [*sic*], and have been free for many years. I was married in front of the Church with Manoel, a slave of the deceased Captain Januario, and my husband is also dead.

From this matrimony we had two children who died many years ago.

As I do not have any necessary heirs, and since I have few possessions, I wish the following:

I establish my heirs to be first José Moçambique, a slave of José Teixeira da Silva Braga, and previously a slave of Bernardo so-and-so, and second the free African Amelia, who in a former time served Francisco Antonio Machado Bueno. My possessions will be divided in equal parts between my heirs José and Amelia.

I name as my executors Lieutenant-Coronel Candido Anunciado Dias e Albuquerque, the Reverend Vicar Scipião Ferreira Goulart Junqueira, and Manoel Luiz Ferreira, all of whom bear the weight of carrying out this will in this order, and if one is unable, the following will do so.

And it is in this form that I conclude my testament, for which I ask Francisco Antonio Ferreira, who writes on my behalf and at my request, on account that I do not know how to write, to compose this as an expression of my will.

—Santos, 28 of August, 1879[38]

Januaria was connected to Proost, who had once been her master, and to José Teixeira da Silva Braga, who owned her first-named heir, José Moçambique. She was connected to Francisco Antonio Machado Bueno, who had once owned Amelia, the second named heir, and to Candido Anunciado Dias e Albuquerque, Scipião Ferreira Goulart Junqueira, and Manoel Luiz Ferreira, all three of whom must have given approval to be named as executors for her will. All of these men were found in Proost's small network (Figure 1.8). Januaria's scribe also shared connections with a number of these men, but was not included in the network because the nature of his relationship to her is uncertain. He may have impersonally acted on her behalf for a small fee or he might have known her well. The others were part of a network of relationships with Januaria. In fact, if all the slaves, *libertos*, and low-ranking whites whom Januaria and the group of prominent townsmen knew were excluded, this network would resemble an upside-down pyramid with her at its bottom tip. The pyramid's crown would be a network of people characterized by shared status that included family members, neighbors, and colleagues of various organizations.

Januaria was not an oddity; many free people of color, including former slaves, became property holders, married in the church, and maintained relationships with their former masters and with other slaves.[39] She did not provide a list of the property and belongings José Moçambique and Amelia eventually inherited, and any such list, if ever drawn up, is lost or inaccessible. Januaria likely left this couple a house and maybe more, since the tax rolls show her as a partial owner of a home on Rua Itororó (neighborhood #4, Figure 1.5), a few years prior to her death. It is fitting that Januaria's neighbor on Itororó was none other than Braga (who had once been a neighbor of Januaria's owner Proost). Braga's house was larger and undoubtedly fancier, but the two houses may have shared a wall and perhaps a connecting gate between their backyards. Tax collectors assessed Januaria's property tax in 1874 at one *mil-réis*, while Braga paid seven times that amount.[40] Was Braga's house home to Januaria's heir, José Moçambique? By giving part of her house to this slave and Amelia—who was probably José's *amazia*—did she provide them with a way to live closer together? We can only speculate on these intimate details.

When Januaria paid the tax on her property in 1874, another man named Jorge Avelino was listed as a secondary co-payer, meaning they probably lived together. Avelino operated a grocery store in town and later ran a small factory processing lime.[41] He was Santos-born, owned several slaves, and may have been of color. One of his slaves was a thirty-two-year-old African (*nação*) washerwoman named Belizarda, whom Avelino bought in 1865 from a man in São Sebastião for 400 *mil-réis*.[42] In this purchase, Avelino relied on the assistance of Theodor de Menezes Forjaz, the township councilman, who served as a commissioned proctor between Avelino and the seller in São Sebastião. Returning to Proost's network, Forjaz also served on the Santos Charity Hospital board along with Junqueira, the man who administered Januaria's will. Perhaps Belizarda lived with Januaria and served her and Avelino together, or she may have been rented out in town and a part of her income paid the small property tax. Belizarda remained Avelino's slave in 1881, when she entered the hospital suffering from bronchitis and died soon after.[43] Januaria and Belizarda were probably around the same age when they died and could no doubt recall earlier years in Africa and the long Middle Passage. Due to different circumstances, however, Januaria died a free and relatively well-off woman with a number of powerful connections. Belizarda died a slave.

To conclude, this chapter began with the descriptions of several slave owners, their neighbors, and their slaves, showing the differences between neighborhoods in Santos. These microareas shared many internal characteristics including demographic and occupation similarity of owners and their slaves, but also differed with respect to each other. Neighborhoods served not only as areas of homogeneity, but also as places where social connections were made through physical proximity. Despite their uniqueness, neighborhoods were not social islands, and Santistas were bound to one another in many ways that transcended not only geography but also class and race. The example of the kinship network between Cypriano Proost and his former slave, Theresa de Jesus, serves to illustrate what might be called "interdependent stratification."[44] This term is useful to describe a local society that was horizontally layered into differing ranks of people, but whose members, at least through the mid-nineteenth century, shared many vertical ties that transected these ranks. Furthermore, both horizontal and vertical ties could occur between neighbors. Clearly, Santos had a high degree of sociability, but also defined ranks of wealth and status.

The web of relationships stretched across the city and township, linking almost every resident in every neighborhood, despite their differences. In fact, Proost's network can be expanded to include Luis Pereira Machado of the Four Corners neighborhood and Francisca Maria das Chagas of the Áurea Street neighborhood. Machado's executor was the father to a man who served as a councilman with three men in Proost's network. His term on the council coincided with that of Forjaz between 1873 and 1877. Moreover, when Chagas's inheritance case faced a claim from relatives in the northeastern province of Pernambuco, a judge assigned José Justiano Bittencourt to help with the case. Bittencourt served in a wedding with Albuquerque (of Proost's network) in 1863. Bittencourt was also a township councilman with Forjaz's father. Still, one noticeable difference stands out between these two extensions of Proost's network. The tie between these men and Machado was of the horizontal type, since the executor had undoubtedly agreed to this important role. Bittencourt, on the other hand, was appointed to Chagas's case when complications arose, creating a vertical tie between Bittencourt and Chagas's widower.

CHAPTER TWO

Material and Demographic Changes

In the earliest days of colonization (1500–1600), Santos (then known only as a small part of the central coast of the Captaincy of São Vicente) was one of the first regions in the Americas to have a viable and renewable export for the European market. Sugar production took root largely through the exploitation of indigenous labor and, later, African slaves. These forced laborers cut down or burned the *tamanqueiro*, hog plum, Biriba, and other trees of the thick Atlantic Forest to plant fields of cane, all the while battling predaceous ants and quickly creeping weeds with rudimentary tools. Cane pests were one of several problems facing these early planters, but it was the variable climate, moderately fertile soil, and relatively high shipping costs that eventually hindered the early colonial Paulista sugar operations. Many of the large, old sugar *engenhos* (sugar mills) of São Vicente fell into ruin when they could no longer compete with planters in other parts of the Americas, including the Brazilian Northeast. The economy, which had been producing for both the external and internal market, turned inward as small communities along the township traded with one another for cassava flour, *aguardente*, fish, rice, fruit, and mostly locally produced tools, furniture, and cloth. There was also sufficient trade with the nearby highlands for beans and beef. The loss of a viable world commodity market did not lower the number of slaves along the coast, however. In fact, the ratio of slave to free, initially high due to the sugar economy, increased more in this region relative to the rest of São Paulo. Few to no bags of sugar passed through the port en route to European merchant houses, but local residents demanded and purchased a surprising number of African slaves for what appears to have been a growing domestic economy. Between 1777 and 1829, the percentage of slaves of the provincial population rose from 22 to 28 percent. Much of this increase was due to the large groups of slaves brought in to fill the new sugar plantation *senzalas* (slave houses) on the northern Paulista coast, but the number of slaves also increased as a percentage of the population of the township of Santos, rising from 30 percent to 33 percent.[1]

The hundreds of slaves involved in the township's local commerce lived in diverse environments and were surrounded by a great range of objects that were often at the center of their toil. This chapter focuses on the people and the objects they used. Even as populations shifted, technology changed, and new objects found their way into the daily life of city residents, slavery remained an unequal institution. In this chapter this picture of society is developed by analyzing material culture and changing demographic patterns. In the first section, a brief summary of the colonial history of Santos provides a backdrop for a description of the common material world that surrounded slaves in the township by the nineteenth century.

THE MATERIAL AND DEMOGRAPHIC PICTURE (1810–1850)

Before Brazil's independence in 1822, Santos was a minor port of low economic importance to the nation. The city was most known for its proximity to the growing, yet still small city of São Paulo and as one of the entryways over the steep escarpment that separates the province's high temperate plateau from its low tropical coast. Santos shares part of an island with the neighboring township and city of São Vicente, but the two are divided by steep hills that split the island in half. São Vicente was one of the first settlements in Brazil and one of the oldest continually inhabited European settlements in the New World. By Royal Portuguese decree, São Vicente became the administrative center of a vast area of mostly unexplored land (at least from the point of view of the colonists) that included the provinces of Rio de Janeiro, São Paulo, Paraná, Minas Gerais, Mato Grosso, and Santa Catarina. São Vicente remained the administrative center of nearly all of southern Brazil until 1681, when the captaincy was divided and the governor was transferred to São Paulo.[2]

In the first fifty years of the captaincy several sugar mills were established using enslaved indigenous labor. In 1548, Luís de Góis, an early explorer and colonist, reported in a letter to the king of Portugal that six hundred free inhabitants and three thousand slaves worked and lived in and around six sugar plantations. But disease and warfare soon eliminated many indigenous slaves, crippling the labor force that planters relied on and leaving no alternatives for a labor force in this lightly settled part of the Portuguese colony. Indigenous slaves became too expensive while high transportation costs pushed African slave prices higher in southeastern Brazil than in northeastern Brazil. In other parts of Brazil, especially the Northeast, trade routes with Europe, the Caribbean, and Africa were shorter than in the south and sugar may have fetched better prices due to lower transportation costs. The soils and climates in the Northeast were also highly suitable for growing cane, and the region soon overtook the Paulista coast in the sugar market.[3]

The colonial period of Brazil was marked by fluctuations in the fortunes of primary products, and the waxing or waning of each product caused population and power to shift between the regions of the large colony. This was apparent when gold was discovered in the interior of Brazil in the last year of the seventeenth century, sparking a rush that attracted Brazilians and immigrants from many parts of the world. With prospectors' wealth and an infrastructure created to feed, house, and supply the miners, many neighboring regions, including São Paulo, benefited economically. The political center of gravity slowly shifted southward, and Portuguese reformers moved the capital from Salvador to Rio de Janeiro in 1763. As Rio expanded and shipping technology improved, its residents became better able to export goods less expensively and to consume products grown or manufactured along the coast. This had a profound effect on coastal São Paulo, where sugar once again took root as a result of strong prices, improved cultivation, and more secure maritime networks with Europe. But the planters who used thousands of African and Brazilian slaves to expand their cane fields chose two townships to the north of Santos and south of Rio de Janeiro, rather than the old zone of sugar cultivation of the early colony. Residents of the Santos port needed to take only a short horseback ride to find the ruins of the old São Jorge dos Erasmus sugar mill, founded in 1533. Finding productive fields of sugarcane destined for European markets, on the other hand, required a one- to two-day canoe or packet boat trip to the north.[4]

With increased sugar production and more coastal trade, the townships on the northern coast of São Paulo became wealthier than rural regions to the south. Plantations in the north augmented sugar profits with earnings from rice, coffee, indigo, cassava, corn, beans, and cotton destined for the Rio and São Paulo markets. The region near the port of Santos did reasonably well producing *aguardente* and by growing cassava or catching fish for the local market. Spirits had long been a regular business for many southern counties. The governor of the captaincy, General Antonio Manoel de Mello Castro e Mendonça, reported eighteen farms producing sixty *pipas* (large tin funnels) of *aguardente* at the end of the eighteenth century. Since the townships to the north had better lands for large-scale sugar farming and their transportation costs to the Rio de Janeiro market were lower, the most prosperous farmers from these parts had on average twice as many slaves as those in Santos township. Further south and below the Santos township were poor towns like Itanhaem, Iguape, and Cananea. According to one visitor, inhabitants in the southern towns "lived miserably, having only fish, a little cassava flour, and timber to sell."[5]

Between the large new sugar plantations on the northern Paulista coast and the poor regions in the south, Santos Township provided sufficient opportunities for agriculture and fishing for the regional economy. Slaves remained the preferred people to get this work done. The percentage of slaves relative to the general population increased in the eighteenth century. Between 1777 and 1825, before and just beyond Brazil's independence in 1822, the number of slaves in the township increased from 1,748 to 2,224.[6] After this point, however, the slave population held steady as planters tended to newly planted coffee trees and sugar fields in the fertile lands below the escarpment. By 1854, Santos had nearly twice as many free inhabitants as slaves, a noticeable change from 1825, when the free inhabitants only slightly outnumbered the slaves. By 1872, the percentage of slaves had dropped to less than a quarter of the population, in large part due to the forced end of the international slave trade to Brazil in 1850.[7] The city continued to rapidly expand so that by 1890—two years after slavery was abolished—there were over 13,000 residents (see Table 2.1).

In terms of distribution of slaves, small-holding remained the norm. In 1817, almost 50 percent of all households listed slaves, and 87 percent of those had ten or fewer slaves. By 1830, the number of households with slaves had dropped to 43 percent, and 83 percent of this group had ten slaves or less. For São Sebastião, to the immediate north, the number of households with slaves was much smaller, about one-third of the 1813 total. Unlike the 1798 census, the 1817 census for São Sebastião does not list any owners with more than ninety slaves.[8] It is not known whether several large sugar plantations were overlooked or if these owners sold many of their slaves. Keeping in mind these reservations, 45 percent of households had slaves, of which 87 percent held fewer than ten slaves. These figures appear to make this neighboring township more demographically homogeneous in terms of slaveholding by the time the country declared its independence.

Despite the strong presence of farming in Santos and São Sebastião townships before 1850, large plantations with many slaves were relatively rare. As in other parts of Brazil, slavery was remarkably widespread among economic and social groups and was one of the least concentrated forms of wealth.[9] Half of all men and women in the lowest or poorest one-third bracket owned one or more slaves (see Table 2.2).[10] Enslaved men, women, and children were relatively inexpensive, at least before 1860, lowering the barriers to entry into the slaveholding world. In other words, men and women of humble origins and meager means (including Africans who had once been slaves themselves) often saved enough to buy a slave. Others who might otherwise appear to be in no position to afford slaves inherited them from their parents or spouse. But in these comments we are restricted by a small sample size of primary sources and the limitations these sources put on historians.[11]

For all wealth-holding groups, farming and fishing figured prominently in city life in the first half of the nineteenth century. Items that separated people from one another within the social hierarchy were often related to farming. Mills and distilleries, houses, stables, large structures covering mills, implements, and other types of possessions created the markers that separated those with little means from those who were wealthy. For example, only the local elite owned homes and profitable real estate in Santos, and property divided people into social categories. Within the countryside, there were many humble abodes of squatters and poor individuals with little more than four thin walls and roofs made of straw. Far fewer people owned "proper" houses—sturdy structures built with wooden beams, stone, and lime, with whitewashed walls, thick wooden doors, earthenware tile roofs, and windows framed by shutters.[12] Other

TABLE 2.1

Population of Slaves and Free Inhabitants in Santos

	1825		1854		1872		1890
	Number	Percent	Number	Percent	Number	Percent	Number
Slaves	2,224	45	2,420	38	1,627	18	0
Free	2,729	55	4,030	62	7,460	82	13,012
Total	4,953	100	6,450	100	9,087	100	13,012

SOURCES: Census lists, 1825; Brazil, *Discurso com que . . . de Fevereiro de 1856*, 991; Brazil, *Recenseamento da População . . .de Agosto de 1872*; Brazil, *População Recenseada . . . de 1890*.

TABLE 2.2

Categories of Poor, Middling, and Wealthy Inventoried Decedents (in Mil-réis*)*

	1820–1850			1851–1880		
	Upper Limit	Deflated	Number of Decedents	Upper Limit	Deflated	Number of Decedents
Poorer*	1,140	1,007	(N=18)	1,014	778	(N=23)
Middling	4,125	3,587	(N=17)	2,840	2,723	(N=22)
Wealthier	22,840	24,080	(N=18)	186,581	162,248	(N=23)

SOURCE: Inheritance records, 1800–1880, CCS, FAMS.

important markers of social division included the tools and equipment township residents used to produce the staples of the local economy. A wheel for crushing cane, a building to cover a mill and keep it dry, and a distillery to turn the cane juice into the strong *aguardente* were entry points into new economic positions. Other markers that could distinguish the poorest from the poor included a small boat and a large hand-knit fishing net, a strip of healthy coffee trees, or the muddy freshwater shallows that grew rice.

Since expensive material items were often crucial for success, status, and power in the agriculturally centered economy, slaves were not always the best marker of wealth. Numerous cobblers, laundrywomen, carpenters, vendors, or subsistence farmers owned a handful of slaves but had to rent their home from someone who was clearly wealthier. Some poor farmers outside of town lived in single-room dwellings, owned a cassava press, an oven and large pan for turning the wet cassava root into dry flour, and as many as ten slaves. In the following descriptions of material possessions it is clear that even five or six slaves bestowed less status upon a person compared to someone with the same number of slaves but who had homes in both the city and country.

The poor but slave-owning men and women can be distinguished from other farmers who owned land or equipment that allowed them to sell a variety of crops and avoid the downturns in price of single commodities. Property ownership in the city may have created one of the best markers between the elite and nonelite; residents who did not own property greatly outnumbered the property holders and were much more likely to be involved in local governance. The rest depended on this small group for their shelter. The town property rolls for 1839 show that roughly three hundred individuals owned one thousand buildings. Of these, more than two-thirds were men. On average, for every twenty residents in Santos, one property owner held three buildings. In the rural parts of the township, on the other hand, it was easier for a poor person to build and eventually claim rights to a simple home or shack. Around half of the poorest third of wealth holders in the inheritance records owned houses, and the majority of these individuals lived on small farms.[13]

A number of small and midsized farms occupied the banks of the Enseada de Bertioga, a long stretch of beach that ran from the village of Bertioga, southward. The beach was ten kilometers long and its southernmost farm was twenty-five kilometers from Santos. Bertioga sits at the mouth of a canal that separates the neighboring island of Santo Amaro (Guarujá) from the mainland. Another important regional river, Rio Itapanhaú, releases its waters at the canal near its opening to the Atlantic Ocean. Here indigenous and African slaves and free Portuguese and

Brazilians built two forts in the sixteenth century to provide an early line of defense against Spanish, Dutch, or English pirate vessels that sought to capture São Vicente and the captaincy. By the eighteenth century, the threat of the rival Europeans had declined when the Portuguese and British navies had eliminated most pirates. Now functionless, the forts fell into ruin, even as the surrounding village grew. There were no large dockside warehouses or official port area as in Santos, only a collection of small sailboats and canoes that the few farmers, shop or tavern owners, and fishermen used to transport their goods.

Looking closely at the homes in the community, several poor to middling families who farmed in Bertioga between 1830 and 1835 exemplify both the homogeneity of these rural neighborhoods and also how a townhouse or proximity to the port made a big difference in their lives. The smallest among these was a farm owned by Prudente Antonio and his sons and daughters, who lived on an acre or so of land. Included in the family property was a copper stove, a wide-lipped cauldron, a pot, a "wheel" or simple grinding mill, and a press for preparing cassava root. They lived in a small house, probably with only one room, covered with a clay tile roof. A stable shared one of the outer walls and was covered by a straw roof. Since horses and cattle were not listed among their possessions, the stable may have been occupied by their nine slaves. Collectively, their goods, including the land and house, were valued to be 1,800 *mil-réis* in 1835, but a remarkable 90 percent of that was in the value assigned to the slaves.[14]

A mile or so to the north was another farm owned by José Lopes de Jesus and his wife Gertrudes Maria de Conceição, another family that was similar in wealth holding and status to Prudente Antonio's family. Jesus and his family had for many years neighbored a small fort run by an old Lieutenant Colonel, his family, and fifty contracted slaves who guarded a cache of arms. The provincial government did not maintain this colonial remnant after Brazil's independence and was vacated. Nearby, the small farms continued as they had done for centuries. José's brother had owned the farm to the south, and their two properties were the consequence of their father's divided inheritance. Jesus lived on a cassava farm quite similar to the one held by his neighbor, Prudente Antonio, but his was a bit larger. He produced forty-eight *alquieres* (1,740 liters) of cassava flour in 1817, nearly five times as much as Antonio. He also supplemented his income by growing cane. The juice of this cane, squeezed from the thick stems, was boiled until it became the thick sugar syrup that he and his slaves fermented and distilled into *aguardente*. His slaves also picked beans and fruit in a small grove of coffee and orange trees, adding another source of income.[15]

Jesus's most valuable possession—listed first in his inventory—was his copper *lambique* (distillery), a simple apparatus that evaporated water and other vapors and collected potent spirits at the bottom of a still. He also owned a number of farm tools such as hoes, axes, and several scythes or *fouces* (machetes) used to cut cane. Among his furniture and household goods was a simple folding cot good for travel, five stools, eighteen *pó-de-pedra* (earthenware) plates, six teacups with platters, one teapot, and one mug. Unlike other households, Jesus's family did not list any silverware and may have used valueless wooden implements to eat simple meals of rice, beans, and cassava. He and his wife had no children, but they did own twelve slaves in 1830. Jesus probably used the cot while his wife and slaves slept on the floor, but they all may have shared the stools when they ate. He also owned a large, old canoe he used to take his flour, spirits, fruit, and coffee to market. Finally, there was a small oratory with two images of saints the family hung from a nail on the wall or placed on a box or table.[16]

Jesus's household was remarkably stable for nearly two decades. Rarely did a household go for so long without a death or sale of one of its slaves. The group of slaves, numbering eight in 1817, added two children (most likely offspring of the slave Maria) and two Africans who were purchased over the next thirteen years. None of these slaves were lost. Many of the slaves may have been passed down from José's father, since they were all Brazilian-born, except the two adults Jesus purchased after 1817. When the inheritance records were drawn in 1832, not one of his slaves was listed as sick or infirm. As for their sleeping quarters, they may have passed the cool, rainy winter nights in a separate two-room millhouse, while Jesus and his wife slept in their simple house. The house was so basic, in fact, that it was valued in the same category of buildings that lacked roofs or were in half ruin. Jesus's most valuable slave, João, was worth five times the amount of his house.[17]

Neither Antonio nor Jesus owned a home in town, but some of their more prosperous farming neighbors did. Nearby, João Antonio de Souza owned a farm called Morro Alto (Tall Hill) off the Bertioga stream, and this is the third example of this rural part of Santos. He also owned a house in town on Rua Santo Antonio. His rural property was similar to Antonio and José's, except he also ran an operation growing rice and picking bananas. Besides the cassava press, small sugar mill, and distillery, he owned two large pans for drying rice and seven boxes for its storage. Antonio, Jesus, and Souza's farms produced a remarkable array of goods for the local market. They show the diversity of an economy that was largely driven to produce for the township and region. Souza also listed a large number of containers such as boxes, jugs, tin funnels, barrels, sacks, and flasks, indicating he had a variety of products that needed to be packaged and shipped.[18]

Despite having the most prosperous farming household of the three, João de Souza owned fewer slaves than Antonio and Jesus in 1817. Among his seven slaves there were two couples: Cecilia and João Nação, and Felizarda and Joaquim. Both slave couples were officially married but had no children within the household. Besides the slaves, a small *agregado* (dependent or additional) family took care of the house on Rua Santo Antonio, where one of two freeborn teenage sons worked as a cobbler.[19] This family was connected to João de Souza's family in a way that was similar to the slaves' association since they also worked for the cobbler shop in exchange for shelter, food, and space. The freeborn family, however, was never obligated to stay, and they may have known that dependencies sometimes can reverse. When Souza died, his widow moved into the town house and managed a frugal life from the income of two slaves. The young cobbler probably added his small profits to the dual family income, belying the old widow's claim to the census taker that she lived off her "own agency." João Nação and his wife Cecilia, who had both served as slaves for their mistress for almost two decades, were the only two slaves who remained with the family.[20]

In terms of slaveholding, these three farmers were nearly alike. They each had a moderate number of slaves of similar value, and their wealth was nearly entirely concentrated in their slaves. Because of the town house, only Souza had nonhuman property that exceeded the combined prices of his slaves. The other two farmers, like the majority of poor or middling households in Brazil, seemed willing to bypass even the most rudimentary material goods, such as furniture or simple farming equipment, in favor of slaves. As these men and their families in Bertioga show, an equally important marker of social position in the Santos township before 1850 was real estate and agricultural production.[21] Real estate owners could be divided into two groups, with one side including those of little or moderate means who could afford to rent or own a house in either the city or the countryside, and those with moderate to wealthy means who owned houses in both places. As far as any conception of "elite" existed among the farmers of Bertioga, property and agricultural output were equally or more important than slaveholding size.

The farms at the Enseada de Bertioga had a degree of homogeneity resembling small areas within the city such as Machado's Four Corners or Chagas's Áurea Street. In the country, however, neighborhoods stretched over long coastlines, peninsulas, or portions of islands. Since most of these neighbors lived off the land, their similarities were often based on the types of products they could grow. The final example of a Bertioga family household is Antonio Damazio, who lived up the coast from the ruined Bertioga forts. Like his neighbors, he ran a small cassava farm using several slaves who planted, harvested, and processed the plant's root into flour to be sold in Santos. Damazio or his slaves packed their canoe with their flour and traveled to the Santos market via the natural canal behind Santo Amaro, a journey that would have required a strenuous day of paddling and poling. Presumably, they spent the night in Santos with friends or on the rough floor of their canoe—under a leather canvas if it rained—before making the journey home.[22]

Damazio lived with his wife, Joaquina, and three slaves. He and his wife were *pardos*, while his slaves were black. The oldest of his slaves, Joanna, was the mother of two slave children, Baldoina and Engrasia. Engrasia, a one-year-old infant in 1818, disappeared from the census records; like many infants her age, she probably died. Joanna gave birth to two more sons, Joaquim and João, who remained in the household with their mother, all as property of Antonio Damazio until his death. Antonio's young grandson, Francisco, moved into the household sometime around 1825. Since he was only one year younger than Baldoina and two years older than Joaquim, this group of children, free and enslaved, were most likely playmates that explored the thick forest behind their house or waded in the cool waters of the stream after they finished their numerous household tasks. The census documents do not indicate who fathered Baldoina, Joaquim, or João, but it would not be unreasonable to guess that their master was also their father since they are, unlike their mother, listed as *pardo*.[23]

After 1820, Antonio Damazio moved his family and slaves to a farm much closer to Santos, shortening the canoe trip to only an hour or two. His new plot of land, on the Island of Santo Amaro, rose from a shoreline rimmed by tall boulders and was probably as thick with vegetation as it is today. The soil in this area is sandy and acidic and really only good for manioc. Somehow, though, he expanded the farm to include the cultivation of rice by 1828. Antonio was sixty years old by then, two years older than his wife, Joaquina. They probably depended on the labor of their slaves and their slaves' children for much of the work. The children, both slaves and free, ranged from seven to twelve years old. If their family was like poor Brazilian rural families today, they lent much of their energy to the tiresome task of pressing and drying the manioc, feeding the chickens or hogs, and sweeping the mud floors of their house. The hardest jobs, however (including that of raising four children), must have fallen on the shoulders of slave Joanna.

Before Damazio moved, eight *pardos*, four whites, and one black made up the racial profile of the Bertioga neighborhood. Most were married and older, averaging fifty years. In terms of marriage and age, this rural neighborhood bore resemblance to Four Corners, but in terms of household size, slaveholding, and race it was like that of the Áurea Street neighborhood. One visitor to the coast of São Paulo wrote, "The poorest make their home, that is, a house with earth supported by cane and covered by straw, at the foot of the mountains and near rivers. Household goods include a pipe, a fusil, and two nets—one for sleeping in during the night and afternoon and the other for fishing. With the fusil they eat what they hunt."[24] Damazio had slaves and could afford a more permanent house and more possessions; the homes of a few of his neighbors probably fit this description as well.

Antonio Damazio may have moved because it made it easier and cheaper for him to get his cassava to the market. His new land also allowed him to diversify his risks by growing other products. Damazio's new neighborhood at Gois Beach also had more non-slave-owning cassava and rice planters than slave owners. But the households of this neighborhood were generally larger and had more dependents or family members to help. Gois Beach was a little more prosperous because its farmers did not have to rely on only one crop; in fact, one neighbor had a productive distillery. This neighbor's production of spirits in 1830 even surpassed the volume produced by the wealthy Machado family.[25]

After Damazio died in December 1838, almost five *mil-réis* were subtracted from the inheritance because of fees owed to the city jailer. The interim judge working on the case, João Baptista Rodrigues da Silva, wrote to the assessor, "It was not possible to have the slaves Joanna and her sons João, Matheos, and Ruffino present for assessment because following the death of the husband [Damazio], they do not recognize the suppliant as their legitimate master, and as they do not obey her, the suppliant asks that you travel to a place called Tegereba, where the slaves will be found incarcerated." Perhaps Joanna knew that Joaquina would sell her and her children off to different parts of the township or country and attempted to run away from her. This might also be another clue as to the mystery of her children's father, who might have been Antonio Damazio himself, a situation that would have caused rivalry and grief for Joaquina. Joanna and her sons were sold, for a little less than one *conto* total, and it is not known whether they continued to remain as a family or were broken up and scattered like so many other slave families.[26]

These four farming families present a good idea of the homogeneity that existed in most of the small rural communities. Moreover, their slaves were similar in characteristics related to race, sex, and age as well as in opportunities toward forming families and the kind of work they were forced to do. There were differences between these families as well, with the most notable being the degree of access to Santos and its port. If João

Antonio de Souza had not owned a house in town his eventual widow may have been much harder pressed to get by merely on the cobbling skills of her live-in freeborn dependent. Similarly, when Antonio Damazio moved out of the village of Bertioga and into a rural neighborhood much closer to the port, he soon resembled his new neighbors in the products he grew. Damazio's family also gives a sense of the degree of mobility that existed for those who could afford it, but which could sometimes have terrible consequences for their slaves.

Slaves owned by people who were poor or of middling wealth were not restricted to farming or even city occupations. Many Santos residents made their livelihoods from the ocean and spent more time aboard ships than on dry land. For instance, the four slaves owned by José Gregorio do Nascimento sailed a two-masted schooner. Nascimento owned the boat with a partner named Joaquim Arcenio da Silva. Judging from the will Nascimento left and the contents of the boat, these two men and four slaves had traveled from Europe and might have intended to return. Nascimento left his share of the boat to his sole heir, his mother, who lived in Lisbon. He stipulated, however, that his partner, Silva, would have the right to use the boat and his possessions for eight years. Nascimento also mandated that the four slaves would be freed, but not before serving his partner for three years. A number of items on the ship give clues as to how these men, including the four slaves, lived and worked. A locked trunk contained a cloth bag full of Spanish pesos, along with smaller quantities of gold and silver. Many articles of clothing and linen appear to have been shared among the master, his partner, and the four slaves. There were fourteen shirts, six leggings, nine pairs of socks, seven jackets, four rough bed sheets made of flax, four pillowcases, and seven hand towels. All ranged from "used" to "well-worn," a clue that they were not intended for sale. The combined value of Nascimento's half of the ship plus his possessions was less than the assessed worth of Prudente Antonio's rudimentary farm on Bertioga Beach, yet their slaves may have been able to speak several languages and were familiar with cultures far removed from this corner of Brazil.[27]

Other slaves whose lives were not comparable to small-farm workers were those who served as house servants to the most wealthy town residents. As Santos was a little town, largely unassuming and unimportant to the nation before 1850, visitors who knew Rio de Janeiro or Salvador probably regarded wealthy Santistas as paupers posing as princes. Nonetheless, the slave chambermaids, livery men, cooks, and housekeepers that labored for the Santos elite knew how to use or preserve objects most slaves never saw. For instance, the most trusted female slaves (those that emptied their mistresses' chamber pots, for example) handled a variety of precious stones and metals meant for adornment. Slaves pinned silver brooches to mistresses' breasts, inserted aquamarine topaz earrings into ladies' pierced ears, or polished lustrous lockets, taking care not to let the tiny nestled portraits escape. Masters displayed their position and power with golden cuff links, shiny *filigrane* buttons for their overcoats, or silver breast pins in the shape of anchors. Pocket watches were a fine marker of wealth, since their golden chains could conspicuously cross a wearer's waist.[28] The servant of a wealthy owner poured tea in fancy china teacups with silver spoons, carried chocolate truffles on bejeweled trays, and cut roasted veal with fine bone and silver–handled knives. They polished desks and tables, restoring the original dark brown hues of the *jacaranda* or the deep red of native *vinhático* wood. Thick mattresses needed fresh down, mirrors and china basins called for a daily wiping, and hanging portraits required dusting. Slaves handled, preserved, and occasionally stole the luxuries that were the markers of social placement.

Slaves of poor owners operated tools that often performed the same task as the fancy tools of the wealthy, but they were simpler and presumably less effective. For example, equipment for processing manioc appeared in a number of inheritance records, but the equipment belonging to families classified in the lower bracket of wealth was quite unlike that of the wealthier owners. In the humble rural neighborhood of Enseada de Bertioga, Prudente Antonio's total estate was valued at 2,460 *mil-réis* (adjusted to 1850 prices), and this included an old manioc press valued at 2 *mil-réis*. In contrast, Luis Pereira Machado, with an estate of 36,560 *mil-réis*, owned two new presses that each had three screws, effectively tripling the amount of cassava root that could be pressed. These screws were large and were the key component to the press. We can get a better sense of the differences between one- and three-screw cassava presses by viewing the photographs in Figure 2.1. A single-screw press well exceeded the height of its adult worker, while a three-screw press filled a barn. Machado's two presses, likely bearing resemblance to the three-screw press of the photograph, were together worth 27 *mil-réis*. Prudente Antonio also owned an oven with a large iron pan used for drying and cooking the cassava flour. His oven was valued at 8 *mil-réis*. The oven of another wealthier township resident was bigger or in much better shape and was valued at 18 *mil-réis*.[29]

Slaves used other equipment, tools, and furniture that had marked differences in quality. Even fairly small and ubiquitous items like mattocks, a kind of hoe, ranged in price and quality. The same was true of basins, trunks, desks, tables, measuring kits containing weights and scales, knives, chairs, boxes, beds, quilts, mirrors, scythes, flasks, limbecs, axes, hammers, mortar and pestles, wooden kitchen trays, cauldrons, gimlets, tubs,

FIGURE 2.1

One- and Three-Screw Cassava Presses

SOURCES: Instituto Estadual do Patrimônio Cultural, "Casa de Farinha"; (*inset photograph*) http://ademaraigner.blogspot.com/2008_12_01_archive.html .

and many other objects listed in the inheritance records in the nineteenth century. These items give a sense of the common, day-to-day *stuff* with which slaves worked and that defined their days' activities, and tell a great deal about their lives. Slaves who worked with broken or cheap tools toiled much less effectively than those who had access to new and functional tools. The goods listed in the inheritance records point to which slaves were in each group.

After independence, Santos held a little under five thousand people, nearly evenly divided between slaves and free (see Table 2.3). Its main products were cassava flour, rice, and *aguardente*. Coffee, introduced in the eighteenth century, accounted for only 2 percent of the town's total production value.[30] By 1854, the population numbered a little more than seven thousand, with 57 percent free Brazilians, 34 percent slaves, and 9 percent foreigners.[31] By this point, the city enjoyed higher levels of trade than many of the province's other ports, but its destiny as South America's busiest port could never have been imagined. Exported goods from Santos were worth 2,669,804 *mil-réis*, while goods from Ubatuba, the largest port town to the north, were about half that. Both places continued to compete for the flour, rice, and *aguardente* trade. The growing of coffee in the lands above the escarpment that separated the coast from São Paulo's high plateau made few early inroads into the agriculture of the coast below.[32]

Fastidious municipal census takers who walked their neighborhoods in the late colonial and early Imperial periods often counted the number of people in a household and noted the demographic profile and, for families that farmed, the previous year's production. These are valuable records for obtaining a multilayered view of society and economy—from the personal and local to the regional and national—but perhaps these records have been given more confidence than they deserve. The nominal census lists for Santos, for example, make it nearly impossible to identify whether slaves, listed along with the urban residences, were city or country workers and residents. For example, Captain Major João Batista da Silva owned three

TABLE 2.3

Population of Slave and Free in Santos, 1825, 1854, 1872 (Percent)

	1825			
	Slaves		Free	
Age Groups	Males	Females	Males	Females
0–10	10	14	25	22
11–50	85	80	51	61
51+	6	6	24	18
Total	(N=1,435)	(N=789)	(N=1,248)	(N=1,481)
	1854			
	Slaves		Free	
Age Groups	Males	Females	Males	Females
0–10	10	16	29	25
11–50	76	73	57	63
51+	15	12	14	13
Total	(N=1,297)	(N=1,123)	(N=1,990)	(N=2,040)
	1872			
	Slaves		Free	
Age Groups	Males	Females	Males	Females
0–10	19	21	24	23
11–50	73	73	74	75
51+	5	8	3	3
Total	(N=943)	(N=684)	(N=4,068)	(N=3,392)

SOURCES: Census lists, 1825; Brazil, *Discurso com que . . . de Fevereiro de 1856*, 991; Brazil, *Recenseamento da População . . . de Agosto de 1872*.

properties scattered throughout the township, two of which were country estates. On the land he called Morrinho (Little Hill), he ran a small business called Feitoria da Casca de Mangue (Mangrove Bark Factory). This enterprise sent a handful of slaves into the swamps in canoes to gather the reddish-brown bark of the Red Mangrove (*Rhizophora mangle*). The bark was then boiled to extract an amorphous substance used to cure leather for saddlers, cobblers, and harness makers.[33] Many kilometers away, Silva owned another farm called Pernambuco, home to forty slaves. Little is known about this property and these slaves, other than that the beauty of its two beaches and the translucent aquamarine ocean water make it popular for beachgoers today. This property was not located on the Island of São Vicente, where the city and port are protected by a natural bay, but on the neighboring island of Santo Amaro. In the city of Santos, Silva owned a house on Rua Antonia, where he listed sixty-two slaves. The thirty-two males of this residence between ages fifteen and forty might have been rented out, but it is far more likely that they were the same slaves as those listed in the separate rural property register. Slaves such as João, Serafim Carpinteiro, Severino, and others, listed along with Captain Batista da Silva at Rua Antonia, probably either worked the fields at Pernambuco or labored in the swamps near Morrinho.[34]

Similar to these two sites, more than 90 percent of the 154 farms in the 1817 land register were located many kilometers to the north and northeast of the port of Santos. These property owners listed 748 slaves and 118 freeborn dependents (*agregados*) on these lands, a substantial number considering the census counted 2,224 slaves for the whole township.[35] If the families of the property owners are added to the rural population and the number of city inhabitants adjusted to account for the slaves listed at city residences but not living there, we might approximate that around a quarter of the township's population recorded by the census lived in the rural areas of the Santos township. This adds strong evidence that historical sources and contemporaries did not always delineate "rural" and "urban" slaves in the many townships that contained small to midsized towns surrounded by many miles of country.

THE MATERIAL AND DEMOGRAPHIC PICTURE (1850–1890)

The international slave trade was repressed in 1850, and in the following decades European immigrants began to arrive in large numbers. As a consequence, the distribution of slaves by age and sex came to resemble that of the free. Up through the 1850s, there was a far higher percentage of slaves of working age than freeborn of working age, reflecting the prevalence of imported slaves. Additionally, males outnumbered females nearly two to one during the 1820s. In 1852, the sex ratio (male to female) had fallen to about one, yet this ratio again began to climb in the 1860s and 1870s when thousands of slaves entered the province through the internal slave trade. As we will see in the next chapter, most of these imported slaves circumvented or passed through Santos, but enough stayed to make the slave population again resemble its previous "working-age male immigrant" form. European immigrants were also entering the free population. By 1872 both slaves and free people had disproportionate numbers of working-age males relative to females of all ages, children, and elderly.

The growth in the population coincided with the diversification of the economy, the increase in port trade, and the expansion of new agricultural goods, particularly coffee. When coffee trees gradually spread throughout the northeastern and central parts of São Paulo during the 1840s and 1850s, nearly all of the beans were exported to international markets through the port of Rio de Janeiro. Since provincial imports were also funneled through the Imperial capital, European manufactured goods bound for São Paulo would often pass through Rio's merchant houses. Merchants of these goods, who also controlled part of the Santos trade, were sometimes reluctant to create competition to their business in the Imperial capital. In 1852, 73,720, sixty-kilo (132-pound) bags of coffee descended the escarpment for shipment out of Santos. Coffee exports out of Rio de Janeiro, on the other hand, were somewhere between one and two million bags per year.[36]

Why would Rio, a city that was more than four hundred kilometers from the city of São Paulo, ship nearly all of São Paulo's goods, rather than the port of Santos that was only eighty kilometers away? Geography was the most important factor, since the highway that descended the Paulista plateau through the littoral mountains to the coast was often so treacherous that merchants found it safer and cheaper to take the much longer route. Until the highway was improved, only mules (rather than carriages or wagons) could make the hazardous and expensive journey. Even after the improvements and considerable attention by provincial officials, the common winter rains often made the road temporarily impassible into the twentieth century.[37]

The port of Santos, therefore, played a peripheral role in the first stage of Brazil's coffee expansion because of geography and lack of cheap transportation. The exclusion from the early coffee boom also sheltered the littoral trade of sugar, flour, *aguardente*, and rice. Thus, traditional agricultural practices probably continued longer in Santos than in parts of the Paulista interior despite its better proximity to the shipping trade of Europe. But the exclusion from the coffee trade abruptly ended when the British inaugurated an eighty-five-mile rail line between Santos and Jundiaí (through São Paulo) in 1867. The railroad was considered a technological marvel, and European newspapers described its Herculean stationary steam engines that pulled the heavy locomotives over inclines of a 10 percent grade. That same year, the provincial government completed the new trans-*serra* highway that, when not raining heavily, competed well with the railway in the first few years of operation. These transportation improvements helped lower the price of goods and spurred exports. In 1874, Santos shipped 836,426 bags of coffee beans, which comprised over 11 percent of the world's total.[38] The town's population also increased in the years following the railway's construction. A total of 10,120 people claimed Santos as their home in 1872, of which 65 percent were free Brazilians, 17 percent were slaves, and 15 percent were foreigners.[39] Compared to the 1854 census, there was a decline in the number of slaves (from 2,420 to 1,627) and an increase in the numbers of foreigners (from 646 to 1,557). Most of these foreigners were Portuguese, followed by colonists from Germany, France, Spain, North America, and England.

The city was governed by a council of men who drew from the regional elite. In 1837 the council expanded from seven members to nine. The composition of councilmen was also altered, reflecting new sources of power available to men within the shifting economy of the Santos township. Before 1850 there were noticeably more Portuguese councilmen (although birthplaces are more difficult to discern for the later period). Portuguese immigrants certainly arrived in higher numbers after 1860, but these foreigners may not have had the same chances for political power as earlier generations of Portuguese residents. The council also included a number of men in professions that were absent among the earlier generations of councilmen. During the first half of the century, this governing body included two plantation owners and three church officials. In the second half of the century, men of these professions were no longer elected to the council. Instead, businessmen—especially coffee merchants—filled the council chairs. The council appeared in several ways to become more professional after 1850, with more lawyers and men who served in other public capacities.[40]

The composition of the council changed according to the greater shifts in the township's population, economy, and material culture. By the second half of the century, the trickle of new wealth became a torrent when the tiny port monopolized the province's export of the enormous supply of coffee. Farms and agricultural goods disappeared from the inheritance records, while *armazens* and manufactured goods took their place. Slaves became more concentrated in Santos, as poor immigrants moved in and many poor and middling groups sold their slaves inland to the rich plantation owners. Slaves who remained in town were often rented out, frequently to immigrants willing to rent a slave or pay the same amount for a free man's wage. By the 1850s and 1860s the nature of wealth had changed, and those who were making a small fortune by financing, selling, storing, or shipping coffee were no longer as connected to the old agricultural elite. The economy had expanded as well and new objects and commodities became available.

As the types of objects Santistas owned and valued altered, the ways workers and servants went about their daily lives changed as well. This was especially true for the slaves who put the tools into the ground, scrubbed linen and clothing in outdoor washtubs, or placed the pots and pans onto wood stoves. Items that had been counted and assessed with great precision in the first half of the century were largely excluded in inheritance records of the second half. Among the poor and middling groups, clothing became something to be worn and disposed of because it became valueless and unnoted. The same was true with linen and cloth, excluding the large rolls that were sold in stores. Canoes and boats disappeared from backyards while carriages and wagons took their place. Town residents were less likely to possess religious items such as oratories, iconography, and shrines. Decedents stopped leaving firearms and weapons for their heirs, but they did bequeath small objects that would have struck their grandparents as exotic and frivolous.[41] Mademoiselle Camille Barriére, for example, left a long list in 1879 that included shiny velvet ribbons, long braids of human hair, wide hoops for Victorian dresses, white gloves, bonnets, and petticoats. She was Santos's first real French shopkeeper and a representative of new fashions and the novel products of European industry.[42]

In sum, this chapter has explored the ways possessions, including the tools that slaves used, changed over the century. It has also looked broadly at people, such as the composition of the population of the township of Santos as it moved from a sleepy backwater port in the 1820s to an important point of entrance and exit for millions of bags of coffee and sugar and thousands of European immigrants by the end of the century. The number of slaves in town increased during the first half of the century, but the rate of increase was greater among the free population. By the second half of the century, the slave population was in decline, largely due to legal factors, and possibly because the slaves were not able to naturally replenish their population.[43]

CHAPTER THREE

Slave Markets and Networks[1]

The British used to say that every man of affairs in Brazil was involved in some way or another in the slave trade. This view was reinforced by experience in Santos: John "João" Hayden, who served as consul to Great Britain during the 1860s, also traded slaves for his associates and family. He served as a middleman for the sale of an enslaved mason to a peddler making his way to Campinas. This activity was linked to his role in managing European investments in local land and materials for the new railroad because the seller of the enslaved mason was the Baron Mauá, a man organizing an enormously ambitious and expensive project to build a railroad between Santos and the coffee highlands. The consul also assisted a woman who wished to sell her domestic servant to a city local, and he guided his own wife's purchase of a small slave family that included a fifty-year-old maid and her twenty-year-old son. All these transactions took place over a six-month period in 1865, a moment when the final phase of European financing became available to complete the much anticipated railroad.[2]

Consul Hayden may have been untypical among British representatives, but he was a typical participant of the slave market. He traded slaves as a secondary pursuit, but the transactions served to reinforce his network of professional relationships and to provide himself or others with slaves who supplied labor and potentially elevated family status. The Baron of Mauá, for example, agreed to godfather the consul's son soon after their slave trade. Consul Hayden was an older man at the height of his career and a person who knew that an investment in slaves would provide a form of insurance for his family when he could no longer work. He was involved in multiple slave transactions over a short period of time, yet these transactions were part of a social network he had formed mostly through other means. Finally, as for other buyers, these slaves were seen to embody multiple functions. Hayden's wife likely recognized that the enslaved maid and her son would add skills the family desired or could profit from, cultivate their social image, and aid the family by returning capital if the time came that they needed to sell the slaves. She bought the slaves from another city resident, keeping the slave mother and her son on their native ground, a small corner of a township that was probably the only world either had ever known.[3]

Hundreds of mostly older men of varying means in Santos entered into a remarkably decentralized, segmented, yet interconnected system with the purpose of buying, selling, trading, or mortgaging their slaves over the nineteenth century. The market was *decentralized* because it was carried out by a great number of individuals with no formal organization or association. Although a few people traded more than others, the majority of slaves were exchanged between men and women who bought and sold only a few slaves in their lifetimes. Additionally, Santos had no place, such as the Valongo neighborhood in Rio de Janeiro, where slave trading was the primary economic activity. Instead, the commission and merchant houses that traded slaves spent much more of their time and effort trading commodities such as coffee, cotton, and sugar. The market was *segmented* because there were discernable groups (often called "cliques" in the network-theory literature) of slave traders with particular and shared characteristics. Finally, the market was *interconnected* because these discernable groups of men and women were connected to other groups by a few "bridging" individuals.

There are many reasons to believe this model of trade, one that had striking differences from the slave marketplace in Rio de Janeiro, was followed by most Brazilian townships that were rural or had small urban centers. For instance, a similar pattern of localized networks created by the trades of single or small lots of slaves existed in Mogi das Cruzes, a township north of Santos.[4] Unlike the large cities of the Atlantic slave trade during the nineteenth century, places like Santos and Mogi das Cruzes did not concentrate slave trading geographically or within exclusive professions, a remarkable fact considering slavery remained a motor of the economy in the 1860s and 1870s. Indeed, thousands of slaves were moving from regions that were less economically vibrant—including the Northeast—to the booming coffee-growing regions of the southeast. A large portion of these bondspeople were forced through the port and over the highway connecting the township to São Paulo.[5] As we will see, however, Santos residents mostly let these coffles pass, turning instead to neighbors, friends, and associates to buy a slave that usually lived nearby.

This chapter approaches the local market and the port trade of slaves as they rotated in and out of town via canoes, packet ships, and overland in coffles, or as they were traded between households and neighborhoods within Santos. There was no single slave market per se, but a series of complex networks that assisted or constrained buyers and sellers as they made their transactions. The availability of slaves for sale and their range of prices were two powerful but exogenous forces that influenced sales, but slave markets went past these two largely impersonal and structural variables. People entering into slave-related transactions often had to depend on a previously existing network and, hence, their social position. Buyers, sellers, and the slaves they traded had different experiences and acted in different ways, depending upon their position within these networks. This is not to suggest there is no value in performing aggregate studies of slave prices or broad changing characteristics of traded slaves within large regions or over long periods of time. Rather, it is a new way of looking at the slave market that stresses individual owners, their connections to one another, and how these components may have affected the particular slaves they acquired or sold.

I also seek to explain the mechanisms that paired sellers to buyers within webs of relationships that fit within the natural and constructed topography of the city and coastal township. Doing so provides additional evidence that slavery in Santos was hierarchical because the overlapping networks of traders and slaves lent to and fit within a society in which social stratification affected all groups. The social distance that existed between groups, both for masters and their slaves, was manifest in the position of owners and slaves within trading networks. Social stratification also appeared geographically; neighborhoods reinforced and bound groups of slaves and masters within a social and economic hierarchy. Sellers, buyers, and their agents acted within discernable networks that had ties across real space and used a scripted protocol of selling to maintain or advance their social positions and to procure labor for a diverse economy. As a result, particular individuals and groups ultimately sought and traded slaves with certain characteristics and relied on the trading networks to pair buyers and slaves.[6]

TO TRADE A SLAVE IN SANTOS

When people wished to buy or sell a slave in Santos, they followed procedures that were similar to those used by traders in other parts of Brazil. As we will see, most sellers relied on their friends, family, and acquaintances to find trustworthy buyers; others placed an advertisement in the local newspaper. These advertisements give few details about the sellers, buyers, or renters but are a rich source of information about the types of slaves entering or reentering the market. Beginning with its first printing in 1849, the fourth page of the Santos broadsheet, *Revista Commercial*, featured the current prices of primary exports, the daily arrivals and departures of passenger and freight ships as they followed the tides, and classified advertisements of a large variety of products and services, including slaves. Common practice was for advertisers to leave their contact information at the newspaper office in order to retain their privacy. Santos was small enough that even listing a residential or business address might reveal one's identity to the growing number of people who disapproved of such commerce. The newspaper appears, however, to have been the least common way to sell slaves in Santos and other small markets, and more common in Brazil's larger towns and cities.[7]

When a customer answered an advertisement or, as was more common, connected to a seller through an acquaintance, he or she entered the negotiation stage of the transaction. Few documents exist detailing this common event in rural areas or small towns, but a bit is known about the larger slave blocks, such as the Valongo market in Rio or the slave pens in New Orleans. In these places, buyers inspected slaves as they would domesticated animals. They assessed limbs, teeth, gait, and dexterity; but unlike horses or cattle, potential buyers also looked at backs and buttocks for scars of whippings, or ankles for the tell-tale signs of the grip of stocks, as signs of punishment could mean an unruly slave. Sales could also involve interviews. One account from the Valongo describes a buyer who conversed with a slave before making the purchase, and this may have been common to confirm the biography and skills claimed by the seller. It is not a surprise that in big markets buyers and sellers were seen openly haggling over prices, since each deal represented a considerable amount of money.[8] In the local trade that dominated the slave market in Santos, buyers and sellers often knew each other or shared mutual friends, and this probably smoothed the bargaining process.

Once a price had been reached, the buyer had to visit the customs house or town hall to pay the municipal and provincial taxes (*meia-siza*) and receive a receipt of the payment. Transacting parties had to show this receipt to a clerk in a separate notary office to get a bill of sale (*escriptura de compra e venda*).[9] The bill of sale not only established ownership, but also was the best defense for either party in the rare case of an accusation of misconduct or fraud. The contract was written in the notary office, a private institution closely regulated by the Imperial government that documented and stored records of commercial transactions of every type, including manumission letters. Occasionally, the notary officer carried his register, ink, and quill to the house of a buyer or seller to document the trade, but this was done as a favor for a friend or for an additional charge. Notary offices also charged a fee for writing and permanently safeguarding these records. Copies were made for each of the parties, but these were probably sent or picked up days later, after the notary or a clerk had time to transcribe the original. Payment for the slave was made either in the notary office or at the time of the transaction, and most bills noted that payment "had already been received" (*ja ter recebido*).[10]

Imperial law also required the presence of at least two additional adult males to witness the transaction and to vouch for the identity of the parties. If a buyer, seller, agent, or witness could not write, another adult male signed on their behalf. In most cases, it appears that the witnesses had special arrangements with the notary office because fewer than fifteen men in Santos witnessed most transactions. On many occasions, the witnesses were friends of the buyers and sellers, and some of the observers had previously traded slaves with the participants of the transactions they observed.[11]

With traders, agents, witnesses, and notary clerks all crowded into a small provincial notary office, the transactions likely became boisterous and celebratory. There is no evidence that slaves were witness to any such celebration. As long as all parties could testify that name, age, and birthplace (and sometimes skin color and occupation) were correctly written in the bill, this likely sufficed. When a slave was purchased within the interprovincial trade or over long distances within the province, the notary asked for passports or written statements from the seller's local notary office that could give proof of the seller's identity and that the slave was not contraband. Interestingly, the notary officer also recorded whether the trading party was personally known (*conhecido*) to him or simply recognized (*reconhecido*). When a buyer or seller was only recognized, he or she was nearly always represented by an agent who was known to the notary. Since notaries may have refused to draw up a bill for a buyer, seller, or agent whose identity could not be personally confirmed, we get a sense of how important personal contacts were for all kinds of contracts. With the ink of the signatures drying in the register, ownership of the slave or slaves passed, as the bill noted, "the total dominion and rights inherent in the appropriation."[12]

Slave trading in Santos was done on a remarkably small scale. We know now that small-scale ownership of slaves in Brazil was far more common than the largeholdings associated with the *casas grandes e senzalas* (big houses and slave quarters, usually within plantations or ranches), and it is becoming increasingly apparent that infrequent single-slave transactions within local markets were the norm for slave trading in Brazil. Traders during this period more commonly traded one slave than two, while group sales were rare. In Santos, traders averaged 1.2 to

1.3 slaves per transaction. Even transactions involving intra- and interprovincial trade were chiefly composed of small-scale transactions. In fact, intermunicipal transactions averaged slightly more slaves per trade than transactions in this township involving longer distances.[13]

Most trading of slaves in Santos took place between township residents. This is a point that deserves to be highlighted because historians have given considerably more attention to the interprovincial slave trade, especially for São Paulo. Trading across provinces (interprovincial), within the province (intraprovincial), and within the township (intramunicipal) are defined by the residences of who is doing the buying and selling, and clearly the latter two vastly overshadowed the former type of slave trade. The majority of slaves that were bought and sold, therefore, simply moved within and between different neighborhoods. This was true even as Santos was becoming a busy port for coffee, sugar, and imported manufactured goods as well as an increasingly important gateway for imported slaves and immigrants.

When slaves were sold to neighbors, localized trading networks formed. These relationships stretched not only between family members and work colleagues, but also between club and association members and through the ties that developed between two people who regularly exchanged money for goods or services. In the tax records and bills of sale, about a third to half of all buyers also sold slaves. In addition, a vast majority of buyers and smaller majority of sellers were residents of Santos. As a port city and the entry point for thousands of slaves to the interior, Santos did attract peddlers and dealers, even if most of them declared other pursuits as their primary occupations. On the other hand, this book suggests that some of the traditional emphasis that historians have placed on peddlers, *ciganos* (gypsies), *comboieiros* (slave conveyers), or other (presumably untrustworthy) middlemen, may need less emphasis in our general discussion of slave trading.[14]

What kinds of people should the literature emphasize, then? João Batista Rodrigues da Silva, who bought a slave named Manoel in 1832, was a fairly typical buyer. He was married, fifty-three years old (according to an unrelated court case), Portuguese-born (in the small town of Santo Andrião de Padi da Graça, in the archbishopric of Braga), and a self-described businessman. He appears only once more in the records, as an agent for a sale in 1841 between a man named Manoel Mina and a doctor named José da Motta. Silva was typical not only in the fact that he resembled most buyers demographically, but also because he appeared only twice in the records. Manoel (the slave) was most likely an expensive investment, and Manoel Mina (the buyer) surely considered what this purchase would do for his economic and social position in town and for his security in case he was no longer able to work. If he had any potential heirs, they were probably also a consideration when he handed over his savings.[15]

As shown in Table 3.1, sellers differed from buyers in that they were a bit older and more likely to be single, Brazilian-born, and in an occupation other than business. The tax lists and bills of sale are filled with sellers such as José Martins do Monte, who was forty-two years old, born in the interior of São Paulo, married, and a trader of sugar and coffee; or Brigadier José Olinto de Carvalho e Silva who was married, born in the city of São Paulo, and sixty-seven years old when he sold Felisbina in 1843.[16] Although purchasing a slave might have ensured a small in-

TABLE 3.1

Profile of Transacted Slaves in Santos, 1832–1873

	Slave Tax (1832–1859)		Bills of Sale (1861–1873)	
	Buyers	Sellers	Buyers	Sellers
Sex (percent)				
Men	89	85	88	82
Women	12	15	13	19
Commercial or religious associations	3	2	2	1
Age (average, in years)				
One transaction	43	46	46	49
First of multiple transactions	35	37	45	nd
Last transaction	43	43	49	nd
Civil status (percent)				
Single	33	36	13	14
Married	61	53	83	71
Birthplace (percent)				
Portugal	76	63	46	50
Brazil (including Santos)	20	35	52	50
Santos	16	17	33	44
Europe	4	4	0	0
Number with demographic information	(N=53)	(N=60)	(N=35)	(N=17)
Occupation (percent)				
Business	74	71	62	65
Public office	11	20	34	27
Farming	14	15	5	12
Army	7	14	15	15
Total number of individuals	(N=179)	(N=219)	(N=138)	(N=151)
Number of coded individuals	(N=100)	(N=105)	(N=111)	(N=63)
Number of slaves in transactions	(N=396)	(N=398)	(N=242)	(N=242)

NOTE: Numbers in percentage categories may not add up to 100 percent either because of rounding or because of subcategories. See the discussion on methodology in an appendix for the method and meaning of coding.
SOURCES: Slave tax lists, 1832–1859, AESP; bills of sale, 1861–1873, PCNS, SCNS.

come if the buyer became incapacitated, older men like Monte and Silva or the smaller number of female buyers might have been compelled to sell their slaves to provide income for dowries or retirement. Slaves required an amount of capital that came to many only at the peak of a lifetime of earnings, thus the trade was directed by many people who were considered at the time to have been advanced in age.

The large number of buyers and sellers of Portuguese birth in this sample indicates that many immigrants arrived in Brazil before and after Independence. According to the number of Portuguese-born witnesses at court trials, they were a powerful minority, often dominating commerce in Brazilian port towns such as Santos. Because the number of buyers and sellers born in Santos (rather than elsewhere in Brazil or in Portugal) was less than 20 percent of all buyers and sellers, most Santistas could not afford to buy slaves and few had any to sell. This may have contributed to the political tension that existed between Santista and Portuguese factions in town.[17]

As the town moved away from local agriculture to servicing the province's principal port between 1840 and 1870, the profile of buyers and sellers of slaves also changed. Traders remained mostly older, married men, but the Portuguese lost their dominance. More buyers and sellers were born in Brazil, and slightly less than half in Santos; more minor public officials were involved in the trade as the municipal government grew and as a larger liberal, professional class emerged in town life. Army officers also grew in proportion to other groups. Businessmen remained highly active, and those involved in the coffee trade were the most frequent participants in the trade, as owners of either commission houses or warehouses. Small shopkeepers and owners of banks, restaurants, and factories also showed a strong presence. Farmers began to disappear from the bills of sale after 1850, especially among the slave buyers. The fact that there were fewer farmers in the township selling their slaves runs slightly contrary to a commonly discussed urban-to-rural shift of slaves brought by the coffee boom, but such a trend may have been occurring elsewhere. Many slaves were sold from the city into the coffee *planalto* (highlands), as emphasized later in the chapter, but within Santos, some people involved with port work may have offered attractive prices and had personal connections to the township's small cassava farmers, *aguardente* distillers, and fishermen.[18]

THE SLAVES TRADED

What about the slaves, including those who were forcibly removed from loved ones for economic motives? Between 1832 and 1858, the biggest demographic group bought and sold included young men and boys. Most were separated from their families, but some were sold with their parents and siblings. As shown in Table 3.2, two-thirds (67 percent) of the 398 slaves for which a tax was paid were males, and nearly half (43 percent) were children under age sixteen. Many of these men and boys were put to work cutting cane, digging manioc fields, sowing rice paddies, cleaning homes, cooking, or hauling bags of sugar or coffee between carts, warehouses, and waiting ships. They were trained as masons, cobblers, coach drivers, carpenters, tinsmiths, and a great variety of other occupations. A substantial number of these displaced slaves spoke with African ac-

TABLE 3.2

Backgrounds of Transacted Slaves (Percent)

	Slave Tax	Bills of Sale	Advertisements
Years of Source	1832–1859	1861–1873	1851–1873
Sex			
Male	67	56	54
Female	33	44	47
Age (average, in years)	(A=24)	(A=26)	(A=20)
Children	43	21	23
Place of birth			
Africa	55	26	18
Brazil	45	73	82
Santos	0	23	0
Data listed	*51*	*85*	*35*
Color/race			
Preto	6	72	68
Pardo	12	23	18
Mulato	76	1	9
Data listed	*4*	*86*	*26*
Occupation			
Domestic servants	...	30	20
Cooks	...	6	8
Artisians	...	8	6
Farming	...	14	8
Other	...	3	10
No particular skills	...	44	12
Data listed	...	*74*	*64*
Total number	(N=398)	(N=242)	(N=130)

NOTES: "Children" are defined as 15 years of age or under. "Data listed" represents the percentage of documents that listed the information of each category. Total occupations may exceed 100 percent because some slaves were listed with more than one occupation.

SOURCES: Slave tax lists, AESP, 1832–1859; bills of sale, 1861–1873; *Revista do Commercio*, 1851–1873.

cents and could tell the story of how they were captured and endured the Middle Passage. In fact, just over half of them had been born in Africa, many from the regions of Angola, Benguela, Congo, and Mozambique. The rest had been born in Brazil, but the specific locations were rarely noted in the slave trade records.[19]

Men remained the most traded between 1832 and 1873, but the gap between male and female slaves narrowed during this period. The average age of traded slaves increased and fewer children were exchanged. Brazilian-born slaves of both sexes began to outnumber Africans as a result of the end of the international slave trade. There were likely more slave domestic servants in the market, probably because coffee wealth had increased the number of people who could afford to buy them. The new money in the port also enlarged the demand for products and services offered by retailers, and these jobs were occasionally given to trusted slaves. Finally, more exports and imports meant more tax revenue, a larger government, and more government officials who could afford to buy slaves. Many men and women remained faithful to the idea that a slave or two was necessary for joining the middle to upper-middle groups in society, even as the stigma of slaveholding grew in the 1870s.

Traders and tax officials sometimes noted race or skin color. The main categories included *pretos*, *pardos*, and *mulattos*.[20] Before the 1850s, slave owners commonly used the word *preto* (black) interchangeably with the word *escravo* (slave). Tax officials usually did not mention race unless a slave was not dark skinned, since listing slaves as *preto* was redundant. *Mulatto* appeared sporadically in the tax lists, and it may have had a greater connotation of ancestry and blood, bespeaking European or indigenous parents or grandparents. But with such a small minority of tax records even mentioning race (4 percent), we should not overgeneralize. By 1870, with the many Africans slaves replaced by internally displaced slaves, it may have become more difficult for slave owners to equate race with family origin and heritage. By this time, it was common for anyone describing a slave on a government, hospital, or church form to do so by phenotype. In bills of sale and advertisements observations of skin color are frequent, including careful notations of who had lighter and darker or even "yellowish or pale brown" (*fulo*) skin. The bills of sale indicate a higher number of *pretos* than the advertisements, but this could be because owners wished to save money by printing brief ads and thus noted only the more unusual traits of slaves for sale.[21]

Walter Johnson found that a few traders in the big slave blocks of New Orleans nefariously propped up prices by hiding illnesses.[22] There is no evidence of such acts in Santos or other locations in Brazil where buyers and sellers had social and commercial ties. In Santos, slaves were occasionally admitted into the town's charity hospital after purchase, but these admissions occurred in a sufficient amount of time after the trade and involved afflictions that could not have been well hidden during the trade. The bills of sale functioned to prevent trickery and to provide a manner of redress if such acts occurred, just as Johnson had found in the redhibition laws of Louisiana. Some slaves died soon after their purchase. Felicidade, who tended to a fruit and vegetable garden and was owned by a Portuguese immigrant and resident in town, came down with symptoms of dropsy in the late fall of 1869. She died one week after she was brought to the hospital, most likely causing her new owner José Antonio de Souza Guimarães anguish over his lost investment. Only a few other cases like Felicidade are found in the records. It was far more common for slaves to remain with their owners for decades. João was twenty-eight years old when he was bought by Henrique Porchat in 1840. He died and was buried in the city cemetery thirty-three years later, with "old age" noted as the cause of death. He was sixty-one years old at the time of his death, exactly as was recorded by the cemetery register.[23]

A long period of servitude cannot be assumed to be a pleasant one, of course. For some slaves, their masters or situations were sufficiently unbearable that they took the considerable risk of running away. For example, Francisco da Costa Bispo, who was one of the relatively few itinerant peddlers involved in the slave trade, bought three slaves and exchanged two slaves before traveling to the coffee-growing areas of interior São Paulo. In August 1864, he bought Gregorio, a native of a small southern port of Espirito Santo, and a farmer (*roça*) previously owned by a man who ran a coffee and cotton commission house. Bispo bought several more slaves over the next year and a half, including Guilherme, a seventeen-year-old Brazilian native without a skill or trade, and a forty-year-old African mason named Paulo. This slave trader also entered into a rare slaves-for-slaves trade with the city butcher Henrique Ablas. Bispo exchanged Maria (twenty-five years old, Iguape native) and her lighter-skinned ten-year-old daughter, Catarina, for one of Ablas's slaves, also named Catarina (thirty-five years old, from Mozambique). Bispo then left Santos and traveled with this small coffle of slaves and maybe a few other traders up the steep highway toward the city of Campinas. Before they arrived, however, Guilherme escaped on the back of a stolen mule. Bispo thought Guilherme was returning to Santos and, as was customary for slave owners of the interior looking for runaways, he placed an advertisement in the Santos newspaper asking readers to look for a tall black man with "a straw hat, checkered patterned pants and black jacket, carrying a bundle of clothing." He added that Guilherme was "skinny and light or yellowish in color with a small toe that had been scarred by worms and a smile that lacks the top front teeth."[24] The stolen mule had a "small star branded on his forehead." Bispo listed the Spanish vice-consul to Santos as the local contact in case Guilherme was found, giving a clue that Bispo may have been a Spanish immigrant himself.

Some unsuccessful acts of flight prompted owners to try to find another owner for their rebellious slaves. Elias ran away in September 1863, returned or was captured, and was placed for sale two months later. His owner, Pedro Savary, one of the town bakers, described Elias in an advertisement for his capture as "a well-known vendor who works beside the Itororó Fountain," a familiar landmark to residents. Strangely, either Elias's sale was inexplicably undone or documents are missing from the archive, because Savary was again noted as the master of Elias less than a year later. Savary again sold the bread vendor, this time to a coffee company called Salles, Oliveira & Sá.[25] Perhaps Elias ran away from Guimarães, forcing Savary to cancel the sale. The documents do not provide answers, but it appears likely there is a connection between Elias's unusual sale and his attempts at escape.

The baker, Savary, sold Elias to the coffee company along with another slave named Alexandre in 1864. Both slaves were Bahian, *pretos*, bakers, listed as able to farm, and young. It is not known how long Elias was kept by his new owners, but Alexandre remained with the company for many years. In 1873 he entered the charity hospital suffering from syphilis and was hospitalized for several weeks. Finally, in 1881, Alexandre returned to the hospital with liver disease and remained there for a full month before he died.[26] If Elias was still alive and in town he undoubtedly felt a deep loss when he heard of his friend's death. They had shared two previous masters, accompanied each other through large life transitions, and shared a similar background. How many hours, for example, had they spent hellishly feeding fuel and bread into the hot mouth of a large bakery oven in a humid city where temperatures hover around ninety degrees Fahrenheit for months? As they both had come from Bahia when they were young and lived and worked together for years, they may have been each other's only family.

TRADING NETWORKS

Transactions that occurred between city residents within town were most common and may have had less monetary risk because individuals often entered into trades with people they knew in other ways. Bento, a tanner and a slave of fifty years with light brown eyes, tight curly hair, and a full face, was bought by João Bernardes Pereira from João Bernardino de Lima in June 1869. Since Bento's skills had little to do with the coffee business he was probably rented out to a leather shop in town. Soon after the sale, Bento was captured by the town's patrol when he tried to escape and was put in jail for seventeen days. Bento may have not liked his new owner, or perhaps he discovered that his owner planned on selling him or sending him out of the city. Whatever the reason, there seems to be a connection between his sale and his runaway attempt. Both his previous and new owners ran a coffee and cotton commission house out of the same building on Rua Setentrional (Northern Street). Not only were João Pereira and João Bernardino de Lima neighbors and in the same business, but each also had a young wife and maybe a few young children. The price for Bento was extremely low, only 400 *mil-réis* compared to the average price of 820 *mil-réis* for slaves with the same characteristics.[27] Perhaps Bento had broken rules before his sale, a fact that Lima used to lower the price. But there is also evidence that friendship or an exchange of favors might have been in play in this transaction. By selling Bento at less than 50 percent the usual price, was Lima (who was also five years older) extending patronage to Pereira? Bento, certainly, was not endeared by the bargain as he served his term in jail. Or did these owners trust each other enough to lower the official price to avoid a few *mil-réis* in taxes?

Acquaintances assisted in other sales. Antonio Bento de Andrade, who worked in the small city post office sold Luisa, a *parda* of forty-five years, to Maria do Carmo Marques Lopes in 1865. Lopes bought Luisa to help her clean and cook and, perhaps more important, to signal to her friends and neighbors that she had entered the slave-owning world. No other slaves of Lopes appear before or after this time in any other source, and so it seems likely that an additional slave could have been beyond her resources. Indeed, two years later, she sold Luisa to one of Andrade's postal colleagues, Luiz Pimenta. Pimenta and Andrade were two of five men working for the post office in 1865. For both sales, Luisa was sold for less than 50 percent of the average price for a slave of her age and occupation, although it might have been true that some characteristic, such as a disability, kept her price low. Another possibility is that one or both of the men had a close relationship with Maria Lopes and consequently traded her at a low price among the three of them. A further clue that affection or patronage was at work in this transaction is the fact Pimenta wrote up a manumission letter for Luisa ten years later. This may have freed him from his obligation to provide for her in her old age or may have allowed him to grant a favor to a person with whom he had created a close relationship. There were no conditions listed in the manumission letter.[28]

Luisa would not have been such an expensive investment to most Santos residents if slave prices had not increased so rapidly after 1860. Price movements are best understood in neoclassical terms, with changing demand meeting limited supply. Such an understanding, however, does not conflict with an emphasis on social networks, as we will see. The consequence of increasing demand and lowered supply, however impersonal this sounds in the commerce of humans, was a precipitous increase in slave prices, a nearly threefold increase in the slave tax lists and bills of sale, and an almost twofold increase in the inheritance records. On the demand side, the growth of coffee and cotton agriculture in São Paulo province, the entry of thousands of immigrants, and the improved roads between Santos and the interior pushed hundreds of new property holders to want slaves, including relatively large lots of slaves for financed plantations. Considering the supply side, the enforced halt of international slave trade by the British in 1850 brought an end to a relatively inexpensive, abundant supply of African slaves. These factors combined to push up the prices of all categories of slaves, as shown in Table 3.3.

TABLE 3.3

Average Slave Prices

	1830–1850			1861–1870		
	Slave Taxes (in *mil-réis*)	Inventories (in *mil-réis*)	Inventories/ Taxes	Bills of Sale (in *mil-réis*)	Inventories (in *mil-réis*)	Inventories/ Bills
All	372	228	.61	1,155	648	.56
Sex						
Males	377	234	.62	1,183	671	.57
Females	330	203	.62	1,116	631	.57
Age						
1–15 years	281	166	.59	1,009	436	.43
16–40 years	439	243	.55	1,252	907	.72
41+	...	152		604	298	.49
Race/social						
Pretos	...	...		1,140	...	...
Mulatos	345	151	.44	...	...	...
Pardos	...	...		1,190	623	.52
Place of birth						
Africa	366	205	.56	993	305	.31
Brazil	339	222	.66	1,198	649	.54
Occupation						
Skilled	...	378	...	1,204	759	.63
Artisians	...	...	...	1,330	...	...
Domestics	...	...	...	1,228	...	...
None Information	372	221	.59	1,195	625	.52
Total	(N=182)	(N=210)		(N=216)	(N=60)	

NOTE: Data were provided only when there were ten or more cases for each category.
SOURCES: Slave tax lists, Santos, AESP; bills of sale, PCS and FAMS.

As in all slaveholding societies, prices between different groups of bondspeople varied considerably. Strong working-age males (sixteen to forty years old), especially those with artisan skills, were the highest priced. In fact, a young or old female slave could be half or a third of the price of a working-age male, even if she was in good health. Relative to other parts of the province, prices were considerably lower in Santos, probably because the township had much easier and less expensive access to coastal sea routes. Its prices were much less than in Rio Claro, an interior township on the frontier of coffee expansion. There, historians have found the highest prices so far for bondspeople in Brazil during the second half of the nineteenth century. The price of working-age males in Rio Claro was 1,800 *mil-réis* in the 1860s, while in Santos, this group of slaves cost 1,278 *mil-réis*.[29] For Vassouras, a township in the older coffee-growing regions of northern Paraíba Valley and much closer to the coast, the group was 1,590 *mil-réis* on average. Considering this range, it seems reasonable to consider that overland transportation added a considerable amount to the price of slaves. If an owner on the coast could sell a working-age male slave to someone in Rio Claro for 140 percent the price in town, what incentive was there to sell locally? The reason, I believe, was a pragmatic one. Buyers and sellers normally preferred to exchange slaves with people they knew, easing what was a risky process. This explanation will come into better focus when we return to the relationships that existed between many buyers and sellers, and the networks they formed.

Comparing prices from various sources gives different prices for the same groups of slaves. In fact, the prices of slaves in the Santos inheritance records were about two-thirds those recorded in tax records and bills of sale and remained fairly constant between 1830 and 1870. Such a discrepancy would have ramifications for studies that have relied on only one of these sources for economic or social analysis. True, buyers and sellers of expensive slaves were more likely to look for guarantees that the transaction could be backed by a court of law if necessary. Thus slave taxes and bills of sale may be slightly biased toward more expensive slaves. There does not appear to be one particular group that is over- or under-represented in the bills of sale or tax records. At the very least, historians might take care before comparing slave prices between different locations if they are relying on different sources for these prices.

Among slaves sold in the local market females became nearly as expensive as males, average prices of children increased as a percentage of the total average, and prices of Africans dropped significantly relative to Brazilians. All three of these changes have to do with the ending of the African slave trade in 1850. After this point the steady supply of African adult males ended, compelling slave owners to rely more on women and children as sources of labor. It may also be the case that the growing service sector helped level prices because labor was not as tied to brute physical force, which had previously favored males. This is not to say that there were plenty of service-sector jobs, such as portering and stevedoring, which required much muscle and were typically given to males. Nor is it to say that male slaves worked harder than female slaves. More buyers in Santos, and perhaps in other provincial cities, wanted slaves who could perform housework, and women and children were usually preferred over adult men for these jobs.[30]

Variables such as age, sex, occupation, and color or race affected the prices of slaves. Other characteristics cannot be discerned well from the documents: healthiness, physical beauty and attractiveness, manners and disposition, evidence of punishment, and whatever personal history the seller (or slave) was willing to reveal in pre-sale interviews. As Johnson argued for the New Orleans slave market, what slave owners "projected onto their slaves' bodies served them as public reflections of their own discernment: They were the arbiters of bearing and beauty; their slaves were the show pieces of their pretensions."[31] The image that owners cultivated with their slaves could earn public respect among some peers and fulfill their ideal of their proper place in society. But it is easy to go too far with this idea, since many owners looked first and foremost for specific skills and jobs a slave could perform. For instance, families in Santos were sometimes desperate to find slave wet nurses, and they placed advertisements as far away as the provincial capital. Owners could not always afford to be picky when it came to the outward appearance of a slave.[32] It is reasonable to assume, moreover, that some households purposely avoided beautiful slaves, believing that attractiveness could interfere with practicality.

Slave prices mostly conformed to prices that were expected over the wider region. Prices that differed slightly from the average were often due to the experience of the buyer and seller. For example, buyers were more likely to purchase a slave at an amount above the average market price if they appeared in the tax lists or bills of sale only once, or if it was their first time buying (see Table 3.4). Conversely, sellers were more likely to sell a slave under the market price if the sale was a single transaction or if it was the first of multiple sales. Buyers and sellers became savvier in finding a price that conformed to the market as they bought and sold more. By their final transaction, these repeat buyers and sellers tended to buy or sell at a price much closer to the average price of slaves with similar sex, age, race, and occupation characteristics.[33] There are some caveats to this finding. Single-transaction or first-time buyers and sellers may have been more likely to buy or sell slaves who had some unlisted characteristic that lowered the price, such as a physical disability or illness. Or these buyers

TABLE 3.4

Average Deviations of Purchase or Sale Prices from Market Prices

	1830–1850		1850–1870	
	Deviation from Market Average	Number of Slaves	Deviation from Market Average	Number of Slaves
Buyers				
First or single purchase	-6	23	-29	93
Repeat purchases	-3	33	-21	42
Last purchase	...	...	-16	40
Sellers				
First or single sale	-32	21	-90	56
Repeat sales	4	36	2	102
Last sale	...	...	34	17

NOTE: For the period 1830–1850, there was insufficient data to separate "repeat purchases" from "last purchase" for both buyers and sellers. These two categories were collapsed for this period but remain discrete for the second period.
SOURCES: Slave tax lists, Santos, 1830–1855, AESP; bills of sale, 1862–1872, CCS, PCNS, SCNS.

may have had ulterior motives in purchasing a slave, which may have been the case for the two neighbors João Pereira and João de Lima, or for the two postmen and Luisa. The ulterior motive could have been to further strengthen bonds of friendship, or to pay or repay a favor.

For Consul John Hayden and the Baron Mauá, the two neighboring coffee merchants, and the postmen who traded Luiza, a network of relationships facilitated the sales of slaves. Again and again, slaves were traded between people with business, occupation, or distant family ties. These small webs of connections were in turn themselves linked, placing the majority of buyers and sellers into networks that stretched across the city and region. In key points in this trading network were important traders who contributed enormously to its cohesiveness. The local slave-trading network of Santos, as in Brazil and other parts of the world, was held together by intermediate agents. Slaves, after all, were an expensive acquisition for most people, and both buyers and sellers had to depend on specialists familiar with the process of transacting slaves and who knew the right people to obtain a slave that fit the wants of the buyer (or who could convince the buyer that the slave was suited to his or her needs). These men were the anchoring points of a structure that displayed areas of semihomogeneity and had a strong effect on which slaves were traded between whom.

The local slave-trading network in Santos during the 1860s can be illustrated using computer programs that are often in the toolbox of sociologists working on network theory.[34] These tools offer a means to analyze network density and identify central individuals, but their best feature may be in visualizing a pattern of activity and relationships that is nearly impossible to detect in the sources alone. Figure 3.1 illustrates a network created by buyers, sellers, and agents that appeared in the bills of sale. The diagram brings to light the position of various buyers and sellers with respect to the entire community of traders. The arrows represent the sale of one or more slaves between two individuals (represented by the points) be-

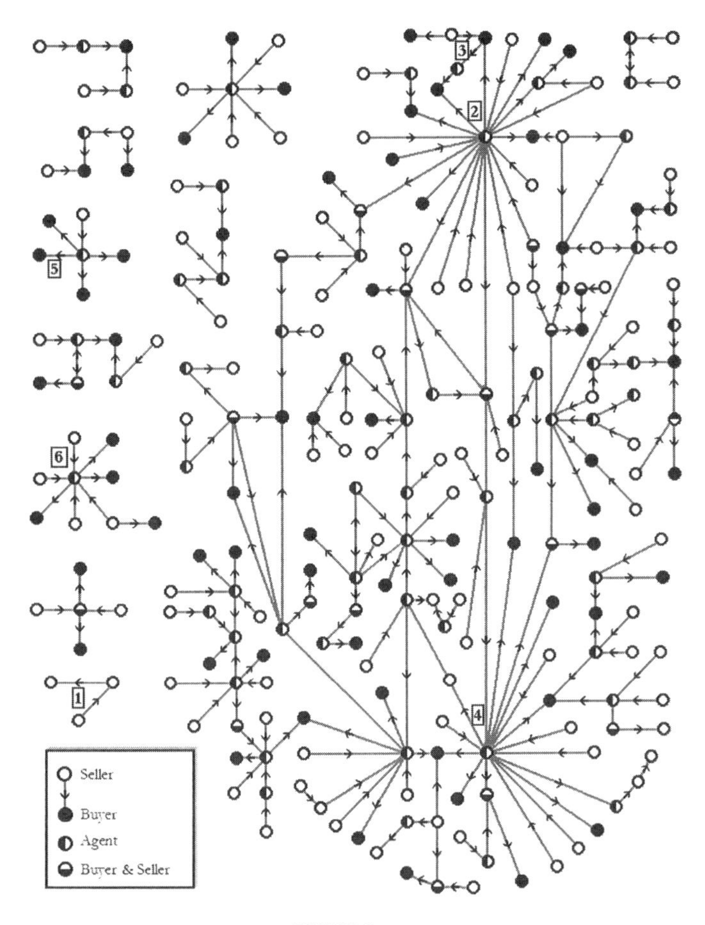

FIGURE 3.1

Network of Buyers and Sellers Involved in Slave Transactions, 1861–1870

NOTES: #1 refers to Luisa (slave of Postmen Antonio Bento de Andrade and Luiz Pimenta, and Maria do Carmo); #2 refers to Gregorio Innocencio de Freitas (Portuguese businessman and the most connected trader); #3 refers to Bento, the tanner (slave of João Bernardes Pereira and João Bernardino de Lima); #4 refers to Scipião Ferreira Goulart Junqueira (township vicar and second most connected individual); #5 refers to Elias (slave of Pedro Savary, the baker); #6 refers to José Justiano Bittencourt (slave dealer on Rua Direita). Eleven pairs were excluded from the graph.
SOURCES: Bills of sale, 1860–1871, CCS, PCNS, SCNS.

tween 1861 and 1870. The arrow follows the direction of the slave in the transaction, unidirectional for sales and bidirectional for trades. Squares were placed over individuals who acted as agents between buyers and sellers, but these same men also may have bought or sold slaves themselves.

As the network shows, the majority of men and women who bought and sold slaves belonged to networks much larger than their single transaction.[35] Since only men and women found in multiple sources were coded, many others were excluded. Thus the network represented in Figure 3.1, albeit dense and complicated, is only a small part of a larger network that must have existed.

Certain individuals were highly active slave traders and thus had central roles in the local slave-trading network. Captain Gregorio Innocencio de Freitas (no. 2 in Figure 3.1) and Father Scipião Ferreira Goulart Junqueira (no. 4) were the most connected individuals, and each was involved in ten or more transactions. Freitas operated a coffee commission house on Rua São Bento, but must have also made a considerable part of his income from slaves. He also lived in Iguape, a smaller port town fifty miles south, and he profited from having connections in both cities. He served as agent for many sellers in Iguape and buyers in Santos. Most of his slaves had been born in Iguape or another town on the southern coast of São Paulo.[36] Junqueira listed Santos as his primary residence, but his job as township vicar took him to other parts of the township and state. He administered wills and testaments and was privy to estate assets before they were sold in auctions or sales. Most important, his clientele and the slaves who he agented differed in various ways from those of Freitas because of their dissimilar personal characteristics, occupations, and positions within the slave trade network.[37]

The groups of buyers, sellers, and clients of these two men shared traits and bought particular slaves who were similar to one another. In fact, there was a greater degree of homogeneity among owners and slaves who had one or two degrees of separation than between men and women further removed. In other words, those who traded with one of the principal sellers, or who traded with someone who traded with the principal seller, were likely to share more characteristics than those who had a distant connection to the principal seller. The regional slave network thus had within it what might be called market nexuses, or groups of people who shared traits and sought similar slaves partly due to their common relationships. Two nexuses can be identified with Gregorio Freitas and Scipião Junqueira at their centers. Many of the men and women who bought slaves from or used the services of Freitas (or someone connected to him through a sale) had been born in Portugal and were involved in similar commercial pursuits.[38] In fact, four others shared with Freitas the business of coffee and cotton commission houses. The slaves they bought were mostly male, *preto*, Brazilian-born, and "without skills." A large number come from Iguape, a port town 150 kilometers to the south, or from other southern coastal towns.

Turning to the nexus of Junqueira, there are fewer men and women of Portuguese birth and less information about these people overall. The few that do have occupation information were mostly army officers, public officials, and lawyers. The vicar even proctored the sale of a young slave to a former African slave with the single name of Ambrozio. The slaves bought from Junqueira were from a greater range of places, yet it appears that the vicar also had a connection to a few towns along the coast. There are more females among these slaves, more domestic servants, and far fewer slaves listed "without a trade" than among those managed by Freitas.[39] A townsperson who bought a slave with the vicar's help was often looking for a maid, while those who went to the captain preferred a strong hand to haul coffee bags. Stronger slaves were priced higher, thus the captain's slaves were on average higher priced than the vicar's slaves, even though there were fewer slaves of prime working age.

The structural cohesion within this network lent a degree of demographic and occupational similarity that, like a palimpsest, layered both masters and their slaves. The small networks of these men, both of which were connected to one another in the wider network, had nexuses of cohesion embedded in this series of relationships and that extended to the slaves they traded. These men and women exchanged slaves with friends, colleagues, and neighbors, and if they did not already know each other through family, job, or association ties, then the sale created a connection. The owners were not the only ones to belong to a group of people who shared a familiarity. Imagine friendly or caring exchanges between Iguapeiro slaves when they saw each other on the streets. Both Santos and Iguape were small enough at this time to permit this common background to be a reason for conversation or at least recognition.

Both the township vicar and the coffee merchant, while demonstrating many differences between themselves and the slaves they administered, had connections to markets that stretched south along the southern coast of São Paulo. This was one of three principal areas where nonresident slave sellers lived and included the coastal towns of Itanhaem, Iguape, Cananea, and towns in the southern provinces such as Paranaguá, Desterro (today Florianópolis), and São Francisco do Sul. Another smaller region was the interior of São Paulo, with its slave sellers from Jundiahy, Mogi-Mirim, and Rio Claro, but this region bought many more slaves than it sold. The third and most important region was the immediate coastal north, including São Sebastião or Vila Bela da

Princesa, both slightly northeast of the old Santos township borders, and the more distant coast to the northeast, including Ubatuba, Angra dos Reis, and Rio de Janeiro. Activity in this third region is evidence that the sellers from towns and cities to the north of Santos were acting as middlemen to sellers from Bahia, Pernambuco, and other northeastern provinces for the interprovincial slave trade. On the other hand, the sale of slaves from the sugar-growing parts of Santos was far more evident during the 1860s than slaves from Rio de Janeiro or beyond. Additionally, the majority of slaves sold into Santos by Carioca (residents of Rio de Janeiro) sellers were African rather than born in the Northeast.[40]

THE GEOGRAPHY OF SLAVE TRADING

Large lots of slaves, marching in chained coffles or unloaded from ships, passed through these two townships. Although agents of slave transfers were not required to register their transactions in the local notary offices, the large port town offered the principal highway leading to the coffee-growing highlands and created a bottleneck where officials could document the movement of slaves. Port inspectors counted between 904 and 2,129 slaves entering the port of Santos per year during the late 1860s. Another 5,680 to 6,034 bondspeople entered at the port of Rio de Janeiro per year during the 1870s, many of them bound for São Paulo on the highway through the Paraíba Valley.[41] Undoubtedly, a large number of slaves crossed the township, but Santista merchants and farmers did not purchase or sell large lots of slaves from (or for) distant markets. Furthermore, slave trading flows were never unidirectional, as is evident in the bills of sale; although slaves were in great demand in the expanding coffee zones, they continued to be sold from inland areas to the coast and beyond. In other words, despite the great attention on slaves who entered São Paulo, there was a steady stream of slaves who were also sold outside of the province.

Geography imposed constraints on regional slave trade by limiting the means and increasing the expense of various routes of travel. But geographical constraints included more than the long stretch of Paulista coastline or the steep escarpment paralleling the ocean. Neighborhoods, city streets and corners, and the location of businesses and dockside warehouses also affected, at the microlevel, the way slave trade worked. Particular areas of the city tended to have more slave sellers than buyers, while townsfolk, who were more inclined to rent slaves, lived in other parts of Santos. Furthermore, the town's rapid expansion and growing importance as a coffee exporter altered the configuration of neighborhoods and the places where buyers, sellers, and renters lived.

During the 1830s and 1840s Santos was not too different from the colonial days: twenty-five city streets nearly all ran toward or connected with a series of wooden dockside warehouses along the muddy shore. As discussed in Chapter One, some of the wealthiest residents lived along Rua Direita and near the Four Corners neighborhood, within close reach of the port business. It is no surprise, then, that most of the Santistas who traded slaves during this period lived in these neighborhoods. Many buyers also lived in this same area, but a greater percentage of sellers lived in areas of town outside the city center.[42] This separation of buyers and sellers was largely a result of an economic shift to coffee from sugar, *aguardente,* and manioc, and the quickening importation of general goods for the interior. Many members of the older sugar and manioc-growing elite lived in the colonial buildings in Four Corners and, as discussed in Chapters One and Two, owned rural property and still made a living from *aguardente* or manioc flour (such as the descendents of Luis Pereira Machado). Buyers of slaves were more likely to be businessmen than sellers and were mostly men who lived in expanding and "gentrifying" areas beyond the small colonial core of the city.

By the 1850s and 1860s, the city had grown threefold, mostly to the east and south where the coast and hills did not limit expansion. Furthering this shift, the customs house moved in 1863, pushing the growing activity of shipping and storing coffee a few blocks eastward. As homes and businesses began to occupy an area that was formerly scrubland and marshes, the majority of the buyers and sellers of slaves remained in the older parts of town. The city was transforming into an important provincial port, but the traders most central to the business of slavery lived in the same neighborhoods where such practices had been conducted under the authority of the Portuguese crown. This is especially the case among sellers who resided in the Four Corners and Rua Direita neighborhoods.[43]

All this is not to say there were not slaves in the newer parts of town. As we can see in the slave advertisements of the era, many residents rented slaves in these areas, but the slaves they rented were often owned by residents of the older downtown. This change reflects the end of inexpensively priced slaves after 1850. The greatest clustering of advertisements was located in the older downtown area. Postings also occurred in the areas to the east and south, but most of these concerned rented slaves. In the peripheral areas, where there were fewer residents with high wealth, most could no longer afford to buy slaves. In Figure 3.2, advertisements are classified into time periods, demonstrating the rapid expansion of residences and businesses that relied on the newspaper to post their advertisements. The farther from the city center, the more likely it was that

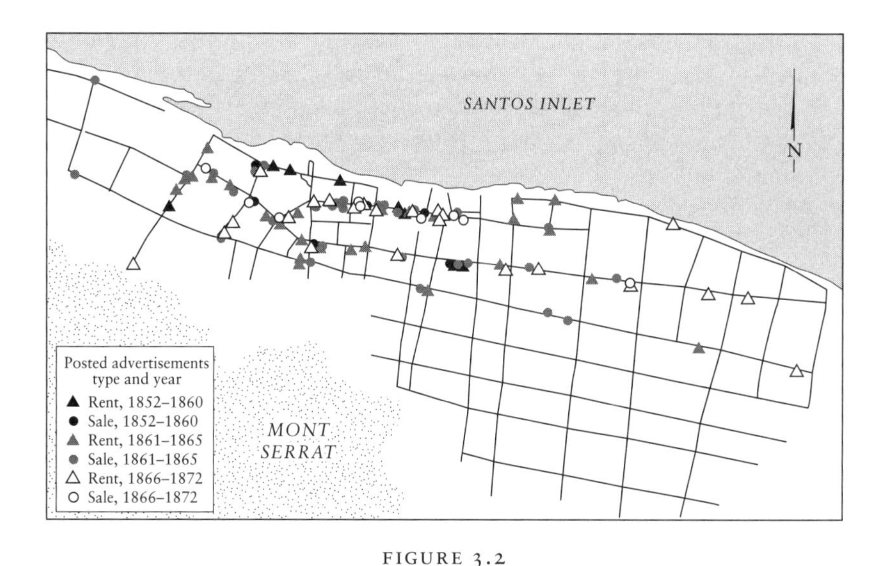

FIGURE 3.2

Slave Advertisements, 1852–1872

SOURCE: *Revista do Commercio* (Santos), 1849–1867, *Diario de Santos*, 1872–1873, FAMS, HS.

postings were for slave rentals rather than purchases. Many of these advertisements indicated the desire to pay either a monthly wage for a free worker or the monthly charge of a rented slave. Visualizing the distribution of notices strengthens the premise that people in particular neighborhoods demonstrated different actions toward or concerning their slaves.

Advertisements often noted the kind of work the slave could do or what kind of work was wanted by a household or business. The most common occupation involved housework, either as servants, cooks, nannies, wet nurses, or chambermaids (*mucamas*). Second in importance were artisan slaves such as masons, carpenters, and coopers. Finally, a number of other occupations were noted, such as warehouse workers and farmers, as well as slaves "without skills." The prevalence of domestic workers, not exclusively female, supports the idea that slavery was important to middling groups in Brazil, even in midsized cities. Households that might not otherwise be able to afford to buy a slave often opted to rent one. In a time when a single slave promoted the social standing of a family, the imagined perception by friends and neighbors may have been equally important as the work performed by a slave. But as the advertisements indicated, a free servant working on a wage may have been a sufficient replacement for owning a slave.[44]

Among those who offered slaves for sale, commission houses predominated, supporting the claim that these types of businesses were the chief agents of slave trade after the 1860s in small towns like Santos, although coffee or cotton commissions were their official or principal pursuit. Shopkeepers also used the newspaper to find households for their slaves. Such was the case of two small tool shops and a clothing store located halfway down Rua Direita, which posted three advertisements in the newspaper, listing one slave for sale and two for rent.[45]

The advertisements were in many ways signals of social and class status, prevalent among particular neighborhoods. When the newspaper notices of two neighborhoods are compared, we find different types of owners who had particular occupations and needs for slaves they wished to buy, sell, or rent. At the west end of Rua Direita, in the Four Corners neighborhood, most of the houses that posted advertisements did so only once during the 1860s, but one—building no. 58—stands out with seven advertisements. Out of this house, which can be identified in Figure 3.3, José Justiano Bittencourt ran a small slave-trading business, primarily by proctoring sales. Bittencourt can also be located in the network of buyers and sellers (no. 6 in Figure 3.1), where he was at the center of a small network not linked to the larger network. Bittencourt's connections probably aided him in his pursuits. He served in a number of official capacities, including police commissioner, township councilman, and administrator of a small port-reconstruction project. During the years he was proctoring slaves, Bittencourt served as the town's *juiz de órfãos* (orphan judge). This was an important post, appointed by the provincial government. Its duties required the administration and care of not only orphans but also African slaves who had been freed because their enslavement had been deemed illegal (for example, African slaves imported after 1850).[46]

Most of the slaves Bittencourt and his neighbors on Rua Direita were seeking to sell or buy were men and women of prime working age, and a few had skills that made them relatively more valuable.[47] Twelve of the nineteen advertisements of this microneighborhood marketed slaves who performed domestic work such as cooking or laundry. One slave was advertised as a farmer, and no skills were listed for several others, and none with artisan skills such as carpentry or cobbling were listed. At building no. 60, two girls were listed for sale as chambermaids, an occupation that would be affordable only to an owner with other domestic servants. It can be imagined the owner carefully trained these two girls to perform the most intimate duties required by a formal lady of a house. Ten years later, across the street, another household sought a male cook, but without explicit regard to whether he was enslaved or free.[48]

A small distance to the southeast was a second microneighborhood where residents also used the newspaper to buy, sell, and rent slaves (see

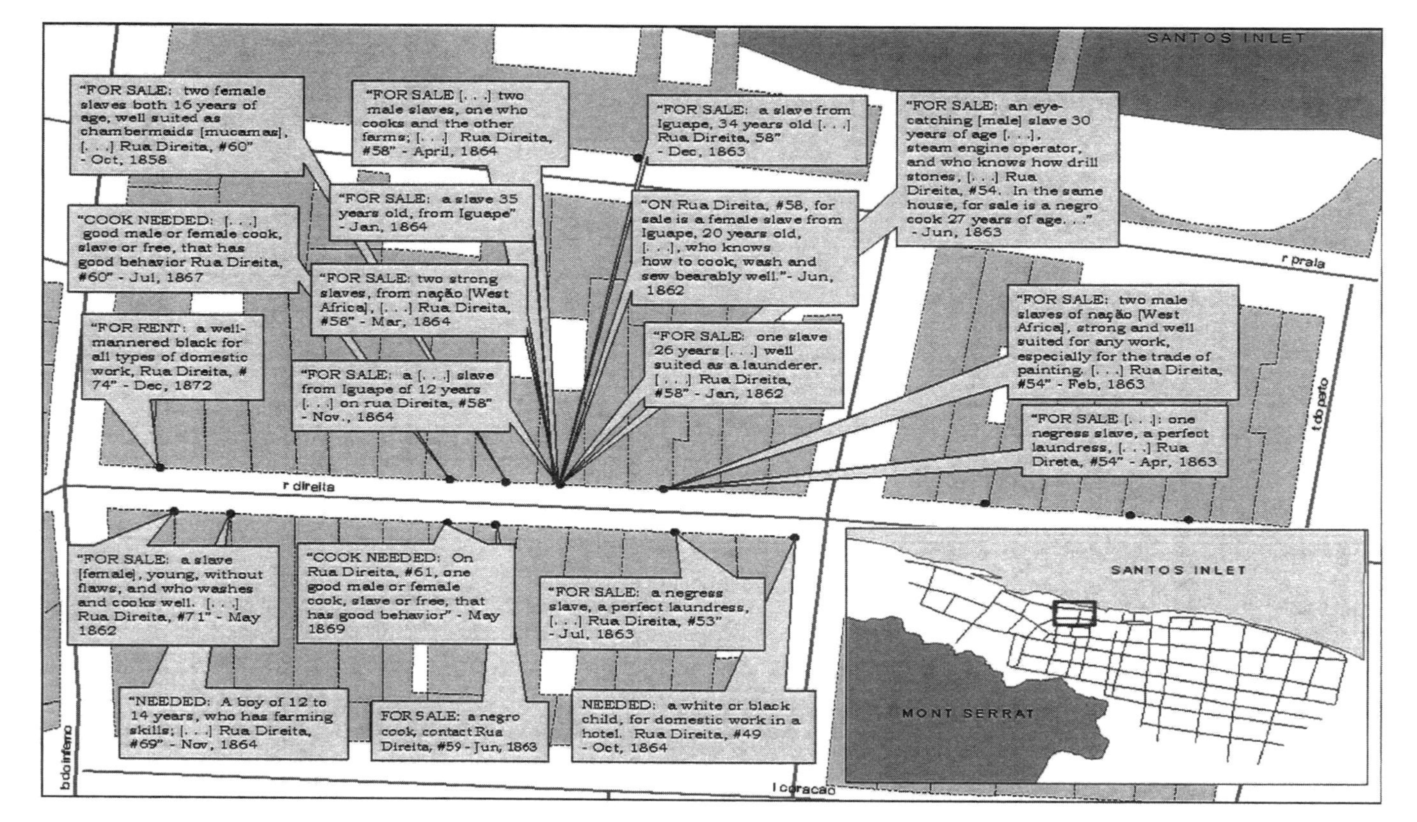

FIGURE 3.3

Advertisements from Rua Direita, Buildings 52–74, 1862–1872

SOURCE: *Revista do Commercio* (Santos), 1849–1867, *Diario de Santos*, 1872–1873, FAMS, HS.

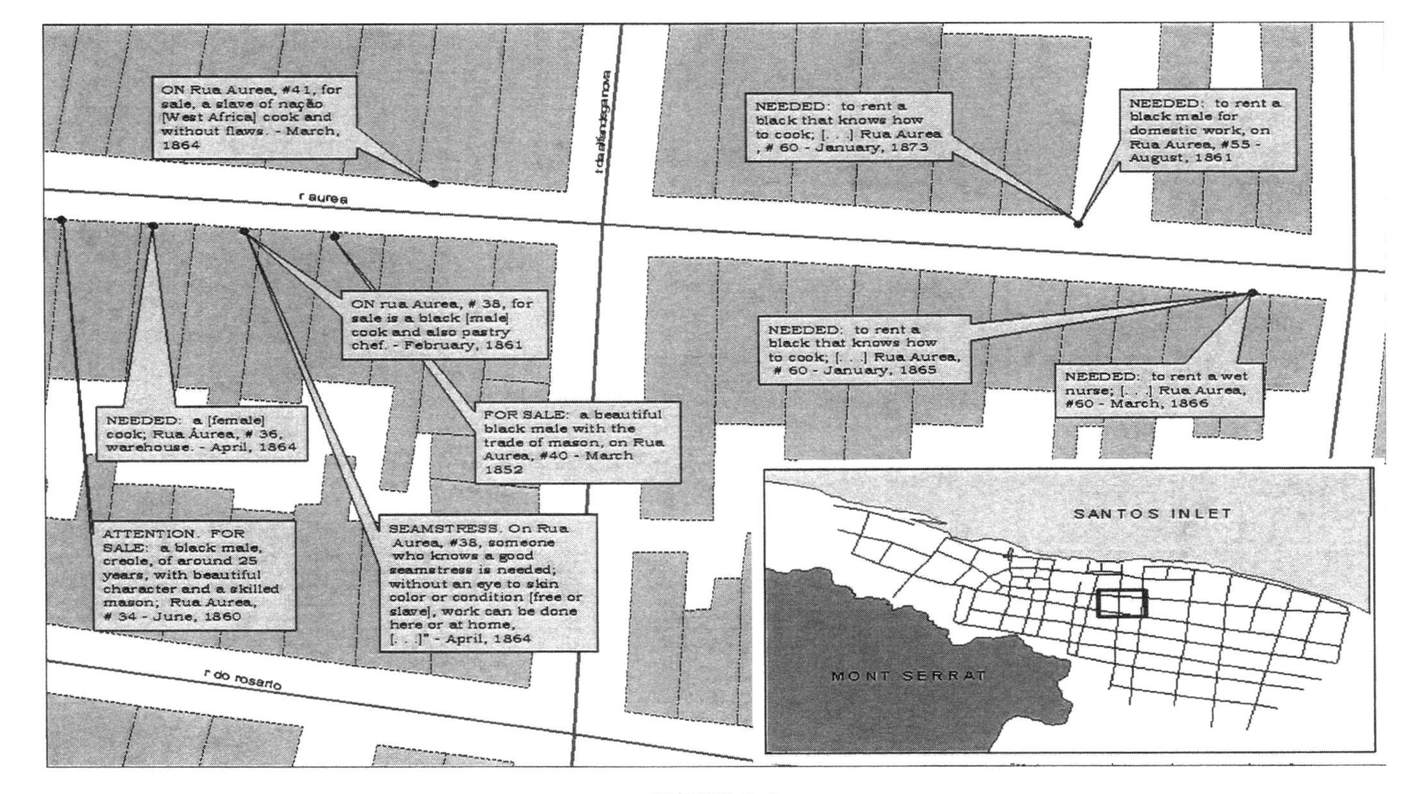

FIGURE 3.4

Advertisements from Rua Áurea, Buildings 34–60, 1862–1872

SOURCE: *Revista do Commercio* (Santos), 1849–1867, *Diario de Santos*, 1872–1873, FAMS, HS.

Figure 3.4).[49] The buildings along Rua Áurea were a bit newer than those on Rua Direita, and there were still many lots that had not been occupied by buildings. This was especially true east of Travessa da Alfândega Nova, where the city made its transition into countryside. Less wealth in this neighborhood coincided with fewer newspaper advertisements. Nearly half of the advertisements posted sought a slave to rent for a variety of jobs, including domestic servant, cook, and wet nurse. Of the five slaves for sale, there were two stone masons, two cooks, and one seamstress. The advertisement for the seamstress clearly indicates the buyer is open to a rented slave or a free wage worker, black or white.

The walk from the house that posted this advertisement to José Justiano Bittencourt's house on Rua Direita would have taken less than ten minutes, yet the differences between the two are noticeable. Slave owners tended to live among others of similar character and were separated from those of different means and wealth by only a few blocks of houses. Comparing the two young chambermaids of Rua Direita to the stone masons of Rua Áurea, it becomes evident that the slaves for sale in these two neighborhoods also differed.

The slave market was an informal institution firmly rooted in the social fabric of town life, even during a period when the institution as a whole was being obscured by more legitimate pursuits. The slave market was rooted first in physical space, as its participants had homes and jobs fixed in a specific geography; even slave peddlers and transient dealers followed common and limited routes of travel. The slave market was also embedded in a network of social relationships with a preestablished structure based on family, friendship, work, association, neighborhood, and economic ties. Forces that acted upon the market were largely outside the orbit of local life, such as the changing prices of slaves of different sex, age, and other characteristics; the number of slaves available for sale; or the collective demand for slaves. But the market was not an impersonal system. It was guided by people who more often than not knew each other in capacities outside the particular sale. There was no formal organization besides the loose set of laws that regulated sales, but certain patterns reflected an organized system of trade.

It is becoming increasingly apparent that similar patterns existed elsewhere, even within some of Brazil's large cities. In a recent innovative study, Zephyr Frank analyzed more than a thousand slave sales registered in Rio de Janeiro in 1869. By geocoding information from buyers and sellers, Frank found that the average distance moved by 238 slaves with location information was nearly 1,500 meters. While this may not seem great, a neighborhood could alter drastically in less than 100 meters in any Brazilian town or city, meaning that the changes of life experience for these common "short-distance" trades were likely significant to the slaves concerned. Frank's study also found that female slaves were more likely than males to be dislocated into parts of the city where property rental prices were higher, while males were most often transferred to lower-rent areas that year. In fact, the median increase in value of property rents for transferred female slaves was 20 percent (and 108 percent, if the smaller number of female slaves who moved to lower-rental value areas is excluded). In a telling example, one enslaved boy, named Maximiliano, was purchased by a small-scale tobacco warehouse owner in Niteroi, from a wealthy doctor in Rio de Janeiro. This boy appears to have moved from the elegant parlor of an expensive townhome to a dank warehouse where he was put to the repetitive work of tobacco rolling. Only five miles separated this boy's old and new homes, but it might have well been a hundred because Guanabara Bay and the expense of the ferry ride prevented any easy return. Indeed, local trades like this one should be understood to have been highly disruptive for slaves. We should not necessarily assume that sales within a province, township, or even city were any less disastrous or disintegrative for communities and families than interprovincial trades. Depending on master largesse, bondspeople may or may not have been able to visit proximate family and friends of previous owners. Slaves who were traded between neighboring rural townships often encountered too many miles of winding road to allow frequent visits. Nor should we assume that the intraprovincial trade had less effect on the demography and economy of these regions than the national trade.[50]

When slaves were traded in Rio or in Santos, the parties involved in the transaction required a great deal of information to make sure they were getting the slave they wanted and that there were no traits of body or character that would jeopardize their expensive investment. After all, most people in the Santos records were able to buy a slave only once or twice in their life. Since the information buyers and sellers needed was hard to come by, they depended on people they knew and could trust when making their purchases. Moreover, they accessed a preexisting web of relationships that linked buyers and sellers and organized the market participants into nexuses of cohesion. Within these groups were a number of coffee merchants connected to Freitas; or politicians, army officers, and lawyers connected to Junqueira. These men stood at the center of a network that also conditioned the types of slaves who were traded, and it was through this network of connections that the hierarchy of masters and slaves maintained itself. The men who bought the mostly male slaves to haul bags of coffee for their export businesses paid a higher price than those who wanted mostly female slaves to clean their houses. But beyond the ability to pay a price, connections between people of similar means and standing were paramount. These groups found cohesion through nationality and occupation and bought slaves who also shared characteristics.

The structural workings of the regional market did not preclude exogenous factors that also shaped the way slave business operated. Supply and demand altered during this period, and prices increased enormously. But we should not lose sight of the individuals involved in these transactions and the importance of relationships in this particular trade. Economic activity is concurrently a social activity. Men and women entered into the market with specific intentions, but found a parameter of action that was delimited by the consequences of thousands of other participants also pursuing their self-interests. We also cannot lose sight of the enslaved men, women, and children who were shuffled over short distances or displaced from families and communities over enormous, unsurmountable distances. For all bondspeople, the slave market was the gateway into a hierarchical world in which status and residential location of their owners tells a great deal about slave actions, prospects, and the treatment they received. The next half of the book will explore slaves who were sent to jail for infractions or for running away, and others who entered the hospital to have a disease or affliction treated. Many died—drowned at sea, struck by the smallpox epidemics, or killed by disasters without description. Others, as we will see, formed families and communities and survived with what they had.

PART II

Slaves and Their Masters

CHAPTER FOUR

Family, Work, and Punishment

Santos's seven discernable neighborhoods were a short walk from each other. Other communities of the township were separated by miles of green forest, thick mangrove swamps, or winding beaches. The appearance and architecture of homes and buildings were often shared within town neighborhoods or small rural communities, as were the demographics and life conditions of their residents. The ways that owners acted toward their slaves also bore resemblance, but differed considerably among these homogeneous areas. When it came to family, work, and punishment, the life conditions that slaves could create with the treatment they received was often unequal, even among a group that is frequently assumed to have been equally abused. From neighborhood to neighborhood, owner to owner, slaves had different opportunities to form families, work particular jobs, and avoid behavior that was deemed offensive and worthy of punishment.

Before about 1840, most slaves worked and produced for a localized and inward-looking world. Some labored to load or unload the ships, to fill or empty dockside warehouses, and to pack or unpack mule troops that carried export commodities down the steep mountains or carried general goods up. Much of the port business came from within or near the township and included shipments of *aguardente*, manioc flour, rice, fish, and fruits from the scattered coastal farms and fishing villages. Even more bondspeople remained under servitude on farms and simple country houses, working to produce commodities for the trade that was centered at Santos. The wealthiest farmers, generally involved in producing and trading products for the world market, often owned a townhome in one of the three middling or wealthy neighborhoods, such as the commercial zone that extended from Rua Direita or the intersection of town houses at Rua Santo Antonio and Rua da Praia. Plantation owners, such as Luis Pereira Machado (see Chapter One), had numerous reasons to take on the expense of a townhome. It was helpful for their businesses to have a direct stake in the day-to-day activity of port, especially since commercial activity was fostered and regulated within a structure of social relationships that frayed with inattention. Men like Machado ran the town government, commanded the coastal army guard, and provided membership for the few town societies and philanthropic organizations. The slowly increasing hum and bustle of town life, especially once coffee, cotton, and sugar were established as important commodities in the 1830s and 1840s, was an enticing attraction to many and an irritation to others who preferred the quiet lives their parents and grandparents had led. The slaves these townspeople owned, at least those not rented out to poorer households or boarded on rural estates, were privy to the activity that surrounded their masters' and mistresses' busy town lives. Far more than spectators, slaves maintained—with much sweat and callus—the stage that composed the theater of their owners' lives.

Over the next half century, local agriculture became increasingly separated from the port's commerce. By the 1880s most of the products handled by Santos stevedores—both imported goods and local products being shipped as exports—were destined to bypass the township rather than remain for local consumption. The service functions of the port expanded enormously, creating wealth that dwarfed what had been previously earned by the richest farmers and producers. The port strengthened its role in international and national shipping relative to other Brazilian ports at the time. In 1779 only 0.3 percent of Brazilian exports came out of the port of Santos. A century later that figure rose to 11 percent, second only to Rio de Janeiro and assuring the port of Santos a key role in national coastal shipping. In 1854 Santos stevedores handled 1.7 percent of Brazil's coastal trade, and nearly 10 percent by 1875. Considering that the port of Santos became busier than those of several larger Brazilian cities and provincial capitals, such as Salvador to the north or Porto Alegre to the south, we can get a sense of why the second half of the nineteenth century is best remembered by frenetic growth and epidemiological disasters.[1]

As the township's economy changed, wealth shifted and new groups of slave owners entered local and regional politics. Servicing the port provided more prestige and wealth for the new elite than any township plantation could possibly do, however large and fruitful. Slave work also changed. Enslaved men and boys were shuffled from the agricultural areas to the city and put to work hauling coffee, loading dockside warehouses, or filling the holds of waiting ships. For some, their masters were the most important people in town, men who rode the technological marvel of British railroad engineering along with tons of basic goods that Europeans and North Americans went to much trouble to obtain. Unquestionably, such owners provided certain opportunities and prestige for their slaves, and maybe a bit of pride. Pride, however, did not lighten the sixty-kilogram bags of coffee or sugar, nor did it thicken the back to the bite of a whip. For the enslaved, the shifting economy and society spurred changes in the opportunities to create and maintain slave families, find jobs that would not injure or kill them, and avoid the shackles or whip of the town jailers.

As the new commercial elite began pushing out members of the old agricultural families who had traditionally governed the township, they displayed their wealth in new ways. Domestic servants increasingly reflected the wealth of their owners: women and girls were provided with brooms and rags for housecleaning and were given the infants of free families to nurse and protect. Men cleaned as well, or were assigned to the kitchen to prepare and serve a family's meals. The people who did these jobs were slaves until price, scarcity, and—by the mid 1870s—stigma made free domestic servants the more reasonable choice.[2] Masters expected their domestic servants, both slave and free, to behave in particular ways in their homes and neighborhoods, ways that reflected a city aspiring to be modern and cosmopolitan. Rules directed at social control were written into the municipality's legal code in an attempt to bring order to the day-to-day life of the increasingly busy streets. Gradually, the language of violence that had long been directed specifically at slaves was dropped. Nonetheless, one need look no further than the town's new jail to find evidence that slaves remained the most disadvantaged group in society. Although bondspeople represented an increasingly small portion of the township population, they were still targeted for arrest at a far higher rate than free people.

SLAVE FAMILIES

While punishment was something to be avoided, and work something to be endured, it was through family and community that slaves found moments of meaning and joy (as well as true heartache and loss). Bondspeople formed families when they had the chance, but doing so depended on the household environment, sex ratios, and the resources slaves had their disposal.[3] Few owners had complete power to force or forbid slave unions, and few slaves had complete freedom to choose unconcealed and lasting relationships. Families and socially and economically durable households were built from negotiation (albeit with vastly unequal terms), compromise, and luck. Historical sources say much less about why some owners encouraged the formation of stable slave families, but the reasons slaves desired families are no doubt similar to why the free population married in Brazil: better emotional stability, a stronger attachment to a place (increasing productivity and loyalty to an owner or patron), a chance to pool resources and to operate collectively, and improved conditions for their children. Some historians have argued that slave marriages were promoted by owners as a way to control their slaves; others have claimed that having families permitted slaves to create their own social space independent of their owners, but these may be two sides of the same coin.[4] The old and prevalent idea that slaves were unable to form families because of cultural norms, male promiscuity, or social instability has been discredited. In the past two decades, historians have concentrated on slave families in Brazil; in fact, their work is the most extensive for any slave society in the Americas. The presence of familial ties in many of these studies is connected to the size of slaveholdings, the type of productive activity, or both.[5]

A handful of studies deal with slave families in the southeastern region of Brazil.[6] In one pioneering study, Francisco Vidal Luna compared the rates of marriage among slaves to the size of slaveholdings and their productive activities in several townships of São Paulo in 1829. He found that slaves on sugar-producing and moderately large plantations (twenty-one to forty slaves) had the highest rates of marriage. Likewise, high rates of marriage among slaves of moderately large holdings were also found by J. Garavazo for Butatais Township (São Paulo) for a later period (1850–1890). Other studies have found the biggest percentage of married slaves on the largest plantations of rural Rio de Janeiro state, Mariana (Minas Gerais), and Campinas (São Paulo) for different years of the nineteenth century. Regarding fertility, however, these studies show that slaveholding size and marriage rates did not have a strong effect on the number of slave mothers with children.[7]

In the numerous studies of slave family formation in São Paulo, none have looked closely at slaves along the lowland coast. Even though the climate, production, and epidemiological risks in Santos better resembled parts of the Brazilian Northeast than the nearby Paulista highlands, slave families in Santos fit the demographic pattern found in the wider southeastern region of Brazil. Slaves who lived within the large and predominantly agricultural slaveholding households of Santos were the most likely to marry (or be purchased after they had married). Rates of marriage may have been higher among the slaves who worked in the fancy townhomes of Four Corners, but the manioc farmers and small-scale liquor producers of the rural Bertioga neighborhood displayed the greatest degree of household stability. Furthermore, slave infants were equally numerous among the small, large, rural, and urban slaveholdings, suggesting that slave women had children in a variety of conditions or were purchased with an infant child to a similar degree by rich and poor owners.[8]

Three neighborhoods exemplify the different ways that slaveholding and household economic activity corresponded with the ability of slaves to form familial bonds. The microareas of Travessa da Alfândega, Rua Josefina, and Bertioga village displayed strikingly varied patterns of slave families and household stability. The two streets, Travessa da Alfândega and Josefina, were within town within a ten-minute walk from one another, but their respective households shared little resemblance in terms of status, wealth, and occupation. Most of the rich men and women who owned town houses on Travessa da Alfândega, in the Four Corners neighborhood, considered themselves to be in a social position far above the poor service-oriented households on Rua Josefina or the small to middling farmers who lived thirty kilometers north of Santos (a canoe trip of several hours) in Bertioga village. This village, not far from the humble homes of Prudente Antonio and José Lopes de Jesus discussed in Chapter Two, consisted of a few rudimentary dockside warehouses and a handful of shops that mostly served fishermen and their families. The farmers in Bertioga planted cassava, rice, or fruit trees or distilled *aguardente* spirits, largely for the local market.[9]

The town's most powerful residents lived in the seven houses on Travessa da Alfândega, beginning at the warehouses and guarded custom house building near the waterfront and ending at the Four Corners intersection. It was a short street, and nearly all its buildings were two stories, neatly whitewashed, and a few had ornate Portuguese tiles and sculpted stone balustrades. With one entrance and a quick dead end at the harbor, Travessa da Alfândega was self-contained but cacophonous with the traffic at the custom house (Figure 4.1). Its wealth was embodied in the number of slaves who labored for the residents of the lane or were rented out in town. Between 1817 and 1830 the average number of slaves increased from twenty-four to twenty-seven per household, mostly in the rural estates of the lane residents. These numbers were low compared to other parts of Brazil where export agriculture predominated, or in cities such as Rio de Janeiro or Salvador. Some of the residents in the Four Corners neighborhood were the largest and most powerful slaveholders in Santos; their slaves were likely to hold skilled occupations and to produce goods consumed by people in distant and foreign markets, while those in the Bertioga village were mostly farm workers.[10]

A few blocks across town, Rua Josefina ran along the eastern edge of the port town. It was a much longer road, had many more free residents, and was considerably poorer than Travessa da Alfândega. Few

FIGURE 4.1

Rua Antonina at Travessa da Alfăndega, in the Four Corners Neighborhood, 1864

SOURCE: Militão Augusto Azevedo, 1864, FAMS.

of these houses had two floors; there was little ornamentation on the building façades, and scrubby lots alternated with neighboring buildings. Rua Josefina provided one of the town's southern exits and paralleled a similar street, Caminho da Barra (Figure 4.2). Residents could walk a good stretch of the street before passing a household that owned a slave. Slaveholding on Rua Josefina averaged only one slave for every three households.

Bertioga village had wealthier households than those on Rua Josefina, in both land and slaves, but its farmers and fishing folk were notably less affluent than the big planters on Travessa da Alfăndega. This rural neighborhood was spread across many more acres of space than the concentrated neighborhoods that held Josefina or Four Corners, but still displayed a similar degree of homogeneity. Not all of its farmers planted the same amount, but levels of wealth, possessions, and slaves were fairly comparable to their neighbors and distinct from most other areas of the city or township. All of the Bertioga farmers listed grew cassava as their principal crops (with *aguardente* usually secondary), and most did not own property outside of their farmstead. Slaveholding was higher in the village than on Rua Josefina, averaging a little more than one slave per household. Within this rural area and on the two urban streets of Josefina and Alfândega, slaveholding increased slightly during the 1820s, perhaps due to the relatively inexpensive price of slaves, numerous chances for upward mobility, and expansion of port activity.[11]

The two groups of slaves on Travessa da Alfândega and within Bertioga were much more likely to appear in multiple years of the census records and to be married. Table 4.1 reflects the number of times slaves appeared in the census records. Considering that more slave couples lived outside of church-sanctioned marriage than within it, a more important indicator of family and community formation is turnover. The speed that slaves moved in and out of a neighborhood was crucially important to their chances in forging familial or community ties. On average, only one slave on Rua Josefina reappeared in a following year of the census records on the same street. The few slaves who lived on that poor street (over a period long enough to be recorded in more than one census) usually disappeared from the records a short time after they first were listed. Slaves were not alone in their short residencies on Rua Josefina; the white households also had a high degree of turnover. Similar to the poor neighborhood of Francisca das Chagas on Rua Áurea, many of the households

FIGURE 4.2

Caminho da Barra, Two Blocks from Rua Josefina, 1864

SOURCE: Militão Augusto Azevedo (2004), p. 108.

TABLE 4.1

Family Patterns for Three Santos Neighborhoods, 1817–1830

	Rua Josefina	Bertioga	Travessa da Alfăndega
Households (average, per year)			
- Number of households	42	62	7
- Number of slaves	12	82	159
Rates of slaveholding			
- Slaves/household	0.3	1.3	24.5
Slave residential continuity (average, per year)			
- Number of slaves who appear in multiple years of the census records	1	52	98
- Number of slaves who appear once in the census records	10	31	61
- Number of households with slaves who appear in multiple years of the census records	1	10	6
- Duration of slaves in households that appear in multiple years of the census records (years)	2.2	6.1	4.7
Slave family patterns			
- Married slaves/total slaves (ratio)	0.01	0.1	0.18
- Slave infants/total slaves (ratio)	0.07	0.08	0.08
Real estate value			
- Taxed income generated by household real estate (in *mil-réis*)	(*R$*=29)	...	(*R$*=142)
Number of years the street or region appeared in census (total)	(N=5)	(N=6)	(N=4)

NOTES: Data for Josefina Street were taken and averaged in the period 1817 to 1828, the years in which this street was included in the census. Bertioga data are from 1817 to 1830, and Alfăndega data are from 1817 to 1828. Slave "infants" are defined as children aged five years or under.
SOURCES: Nominal lists, 1817–1830, AESP; urban property tax rolls (1839), AESP.

in this region rented their homes, and residents were unable or unwilling to remain in a building for even a couple years. The average duration of reappearing slaves was just over two years, about half that of Travessa da Alfăndega and one-third of the Bertioga averages. Most slaves of Travessa da Alfăndega and the Bertioga neighborhood lived in the same household for three or more years than recently arrived slaves who stayed for two years or less.[12]

As displayed in Table 4.1, depending on the neighborhood they lived in, between 1 and 18 percent of slaves were married. Marriage among slaves in all three of the neighborhoods dropped from about 12 percent in 1817 to about 7 percent in 1830, but the latter census excluded many of the wealthier streets that may have had higher levels of married slaves.

Even if there are married slaves missing from these rolls, it is apparent that slaves either found marriage to be more difficult or less appealing. More slaves were married among the Bertioga farms and the Four Corners farming households. In contrast, only one slave on Rua Josefina was married during these thirteen years. The largest group of married slaves lived in the sizable slaveholding households of Travessa da Alfãndega, where nearly one out of every five slaves was married, twice the rate of Bertioga and twenty times that of Rua Josefina.[13]

Although Bertioga had rates that were higher than average for the township, marriage was relatively infrequent compared to many parts of the province. For example, in 1829 three-quarters or more of enslaved residents were married or widowed in many townships in São Paulo. Santos's low marriage rates, shared by the provincial capital to the west, was anomalous. Moreover, only 16 percent of the enslaved were married or widowed in 1829 in São Paulo city. Perhaps an ideology that hampered slave marriage prevailed to a greater degree within the more commercial and urban areas of São Paulo at this time, but as we have seen, Santos was much more agricultural than urban during the first half of the nineteenth century and culturally different than the highlands region where São Paulo city was located. Along the tropical coast to the north and south of Santos, marriage rates were lower than the provincial average in 1829, but not nearly as low as they were in Santos. Four decades later, marriage rates among slaves appear to have dropped considerably in townships that produced commodities for world markets or were commercially oriented. Not coincidentally, these were the most likely recipients of slaves imported through interprovincial slave trade. Marriage rates among the enslaved in Santos and São Paulo city fell to about 7 percent in 1872. Iguape, a coastal township largely disconnected from world commodity markets, showed a rare increase in marriage rates by the 1870s. In contrast, less than 2 percent of slaves were married or widowed in São Sebastião, with its large sugar plantations and relative proximity to Rio de Janeiro. Similarly, Lorena and Areias, two coffee-producing townships in the Paulista Paraíba Valley, had much lower marriage rates than the provincial average.[14]

Table 4.1 also compares the percentage of slave infants in each of these three neighborhoods.[15] The presence of slave infants is another important indicator of slave families. Unlike slave marriages, the percentage of infants did not vary significantly between the three areas. Between 7 and 8 percent (based on a per year average) of all the slaves in these three neighborhoods were children ages five and under. Between 1817 and 1830, 6 to 8 percent of slaves in Santos were infants under six years. By 1873, 4 percent of bondspeople were under six, but because the Rio Branco law had decreed all newborn slaves free two years before, this average reflects only those slaves between three and five years old. In fact, the proportion of children of this age bracket was larger among the enslaved group than it was among the free group, suggesting that by the late 1860s at least, slaves were having children at a higher rate than the free people in Santos. True, this was a time in which an increasing number of single, working-age male immigrants entered Santos, which tended to lower overall fertility rates among free residents. As in all societies where working-age male immigrants predominate, there were far fewer opportunities for having children because of the high degree of transience and lopsided sex ratios. The evidence that fertility increased supports the idea that the opportunities (and willingness) among slaves to bear children improved.

The Bertioga households displayed the greatest stability, due in part to the relatively insulating nature of their productive activity and their geographic isolation. Historians have found similar degrees of stability among the small to midsized tobacco and cassava farmers in the Bahian Recôncavo. Not only did the small size of these northeastern farms blur "the distinction between peasant and slave-based agriculture," but these growers "depended far less on the importation of African slaves and much more on the natural growth of the slave population."[16] We might remember the three Bertiogan farmsteads discussed in Chapter Two, with slaves in residence for more than a decade. Prudente Antonio was the poorest of the group, living in a decrepit house and scraping by on a ragged patch of cassava. Yet, based on the inventories of 1817 and 1835, the slaves Ignacio and Eugenia remained with his family for eighteen years.[17] The other slaves in Antonio's household remained for a period of time that greatly exceeded residency periods of most slaves in other parts of the township. Like the tobacco or cassava farmers of the Recôncavo, Bertioga households appeared to be fairly poor or middling in wealth but exceptionally stable. Historians may find low turnover to be the most formative element for durable families among the enslaved.

The wealth and position of owners and their residential location within the city and township were more important for determining when slaves married than other factors such as race, sex, or place of birth. No racial or color group had a strong advantage over another in marrying in a Santos church or chapel. The ratio of black slaves to *pardo* slaves was slightly higher among the small group of married slaves than among the much larger group of single slaves, but the difference was nominal.[18] Proportionately, there were slightly more married slave women than men, despite the fact that there were more marriages between slave males and free females than vice versa. This was largely due to the fact that slave women lived longer and that until 1869 it was not illegal to sell the spouse of a slave out of the township.[19] Some historians have found that African-born slaves were more likely to marry, even though Brazilian-born slaves—because of better fluency in Portuguese—may have been more capable of mastering the catechistic requirements of a Catholic wedding. Among the small set of slaves married in a Santos church or chapel, for example, slightly more were African-born (but many did not have any birthplace listed), confirming what historians have found for other parts of Brazil.[20]

Neighborhood, and hence owner position and status, corresponded to large differences in slave marriage ratios and turnover rates. The differences between the neighborhoods supports the idea that large-slaveholding and wealthy owners were more likely to buy married slaves or allow their slaves to marry. For example, in 121 inheritance records accessed for this study, slaves were sometimes listed as spouses or young offspring. Among the three owners who died with married slaves listed in their inventories, two were among the wealthiest individuals in the records, while the third fell in the middle spectrum. Nine of the decedents had slaves with children, but their levels of wealth ran the full spectrum.[21] The sample is too small, however, to be more than suggestive. As on Travessa da Alfândega and Rua Josefina and in Bertioga, church-sanctioned marriage for slaves appears to have been a privilege, but childbirth was less restricted.

Another bit of evidence comes from one of the largest slave and property owners in the township. The Carmelite order owned a church and convent on Rua Direita, not far from Four Corners, along with several farms and numerous slaves. In 1865 church officials sold a large group of church slaves to José Vergueiro, the son of Senator Nicolau Vergueiro, who then resold them to coffee plantations in the interior. There was a public outcry over this transaction, and disapproving editorials were printed in the town newspaper. Nevertheless, the Carmelites proceeded with a list of sixty-five slaves to be traded. Remarkably, this list indicated numerous familial ties among the slaves. Nearly every slave on the list was related to another slave; in fact, only three slaves appeared not to be part of the eleven families in this group. The Carmelite slaves included (1) three married couples (two with children), (2) three widowers (one with his children and two with extended family), (3) one widow (with children and extended family), and (4) three mothers with children (two listed as unmarried, one with a husband who was not included). Five of the groupings included extended family such as nephews, grandparents, or grandchildren, and one slave family included a slave *agregado*.[22] In this way, the church was similar to other wealthy slave owners with its high proportion of slaves who were or had been married. This portrait of the Carmelite slaveholding also shows the numerous kinds of family ties not usually found in Brazilian historical sources, including the marriage registers. We should keep in mind, however, that since church officials were under pressure from the public they may have gone out of their way to display an intention to maintain families as units.

Church marriage records maintained by other branches of the Catholic Church in Santos also support the idea that marriage was more common among slaves of rich slaveholding owners in the wealthier neighborhoods. Among the forty-two marriages involving bondspeople in the township, owners of married slaves were involved more in urban occupations than farming, were Brazilian and Santista, and were often wealthy and politically powerful. For example, Henrique Porchat, who was Swiss-born and a longtime resident, owned two slave couples who married. Porchat opened one of the first steam-powered lime factories in Santos and ran one of the town's main dockside warehouses, along with a butchering operation. He was also one of the largest slaveholders in the township during the 1870s. Another wealthy Santos resident, João Octávio Nebias, owned fourteen slaves in 1817 and fifteen city buildings by 1839. Nebias served as a township councilman and a legislator for the provincial government, and in 1851 he permitted a slave couple that he owned to marry. Finally, João Teixeira Chaves, who allowed his slaves Francisco and Sebastiana to marry in 1839, owned sixty-four slaves in 1817 and sixty-five in 1830. Chaves owned a plantation named Paciencia on an expanse of rural land that probably once produced sugar or coffee for international markets.[23]

Most slave weddings took place in the town's *matriz* (the principal location of the Catholic church in a given region); others occurred in the Carmelite Church, the Church of Nossa Senhora dos Pretos (Our Lady of the Blacks), and the Chapel of São José in Bertioga.[24] Among the slave grooms, 37 percent were Brazilian of birth (20 percent within Santos), 42 percent were African, and 22 percent were of unknown birthplace. The brides largely fit this demographic profile, except more slave brides were born in Santos than in other parts of Brazil or in Africa. All Catholic weddings required two witnesses for the marriage to be official, and relatives often served this honored role. Of the fifteen slave marriages that provide names of witnesses, three slaves served for three slave marriages, one of whom was also owned by the groom's master. The other ceremonies were all witnessed by free men.[25]

Slaves who married in Santos were most likely to take another slave as their spouse, but mixed unions were not uncommon. Twenty-four marriages involved only slaves. Ten marriages occurred between slave males and free females. Unions between a free male and a slave female were the least common, with only three instances of this type. Overall, and mirroring patterns found in the census records, slave weddings were rare to start with and became even rarer as the century progressed. A typical year in the middle part of the century saw only one church slave marriage (assuming, of course, that these marriages were regularly recorded and the archive is missing no books).

Marriages among the enslaved appear to have declined in Santos, either because this option became more difficult, was promoted less by church officials and masters, or brought fewer benefits for partners. Among adult slaves who died and whose deaths were registered by the city, married and widowed slaves declined from 11 percent in 1857–1870 to 5 percent in 1871–1886. Free marriage rates held steady during the second half of the century. Slightly more than one in three free adults were married or widowed when they died. For other parts of southeastern Brazil during this period, marriage rates ranged between 1 and 42 percent. Robert Slenes found that the proportion of slaves who were married or widowed increased between the 1850s and early 1870s in several regions of interior São Paulo, but declined during the late 1870s and 1880s. This was also the case for Mariana, Minas Gerais. Santos appears to better resemble Rio de Janeiro then the interior of its province, not only because marriage rates among slaves were relatively low to begin with, but also because they steadily declined during the second half of the nineteenth century.[26]

Even though slave marriages were more likely to take place in households that were wealthy and held far more slaves than was normal in the township of Santos, strong relationships formed between slave men and women with or without church, state, or master approval. Slaves may have had a much harder time maintaining families in poorer areas like Rua Josefina where turnover was high, but slave women still had infants at a level that was fairly constant with the rest of the township. The Bertioga neighborhood appears to have been the most ideal location for slave families since turnover rates were so low, despite its relative poverty.

Historians have argued that the higher rates of slave marriage in the larger plantations was a consequence of better chances for slaves to socialize and find a spouse in environments where there were more potential partners. Since slaves generally married slaves owned by the same masters, the plantations with numerous slaves increased the chances that a partner could be found. This seems like a reasonable explanation, yet it does not explain why more slaves married from moderately large plantations (twenty to forty slaves) than from large plantations (forty or more slaves) in several parts of Brazil at different times. This finding suggests that there were other factors at work besides the chances for socialization. In one study, Heloísa Maria Teixeira cross-referenced hundreds of slaves in several different sources. Teixeira's study focused on the Mariana Township (Minas Gerais) between 1850 and 1888.[27] She found that moderately large slaveholdings were more likely to be stable and have low rates of turnover. The Bertioga neighborhood in Santos, which had small to medium slaveholding and cassava farming, had the most stability. In that part of the township, slaves may not have been able to marry as frequently, but they may have had an easier time creating and maintaining a family, even when the marriage was not officially recognized. The fact that female slaves in Santos and those in other parts of Brazil had children at rates that were not influenced by slaveholding size suggests that plantation size may have had less effect on socialization than scholars have imagined. If many small farms were clustered, or if smallholding slaves lived in a town, then they probably had frequent contact with many slaves of different owners. Certainly, relationships must have been forged in such conditions, despite the smaller chance or even desire to have their union officially blessed by the Catholic Church.

SLAVE WORK

Beyond having different opportunities in family formation, slaves also found vastly different opportunities for work. In fact, slave work is one aspect of slave life in which historians have commonly recognized social hierarchies.[28] In Santos, as in the rest of Brazil, slaves worked as many as a hundred officially recognized jobs and were skilled in multiple trades. The slave workplace, like nearly all workplaces, was rarely egalitarian; many jobs took years to master and workers usually had to respect seniority. This was especially true among the skilled creative trades, such as blacksmithing or cooperage, where apprenticeships were common.[29] For the historian, finding information about occupational status is difficult since slaves were usually broadly categorized into occupations that had many internal ranks. Owners only rarely indicated these ranks, such as *mucama* (head house servant) or "*mestre de obras*" (master builder), and in fact often did the opposite by listing skilled workers in nondescript categories such as *jornaleiros* (day laborers) or *trabalhadores* (workers). Historians also face the challenge of piecing together scattered bits of information gleaned through sources that deal with other aspects of slave life, such as their sale, health, or when they were passed to heirs via wills and testaments. In these sources, indirect information about slave work appears. Nevertheless, it is possible to find and connect sufficient evidence that slave work varied considerably, and that particular slave jobs were concentrated in different neighborhoods or parts of the township.[30] Furthermore, slave labor varied by sex, race, and birthplace and that of their owners. Finally, slaves faced different risks depending on their work. Inequality, then, is clearly evident in labor conditions that depended on the position of their owners and fit within a stratified world.

Between 1840 and 1870, Santos slaves most commonly worked with some type of pole in their hands, such as a broom, a mop, or a hoe. The most prevalent slave occupations in the port city and in the rural areas of the southern part of Santos were farming and domestic service, although a sizable group of slaves moved coffee and goods between mule trains, dockside warehouses, and ships. That agriculture had not yet forfeited its centrality in the township's economy to the service sector is reflected by the high number of farming slaves. Other important occupations included baking, carpentry, cooking, and masonry.[31] Many masters described their slaves simply as *sem oficio* (without a trade) because their slaves did not work one of the skilled creative trades such as carpentry, cobbling, or baking.[32] Owners who posted advertisements in newspapers may have wanted to lure buyers by making their slaves appear adaptable, and thus listed their slaves as *proprio para qualquer serviço* (good for any service). These owners may have had a domestic servant for sale but used a description that would have expanded the pool of potential buyers to include those who wanted an outdoor laborer.[33]

Some slave occupations were concentrated in certain neighborhoods. Chapter Three explored the kind of work slaves did and the job skills obtained in two neighborhoods that posted slave sale or rent advertisements. This chapter extends that analysis by comparing slave advertisements posted by residents of a small portion of Rua Direita and Rua Áurea posted in the local newspaper. The difference between those two neighborhoods was evident in the types of slaves that households bought, sold, and rented. Áurea and Campo streets, which intersected in the Aurea neighborhood, stretched along the town's southern outskirts and included many of the town's poor and middling households, but also had a few wealthier residents scattered throughout. Rua Direita (in the Dockside neighborhood) had only a few poor residents, many middling households, and several wealthy merchants and businessmen. This street ran through the middle of town, connected nearly every neighborhood in town, and was the main route for goods coming in from or going out to sea. Residents in the Áurea neighborhood posted fewer advertisements compared to the Dockside neighborhood and rented more slaves than they sold or rented out (see Table 4.2). On this street, more slaves worked as cooks and masons. In contrast, slaves on Rua Direita were more likely to be butlers or table servants and "jack-of-all-trade" slaves, giving evidence that the work slaves performed was connected to the neighborhoods they and their masters lived in.

TABLE 4.2
Types of Advertised Slaves, 1850–1873 (Percent)

	Rua Áurea to Rua do Campo	Rua Direita
Slaves for sale	32	63
Slaves for rent	15	16
Slaves needed	47	16
Cooks	23	12
Domestic servants	35	29
Masons	10	2
Wetnurses	10	2
Butlers or table servants (*copeiros*)	3	8
Jack-of-all-trades (*todo/qualquer serviço*)	3	28
Total advertisements	(N=32)	(N=63)
Total with occupation listed	(N=31)	(N=52)

SOURCE: *Revista do Commercio, Diario de Santos*, 1850–1873, CCS in FAMS, HS.

Slave occupation also varied regionally, even in areas with similar geography and productive activity. Neighboring Santos to the north, São Sebastião and Ilha Bela de Princesa were two townships that had a similar climate, fauna, and geography. But they differed from Santos in that hundreds of slaves in these townships maintained large plantations that produced sugar destined for markets in Rio de Janeiro or in Europe. São Sebastião was a primary restoring point for large ships between Rio and Santos and offered many of the shops and services that otherwise were only available at the larger port of Santos. Thus besides farming slaves there were also cooks, tailors, seamstresses, and carpenters.[34] But slaves predominantly farmed in São Sebastião and Ilha Bela, and because wealth was more concentrated in the hands of a few large *fazendeiros* (ranchers or planters), there was a smaller base of middling wealth holders who could afford enslaved domestic servants. All in all, though, the economies of these townships were less varied than Santos, creating a smaller range of possible occupations for their bondspeople.

Race and birthplace of slaves sometimes corresponded with the types of jobs slaves worked. Darker-skinned slaves were always the majority among slaves in Santos, but some jobs had disproportionate numbers of lighter-skinned slaves. In all parts of the township, slaves who worked jobs outside of agriculture (such as in domestic service), those "without a skill," and "general worker" slaves were about 75 percent black, which was probably the overall race or color for the total slave population in Santos at this time.[35] The high proportion of *pardos* who worked in carpentry or tailoring and low proportion of slaves of this group that worked as cooks and bakers are therefore noticeable.[36] But, again, this could vary region to region. About an even number of black and *pardo* slaves worked in the cassava-growing and small farmstead region of Bertioga between 1817 and 1830. In contrast, black farming slaves outnumbered *pardos* three to one in São Sebastião. Sebastiano plantation owners had the resources and connections to purchase (and illegally import) many more black African slaves than the smaller and poorer farms that were about three hours away by canoe.[37]

Language and culture may have limited African slaves' access to certain jobs in some instances but not in others. For example, a similar proportion of African-born slaves were servants as among the overall township slave population. This was true among *macumas* (ladies-in-waiting or chambermaids), for example, but among higher-skilled jobs in this township, such as carpentry, cobbling, and tailoring, there were relatively more Brazilian-born slaves than in the general population. Again, regional variance appears, even between neighboring townships. In Santos, native-born slaves did not dominate cobbling and carpentry and Africans appear to have had an easier time entering some of the town's skilled trades. Slave farmers were also often African, most likely because the larger plantation owners bought younger male slaves before the end of the international slave trade in 1850 and because some of the African slaves may have arrived with farming skills. The birthplaces of slaves listed as "without a trade" or as "general workers" were similar to those of the larger slave population.

The sex of the slave owner correlated more to slave occupations than did the birthplaces of the enslaved workers. Women slaveholders, for instance, were more likely to own enslaved farmers. In fact, nearly three out of every four slaves possessed by female owners worked on small garden plots, midsized rural farms, or the large fields of the plantations. Free women inherited property from their parents or husbands and, because women often outlived their husbands, numerous widows continued the operations of their husbands' or fathers' farms. Male owners, on the other hand, owned a higher percentage of slaves who worked the dockside warehouses or serviced the port. The coffee business and import-export trade were, in general, dominated by men, such that when these businesses were inherited by women, they were probably sold. Interestingly, male slaveholders were also twice as likely as women to own domestic servants, largely because women were on the average poorer than men. Other slave occupations were inexplicably concentrated by male or female owners; for instance, women owned more carpenters, but fewer masons. Slave cooks, washerwomen, and bakers were evenly divided among male and female owners. Finally, enslaved seamstresses (remember Francisca Maria das Chagas and her neighborhood on Áurea Street) did almost all of their needlework for mistresses.

The great variety of jobs that slaves worked could be placed into four broad categories: domestic servants, general workers, skilled creative trades, and farmers. These categories, presented in Table 4.3, include the majority of jobs that slaves held.[38] "Skilled creative trade" is a category similar to the often-used category of "artisan slaves," but is broader and includes bakers, carpenters, construction workers, ceramic kiln workers, cobblers, coopers, masons, pastry chefs, seamstresses, ship caulkers, and tailors. We can also place owners into different categories to see the effect of place of birth and age. One increasingly important occupation in town, coffee commissioning, is included in Table 4.3 to demonstrate how the growing service economy affected the kinds of jobs slaves worked.

Slave occupation was connected to other attributes of their masters. Owners born in Santos were more likely to own slaves who transported or stored port commodities than enslaved domestic servants. Portuguese masters, on the other hand, owned relatively more enslaved domestic servants. Owner birthplace had an effect on the number of farming slaves that each group possessed. Since Brazilian-born owners were more likely to own land, the proportion of their slaves tilling fields or planting gardens was higher than other groups. Proportionally, more farming slaves were held by older owners, reflecting the general shift in the local econ-

TABLE 4.3

Types of Working Slaves Held by Different Owners, 1845–1885 (Percent)

	Slaves				
Owners	Domestic Servants	General Workers	Skilled Creative Trade	Farmers	Total
Born in Santos	20	41	15	18	(N=101)
Born in Portugal	38	35	12	5	(N=82)
Age under 50 years	38	36	13	9	(N=77)
Age over 50 years	21	40	19	12	(N=97)
Coffee merchant house owners	18	38	16	5	(N=95)
Identified individuals	26	44	13	6	(N=539)
Unidentified individuals	32	31	12	8	(N=301)

NOTE: "Identified individuals" indicate owners located in multiple sources.
SOURCES: Slave tax registers, 1833–1845, AESP; bills of sale, 1863–1870, CCS in FAMS, PCNS, SCNS; manumission letters, 1844–1875, CCS in FAMS, PCNS, SCNS; inheritance records, 1830–1872, CCS in FAMS; *Revista do Commercio* (Santos), *Diario de Santos*, 1850–1873, CCS in FAMS, HS.

omy from agriculture to commerce. The changing economy and society can also be seen in the fact that older Santistas owned slightly more slaves in the skilled creative trades than younger Portuguese masters and that the younger generations found it more necessary (and within their often growing household earnings) to own a domestic servant.

If we look only at coffee merchants we find that they were most likely to consider their slaves general workers rather than domestics, skilled creative tradespeople, or farmers.[39] Coffee merchants, and the growing number of people involved in the service sector of the township economy, appear to have been among the first to hire *libertos*, free Brazilians, or poor immigrants and to pay a wage for their work in their businesses. Indeed, advertisements for domestic workers show that by the 1870s some township residents preferred wage workers over slaves. As amazingly elastic slavery was to the new forms of production and shifting economy after 1870, we may not want to entirely abandon the old idea that slavery and industrialization were like two intermeshed gears spinning at different speeds. A few of Santos's earliest and most prominent abolitionists (or "manumissionists"; see Conclusion) were coffee merchants, but the majority of this group likely believed into the 1880s that patience, not government interference, was all that was needed to accomplish the transition to free labor. In the meantime, slaves were considered a necessary part of the labor force for a port city that sometimes had trouble finding workers.

The number of bags of coffee doubled and tripled in large part due to the opening of the railroad in 1867. More businessmen took on the role of intermediaries with the interior coffee planters. Carpenters and masons constructed large stores and deposits, and entrepreneurs extended new dockside warehouses into the canal. The Santos supplement for the Rio de Janeiro "Almanak Laemmert" from 1850 listed twenty-five businessmen who specialized in "coffee and sugar." For the first time that year, coffee exceeded sugar in total exports of the province, a monumental shift considering that sugar dominated provincial exports for more than three centuries. Sugar accompanied coffee in the commissioning business in 1850, but as can be seen in Table 4.4, this product had largely dropped out of sight two decades later. Besides coffee, townspeople were also excited about the prospect of cotton at the dawn of the U.S. Civil War. Cotton in Brazil had long been expensive and inferior compared to American cotton, but when the American Union navy blockaded Confederate ports, the English were willing to look for alternatives to feed their steam-powered looms. During the Civil War years and shortly after, many commission houses specialized only in cotton and coffee, with thirty-four such houses in 1870.[40] The railroad also facilitated the custom of a group of "coffee barons" from Sao Paulo of arriving on the morning train in time

TABLE 4.4

Growth in Santos Port Services, 1865–1880

1865		1875		1880	
Number	Type	Number	Type	Number	Type
11	Commission houses (general)	34	Commission houses (coffee and cotton)	55	Commission houses (coffee and cotton)
13	Warehouses (coffee)	10	Commission houses (general goods)	16	Commission houses (general goods)
		18	Import and export Businesses	33	Import and export Businesses
		3	Warehouses (sugar)	2	Warehouses (sugar)
				4	Warehouses (construction material)

SOURCE: Almanak Laemmert, 1865, 1870, 1875, 1880.

to make the commodity exchange meeting in Santos. We might imagine that as the long train twisted through the mountain pass, these men could catch glimpses from their luxury compartments of the long row of sooty cargo cabs carrying their goods and wealth.

As the town's economy diversified, its labor divided into more specialized roles. New technologies, primarily those brought by combustion, altered the set of jobs that slaves worked. There is nothing apparently intrinsic to this incipient industrialization that suggests that the institution of slavery was not so pliant to adapt. What is true is that by the 1870s, slaves worked a different set of jobs than their parents and grandparents.[41] Before, female slaves had mostly kept houses and farmed. Some worked as cooks or vegetable vendors, while a small group was listed as "without a trade." Labor for male slaves had included farming, carpentry, masonry, domestic service, cooking, and shoemaking. After 1870, townspeople increased their demand for specialized forms of labor, jobs that had not been practical when the city was small. Female slaves still largely worked domestic jobs, but there were more cooks and washerwomen than domestic servants. The number of slaves classified as domestic servants dropped enormously, declining in the 1870s and 1880s to about a third of the level it had been in the two decades before. Most male slaves still worked as cooks and farmers, but many slaves began laboring as wagon drivers and warehouse workers.[42] Other new jobs such as shop clerk, pastry chef, railroad worker, factory worker, and tobacco roller appeared. The term "without a trade" was dropped and a new category of "worker" rose to take its place. As the local internal market for slaves began to dwindle and poorer immigrants flooded into town, this term began to be used for the slaves and free wage earners who were working the same tasks, sometimes side by side.

Neighborhoods still retained some degree of homogeneity in terms of slave occupation. As evident from the slave advertisements, more owners in the wealthier Four Corners neighborhood bought, sold, and rented slaves who worked in domestic service or as cooks. A short distance away on Áurea Street, an increasing number of slaves worked as artisans and seamstresses. Much less is known about what happened to the slaves in the Bertioga neighborhood, since the government stopped recording detailed censuses after 1840. It seems reasonable to assume that as coffee merchants in the city were willing to pay high prices for slaves, the cassava and rice farmers in the rural parts of the township sold their slaves. If this happened, the remarkable household stability that had existed during the first half of the century would have been upset when slave families were broken by sales.

SLAVE PUNISHMENT

As slaves worked in shops or warehouses or traversed the city with wagons weighted down by bags of sugar or coffee, they had to be aware of a set of rules that governed their manners and conduct. When Santos was a small town and retained much of its colonial form, the houses on Rua Direita or Hell's Alley (Beco de Inferno) pressed tightly against one another and people had to pass shoulder to shoulder. In such an environment, particular behavior was held by city officials to be tasteless or offensive. Detailed rules were drafted and enforced by officers of the law. Police patrols, the army guard, and plain-clothed cops all had the power to arrest. They were active at all times and especially attentive on Sundays and holidays, when slaves and free people of African descent partook in a variety of entertainments. In the eyes of the white slaveholders, their music and dance inherited from a diverse range of African cultural backgrounds were foreign and anti-Christian, and they often did their best to ban them.[43] Even two or three slaves sitting on a curb after work sharing an old song could have been construed as a punishable offense. Slaves were forced to operate within two sets of norms: the official city laws that everyone, black or white, had to follow; and a second and much stricter set of unspoken rules that applied only to slaves that depended on (1) the situation and crime, (2) the slave committing the act, and (3) the whim of the offended *gente bem*, or "better," who often hauled people of color into jail.

The oldest existing set of city laws, the *Codigo de posturas*, dates from 1847 and gives a picture of many quotidian activities. Many of these rules may not have been strictly followed but, at the very least, they give a sense of how city officials imagined an orderly city and responsible residents to be. For example, city residents annually whitewashed their walls and fixed their sidewalks; they prevented the enormously long trains of mules and muleteers from clogging up local traffic; and they changed the white pans collecting bloody drippings from freshly butchered pigs on a daily basis. Santos residents and visitors were expected to bury their dead 1.3 meters underground, and they could administer torture in the form of whipping slaves who acted offensively or disrespectfully. In 1847 Santos was still a farm town, and many laws applied to the people who came from the rural regions to sell what they had grown or raised or to find the services the countryside did not yet offer. Of the 118 legal articles, twenty-three outlined the ways that houses, sidewalks, fences, and roads were to be maintained and modified. Another twenty dealt with animals, including how they were to be raised, killed, and their meat handled. Nineteen laws applied to medical establishments, sanitation, and burial. Finally, twenty articles regulated the proper street conduct of townspeople, and several of these related specifically to the behavior of slaves.[44]

As the century progressed and the town's economy diversified, city officials added more laws to the books. A few of the older rules were deemed obsolete, but overall the list expanded into 190 articles by the first year of the Republic in 1890. The biggest jump in the size of the *codigos* came between 1847 and 1852, when a commission led by Judge José Justiano Bittencourt debated how to modernize the city laws. The commission added forty-four articles, mostly related to the regulation of business and commerce. This group was motivated by the large changes that were occurring in town. New laws were deemed necessary for the expanding commercial environment and to ensure that the city had the most up-to-date mechanisms of gaining tax revenue from the new forms of business. It also paralleled and mirrored changes at the national level since the Brazilian Parliament approved a detailed commercial code in 1850. In town, Santos officials added a law that permitted factories of soap, liquors, or lime to open only after the owner had obtained the township council's permission and paid a sizable tax. The tax, in fact, was ten times the amount collected from small shops and taverns. Another law prohibited factories opening near residential areas. Article Eight raised the tax on commission houses, and Article Nine mandated a tax for businesses renting out wagons and lifts in town. When Bittencourt's commission sent the new list of laws to the provincial government, Paulista senators approved it with only a few changes.[45]

Another important move of the Bittencourt commission was to exclude the language of violence that pertained specifically to slaves. Before the 1850s, slaves could receive twenty-five lashings if they were caught washing their clothes directly in a public fountain.[46] They were prohibited from loitering in shops or doorways, and their masters were fined for this offense. A more serious crime was the festive gathering of slaves, as mentioned earlier, where many escaped their toil through friendly gatherings that mixed talk, song, and dance. The slaveholders had no patience for these events, referring to them as "barbarous drumming (*toques*) and rude bawling (*vozearia*)." They dealt twenty-five blows for offenders. After 1850, the laws that applied to how men and women acted on the street became more general.[47] Fewer laws specifically mentioned slaves and offensive behavior independent of the doer itself was highlighted. The law code also dropped the language of violence and no longer called for a specific number of whippings. Most likely, whipping carried on in the jailhouse and within the home, as a law banning it from the Empire had not yet been passed.

Even though the crimes and forms of punishment in the updated law code may have become more "democratic" on appearance, other sources demonstrate that there were many unwritten rules that applied only to slaves. Undoubtedly, slaves were the primary target of the town's criminal legal system. An enormous amount of attention and energy went into bringing slaves in line with the dominant system of white (and colored) slaveholding morality. Indeed, slaves were twice as likely to go to jail in 1878 as a free person, and up to four or five times more likely to go to jail than a city resident, as evidenced by jail registers.[48] Most Brazilian jail keepers in the nineteenth century kept track of who entered and stayed behind bars, and a few of these books from Santos, tattered and dirty, remain in the hands of the police today. Besides the name of the arrested party, the crime, and the length of stay, these registers also included physical descriptions of the slaves. The descriptions were, in a sense, nineteenth-century mug shots and are one of the few places in archives that provide a sense of slaves' appearance. For a period of time, the local newspaper also announced arrests, giving short details to the crimes and, if they were slaves, the names of the owners.[49]

Slaves were hauled into jail for a variety of reasons, but most arrests were ambiguously justified by the police as a reaction to "disobedience,"

TABLE 4.5

Reasons for Slave Arrests, 1866–1879 (Percent)

	Male Slaves	Female Slaves
Disobedience	13.4	33.3
Disorder	9.1	11.1
Disrespect	5.0	3.7
Drunkenness	12.2	3.7
Flight	15.1	9.3
Past curfew	17.5	7.4
By master's request	14.4	24.1
Assault or murder	3.6	1.9
Robbery	1.4	0.0
Other	1.0	0.0
Unknown	7.4	5.6
Total	(N=418)	(N=54)

NOTE: "Other" includes trespassing and littering, while "unknown" includes those without description and 25 cases listed as "under investigation" (*para averiguação*).
SOURCES: Arrest registers, 1860–1880, MPCSP; *Revista do Commercio* (Santos), 1866–1867, HS.

"disorder," or "disrespect" (see Table 4.5). The most frequent offenses were breaking curfew, attempted or suspected flight, and drunkenness. Curfew began at nine or ten o'clock in the evening and was marked by the toll of the church bells. Patrols who found slaves on the streets without a note from their masters were arrested. In addition, owners often brought their own slave into jail or asked the police to arrest a slave they thought deserving of punishment. Female slaves were more likely than male slaves to be brought into the jail upon the whim of their masters or mistresses. Gender played an important role in other aspects of arrests. Females were more likely to have been arrested for "disobedience" and "disorder," but less likely to have been behind bars for "disrespect," drunkenness, and attempted escape.[50] Serious crimes such as violent assaults and murder were still quite rare in Santos before 1880, and they caused a good deal of attention when they did occur.

The rates of slave arrests for different categories of offenses also varied according to age and race. A higher percentage of young to mid-age slaves (under thirty years old) were arrested for disobedience, disorder, and violent crimes; while older slaves (over thirty) had a greater chance of going to jail for breaking the nightly curfew or drinking too much. A nearly equal number of young and old slaves were arrested at the request of their owners for disrespect or because they attempted to or were suspected of running away. "Disrespect" was also a reason used to justify the arrest of a higher percentage of lighter-skinned slaves. Darker-skinned blacks, on the other hand, were more likely to "disobey" and were more often taken to the police upon their owner's request. Finally, the offenses committed by mulattos and other lighter-skinned slaves had a greater chance of being put under investigation. Clearly, race played a role in influencing the situational rules that slaves lived by day to day.[51]

Interestingly, slaves who "disobeyed" were more often described as tall and skinny, while slaves who "lacked respect" were more likely to be short and stout.[52] Considering the physical and demographic differences between these groups of offenders, it seems likely that slaves who had a more proximate relationship with their owners, including young black female domestic servants, were more likely to be accused of disobeying orders. Physical appearance and age came into the picture as well. A dark slave with a dominating physical figure—one who was tall and strong—was simply disobedient when he refused a request.[53] A lighter-skinned, short, and portly slave who refused the same request or responded in an unanticipated manner was easily deemed disrespectful. It might have also been the case that lighter-skinned males who worked in more independent capacities ran a greater risk of stepping over the permissible line that their race and status afforded them when confronted with an authority figure.

The jail where these slaves were sent was in an imposing, two-story building that also served for a period of time as the courthouse and as a regional headquarters for the National Guard (Figure 4.3). By the first decades of the Empire, the old jail was far too small and inadequate to handle the increasing numbers of prisoners. The town's criminal judge (*justiça da paz*) sent a letter to the provincial government in 1839 asking for funds to construct a new jail.[54] He wrote:

> The building will have four jail cells for men, two for women, two infirmaries, and two solitary cells that will serve only to harbor inmates who are disturbing the peace or who are punished by being denied their rations, etc. but will also serve as a chapel, for those condemned to death; and finally as a place for the restraining devices (one that weighs almost twenty kilos) and the storage of iron chains and shackles, a space for madmen, and for other uses. [There will be] a workspace where inmates will toil, as they would be required according to the regulations that will be given to the prison. And finally, above the entrance to the jail, near the front balcony, an alter will be placed for the divine offices, used in the very least for the principal days of the year, so as in this form to inspire the religious sentiments in men, or for those that lack this, a place where they can find these sentiments.

The new jail had at its center an open courtyard, and all of the cells and guardrooms were arranged around this space. A single door to the

FIGURE 4.3
The New Jail in 1864
SOURCE: Militão Augusto Azevedo, 1864, FAMS.

building was in the front, where the jailor had his office and guards were posted. Behind the office and to each side of the courtyard were cells for individuals who had committed less serious crimes (*crimes medios*). These prisoners were separated by sex and given a cell and medical clinic (*enfermaria*). The back of the jail was reserved for the most serious criminals. Within one of these back cells, the jailor kept stocks, known in Portuguese as the *tronco* (trunk) or the *namorado* ("boyfriend"), which physically restrained the feet or hands of prisoners. The *tronco* forced a man to remain sitting or prostate and must have caused blisters and wounds where it bit at the ankles over a period of days or weeks. Prisoners who were lucky enough to avoid fetters could communicate with people outside of the jail through barred windows that opened onto every cell.[55]

More slaves were arrested during the drier summer and fall months than in the winter and spring. This was a time when more slaves were circulating and the warmth invited segregation, celebration, and occasional rebelliousness. Arrests peaked in March and April, with the number of arrested slaves nearly three times as high as those arrests in the colder and rainy winter months of June and July.[56]

Slaves were arrested by a number of different groups including the police, army, and even common citizens. Police patrols were the busiest in this task and made nearly half of the total arrests, but slaves were also arrested by order of the *delegado* (police commander) or *subdelegado* (supporting officers). Night police patrols booked mostly curfew and drinking charges, along with sending an occasional slave who lacked sufficient respect for a day or more behind bars. A few *paisanos* (plain-clothed police officers or detectives) worked principally on investigations, but would also arrest slaves for any other crime. Two divisions of the army also made arrests, as did the jail guard and the city block inspectors. The *praça de linha* (imperial soldier) and the *guarda nacional* (national guard) arrested about twelve slaves per year during this period, mostly related to disobedience and disrespect. Finally, slaves were brought into jail by citizens who were not their owners. Slave Narciso was arrested by an "agent" of his French owner, and Nistardo was brought into the jail by an "employee of his owner's [coffee commission] house." On some occasions a slave was escorted to jail by other slaves. Pedro was brought in by two slaves owned by his master and carrying a letter requesting the jail keeper to confine him for unspecified charges.[57] Owners paid a daily rate for their slaves' confinement, and the city jail seemed willing to take both new slave inmates and their master's money regardless of space. With nearly every free male in the city capable of making an arrest, slaves had to be constantly on guard. If their behavior conflicted with someone's mood, they could find themselves behind bars.[58]

Depending on the severity of their charge and the actions taken by their owners, slaves could be released in less than twenty-four hours after being arrested. Others spent months in jail waiting for investigations to conclude or for their owners to believe that they had paid their just dues. A slave named Macias spent almost four months behind bars resulting from a dispute over his deceased owner's inheritance; the disputing party needed a neutral place from where Macias would not run. Most slaves who were interred for more than a month were runaways from other parts of the province, but some were jailed for long periods over a single and often minor offense toward their owners. São Paulo slaves condemned to the gallows in Rio de Janeiro spent time in the Santos jail on their trip north. One slave named Narciso had already served twelve years in prison when he was escorted through Santos in 1879.[59]

The length of time a slave spent in jail usually depended on the charge. Those charged with curfew violations or drunkenness were usually free within twenty-four hours. On average, slaves arrested for disobedience or disorder were released within a shorter time than those charged with disrespect.[60] Apparently, a slave who failed to serve a master's request was treated with less severity than a slave who acted with an attitude unbefitting their color and position. The most powerful people in town had many means of making sure that the lines of race and status were not crossed. Moreover, the more powerful the individual, the more discretion he or she had as to whether a slave was acting disrespectfully. Slaves arrested at their owner's request served both short and long terms in jail, as did runaways. Overall, two out of every three were released in under a week.

A handful of slaves were arrested more than once. Of the twelve who can be identified with two charges during these two decades, only one slave was arrested for the same offense.[61] About half of these multiple offenders were arrested twice within a period of a year, and one was arrested for disorder eight years after his first offense.[62] Surprisingly, most of these slaves did not serve a longer period of time on their second stay in jail.

Some historians have speculated that punishments were so severe that some slaves were killed or had to be treated for injuries. Of the fifteen slaves who appear in the jail and hospital or cemetery records, or in all three between 1860 and 1880, however, none entered the hospital or died in the same month of his or her arrest.[63] This sample is, of course, too small to produce any firm conclusions, but it seems likely that the connection between punishment and severe injury was not widespread. Many owners did not want permanent physical injury inflicted upon their slaves because such wounds could affect their work or their price on the market. Scars from whippings, for example, lowered the price of a slave because they signaled unruliness. Owners could, at their own discretion, inflict punishment or torture that left no scars, though it appears likely that a master would sell a slave who presented too many problems.

Slaves were targeted by the legal system partly because many owners were unable or unwilling to punish their slaves themselves and preferred to send them to the jail for an affordable fee. Slaves faced many more rules than the free, including curfew and runaway laws, but also had to maintain strict decorum before more powerful men and women who could easily interpret their actions or expressions negatively. By the late 1870s, however, slaves were becoming a small minority within the expanding city population, and the police spent more of their patrol time arresting drunken mariners and rowdy wage workers than attending to disobedient slaves. Free men and women could also be arrested for disobedience and disrespect, but such cases were rare. "Disorder" was the charge given to 15 percent of the free people arrested, and probably included bar room brawls, back-alley fights, and other activities for which mariners were infamous throughout the world. Many of the activities leading to arrest were driven by impaired judgment after excessive drinking; in fact, one out of every two arrests between 1875 and 1880 carried the charge of *ebrio* (drunkenness). Twenty-six free men went to jail upon the request of a consul general. When one of the several foreign consuls based in Santos received complaints regarding their countrymen, they rarely hesitated to order their arrest.[64]

Slaves lived in an unequal society and were held by a great diversity of owners of differing levels of wealth, occupation, and background, and these factors affected which slaves went to jail. Slaves owned by females went to jail more often for refusing to obey, shirking their obligations ("disobedience"), or creating a scene that was beyond the control of the mistress or other authority figures ("disorder"). A higher percentage of female slaves than male slaves were sent to jail upon the request of their owners, but masters were more likely than mistresses to make this request. Finally, a higher percentage of slaves of male owners than those of female owners were charged with breaking curfew and running away. These differences often related to the jobs that slaves performed. Slaves owned by females tended to be farmers, while more slaves owned by males were warehouse and port workers. The division between slaves of men and women also reflects a division between slaves working and living in different parts of the township.[65] Owners with slaves in town could call on the authorities to bring their slave in for punishment more easily than those living in rural settings. Furthermore, townspeople of differing class and status regularly passed one another on the street, allowing for a greater likelihood of situations that involved honor and respect and the perceived lack thereof. Finally, city slaves were more affected by the curfew laws.

By the 1870s, many slaves were owned by companies or groups of people, mostly involved in business.[66] Most of these companies revolved around the speculation of coffee investments and the storing, loading, and shipping of coffee. The growing number of these companies relied on the jail to punish. Between 1866 and 1870, 18 percent of arrested slaves were owned by companies. After 1870, and until 1878, 28 percent of jailed slaves were "company slaves." Beyond the rise of these corporate entities, it is clear that private and public institutions were interacting to a greater degree than before in managing the lives of slaves.[67] Discipline and punishment were becoming increasingly contracted and institutionalized, further divorced from the realm of the family and the responsibility of the owner.

Slaves owned by Portuguese immigrants were more likely to be arrested for curfew violation and drinking. As discussed, this large group of foreigners had relatively more slaves working as domestic servants and in general port work, and far fewer slaves working on farms. Brazilian and, specifically, Santista slaveholders tended to make a greater percentage of charges of disobedience and disrespect and of suspicion of escape.[68] We cannot tell whether Portuguese owners were better able to apprehend their slaves when they escaped because of stronger community ties, or whether the slaves of these owners were less likely to run away because they were in a relatively better position in terms of jobs or resources.

The occupations of many owners of arrested slaves can be found in other sources, giving further detail into this inequitable and highly disciplining society. Among the more than two thousand individuals identified in sources with occupation information for the 1860s, nearly one-third were involved in a business or port commerce. About an equal percentage of the owners whose slaves were arrested were businessmen or commercial agents. This is a clue that this group was not more likely than other slaveholders to have their slaves arrested. Of all the identified free male residents and visitors in town in the 1860s and 1870s, including slaveholders and those without slaves, about one of every ten was involved in public life, as township councilmen, judges, customs house workers, block inspectors, postmen, or a myriad of other local or distant government jobs.[69] Moreover, the number of public officials and the liberal professions were growing at this time, while farmers and religious occupations were on the decline. Relative to their overall numbers, slaveholders who were public officials or in the liberal professions had a disproportionate amount of slaves enter the jail.[70] One out of every six owners of jailed slaves belonged to owners of this profession. This makes sense because these owners were more likely to have connections to the police or jail and could most easily call on a friend or associate to arrest their slave. Again we see that as the town's economy modernized and incipient industrialization emerged, old institutions were quite adept at playing a role in reaffirming slavery.

Between 1850 and 1870 Santos grew at an accelerated rate, driven by coffee exports and the quantities of imported and manufactured goods that coffee money could buy. But with around seven thousand inhabitants the city was not yet large, and city officials probably still knew or recognized most of their neighbors and townsfolk. The "disrespect" charge, common in the early 1860s, seems to have been applied to slaves who had regular day-to-day interactions with townspeople, in particular situations in which their interactions were deemed inappropriate. A new slave, unknown to everyone, could also be perceived as disrespectful based solely on unfamiliarity and his or her skin color, but the charge usually implied a broken protocol among residents of a close-knit community. The last year from which there is a surviving nineteenth-century jail register is 1879. That year, the number of warehouses and commission houses doubled, and epidemics of yellow fever and smallpox struck the city with unaccustomed virulence and terror. In the eyes of some officials, the city was spiraling out of control. This is reflected by the types of charges placed against slaves during this period. During the 1860s less than one in ten arrests carried the "disorder" charge, but by the late 1870s, it was applied to nearly a quarter of all arrested slaves, while "disrespect" nearly dropped from the books. Perhaps the scripted roles that slaves were supposed to follow, steeped heavily in patrimony and honor, had begun to break as hundreds of foreigners migrated to the town, greatly increasing the population and tempering the spirit of sociability. A slave named Salvador, arrested on an April evening for disorder, was the last slave on record to receive such a charge. Salvador was a forty-year-old light-skinned slave (*fula*) owned by Dona Balbina Nébias.[71]

In sum, three important aspects of slave experience were considered in this chapter: families, work, and the rules they had to obey. Depending on their characteristics, the status of their owners, and neighborhood location, slaves had different options in forming families, working jobs that would not immediately injure or kill them, and avoiding arrest. In terms of families, Santos confirms much of the evidence that historians have gathered for many parts of Brazil. The wealthier, primarily export-producing households were more likely to have married (and widowed) slaves, while the poorer, urban neighborhoods had almost no married slaves at all. In addition, marriage rates among slaves declined, fitting patterns found for other parts of southeastern Brazil. Household stability, perhaps a better indicator of slaves' chances to form informal families and communities, was the greatest among the small and largely isolated subsistence-producing households of the township. Neither marriage rates nor household stability, however, corresponded with the frequent incidence of slave mothers and infants. As much as the historiography has appropriately moved away from the idea that slaves could not form families, historians continue to put too much emphasis on Catholic marriage among slaves, a symbol of family that was restricted to a minority of more privileged slaves.

Most slaves in southern Santos worked as farmers or domestic servants, whereas the percentage of farming slaves was considerably higher in the large sugar plantations of São Sebastião Township, just to the north. Besides regional concentrations, different neighborhoods had more slaves working in particular occupations. Certain demographic groups of bondspeople were more likely to work particular skilled trades, but since there was variance between Santos and São Sebastião, concentrations of occupation by race or color occurred more by chance. Owner characteristics also had an effect on the type of work slaves did, and this was particularly evident in the differences between male and female owners. Since women rarely operated commercial ventures in town, but commonly handled the largest plantations in the township, slaves of mistresses were more often farmers. By the 1870s, the commercial elite of Santos regularly purchased bondspeople to haul and store their goods. This is reflected in the drop in slaves listed as "without a trade" and the increase in the label "worker," a better word for the times.

The final section of this chapter considered the rules and punishment of slaves. It also found that depending on a slave and owner's characteristics, a slave had different chances of being arrested, being booked with a certain type of charge, and discovering that their sentence would be tolerably short or dreadfully long. By the 1860s and 1870s, institutions in Santos were handling the affairs of slaves to a greater degree, and the coffee merchants, who often did not live in town, had discovered the convenience of paying for someone else to punish their slaves. Capitalism made allowances for slavery, as we will see in the evolving medical treatment of slaves.

CHAPTER FIVE

Illness, Recovery, and Death

André and Hermenegildo hauled bags and crates and worked a small tavern located next to the warehouse and offices of their owner, a coffee and cotton commission house on Rua Santo Antonio called Monteiro, Prado & Wright. They appear to have been friends, since the pair was arrested for inebriation by the night patrol in 1870. Hermenegildo was thirty years old, with brown eyes, tall, and noticeably thin in the face while his companion André was shorter and younger, with rounder features.[1] Four years after their night in jail, André entered the hospital suffering from chest pains or weakness. He died six days later. The doctors claimed his death was caused by a hypertrophic heart, a condition known as cardiomyopathy today. In the twenty-first century, cardiomyophathic diseases usually affect people of advanced age, but they may "be secondary to infectious disease, exposure to toxins, systemic connective tissue disease, infiltrative and proliferative disorders, or nutritional deficiencies."[2] The doctors were particularly precise with his case, but they may have misdiagnosed, especially considering the rarity of heart disease among young adults. André's companion Hermenegildo entered the hospital a few months later. In fact, this was Hermenegildo's second visit to the hospital within five years. Fortunately, he did not suffer the same fate as Andre: after battling smallpox for nearly two months, he was released, likely cured.[3]

Andre's battle with smallpox was repeated many times over by other individuals in Santos, especially during the numerous epidemic years of the second half of the nineteenth century. When the hospital records, death certificates, and cemetery registers are used in combination to explore cases like these, we learn much about the illnesses, injuries, general medical treatment, and deaths of slaves and free people in Santos. As with these two men, the historical sources allow us to follow some individuals from the first signs of an illness to the time they recovered or, more unhappily, to their burials in the town cemetery. Town almanacs, annual reports made by São Paulo's president, and a range of other sources give us the broader context to make sense of local changes, such as the worsening epidemics striking the province, new expectations about public health, and the role of the state.

OLD MEDICAL INSTITUTIONS, NEW DISEASES

Until the 1860s, for example, charitable medical care was mostly organized by the Catholic Church and financed by the philanthropy of the elite in a way that left this system largely autonomous from the state. In ports with hospitals that assisted foreign mariners, the public medical system was subsidized by a small tax levied on shipping companies. This system managed reasonably well when cities were small, the movement of ships and goods low, and populations better sheltered from destructive epidemics and pandemics. By 1860, however, Santos faced an altered epidemiological environment, much stronger trade linkages with foreign ports, and a rapidly growing population. This put enormous strain on its traditional charitable system, leading to medical services that were tragically inadequate relative to other towns. Filling this vacuum in health care, private doctors became increasingly important in the lives of town residents, including slaves. Yet even this system of private health care were insufficient relative to standards established elsewhere at this time, especially when it came to preventable diseases such as smallpox. Thousands of slave deaths might have been prevented through a better water supply, cleaner instruments for midwifery, and fewer crowded houses, each of which had an equally terrible impact on the town's numerous free poor.

Most slaves in the township of Santos were killed by a handful of diseases that derived from the environments in which they lived and the treatment they received. Causes of illness and death, along with uneven medical treatment, point to an unequal society in which slaves had dissimilar access to resources, opportunities, and humane treatment. The types of illnesses and afflictions, the range of treatment, and the hope for recovery often corresponded with slaves' sex, age, race or color, and a number of variables related to their owners. Some slaves had a very good chance of avoiding disease in the increasingly risky health environment of the tropical port of Santos. These bondspeople were more likely to receive medical care that helped them recover from illnesses. This was a time when doctors knew less about the life-threatening diseases of the region and even prescribed treatment or performed operations that increased the risks. Judging from hospital recovery rates that ran between 80 and 85 percent, doctors and nurses were generally helpful, even toward their enslaved patients.[4]

Until recently, historians have shown little interest in the health and healthcare of the slaves and the free poor. One popularly believed but unproven assumption is that slaves suffered from a different and worse set of afflictions than the general population, and if they received any western medical care at all, it likely harmed more than helped. Furthermore, the concept of owners providing medical assistance to slaves seems to evoke the outdated notion of benevolent slave owners, especially in Brazil, where prominent historians have argued that the institution of slavery was less cruel overall than slavery in the United States.[5]

As a result of a wave of new studies, mostly by Brazilian graduate students, we now know more about what diseases and afflictions harmed or killed slaves and how these altered over time or differed from place to place. Yet the idea that slaves suffered more and from different afflictions than the free population has not been confirmed because the free population is still rarely included in studies. During the second half of the nineteenth century slaves became more concentrated in the hands of wealthy owners, and the population of free poor (many of them former slaves) grew despite increasingly fearsome threats of tuberculosis, yellow fever, smallpox, and cholera.[6] This is the first investigation that crosses Brazilian hospital and death records to examine the multiple causes illness, injury, and death among slaves and free people and the types of health care that these groups were provided—or denied—during the second half of the nineteenth century. Such an analysis is valuable beyond filling a lacuna about the general health and medical treatment of this population. Historians of Brazil have argued that infectious diseases worsened in this period, quickening the transition to free labor through a mortal attrition of the slave population. Furthermore, the problem of deteriorating health is important in the political history of Brazil since it has been offered as one of a handful of reasons why the republican movement overthrew the seven-decade-old monarchy. Considering the centrality of these claims to two of the most important social, economic, and political transitions in Brazilian history—the switch to free labor and the end of the monarchy—it is worthwhile to explore the large number of historical sources related to the health and death of free and slaves that are often available yet rarely consulted in hospital, municipal, and state archives across Brazil.

Some diseases that sickened and killed Santistas appeared irregularly and caused panic at the first sign of infection. An "epidemic" is most often defined subjectively and relatively as an outbreak of a disease that exceeds normal expectations and creates a wellspring of fear. Brazilian epidemics of the nineteenth century shared many characteristics. At their worst, they emptied busy streets and markets of their pedestrians and vendors, overfilled the hospital, brought general commerce to a standstill, and prompted nearly every mobile inhabitant to leave town altogether. The government published lengthy reports written by doctors about the latest scourge, politicians heatedly debated the efficacy of quarantines, homeopaths blasted the chicanery of allopaths or vice versa, and imperial lawmakers shifted their views on slavery, immigration, and sanitation in light of epidemics.[7] Nonetheless, endemic diseases sickened and killed far more people in Santos than epidemic diseases. Afflictions such as tuberculosis and malaria fluctuated year to year, but even in their worst form these ailments were not considered epidemic.[8] Today, after two centuries have turned, the high death tolls and the widespread reputation of the region as a vast international cemetery remain as a somber legacy.[9]

During the first half of the nineteenth century, Brazil did not experience many problems with diseases that caused terrible epidemics elsewhere, such as cholera, yellow fever, or the plague. Compared to the United States, in fact, Brazil was far less harmed by some of the major infectious diseases that circled the globe between 1790 and 1850. Yellow fever epidemics struck Philadelphia and New York between 1793 and 1803, before moving southward to the Gulf Coast, where this virus perennially crept into the Deep South when its vector was carried by steamboat or railroad. Cholera killed thousands in the United States in 1832 and 1848, as did influenza in 1847. In sharp contrast, Brazilian seaboard cities were spared these pandemics of cholera and influenza and epidemics of yellow fever until 1849. This may have been because the nation was too isolated from trade and migration to allow much disease exposure on a global scale. Ships were still slow enough to allow epidemics to run their cycle on board before arriving, and the nation's population was too diffuse and rural to allow a fertile ground for these diseases. Finally, excluding cholera, there were more global epidemics overall during the second half of the nineteenth century than the first half because of the increasing pace of globalization and colonization.[10]

Travelers and government officials commented on and celebrated Brazil's unusual exclusion from the worst rounds of these three diseases. Visitors to the country in the 1820s and 1830s, including John Mawe, an English geologist, and the pair of Swiss naturalists, J. B. von Spix and C.F.P. von Martius, could offer no strong opinion as to why the terrible scourges of Europe, the United States, or the Caribbean were not present in Brazil. Some travelers believed certain provinces to be healthier than others. This was also the view of São Paulo officials, who boasted to the president that they enjoyed a special status of good health within the Empire. The Emperor's personal medic, J.F.X. Sigaud, promoted the climate and general health in Brazil during his tenure in the 1830s and 1840s, but he also claimed that recently arrived Europeans faced a period of hardship and risk before they "acclimated."[11] Mary Karasch's research on the enslaved patients of the Misericórdia Hospital of Rio de Janeiro in the 1830s and 1840s gives additional support to the opinions of these travelers and officials. The four diseases that Brazilian officials would later attribute as causing the worst epidemics—smallpox, yellow fever, cholera, and bubonic plague—did not have the presence in Brazil that they would after 1849. The leading causes of slave death were, in order of frequency, tuberculosis, dysentery, diarrhea, gastroenteritis, and pneumonia. Moreover, two out of every three slaves buried by the Misericórdia Hospital were killed by one of these top five diseases. As Karasch makes clear, despite Brazil's avoidance of the major pandemics and yellow fever, slaves faced enormous risk due to their unhealthy environments and dealt with the death of children, spouses, and other loved ones with heartbreaking frequency. Free people, a population not included in Karasch's studies, may have faced this risk and loss equally, especially among the poor.[12]

In 1849 Brazil's rosy reputation wilted when yellow fever appeared in Bahia, prior to sickening and killing with high virulence in nearly every large and midsized Brazilian coastal city by 1852. Cholera struck soon after, spreading even faster and deeper into the interior than yellow fever. By the end of 1856, it had killed tens of thousands, mostly among poor people of color and slaves. Cholera became a deadly threat along the thousands of miles of coast and major river systems such as the São Francisco and Amazon, but spared lightly populated interior regions that had no direct or uninterrupted river connections to Brazil's ocean ports. Smallpox and gastrointestinal illnesses appear to have worsened in the hundreds of growing towns and cities in Brazil, as more people crowded into urban or semiurban areas that lacked effective vaccination programs or uncontaminated water sources. Finally, contemporaries noted that cholera and smallpox killed relatively more slaves and people of color, while yellow fever and malaria were worse among whites and free people. All of these details are nearly lost in the haze of posterity and disinterest, despite their impact.[13]

A few contemporaries claimed that yellow fever and cholera were present in Brazil before 1849.[14] There is no doubt, however, that the proportions these diseases assumed in the second half of the nineteenth century were like nothing seen or felt before, regardless of their uneven impact, both geographically and socially. Yellow fever was especially destructive in the 1850s, 1870s, and 1890s. Like cholera, it also spread inland, but much more gradually, and was appearing in coffee towns along the railroad in São Paulo and Rio de Janeiro by the 1890s. During the lull decades, government officials became self-congratulatory about their urban sanitary reform programs and more lax in health measures such as quarantine and vaccination. During the 1860s and early 1870s, for example, quarantine was rarely practiced. After a terrible resurgence of yellow fever and the diminishing power of the conservative cabinet, the quarantine process was reinstated and reaffirmed by law in 1876.[15] Quarantine remained mostly ineffective in keeping disease out because it did not prevent the movement of mosquitoes, yellow fever's carriers. Foreign transportation companies nevertheless continued to send their ships into ports like Santos, despite the near certainty that large portions of their crews would have to be replaced after death had done its rounds. An ever-growing amount of coffee was flowing out of this port and foreign shippers were aware of the considerable profit that successive loads of coffee would bring. Sailors were caught between the pursuit of profit, the pressing need for a job, and the natural reaction of a virus among an adult population that lacked resistance. Those who survived told tales about it, and Santos acquired the reputation as an especially notorious "yellow fever port" in the 1890s. Thousands of sailors and ship officers were killed, and their collective story became part of maritime lore. John Masefield, for example, wrote:

It's a cruel port is Santos, and a hungry land,
With rows o' graves already dug in yonder strip of sand,
'N' Dick is hollerin' up the hatch, 'e says e's' goin' blue,
His pore teeth are chattering, 'n' what's a man to do?—
It's cruel when a fo'c's'le gets the fever![16]

Cholera was Brazil's second new and frightening health problem in the second half of the nineteenth century. Its epidemics were less frequent but more deadly than those of yellow fever. Before 1855, some believed that the "intense heat of the equator, or the vast expanse of the Atlantic ocean, somehow offered an effective buffer" against the spread of cholera from North America, the Caribbean, or commonly used Atlantic layover points such as Cabo Verde or the Madeiras.[17] This belief was discredited when cholera, like yellow fever before it, spread down from Pará, a far northern province, in 1855. By the time it reached the Rio Plata on Brazil's southern border with Uruguay in 1856, it had killed more than 200,000 Brazilians, most of whom were poor and black. Large cities such as Porto Alegre (Rio Grande do Sul), Recife (Pernambuco), and Santo Amaro (Bahia) were struck so hard that for weeks the dead went unburied in streets and homes. One doctor returning to Santo Amaro found nearly 300 bodies in putrid states of decomposition. This was one of many images that composed cholera's "theater of horrors," as the Bahian provincial president wrote in his annual report to the Emperor.[18]

The final infectious disease that would appear, again allegedly for the first time in Brazilian history, was bubonic plague. With this disease, Brazil fit within a circuit of countries visited by the plague during its third pandemic. Originating among a rodent reservoir in the Himalayas, it had spread from Asia to Europe, arriving in Porto, Portugal, in the summer of 1899. It then jumped across the Atlantic in late fall, appearing first in Paraguay, and then in Santos in early October 1899. Some in this deeply Catholic country may have wondered if this "biblical disease" was going to be the next catastrophic epidemic on a par with yellow fever or cholera. These fears proved unfounded when the plague never took epidemic proportions, but it did spread northward and was a regular cause of death among residents of the many seaboard cities of Brazil well into the twentieth century. Ironically, Brazil may have been spared major epidemics of plague through largely ineffective sanitary efforts to rid its cities of yellow fever. Among the many reforms of this period, two common measures were to move stables to the outskirts of cities and provide public trash removal services. While these efforts would have had little effect on yellow fever (because mosquitoes used common receptacles and cisterns as breeding sites), they may have reduced the breeding populations of rats that carried fleas infected by the *Yersinia pestis* bacilli. The outbreak of plague also advanced the career of Oswaldo Cruz, Brazil's most famous public health officer, who was part of the team from Rio de Janeiro that visited Santos in 1900 to confirm the presence of bubonic plague. Finally, the plague spurred efforts by the young Republican government to improve public health, such as increasing funds for hospitals and sanitation campaigns, which became effective in the early 1900s, partly under the guidance of Cruz.[19]

By the time the bubonic plague appeared in Santos the government had constructed a special "isolation hospital" that it used to treat contagious diseases. This new hospital was an example of the remarkable expansion in health care services that occurred during the second half of the nineteenth century, often through the hybrid efforts of state, church, and civil organizations. Before 1850, there were less than twenty-five hospitals in the whole Empire, including clinics run by the army, navy, and Catholic Church. Of these, the Misericórdia Hospital at Santos (Santa Casa de Misericórdia de Santos) was the oldest and one of the first hospitals to be founded in the Americas.[20] It was inaugurated in 1543, one year before Brás Cubas received the captaincy of São Vicente. Santos was barely a village at that point, overshadowed by the larger neighboring colony of São Vicente, but it was located at the edge of a deep harbor that made it a far more capable port. The hospital was intended to provide care for local residents and sailors. It took its name and purpose from Portugal's Irmandade da Misericórdia, built in Lisbon in 1498. The hospital was mostly funded and operated by the Santos Misericórdia Society, which constructed a new building in 1665. That year this prestigious group of town elite received a grant from the colonial governor, Jerŏnimo de Ataíde, who recognized the importance of the hospital because Santos was "the point of entry and exit for all of the captaincy's commerce and also because there is a great need by the poor for [the hospital's] services."[21] Throughout the eighteenth century, the hospital remained with few changes, located in the center part of town and a few blocks from the customs house. In the 1830s it was moved southwest to the outskirts of the city and a new building was built at the base of São Jerŏnimo hill. The most recent Misericórdia Hospital was constructed in 1928 on the other side of the same steep hill, where it remains the region's most important hospital.

In the first half of the nineteenth century, the Santos Misericórdia Hospital and its sister hospital in São Paulo were the only two nonmilitary hospitals in the province. The São Bento monastery had long provided care for some of the poorest in society, but it was a small rudimentary hospice without, it appears, a medical doctor. In the 1870s, the cemetery recorded which institutions had provided care to the deceased prior to their death. About twice as many bodies came from the Misericórdia Hospital as the São Bento Monastery. Several years later, São Bento ended the operations of its clinic.[22]

Following the midcentury wave of epidemics of unfamiliar and deadly diseases, the provincial and municipal authorities began constructing several new hospitals. The province's population and number of municipalities also increased, largely due to the advances of coffee into the interior of the state. In 1855, hospitals opened in Itú and Sorocaba, two towns in the interior near the city of São Paulo. A third hospital opened the next year in the northern coastal town of Ubatuba, a provincial port and frequent stop for coastal shipping between Santos and Rio de Janeiro. The new hospitals were small compared to the older hospitals, but had disproportionately larger operating budgets. Expenditures per patient for the Sorocaba Misericórdia Hospital in 1861, for example, were more than double that of Santos. Between 1855 and 1866, six new hospitals opened in the province. The expansion of state-sponsored institutional health care is remarkable, considering that in the previous 350 years provincial officials had funded only two public hospitals. Hospitals also became specialized. One São Paulo hospital treated only the mentally ill and another cared for patients with leprosy. Moreover, hospitals were divided by class during the 1870s and 1880s. In 1874 the Beneficent Portuguese Hospital opened in Santos, giving care mostly to prominent Portuguese residents who were part of the Portuguese Society or to those who could pay the higher daily hospital fees. In the capital of São Paulo, a new hospital for the poor began operations in 1884.[23]

Framed by the steep São Jerŏnimo hill at the edge of town, the Second Misericórdia Hospital (1835–1928) had fifty beds for patients, most or all in the dormitory style that was typical before the risks of infectious diseases were known. We can see an image of this building in Figure 4.3 as it stood in 1864, by looking at the building with the steeple to the left of the new jail. It consisted of two floors and several large, leaded-pane windows that brightened its interior. It was notoriously overcrowded and overcapacity, however. Between 1878 and 1880, the hospital clerk recorded, on average, 108 patients at for its fifty beds. In 1881 the hospital expanded (probably with an added annex) and added another twenty beds, which relieved the crowded conditions only temporarily. By 1885 the number of patients again constantly exceeded the official number of beds. In fact, between 1878 and 1885, the hospital was at 125 percent official capacity more than half the time. During the 1878 smallpox epidemic it admitted 294 patients in one month, 244 more patients than it had beds. Patients may not have gone without beds, however, since it was common for township governments and local hospitals to erect emergency infirmaries in churches and convents during epidemic years.[24]

Like all Brazilian public hospitals of its day, the Misericórdia Hospital of Santos cared largely for the poor. People with access to their own bed avoided, or were denied permission into the hospital. This is evident by the fact that none of the more than two thousand freeborn individuals who were recorded in other historical sources of the township (see Appendix) entered as a patient at the Misericórdia hospital. Even though the hospital offered a "first class" service of treatment, Brazilians with a small amount of money, or with access to loans from friends and family, avoided the hospital. They did so because medical care was viewed as something best provided at home. Little distinction was drawn between domestic service and nursing, and slaves or free servants who cleaned their owners' houses were also drawn into the role of caregiver. Illnesses and injuries that required medical care were served by the city doctors that residents could call on. In the township's rural regions, the sick had to rely on neighbors or pay the fees for a doctor to travel to their bedside.

Approximately five thousand slaves were admitted into the town hospital during the nineteenth century, but they were far outnumbered by mariners and destitute free persons. In 1859 the Misericórdia Hospital reported to the provincial government that it had treated 332 people, half of whom were destitute. After 1860 (when patient lists become available) for every slave patient that entered the hospital there were an average of three sailors and twelve free poor patients. Slaves were admitted in increasing numbers up through the late 1870s, at which point the increasing demand by slave owners for the hospital's services no longer surpassed the decreasing number of slaves in town. By the mid-1880s there were so few slaves in the hospital that most free patients never encountered them. By 1886, the total number of hospital patients had more than tripled, and nearly 82 percent of them were too poor to pay for their care. There were also barely any slaves left in town to receive the hospital's services: only sixteen slaves entered that year. The many mariners or immigrants that were treated in the hospital may not have met slaves, they undoubtedly met many Afro-Brazilians, including former slaves.[25]

Slave owners generally believed that their sick or injured female slaves were better off at home than in the hospital among the rowdy mariners and poor males of questionable morals. This belief is supported by the numbers: three of every four slaves who entered the hospital were male. The city as a whole had more male slaves than female slaves, but the hospital's male-female ratio was much higher than that of the city population. During the 1860s and 1870s, the ratio of male to female slave patients increased, but so did the overall sex ratio of both free and slaves in the city population. Male slaves did not necessarily get sick or injured more frequently than female slaves, even though more slave men worked out-of-doors and in occupations that could have exposed them to a greater range of risks. As we will see, the most common illnesses and causes of death were shared between both sexes. Moreover, females faced the risky prospect of childbirth. Risk and health aside, there may also be an economic explanation: male slaves were priced higher than females and owners probably considered the value of their property when deciding whether to pay for hospital care. Another contributing factor was the common view that the Santos Misericórdia Hospital, like many hospitals of its day, was a masculine place unsuitable for girls and women, regardless of whether those females were enslaved. Free female patients avoided the hospital to a greater degree (or were excluded from it), comprising only 13 percent of the hospital's free patients.[26]

Because the hospital treated globe-trotting mariners, African slaves, and recent European immigrants, hospital rolls reflected patients from all over the world (see Table 5.1). The 1860s showed more enslaved patients of African birth, but this declined by the 1870s as a consequence of the end of the international slave trade in 1850. Among native-born slaves, we can see evidence of the large interprovincial movement of slaves as more slaves born outside the township were treated after 1870. Santistas probably never made up a majority of patients even among the free patients. After all, the hospital was founded by Bras Cubas with "an eye to the sea." As coffee became more important and Santos took over much of the provincial trade, foreign sailors and immigrants increasingly found their way to the city hospital. In 1861, for example, 106 Europeans were hospitalized. In 1881 the hospital gave service to an astonishing five hundred Europeans, the vast majority of whom were sailors.[27]

Patients were categorized into several classes that depended on the source of their payment. Those who were too poor to pay anything made up the largest group, followed by sailors. The hospital collected money from ships and trading companies that covered the expenses of most maritime workers. Other categories of care during the 1850s and 1860s were the first, second, and *pobre* (poor) classes. The second-class category was the type of care provided for most slaves, but by 1870 one out of six slaves was placed in the first class and eighteen slaves were classified as poor. There is no clear reason why a small number of slaves were put in the first and poor classes of service. This becomes even more mysterious when we look closely at their owners. Nearly the same number of wealthy owners (as measured by rough estimates of slave and property ownership) had slaves in the first class as in the poor class of treatment. For instance, Dona Emilia de Jezus Cortez, who became one of the town's

TABLE 5.1

Birthplaces of Patients in the Santos Misericórdia Hospital, 1861–1883 (Percent)

	1861–1870	1871–1883
Slaves		
Africa	41	30
Brazil (including Santos)	43	65
Santos	17	14
Unknown	15	6
Total	(N=568)	(N= 741)
Free		
Africa	6	5
Brazil (including Santos)	28	31
Europe (including Portugal)	41	59
Portugal	15	19
Santos	11	10
Unknown	24	5
Total	(N=1,999)	(N=3,228)
Total	(N=2,567)	(N=3,969)

NOTE: Totals exceed 100 percent because the "Brazil" category includes people born in Santos.
SOURCE: Hospital patient registers, 1861–1883, ASCMS.

biggest slave owners in the 1870s, placed Julio, an African slave, in first-class service for a week in 1869 for the treatment of "*cravos nas pez*" (plantar warts). Three years later, Cortez sent Julio back to the hospital for a stomach ulcer, but this time he was treated in the poor class. In 1875, Julio returned to the hospital for a third and final time after what was likely a stroke (*apoplexia*). This time he entered the second class of service, like most slave patients, but unlike most, he did not recover. Why Julio and other slaves received the "first class" or "poor class" of treatment remains unexplained. It is important to note that Julio's chances of entering *any* class of treatment in the hospital would have been much lower if he was not an adult male.[28]

In 1870, a "state" class was added to record the patients whose treatment was paid for by the government. Additionally, hospital officials gave slaves their own class of service in 1877, probably as a consequence of the increased official attention that turned toward the diminishing number of slaves after the end of the African slave trade in 1850 and the Rio Branco Law of 1871–72. I found no evidence, however, that the addition of this new category in the patient registers indicated that the slaves were isolated or even treated differently from other patients, only that they were better tracked for statistical and reporting reasons. After 1870, the number of patients admitted in the first class of service dropped precipitously. The hospital was facing greater competition for health care from private doctors and clinics in town and from a more modern hospital built by the Portuguese Society. Slaves given first-class treatment decreased to only about 2 percent of all slave patients by the late 1870s.[29] The Portuguese Society Hospital may have also treated slaves, but since they have not opened their books to researchers, no one can tell.

In 1859, one-quarter of patients received the funds for their treatment from the state or maritime companies, another quarter by philanthropic donations, while the rest paid their own fees. A slave owner or person renting a slave customarily paid for a slave's medical care, but the records do not specify who provided the money. A slave's short-term visit to the hospital was not costly, but a stay of longer than a week could become quite expensive for a slaveholder. The daily fee was about two or three times the daily rate of unskilled wage labor, and a month of treatment cost around a tenth of the average price of a slave. In 1842, the hospital charged Maria Apolinario one *mil-réis* per day for the treatment of her slave Niterio. After eighty days and one surgical operation, Niterio recovered and was released. Perhaps the bill was too onerous or seen as unfair, or perhaps some hardship had befallen Maria Apolinario, because she neglected to pay the charges. The Misericórdia Hospital had to bring her to court to try to recover its 180 *mil-réis* bill.[30]

It is unknown how much better the first-class treatment was compared to the other classes. Patients in the first and second classes were, on average, in the hospital for less time than those in the third class. Sailors had the shortest period of treatment—about ten days—probably because they returned to the care of their ship medic at the first sign of improvement. In terms of mortality rates, 20 to 22 percent of the first-, second-, and poor-class patients died while in the hospital. Surprisingly, sailors and slaves in the post-1877 slave class of service died at much lower rates (8 percent and 13 percent, respectively).[31] We cannot go too far with these numbers because disease environments, immunity rates, and propensity to use the hospital services differed among groups.

In the 1860s, about the same number of slaves entered the hospital as were buried in the cemetery. By the 1870s and early 1880s, the ratio had increased somewhat, with about six slaves entered into the hospital for every five slaves buried in the cemetery.[32] These numbers speak to two facts. First, since most of the slaves buried in the cemetery were not slaves treated in the hospital, many if not most owners did not send their slaves to the hospital, though we should not assume that these slaves received no care, as we will see. Second, this small increase in the hospital-to-cemetery ratio reflects a growing opinion among slave owners that hospitalization could better guarantee the perpetuation of a valuable investment, return a slave to a condition where he or she could continue contributing to a household or firm, avoid the death of a person who they had gotten to know very well and perhaps cared for, or a combination of these reasons.

Increased faith in paid medical services was by no means only directed toward the hospital. Private doctors played an increasingly important role in the lives of city slaves. The perpetual overcrowding and poor reputation of the Misericórdia Hospital certainly must have contributed to the growth of alternative options. In fact, the number of individuals involved in the private medical system grew much faster than the town's population. Between 1872 and 1885 the town's population increased 170 percent (9,151 to 15,605), while the number of doctors and barber/bloodletters grew almost threefold. In 1850, there were four doctors in town, two dispensaries, and less than twelve dentists, bloodletters, barbers, and midwifes. By 1885, the there were fourteen doctors, two midwives, seven pharmacists, three dentists, and fourteen barber/bloodletters. Most, perhaps all, doctors who began new practices in the 1870s practiced medicine on the town's slaves for a fee paid by the owner or the slave patient.[33]

With this expansion of public and private medical services, we might reasonably guess that two adult male slaves out of every three that were infirm or injured received public or private (Western) medical assistance by 1860. Since such services were much less available for enslaved children and women, it is also reasonable to guess that the majority of these slaves did not receive medical care. These rough estimates are based on a comparison of the number of slaves treated to the number of slaves who were likely sick or injured. In 1872, for example, 1,627 slaves lived in Santos, composing 18 percent of the population. If about 10 to 12 percent of Brazilian slaves became infirm or suffered from an injury during the year, then 150 to 200 slaves needed some medical care that year.[34] This is a good deal more than the eighty-two slaves that were admitted into the hospital in 1872. Male slave patients outnumbered females three to one, making it likely that female slaves who might have needed hospitalization did not receive it. Additionally, it was rare for a child under ten to be admitted, even though this age group of slaves (and free) had exceptionally high mortality rates.[35] Some owners paid an extra amount to have a slave cared for in the first-class service, others paid for private doctors to treat their favored (or high-value) slaves. Bondspeople sometimes managed to save a considerable amount of money, often with the intention of buying their freedom; thus some may have paid for their own medical care. At least among adult males, it appears that only a minority of slaves with serious illnesses or injuries found no hopeful remedies at all. Irrespective of age or sex, slaves commonly sought the help of relatively inexpensive *curandeiros* (folk doctors often of African heritage) as a supplement to or substitute for western medical attention.[36]

About four in every five patients (enslaved and free) who entered the Misericórdia Hospital in Santos recovered to a sufficient degree to be released. While comparable data for other Brazilian hospitals is scant, it appears that hospitals of this period were on average riskier than English hospitals, yet less so than might be assumed for the era before knowledge of bacteriology or common etiology was widespread. Doctors knew far less about what caused life-threatening diseases, and some prescribed treatment or performed operations that may have increased the risks for their patients. Yet overall, doctors were able to provide services that helped many recover from their illnesses and injuries. A break from a grueling work schedule, a bed (when available), and two or three meals a day may have been the best medicine. Staff at the Misericórdia Hospital operated on more bodies and prescribed a greater range of medicines to ailing patients in the 1860s and 1870s than during the first half of the century, but we cannot know if this lowered or raised mortality rates since epidemiological conditions fluctuated greatly. Common procedures of the day included lithotomies, hernia operations, and amputations. The use of anesthesia, such as ether, was well known to European doctors, along with the importance of antiseptics like alcohol and iodine, but these may have not been common in Brazilian hospitals. Some doctors dispensed medicines that further impaired their patients. Calomel, containing mercurous chloride, was commonly recommended by the European medical books that Brazilian doctors collected. Other drugs were effective, such as quinine for malarial fevers or morphine for pain.[37]

Few records exist on the success rates of private doctors; thus it is difficult to speculate on the quality of that care. Private allopathic doctors performed many of the same procedures and prescribed the same medicines as the hospital doctors. Few to none believed that a bedroom or hotel room may have posed additional, unseen risks than a hospital ward, and most probably thought that a familiar and comfortable yet well-ventilated location was the best spot for recovery. Homeopathic doctors, who became popular in the township by the 1870s, prescribed products that were so diluted that they were, for all practical purposes, indistinguishable from the largely benign liquid that held them (usually water, sugar, or alcohol). It is hard to believe that this helped patients much, but these products were far less harmful than calomel or other heavy metals prescribed in small doses by traditional doctors. Additionally, the water or harmless sweet liquids that usually composed more than 99.9 percent of homeopathic medicines may have helped hydrate patients.[38]

COMMON CAUSES OF SICKNESS AND DEATH

The afflictions that sent slaves and free people to the hospital were usually not the same that sent them to their graves. Furthermore, a close look at the leading causes of illness, injury, and death shows that three basic demographic traits—sex, age, and place of birth—had a more profound influence on disease propensity then than the judicial and social categories of enslavement and freedom. This discussion will only summarize findings published elsewhere, but in doing so, I hope to show that the health environment and medical treatment that different segments of the population received conformed with and reinforced the hierarchical divisions that are the theme of this book. Depending on a slave's owner, a slave lived in a particular neighborhood and worked particular jobs. These locations and kinds of work, in turn, exposed slaves to certain health risks and dissimilar medical treatment. Therefore, environment and manual labor also played an important role in contributing to a world for slaves that was far from equal.[39]

The great endemic killers of the day—tuberculosis, tetanus, gastrointestinal diseases, and parasitic worms—took the lives of most slaves and free, yet these diseases were accepted almost as much a part of life as the setting sun. Tuberculosis (TB), commonly known to its contemporaries as "*tísica*" in Portuguese or "consumption" in English, was the greatest killer in Brazil and, likely, most other parts of the world in the nineteenth century. Nearly everyone of normally good health had TB bacteria suspended in tiny capsules produced by the lung's immune system, but these germs broke free from time to time, especially when health was jeopardized by other afflictions, risky behavior, or old age. It then waged a slow war on the body's natural defenses, marked by battles that the body sometimes won. Thus, it could mysteriously appear and disappear, and until Robert Koch discovered the microscopic *Tubercle bacillus* in 1882, little could be done to prevent or defeat it. Slaves and free people rarely entered the hospital with TB, yet the disease killed both groups in high proportions until the 1870s, when smallpox surged ahead. Slaves were a bit more prone to the disease than free people, but it was a large risk for both groups. Doctors prescribed quiet bed rest and good ventilation for late-stage TB sufferers, an environment that the hospital lacked. The hospital treated one TB patient for every eighteen deaths between 1865 and 1883, demonstrating that the Santa Casa de Misericórdia was generally avoided when it came to this affliction. As shown in Table 5.2, females of working age (fifteen to forty) were the most prone to its fatal effects, but both men and women of this age bracket were increasingly killed by TB during the 1860s and 1870s. Others have documented the same phenomena in areas that were urbanizing and industrializing. Not only did a denser population more easily spread the disease through human contact, but the increasing amount of urban pollution likely weakened the ability of lungs to contain the bacteria within granulomatous lesions.

Tuberculosis was sometimes romanticized in the Victorian period due to its gradual effects that caused people to slowly sink into themselves, with life's candle dimming to only a flicker before darkness. Other diseases wrenched their victims in bed, contorting them in unbearable agony or causing the expulsion of bodily fluids that would have been difficult for any witness to paint in romantic terms. The other top killer of the day, neonatal tetanus, was of this variety, since it caused newborn infants to develop trismus of the jaw and spasms of the back. Death from starvation or strangulation often came within a week, because tightened muscles prevented a baby from feeding or breathing—a deeply disturbing scenario that was repeated a hundred times over in similar proportions by the free and enslaved in Santos over the century. Tragically, this was an easily preventable disease, since it was most often caused by an infection that entered infants' bodies where the umbilical cord was cut. Doctors in the nineteenth century were becoming increasingly aware of the need to use antiseptics, even before the germs of various diseases were catalogued with the help of microscopy. Yet since childbirthing remained tradition-bound and in the hands of midwives who had the propensity to add all sorts of contaminated poultices to the cut cord on the bellies of newborns, tetanus was one of the main reasons why one child (enslaved or free) out of three never made it to his or her first birthday. After the first

TABLE 5.2

Top Causes of Hospitalization and Death among Enslaved and Free People

	Affliction Type	Pathophysiology	High Propensity Groups
Hospitalization			
Smallpox	Infectious diseases (virus)	Human-to-human contact and inhalation of airborne particles	All
Yellow fever	Infectious diseases (flaviviruses)	Mosquito vector	Free people, especially foreigners
Fractures and wounds	Injuries	Accidents; violence; negligence; cruelty	Free and enslaved people of working age (15 to 40)
Common colds	Infectious diseases (respiratory virus)	Human-to-human contact and inhalation of airborne particles	Slaves
Rheumatism	Musculoskeletal and connective tissue disorders	Repeated physical stress; autoimmune reaction; alcohol	Free and enslaved adults; people over the age of 30
Death			
Tuberculosis	Infectious diseases (mycobacteria)	Inhalation of airborne particles	Free and enslaved females of working age (15 to 40)
Smallpox	Infectious diseases (virus)	Human-to-human contact and inhalation of airborne particles	All groups
Tetanus	Infectious diseases (Anaerobic bacteria)	Infected wounds, cuts, and umbilicus stumps	Free and enslaved newborns
Gastroenteritis	Viruses, bacteria, or parasites	Contaminated water and foods	All groups
Parasitic worms	Infectious Diseases	Contaminated water and foods, hand to mouth, abrasions on the foot	Free and enslaved children

SOURCES: Hospital patient registers, 1861–1883, ASCMS; cemetery registers, 1857–1886, FAMS.

birthday, Santistas were rarely struck by adult tetanus (lockjaw), despite the fact that slaves and free people often went barefoot, risking infection through abrasions on their soles.[40]

Three other common endemic killers were gastrointestinal disorders, edema, and parasitic worms. Gastrointestinal disorders, including dysentery and diarrhea, were, as a broad set of afflictions, one of the top killers among free and enslaved, but killed higher proportions of free people compared to other diseases. This was a category that included many kinds of bacteriological, viral, or parasitic disorders and was generally spread through contaminated water and foods. It was common practice to clean and bathe in the same streams and rivers where one drew water for drinking, washing food, or cooking. Water was sterilized by boiling (and by distilling or fermenting), but without this knowledge and without going to the expense and inconvenience of heating water in a port city that was often hot and humid, few gave any thought to invisible organisms entering their bodies through the water they drank. Another common endemic killer was edema, known as "*hydropesia*" in Portuguese or "dropsy" in English. Like gastrointestinal disorders, this was seen as a unique disease in the nineteenth century, but today is believed to be a combination of symptoms of several diseases. The word's root is the Latin *hydropisis*, which means "a water condition." For centuries, people had referred to any marked swelling and collection of liquids in tissues as edema, hence a condition related to water. It is now known to be caused by a number of factors, including malnutrition, problems in the liver or lymphoid organs, and heart failure. Finally, parasitic worms abounded, and these could enter the body in all sorts of ways. For some medics in nineteenth-century Brazil, worms of the *Aschelminte phylum*, including the guinea worm, tapeworm, roundworm, hookworm, and pinworm, were so prevalent that they were seldom listed as a cause of death. Children faced much greater difficulty than adults in competing with their worms for nutrients, and nearly 90 percent of those who died with worms were five years old or younger. *Aschelmintes* affected the young, old, male, and female categories of the free and enslaved populations in similar proportions.[41]

The growing problem of epidemic diseases also took many lives. Between 1861 and 1870, a decade when yellow fever mysteriously receded from Brazilian shores, smallpox also appears to have lessened in virulence. During this decade it was not found among the five deadliest afflictions, but between 1871 and 1883 it became the top killer, temporarily surpassing tuberculosis. On average, slaves were a bit more likely than free people to enter the hospital when this disease developed, but it killed free patients in slightly higher proportions. Slaves may have entered the hospital sooner, perhaps before the stage of skin eruptions, while free people avoided the hospital until the last stages of the disease. Smallpox was similar to most afflictions in the sense that the judicial and social line that separated free from enslaved created no obstacle in its deadly effects, and unusual in that it sickened and killed different demographic groups in similar proportions. In other words, neither age, sex, place of birth, nor legal condition had much of an influence on who contracted this disease.

Doctors and health officials had undeniable evidence that smallpox was one of the few diseases that could be effectively battled through public health programs. Incidence of the disease was greatly lowered in some parts of the world through vaccination incentives, but in Brazil, unfortunately, the multiple levels of the state did not have the power, will, or resources to implement successful campaigns. Brazilians vehemently resisted the idea of vaccines throughout the nineteenth century, a resistance that came to a head during the vaccination revolts in Rio de Janeiro in 1904. The resurgence of smallpox in Santos during the 1870s coincided with the town's unprecedented gains in global commodity markets, thus the nonchalant attitude of provincial officials could have stemmed from a reluctance to tap government treasuries, even in the face of what had become the most fatal disease in the township.[42]

Smallpox, like tuberculosis, was spread through interpersonal contact. Debates may have flared between contagionists and environmentalists, or miasmists, about how and why other diseases appeared, but smallpox, measles, and colds were readily accepted by most as communicable and typically spread within families, workers, and neighbors. Yellow fever, on the other hand, muddied the debate because it provided ammunition for both sides. Until the *Aedis aegypti* mosquito was confirmed as its vector in 1900, yellow fever appeared to spread from port to port, sometimes after the arrival of a contaminated vessel, yet it could sicken new victims who were known to have had no direct contact with the bodies or items of other victims. Yellow fever's symptoms are often flulike but can culminate with bilious vomiting and death. Mortality rates depend on whether the disease is endemic or epidemic within an affected population. In areas where yellow fever reappears with frequency, mortality rates range from 5 to 10 percent, but it can be as high as 50 percent in places where it becomes epidemic. Infection results in a lifelong immunity, and populations that have not been exposed to the disease are the most susceptible to higher rates of infection. Children usually suffer from a minor form of the disease, reducing the chances of high mortality rates and sharp fluctuations of incidence that are observed in places where the virus is introduced to virgin populations. Finally, there is overriding historical and biological evidence that particular genetic groups have better resilience to the disease, thus reducing the mortality rate in some places where the disease is endemic.[43]

Several epidemics struck Santos during the second half of the century, swelling the hospital far beyond capacity, causing general panic, crippling businesses, and forcing authorities to implement quarantine procedures on ships and infected homes. Slaves were rarely infected or killed by yellow fever, but the free population, especially people of European origin, were infected at high rates. In 1874, for example, twenty free patients died from yellow fever but not a single slave. Brazilians in the "mixed groups" (*mulatos*, *fulos*, and *pardos*) were infected at a slightly higher rate than slaves, suggesting that genetic resistance was weakened or lost among children with mixed African and European heritage. The much lower propensity for yellow fever among Santos slaves is not an isolated finding; in the U.S. south and the Caribbean the disease has also been found to inflict more damage on the free population than among slaves.[44]

Epidemics were frightening when they struck; other illnesses and injuries were part of the normal rhythm of life. Some such afflictions deserve mention because they were intimately connected to the jobs that slaves and free people performed and to the social environments in which they lived. For example, joint disorders were the second most common reason for admission in to the hospital, after gastrointestinal diseases. These problems were broadly called "rheumatism" or "rheumatic fevers" in the hospital patient lists and are known today by doctors as osteoarthritis (OA), rheumatoid arthritis (RA), and gout. The pathophysiology of OA and RA differ markedly. RA is a systematic autoimmune disease that may be caused by trauma, while OA (or degenerative joint disease) is largely noninflammatory and caused chiefly by the loss of cartilage in synovial joints such as shoulders, elbows, hands and knees. RA can have acute onset, accompanied by flulike symptoms, while OA usually has gradual onset of pain in joints commonly used for physical labor. This disease often causes agony for people over forty, but was by no means restricted to this age group. Joint disorders developed in younger people may result from traumas that trigger RA, heavy drinking that cause gout, or physically demanding and repetitive work activities place unusual stress on joints, leading to painful OA arthritis. Again, we observe that the free population suffered from joint disorders at nearly the same rate as slaves before 1870. After 1870, the number of rheumatic free patients increased relative to slaves, even though slaves were an aging population and not self-reproducing. We might imagine the many backs bent by tilling fields, elbows stressed by years of repetitive hammering, or knees that bore the weight of a thousand heavy loads. Yet the general homogeneity of incidence rates for older enslaved and free people shows that such actions were not reserved for any group based on legal condition or sex. Rather, the crucial factor in propensity for this affliction was simply age.[45]

Another crucial factor for some deadly illnesses was residential location and type of work. Slaves who lived and worked as stevedores and warehouse workers faced a special set of risks that was not shared by the general population. Of 304 slaves that entered the hospital between 1869 and 1873, fifty-eight were owned by men whose addresses were listed in the detailed *Almanak Luna*, published in 1872. It can be assumed that most of these slaves lived and worked at their owners' addresses, though some may have been rented out or worked in other locations. Out of this group of fifty-eight slaves, nineteen lived on Rua Direita, the main commercial thoroughfare that connected the Four Corners neighborhood with the Dockside neighborhood. These slaves fit a very urban profile, since they had a good deal of autonomy, worked physically onerous jobs in a piecemeal way, and used their free time and extra earnings to engage in activities frowned upon by the elite. As a result, only two afflictions—traumas and syphilis—brought this small group into the hospital more than 50 percent of the time, a rate that was far higher than that of the general population.[46]

Trauma was not uncommon among slaves from all parts of the township. In fact, slaves from all over entered the hospital with broken limbs, open wounds, contusions, and paralyzing spinal cord injuries. Most of these were work related, as port, maritime, and farming environments each had their numerable dangers. Some were victims of violence, but the hospital diagnoses do not give the exact cause of injuries. In fact, based on the increase in the proportional number of slave patients with injuries, Santos appears to have become a more dangerous and violent place by then end of the 1870s. More people—enslaved and free—died from accidents such as tall stacks of crates collapsing in warehouses or heavy bags of coffee or sugar falling from ships. By the early 1880s, Santos also had a few steam-driven factories of lime and soap in operation. The thick gears of their machinery could catch and pull or steam boilers could explode. On the streets, kicks from mules and horses could cause injury, and it was not uncommon for the new trolley in town to run over pedestrians caught unaware. These kinds of injuries were more common among enslaved men than enslaved women. Contrary to expectations, the free population had higher rates of injury than slaves throughout the 1860s and 1870s. Injuries were the cause of admission for about 6 percent of free patients during the 1860s. In the 1870s, they became the third-leading cause of admission for slaves and the fifth-leading cause for free patients.[47] Among the slaves on Rua Direita, most entered the hospital suffering from hernias, a painful condition prevalent among those who lift and strain under heavy loads.

The other unusually common disease among the Rua Direita slaves was syphilis. This sexually transmitted urogenital infection is caused by the bacterium *Treponema pallidum*. In the first stage of syphilis, the bacteria multiply at the site of invasion, leading to a tissue reaction that is noticeable but often painless. If syphilis comes to its final stage the disease can destroy skin, bone, and soft tissue and, at its worst, cause aneurysms, heart failure, and a wide array of neurological deficits (called nuerosyphilis). Most hospitalized patients must have suffered from the secondary stage of syphilis that is typically accompanied with a "low-grade fever, malaise, sore throat, hoarseness, anorexia, generalized adenopathy, headache, joint pain, and skin and mucous membrane lesions or rashes."[48] Overall, the incidence of syphilis held steady among slave patients during the 1860s and 1870s. Among free patients, the rate of infection was slightly lower than that of slaves during the 1860s but exceeded the slave rate during the 1870s.[49] With the influx of single European men in town, many of them sailors or recent immigrants, an increase in involvement with prostitutes is likely.

Not far from the urban slaves on Rua Direita was another localized cluster of syphilis patients. The sufferers were a group of women who worked a brothel run by Camilo de Andrade. Located on the corner of Rua Consulado (formerly Beco do Inferno), this establishment was no more than a five-minute walk from Rua Direita. Andrade was labeled as *gerente* (manager) of a large group of enslaved women, twenty of whom entered the hospital (and one who entered the cemetery) between 1871 and 1876. Besides syphilis, these women were treated for afflictions likely acquired in their exploitation. For example, Andrade's slave, Maria, entered the hospital in 1875 with a difficult pregnancy. Two very young infants, possibly born to one or two of Andrade's prostitutes, were killed by tetanus and parasitic worms. His slave Celestina entered the hospital three times, each time suffering from syphilis. On two of these visits, however, she was registered with different owners. She may have been bought and sold as part of a sex ring, or her ownership disguised to avoid attention. The bouts of syphilis these women suffered may have resulted from contact with some of the enslaved men on Rua Direita as well as the numerous free poor who also frequented the brothels, such as the many European and American mariners who partook in such activities when released into any world port.[50]

Looking at the slaves on Rua Direita provides further evidence that owner occupation, residential location, and slave afflictions were intertwined. Some of these slaves were owned by one of the coffee or cotton merchants, at a time when men in this line of business were filling the ranks of the town elite. Between 1861 and 1883, 121 slaves owned by coffee and cotton merchants entered the hospital. Merchants had fewer females in the hospital than average, probably because they relied more on male slaves to haul or store coffee bags and other exported or imported goods. Smallpox was the main affliction that sent commission-house slaves to the hospital for treatment, and in general they were hospitalized in numbers lower than the overall slave average. Syphilis was the second leading treatable problem that commission-house slaves suffered, followed by *delirium tremens*. This latter resulted from overuse of alcohol, and slaves that suffered from this ailment may have frequented the numerous taverns that neighbored their owners' *armazens* and *trapiches* (waterfront warehouse and pier). This sample of urban slaves surprisingly suffered little from arthritis, a condition that may have been more connected to outdoor jobs that had limited and repetitive tasks, such as hoeing or cutting cane.[51]

Whether an illness was transmitted by sexual contact or an injury caused by a violent blow or accident, slaves were not alone in facing severe danger and the many cruelties of nineteenth-century life. The city was filled with free people of little means who scraped by on uncertain sources of income and who were willing to take on dangerous work in order to stave off hunger for themselves or their families. These destitute people were also compelled to crowd into tight and insecure quarters, sleeping in close proximity to people who were possibly infected with a severe ailment such as smallpox or tuberculosis. In contrast, some slaves managed to avoid the clearly dangerous environments faced by the poorest free. As we have seen, most diseases and afflictions, including yellow fever, syphilis, and arthritis, affected particular groups of slaves and free people to different degrees. People suffered from a variety of ailments that depended more on sex and age than on slavery or freedom, reinforcing the view that poverty was its own kind of powerful enslavement. The range of risks that slaves faced was connected to their day-to-day environment and the treatment they received from their owners.

BROTHERHOODS AND BURIALS

Even after death, slave bodies were treated differently depending on their status and the resources afforded for the funeral. When slaves and free people died, friends and family transported their bodies to Santos's only Catholic cemetery in funeral processions that were sometimes highly elaborate and festive. In fact, when the city became overly congested and busy in the 1890s, the government restricted funeral processions to hours of the day that did not coincide with the periods of heavy traffic. Some bodies were carried in simple plain boxes in a police cart, others hefted on the shoulders of loved ones. The trolley was a favored choice and, in fact, this means of conveying corpses became so popular that the trolley company created special procedures for funerals, including a specific funeral route to the cemetery. Some slaves brought elaborate and varied traditions from Africa to the procession and ritual of burial; many others were buried with little notice and at the cost of the township government. As João José Reis explores in his book, *Death Is a Festival*, the funerary economy was complicated in the Imperial days, demonstrating again that some slaves were in a better position in this economy even after death.[52]

Municipal rules on slave burials tightened as epidemics increased and officials drew stronger connections between the spread of diseases and the ways in which decomposing bodies were disposed of. Before 1850, bodies of both free and slave were buried in the floors of churches, often near the small altars dedicated to various patron saints that were maintained by the church sodalities (brotherhoods and sisterhoods). These small enclosed spaces, with their often ornately decorated shrines to patron saints, ran along each side of a church and faced onto the pews. Burials had their own social geography, and many Brazilians believed that the spatial placement of the dead could influence afterlife and give benefits for their descendents. Historians have written about the social functions of sodalities, including the maintenance of practical and meaningful communities of free and slaves.[53]

In 1850, new Imperial and provincial laws prohibited church burials. Bodies were temporarily buried behind the Saint Anthony church until a better space could be found and prepared. Since men and women were sometimes buried in their finery and with personal objects such as metals or jewelry, the city could not bury its dead in a space unprotected by high walls and under the watch of a guard. The official commission put in charge of the new cemetery decided that because the Saint Anthony church neighbored the harbor and was only two meters above sea level, it was not a suitable place for the public cemetery. They settled instead on a piece of land on slightly higher ground that neighbored a small, private Protestant cemetery. The new Cemetério do Paquetá opened in 1854 and its arrival did not come too soon. When the 1855–56 cholera epidemic struck, the dead quickly filled a quarter of the new cemetery's space.[54]

The church and some townspeople objected to the 1850 law and the striking change in custom that it represented regarding burials. Their objection was largely cultural and religious since some believed that removing the sacred act of burial from the auspices of the church was sacrilegious. Another objection, often overlooked by historians, was financial. Church burials were a major source of income, and the church was reluctant to cede that money and power to the government. Undoubtedly, the church lost a source of income but sodalities probably fared better under the new arrangement. As we can see from the map of the cemetery in Figure 5.1, sodalities were given a sizable portion of the new cemetery and could profit on the graves there as long as they paid the city a small tax. Of the 25,000 square meters of ground that Paquetá occupied, 10,400 square meters were used by Santos's eleven brotherhoods and sisterhoods. The sodalities were also given the front half of the cem-

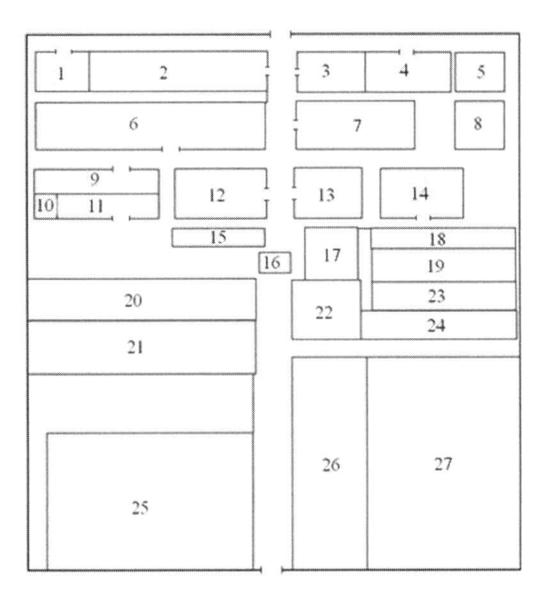

1. Plot (Jazigo) 3ª, Irmandade SS. Sacramento Novo
2. Plot 4ª, Irmandade de N.S. do Carmo
3. Plot N. 3 (velho), S.S. Sacramento Irmandade
4. Plot N. 2, Irmandade de S. Francisco
5. Field plot 1
6. Plot N. 6, Irmandade N.S. dos Passos
7. Plot 5ª, Irmandade de N.S. Rosario Apparicida
8. Field plot, ossuary
9. Plot N. 11, Irmandade de S. Benedicto
10. [Illegible] 15ª
11. Plot N. 15, Irmandade N.S. do Rosario dos Homens de Cor
12. Plot 10, Irmandade de N.S. da Boa Morte
13. Plot N. 9, Irmandade N.S. do Terço
14. Plot 12ª, Irmandade N.S. do Amparo
15. Plot N. 1, infant burials (sepulturas casos de anjos)
16. Chapel
17. Plot N. 1, infant burials
18. Plot N. 2, infant burials
19. Plot N. 3, infant burials
20. Field plot, N. 100
21. Plot N. 2, adult burials (sepulturas casos de adultos)
22. Plot N. 20, adult burials
23. Plot [illegible], infant burials
24. Plot N. 5, infant burials
25. Plot N. 7, infant burials
26. Unlabeled
27. Plot N. 6, infant burials

FIGURE 5.1

Map of the Paquetá Cemetery and Sodality Plots, 1898

SOURCE: Cemetery registers, 1897–1900, FAMS.

etery and would have been most visible and well accessible from the front gate. The back half of the cemetery, behind the chapel, held the numerous burials unconnected to any sodality. With these changes, the biggest beneficiary of Paquetá clearly was the municipal government, and it registered a net profit from the cemetery's income several years later.[55]

The creation of public cemeteries was an enormous break from centuries of Roman, Portuguese, and Brazilian burial practices; but while the graves had moved, the ways that townspeople put their dead into the ground did not change much. Those with a little bit of money sometimes requested that their bodies be buried in a grave site maintained by their favorite sodality. Before and after enactment of the cemetery law, the police were notified when someone died or was found dead, especially when violence was suspected. The dead were carried to the church and later the cemetery, in a closed rather than open box, and wrapping and carrying corpses within nets was prohibited. Gravediggers buried the dead six *palmas* (palms, or handwidths) under the church floor. This depth was also standard for cemetery burials. There was neither an explicit rule against reusing caskets nor a law dictating how the cemetery was to be organized or maintained.[56]

Larger changes in burial practices did not occur until the 1890s, when the cemetery began to overflow and there seemed to be no limit to the population boom, expanding coffee economy, and waves of deadly diseases. City officials responded to the excess numbers at the Paquetá Cemetery by adding several laws and altering others. In the 1895 municipal code, police required proof of an official autopsy, greater vigilance in inspecting the cemetery, and a numbering system for graves. Cemetery caretakers followed municipal laws that better organized the cemetery space and limited grave sites to a small plot of ground. It had long been practice for church and cemetery gravediggers to not disturb a grave site's remains for two years, but by 1895 Paquetá had so filled to capacity that cemetery caretakers were allowed an exception to this rule.[57] There are no data on how many people were removed in less than two years from burial, nor do we know what was done with the remains. Most bones of the poor and perhaps those of some of the more powerful families must have been taken out of the cemetery if it filled to quarter capacity in only its third year (when the city had half the number of people as it would in the 1890s).

Those who neared their deaths were frequently concerned about the fate of their souls, and some wished to be buried in the sacred spaces maintained by the town's brotherhoods. Most slaves, however, may not have believed that this was necessary or never had the opportunity to associate with a religious sodality. Eleven sodalities received the recently deceased to be buried in their sacred sections of the public cemetery. These secular groups (with religious affiliations) had existed in Brazil since the first years of the colony and can be found in Portugal as early as the thirteenth century. They consisted mostly of laypersons who elected an administrative board to carry out meetings, control the treasury, and organize funerals among other activities.[58] Sodalities had long admitted slaves and people of color and according to João José Reis, "provided an alternative form of ritual kinship." This "family" was "responsible for giving its members a place of communion and identity as well as help in times of need, providing support when striving for manumission, offering a means of protesting slave owners' abuses and, above all, celebrating dignified funeral rites."[59] Between 1870 and 1875, cemetery officials noted which sodalities received bodies for burial. In 1874, one out of every four nonslaves buried by the cemetery was done so under the auspices of a sodality. Far fewer slaves had connections to these groups, and only one out of twenty slaves was buried with a sodality in the Paquetá Cemetery.[60] Such a low number suggests that by the 1870s the majority of slaves did not have strong connections to the sodalities.

The sodalities that carried the most dead into their grave plots in 1874 were Nossa Senhora do Terço and Nosso Senhor Bom Jesus dos Passos. N.S. do Terço accepted one slave and twenty free people in 1874, while N.S. Bom Jesus dos Passos accepted only the free. The single slave buried by the N.S. do Terço sodality was André, owned by the Monteiro, Prado & Wright Company, whose medical care and death was described at the start of the chapter. N.S. do Terço had accepted a few slaves in other years, and, like André, all were slaves owned by prominent masters. Besides N.S. do Terço and São Benedito, only one other brotherhood—Irmandade do Rosário dos Homens Pretos (Brotherhood of Black Men)—accepted slaves into its cemetery plot. If we look closely at the owners of the slaves buried in these three sodalities we find that they were almost all prominent city businessmen who owned multiple slaves. This gives evidence that owner status had a part to play with the slaves who were buried by one of the sodalities. The slaves themselves, however, did not differ greatly in terms of demographics from the slaves buried in the secular parts of the cemetery during this time.

Santos had no sodalities exclusively for slaves in the early 1870s, but eight sodalities accepted only free members. These attracted mostly small shopkeepers, minor government officials, and artisans. Each buried at least one person of high status during this period—either a township councilman or a coffee commission house owner. It appears that religious factors, more than class, status, or sex, appealed to city residents when they chose or were invited to join a sodality. Race or skin color was certainly important for some groups, but evidence on this point is hard to find for Santos since so few sources give racial or color data during the second half of the century. For example, N.S. do Terço buried Ritta, a freed slave of eighteen years, and Anna Maria do Espírito Santo, who was listed as *parda* in the marriage records. São Benedito, another sodality that accepted slaves, also buried two freemen who were African. Conversely, the Irmandade do Rosário dos Homens Pretos, a group traditionally of members of color, buried Albino da Silva, a seventy-year-old Portuguese immigrant. It is unlikely that da Silva was as dark-skinned as his brothers. Besides race, sex was important in the small sisterhood in town, Nossa Senhora do Amparo, which buried four women, all of whom were middle-aged or elderly. It was within the church, and especially in sodalities, where some of the integral vertical links "interdependent stratification" (see Chapter One) were created and maintained. Santos looks likely to have fit within a national trend in which brotherhoods were less divided ethnically by the middle part of the nineteenth century. Additionally, whites of different backgrounds were no longer excluded from specific confraternities and even joined *preto* and *pardo* brotherhoods. One thing did not change: many white brotherhoods continued to exclude people of color.[61]

Payments for burial demonstrate the high levels of poverty that existed in Brazil at this time and suggest that the cemetery contributed a portion of its income to providing burials to families that could not afford them. The cemetery regularly charged a small fee (*emolumento de fábrica*) for burying the dead in either the religious or secular sections. For the deceased who had been in a brotherhood or sisterhood, part of this money was passed on to the sodalities. In the late 1870s, caretakers began entering the payment amount next to the name of the deceased. Payments ranged between "five" and "one-half" (probably indicating five *mil-réis* and 500 *réis*), but most were less than one, including hundreds of "zero" payments. The range of payments likely reflected a sliding scale based on families' income, so that the poorest and least known were exempt from the cemetery fee. Between 1878 and 1886, the cemetery received no money from 58 percent of its 4,200 burials. Slaveholders, on the other hand, nearly always paid the "one" or "one-half" amount for their dead slaves. With the steep rise of slave prices by the 1870s, fewer owners could claim they were unable to afford the small fee. This trend mirrors the growing numbers of slaveholders who paid for their slaves' hospital bills. Occasionally, police brought to the cemetery the corpses of free people who had no available kin or friends. This small group rarely registered a payment. Cemetery clerks also collected less money from free adults who had single names, most of whom were free slaves or their children.[62] Thus, despite the general homogeneity among the groups that paid or did not pay, there is some evidence that the unknown and destitute were more likely to have their burials paid by the township.

As with slaves, most of the free people buried in Paquetá Cemetery were not patients who had died in the Charity Hospital. In 1865 cemetery caretakers buried 268 bodies of free people in the cemetery, but only thirty-seven free patients died in the hospital. This ratio (seven to one) is higher than that for slaves, partly because many of the nonslave bodies in the cemetery were mariners who died on ship. Nevertheless, the difference between slave and free deaths also suggests that the free were more likely to receive private medical care, while the slaves were more likely to go to the hospital when sick or injured. Almost a decade later, a higher proportion of the free buried in the cemetery had died in the hospital. In 1878, 18 percent of the bodies of free and slave came from the Charity Hospital, and eight years later 23 percent of the dead were recently patients in the public hospital. The small hospice in the old São Bento monastery sent thirteen bodies to the cemetery during several months of 1878, 12 percent of all the bodies received. By 1886, however, this monastery was no longer listed with any of the names of the deceased.[63]

This chapter has covered a range of topics from the illnesses slaves and free people battled to the treatment they received and the funeral customs that followed for those who did not survive. I have presented additional evidence of the steep hierarchies within slavery when they struggled against fatal illness and injuries. The afflictions that slaves and free people suffered varied little, with the notable exception of yellow fever and to a smaller degree, smallpox. Thus the judicial and social categories of slavery and freedom did not greatly impact illnesses and injuries; rather, basic demographic variables were the main deciding factors when it came to propensity to health risks. Additionally, occupation and neighborhoods again had an effect on the life conditions of slaves. The male slaves on Rua Direita, or the female slaves working Camilo de Andrade's brothel endured sexually transmitted diseases and physical injuries disproportionately. Females working as maids or servants in one of the town's homes, on the other hand, were most likely to fall ill to tuberculosis, a disease that took from the ranks of all people in Brazil during the nineteenth century. Even after death, the bodies of slaves were placed into graves that depended to a certain degree on the status of their owners. A slave buried in one of the cemetery plots reserved for a sodality, for example, was usually owned by an owner with status.

CHAPTER SIX

Pathways to Freedom: Manumission and Flight

Late one Wednesday evening, June 2, 1858, under the cover of darkness, two slaves slipped out of their house in Santos and stole away from town. The runaways were from Africa. Jacintho was a tall man from West Africa (Mina), thirty years old, with light brown skin. Francisco was slightly younger and darker, had a firmer grasp of Portuguese, and came from southwestern Africa (Congo). As coopers, they tapered and beveled wood staves, squeezing them into two or three stiff metal hoops to make watertight containers. Gaps or imperfections between these staves, even those too small to be seen by the naked eye, could ruin a barrel. In this craft, skilled workers were hard to find and their work took years to master, commanding respect when it was done well. The two men may have previously discussed how extra work might bring savings for manumission letters, or they may have talked about the ways they could use their skills and savings in order survive on the run. If Jacintho and Francisco had never left Africa, they might have seen the other's customs and primary languages as strange or exotic, as their homelands were separated by many hundreds of miles of rough terrain. But in Brazil and in the dimness of a waning moon, they were compatriots and united in their risky pursuit.[1]

Two weeks after their disappearance, Jacintho and Francisco's owner, José Teixeira da Silva Braga, posted an advertisement in the local newspaper asking readers to help him find these two runaway slaves (Figure 6.1).[2] He promised fifty *mil-réis* (equivalent to more than a month of unskilled wages) to anyone who found them, plus compensation for expenses incurred during their capture and return. Braga had reason to believe that a fellow townsperson could accomplish the task since he had heard rumors that the fugitives had returned to Santos once or twice at night. His advertisement may have had its desired effect, as Jacintho was later captured or voluntarily returned. Less is known about Francisco, who may have found tenuous freedom.[3] Slave runaways were often punished, and the skin, tissue, and muscles of Jacintho's back may have been severely cut by 100–200 lashes of a whip. Or he may have served a week or more in stocks at the city jail.

At the time of this attempted escape, Braga owned several other slaves, including a woman named Benedita. Upon her death in 1875, Benedita may have been relieved to know that at least within her family bondage had ended with her, as Braga had signed a letter of manumission to free Benedita's two-year-old daughter Carolina four years earlier.[4] Braga granted the manumission letter to this little girl without conditions, stating that it was to reward the good service that Benedita and her two enslaved brothers, Izidoro and Antonio, had given his family. Izidoro, a tailor who had a regular stature and "catlike eyes" (*olhos gateados*), may not have felt much lasting gratitude because Braga ordered him arrested and investigated for an unstated crime several years later. About the same time that young Carolina was freed, Braga wrote a manumission letter for another slave in his posse, a teenager named Amelia. As an older girl, Amelia was much more expensive on the slave market compared to the enslaved toddler, Carolina. Most likely as a result of this price difference, the manumission letter carried an important stipulation: for ten years, Amelia would continue to labor with great restrictions to her

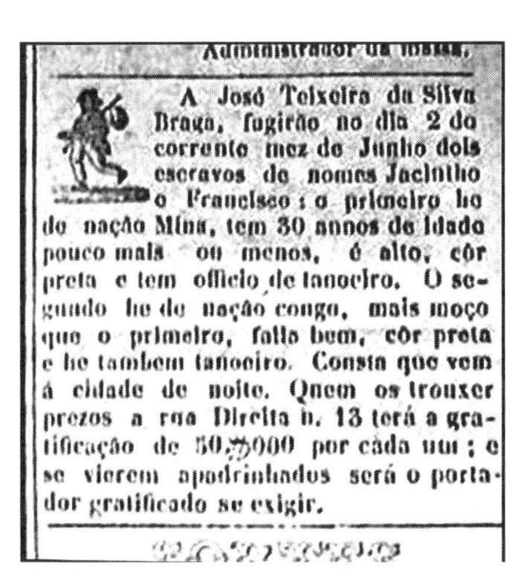

A José Teixeira da Silva Braga, fugirão no dia 2 do corrente mez de Junho dois escravos de nomes Jacintho e Francisco; o primeiro he de nação Mina, tem 30 annos de idade pouco mais ou menos, é alto, côr preta e tem officio de tanoeiro. O segundo he de nação congo, mais moço que o primeiro, falla bem, côr preta e he tambem tanoeiro. Consta que vem á cidade de noite. Quem os trouxer prezos a rua Direita n. 13 terá a gratificação de 50$000 por cada um; e se vierem apadrinhados será o portador gratificado se exigir.

FIGURE 6.1

Jacintho and Francisco's Runaway Announcement

SOURCE: *Revista do Commercio* (Santos), 6/1858, HS.

liberty under another man. This new master, in fact, was a freed slave. While Amelia and her new boss had both legally exited the condition of slavery, they were located at very different points within a bondage-freedom continuum that included slaves and *libertos* (freed slaves). Unlike the kind of freedom enjoyed by her new master, Amelia could not quit or leave without permission. To do so might risk reenslavement and put her and any children she bore back in Braga's hands.[5]

Braga's slaves show us that there were three broad paths to freedom: flight, manumission with strings attached, and uninhibited manumission. Most people who were born enslaved died enslaved, but a minority of slaves took one of these three paths. Each path, furthermore, was taken by different groups of slaves, depending on a range of characteristics. Runaways were mostly valuable skilled males who had the resources or the know-how to survive on the run. This group, at least in Santos, was the least likely to receive a manumission letter. In contrast, the group least likely to run away—enslaved girls and young women—was the most likely to receive a manumission letter free of stipulations. As we saw in the manumission of Amelia and Carolina, these letters could be granted without conditions or could carry very burdensome obligations; this too usually depended on the slave price (and, hence, demographic and physical characteristics of the slave). That certain pathways to freedom were almost entirely closed to large groups of slaves indicates that the hierarchies within slavery may have been felt more acutely in society's ultimate reward: legal freedom.

Jacintho and Francisco took one particular pathway to freedom when they "stole themselves" by running away. Escape was a manner of attaining freedom that was relatively rare until the last five years of slavery in Santos. I argue in this chapter that running away from owners not only carried considerable risk and separated slaves from caring communities of families and friends, but required resources and skills that most slaves did not have. Slaves of wealthy owners were more likely to take the risk of losing connections to loved ones, violent punishment, and even death through flight because they were more likely to have marketable skills they could sell as well as enough education to help them navigate their way to safety.

ESCAPE THROUGH MANUMISSION

Another pathway to freedom, that taken by Braga's enslaved domestic servants, was manumission. Some manumission letters were freely given, and once received, former slaves (*pretos forros*) had nearly every political right as any other Brazilian citizen, but usually had very little economic leverage. Some kinds of manumission allowed slaves to pay for their freedom or conditionally stipulated a future payment or obligation of labor. These conditional letters often did not give immediate freedom for slaves but they did provide some worthwhile benefits.[6] For example, slaves usually could not be sold once the onerous process of manumission had begun. Manumission could also be purchased, but this often carried a high price that left some former slaves in precarious financial positions. Furthermore, if owners did not receive expected payments for a manumission, or the slave did not provide the stipulated labor or behavior of a conditional manumission, or if any manumitted slave displayed "ungrateful" behavior, these formerly enslaved men, women, and children could be forced back into slavery. While revoked manumissions were rare, it is clear that recently manumitted slaves could not feel entirely secure that legal freedom was theirs to keep.[7] Despite these important limitations, freed slaves of childbearing age looked toward future children and grandchildren. Daughters born to freed slaves could bear children that faced no legal possibility of having to reenter slavery. Sons born to freed slaves, however, might father enslaved children if their wife or partner was a slave. For most people of African heritage and little means, slavery and freedom were not far apart.

Rosa, who acquired a conditional manumission letter in 1844, may have held hope for the future of her children as she labored under the thorny conditions of unfamiliar freedom. Rosa paid 511 *mil-réis* to her owner, Antonio de Freitas Caldas, to receive her letter. Caldas contributed another 77 *mil-réis*, which could have been a loan or a gift. The letter specified that Rosa still owed another 332 *mil-réis* and that she would have to pay this amount while serving Caldas over the next six years. Annually, Rosa would have to pay 55 *mil-réis*, which was more than a month's wage for a common laborer in 1844. Rosa may not have had more than a month of income to spare, however, since her manumission contract stipulated that she had to continue to give her time to Caldas in exchange for his bestowal of the letter. Rosa's difficult situation may not have been hers alone; slaves like Rosa borrowed the initial payments toward manumission letters from friends, family, or acquaintances, debt that they may have found difficult to pay. As for her former owner, it cannot be assumed that Caldas granted the letter only as a gesture of goodwill. A plausible scenario is that at the moment Rosa was able to make the initial payment for her letter, Caldas needed the money. This large sum of cash came with little short-term loss, moreover, since Rosa would continue laboring in the same way as she had done as a slave. It was not uncommon for free people of even moderate means to have more than fifty small and large debts when they died, and the money that Caldas owed his friends and neighboring shopkeepers may have been a pressing concern in 1844.[8]

In this case, the decision to manumit or not was in Caldas's hands. For most of slavery's existence in Brazil, in fact, slaves had little chance of forcing a master to accept manumission. As Perdigão Malheiro commented in 1866, "Among us no law guarantees the *peculio* [anything of value saved by a slave]; and even less its free disposal by means of a will or through inheritance, even when the slave is the property of the state."[9] Only when abolitionist pressure increased and the Rio Branco law of 1871–72 passed, declaring newborn children of slaves to be free, was this centuries-old system undermined. Owners may have commonly resisted the proposal of a paid manumission because a freed (manumitted) slave did have partial legal recourse. As mentioned, in most instances, he or she could not be sold and the manumission contract had to be maintained in the case of a transfer, such as an inheritance. By the 1870s, more lawyers and judges supported slaves' efforts to initiate a manumission process with even small amounts of money. When successful, slaves gained the ability to halt an imminent or future sale and a potentially catastrophic disruption in their lives and the lives of their loved ones. Yet even at this end stage of slavery, a freed slave could be reverted back to slavery if a judge determined that a manumission letter, made years earlier, was legally void. Indeed, lawsuits that successfully reenslaved freed slaves increased in number after 1850 in Rio de Janeiro, before declining after 1870.[10]

Among the various stacks and bundles of old documents relating to manumission that have been preserved in Santos, some are tattered and illegible, but enough exist to explore the legal route to freedom. Several categories of letters depended on the institution that regulated the letter, quality of original or transcription in the archive, and type of letter. The notary offices and municipal archive hold 466 manumission letters written between 1802 and 1877, but we must rely on the transcribed copies of nearly one-third (174) of these because the originals were either lost or unavailable. The man who transcribed these documents in the 1940s and 1950s, Costa e Silva Sobrinho, included the names and demographic information of the owners and slaves involved, but usually excluded the type of manumission letter (freely granted, purchased, or conditional). For this reason, two-thirds (294) of the notarized letters could be used for an analysis of the participants of the manumission involved for each kind of letter, but this is not possible for the total set of letters (551). We also had access to eighty-five baptismal manumission letters found in the church records of 4,996 regular baptisms of slave infants, children, and adults between 1832 and 1870. Baptism records are rarely included in studies of manumission, although as James Kiernan first demonstrated for Paraty, these were a central element in the overall manumission process.[11]

Enslaved adults and children who wished to escape slavery legally in Santos commonly had to meet one of three conditions: they had to be able to earn, save, or borrow enough money to cover their own price; they had to find someone else to pay; or they had to negotiate with their owners a future exchange of labor for partial or full freedom. We can see evidence of the burden most manumission letters entailed when the types of manumission letters are distinguished (see Table 6.1). As mentioned, some slaves were manumitted at baptism, but far more bondspeople received their manumission letters through purchase or with the promise of contracted labor over an extended period of time. Excluding the baptismal records, there were 294 descriptive letters written for enslaved adults and children.[12] Of these, 22 percent were given freely or listed no conditions. These were manumissions with no (known) strings attached. But a larger share, 27 percent, forced the slave to comply with some condition, usually in the form of pressed labor over many years. Another 34 percent

TABLE 6.1

Manumission Types, 1810–1880

	Number	Percent
Free		
Explicitly free	18	5
No conditions mentioned	47	12
Purchased (onerous)[1]		
Self-purchase	105	28
Family or third-party purchase	21	6
Conditional[2]		
Serve until death of master	52	14
Serve a fixed time	7	2
Other	6	2
Unknown	13	3
Purchased (onerous) and conditional	25	7
Baptismal		
No payment mentioned	80	21
Purchased	5	1
Unknown	25	7
Total	379[3]	100[4]

NOTES: 1. Includes 25 letters that were purchased and had conditions; 2. Excludes all purchased letters; 3. Includes 294 detailed notarized letters and 85 baptismal records; 4. Figures do not add to 100 percent because "purchased" category includes "purchased and conditional" letters.

SOURCE: Manumission letters, 1810–1880, PCNS, SCNS, CCS, FAMS.

of the letters allowed the slave, a family member, or a third party to pay money for the manumission letter.[13] If free baptismal manumission letters are included the percentage of unpaid and unconditional manumission letters increases slightly, to 38 percent.

The relatively low number of unconditional manumission letters in Santos was similar to other parts of São Paulo during this time. For São Sebastião, the neighboring township to the north, Rosangela Dias da Ressurreição, found that conditional letters were the most common.[14] Peter Eisenberg found a higher number of purchase letters (*onerosas*) for slaves in Campinas: 60 percent of letters were of this type between 1798 and 1885. Only after 1886, when slavery seemed fated to end for some, did unpaid letters surpass purchased letters in Campinas.[15] Nineteenth-century São Paulo is unusual in this respect, since many other parts of Brazil had proportionally more unpaid manumissions than paid.[16]

Historians have often distinguished between the three types of manumission letters and have argued that they were largely "separate but related" systems of granting freedom. I believe this is true, but two comments must be made about the data available on slave manumissions in Santos. First, among the transcribed letters from the two notary offices, nearly a third do not fit neatly into one of the three categories. For example, 7 percent of the letters were both onerous and conditional (Table 6.1). In these cases, in addition to the conditions attached to the manumission letter, the slave or someone else paid or vowed to pay a sum of money. Another 16 percent of the letters did not explicitly state whether the manumission was free or if there were conditions attached. These "ambivalently free" manumission letters became increasingly common after 1860 when the notary officers composed shorter, more formulaic, and less detailed letters.

Second, slaves who paid or found a third-party payer were sometimes given a separately contracted lease on their labor (*contratos de locação*). These were nothing other than indenture contracts, a term rarely seen in the historical literature because such contracts have been uncommonly found or given attention. Leases were written separately from the manumission letters, and were also closely connected to them.[17] In one example, a slave named Juliana was manumitted by Anna Luisa in 1864 in a letter that mentions a 400 *mil-réis* payment but no payer. The notary office holds another document from the same year and for the same amount, contracting Juliana to serve Joaquim Soares Gomes for four years.[18] Evidently, after negotiating with Juliana, Gomes initiated the process and paid Anna Luisa the amount of Juliana's manumission. He then entered the former slave into indentured service in a contract that was written separately from the manumission letter. The indenture contract, in fact, makes no mention of the manumission contract, or vice-versa. In another case, a slave named Joaquim paid his mistress, Virginia Maria Nebias, 800 *mil-réis* to purchase his freedom in 1862. The letter also documented that Nebias's husband, Captain José Raggio Nobrega, had paid an additional 700 *mil-réis*. The notary office holds an indenture contract, written on behalf of Nobrega, stipulating that Joaquim would give eight years and four months (one hundred months) of his labor for 400 *mil-réis*. Clearly, Joaquim did not have enough funds to pay his purchase price and offered an indenture for the monies. Why the *locatório* (indenture contract) is 300 *mil-réis* less than the amount listed in the manumission letter is not given.[19]

When approaching manumission letters, we should keep in mind that some letters were unclear as to whether they were free or conditional, others were both onerous and conditional, and a few were onerous but excluded information on conditional indenture service contracts written separately in the notary office. Nevertheless, the different manumission categories can be discerned for many of the letters, but only if we include a few additional categories that do not hide the ambivalence of the data.

Among the conditional letters with no mention of payment, two-thirds stipulated that the contract would end with the death of the owner. Some conditionally manumitted slaves were transferred before they met the terms of the contract or when a master died. Some contracts ran until the ex-slave reached adulthood or was married, while others stipulated specific periods of time ranging from two to ten years. Of seventeen manumissions in 1866, the second year of a difficult five-year war against Paraguay, eight slaves were "freed" in order to be conscripted into the war effort. The slaves were donated by families to serve as substitutes for eight family members. Over the century, the proportion of free, paid, and conditional manumissions remained fairly steady.[20]

Conditionally freed slaves occupied complicated positions somewhere between slavery and freedom, a changeable and nuanced condition that was not always acknowledged by township officials. For example, some conditionally manumitted slaves in Santos were listed as slaves in other documents years later. Clemente and Domingos are listed as slaves in the 1817 nominal list, though they had been conditionally manumitted four and eight years earlier, respectively. Urçula appeared in the nominal list in 1817 as a young slave owned by Antonio Joaquim de Figueredo. She was manumitted by Figueredo three decades later, but then sold as a slave a short time after.[21] This sale was different from the indenture contracts mentioned earlier. The *meia-siza* (tax) record in which Urçula appears for the third time was exclusively for the transfer of slave ownership, while a sale of an indentured labor contract could have taken place in the notary office.

As shown in Table 6.2, among the purchased manumissions, those bought by a family member or a third party were less common than self-purchase, but this may have been because the letters did not always mention who paid for the manumission. For example, eighteen out of fifty-eight letters manumitting slave children involved purchased freedom between 1811 and 1880, but none gave information on a parent, relative, or third party. It is inconceivable that a child would be able to pay for his or her own manumission, yet in a third of these letters there is no mention of the source of funds. Manumission letters of children were certainly not the only ones missing information on who paid. It appears likely that among the "self-purchase" manumission letters, some slaves received money from friends, family members, or people, some who might have wished to use them as indentured servants.[22]

Female and male slaves were fairly evenly divided between all types of letters, although males are slightly higher among purchased letters. This matches findings from other parts of Brazil and gives further evidence that male slaves had better earning power. Too many of the letters are

TABLE 6.2

Backgrounds of Manumitted Slaves, 1810–1880

	Free	Purchased	Conditional	Purchased and Conditional	Baptismal
Slave sex					
Male	32	66	38	13	44
Female	33	60	40	12	41
Slave age					
Child	13	20	20	2	85
Working age	16	35	27	6	0
Elderly	7	10	4	17	0
Unknown	29	61	27	0	
Slave birthplace					
Brazil	18	35	25	6	85
Africa	11	38	12	6	0
Unknown	36	53	41	13	0
Owner information					
Male	44	76	36	16	39
Female	18	42	40	9	44
Couple	3	4	2	0	0
Carmelite Church	0	4	0	0	0
Total	(N=65)	(N=126)	(N=78)	(N=25)	(N=85)

NOTE: "Free" includes both letters that specify explicit freedom and those with no conditions mentioned.
SOURCE: Manumission letters, 1810–1880, PCNS, SCNS, CCS, FAMS.

missing information on birthplace to come to any strong conclusions, yet it does seem that African-born slaves were more likely to have purchased their manumission while Brazilian-born slaves were granted more conditional manumissions. Slaves of working age were the most commonly manumitted slave in purchased and conditional letters, and children more frequently appeared among the freely given letters, perhaps because their lower prices made it easier for family members or third parties to pay.

Except for conditional manumission letters, male owners were most frequently involved in the manumission process. Perhaps masters placed more emphasis on the financial return of slaves while mistresses were more concerned with the future labor they would receive. As discussed in Chapter Four, male owners were more likely to be involved in commercial ventures and businesses while female owners were more likely to have slaves tending plantations or farms. These different occupations may have influenced the ways that owners and their slaves approached manumission. A handful of couples manumitted their slaves jointly, usually favoring free manumission and perhaps signaling that both spouses were inclined to be involved when bestowing letters that carried no obligations or collected no money. Three of the paid manumissions made by the Carmelite Convent were made by a third person who probably expected a return in labor for the former slave. After 1871, slaves had a much better ability to enter into a verbal agreement that gave them the right to demand (and sometimes sue for) their freedom once they had saved and offered a sufficient amount of money for self-purchase.[23] Even when "activist" judges became more open to slaves seeking freedom through liberty suits in the 1870s and 1880s, devious owners still had legal tactics to reject self-purchase monies and their slaves' freedom on the grounds of property protections and centuries of tradition.[24]

Many owners were open to manumission, but this freedom process could mean very different things for the owners and slaves involved. In distinguishing free, conditional, and paid manumission, I have excluded letters that either had missing data on these categories or were manumissions granted at baptism. Including this wider set of manumission documents, however, provides additional information on the sex of the slaves and owners involved in all types of manumission, and suggests the important role of baptismal manumissions. Considering this whole, Brazilian-born female slaves in Santos were the most likely to receive some sort of manumission letter. Historians have found this to be true in almost every systematic study of manumission in Brazil. As we can see from Table 6.3, these studies show that Brazilian-born females received the most letters, even though in the general population they were vastly outnumbered by African-born males until late in slavery's existence.[25]

TABLE 6.3

Studies of Manumission by Location and Period

		Groups Most Likely to Be Manumitted (Percent of Manumissions)			
Location	Period	Female	Black[1]	Native-born	Adults[2]
Salvador, Bahia	1684–1745	67	54	69	55
Salvador, Bahia	1779–1850	62	77	51	89
Salvador, Bahia	1808–1884	57	nd	53	nd
Paraty, Rio de Janeiro	1789–1822	66	62	84	54
Rio de Janeiro (capital)	1807–1831	64	69	59	45
Santos, São Paulo	1800–1871	54	nd	68	46
São Paulo (capital)	1800–1888	58	nd	69	nd
Campinas, São Paulo	1798–1888	52	58	76	66

NOTES: 1. "Black" includes "*preto*" and "*negro*"; 2. "Adults" were defined as 16 years of age and older, except for the Salvador study, which included slaves 15 years or older, and the Campinas study, which included slaves 10 years and older.
SOURCES: Schwartz, "Manumission of Slaves"; Mattoso, "A Propósito de Cartas"; Nishida, "Manumission and Ethnicity"; Kiernan, *Manumission of Slaves*; Karasch, *Slave Life*; Eisenberg, "Ficando Livre."

Before the last two decades of slavery, African-born males appear as the majority among slaves in most historical sources from Santos, including census lists, inheritance records, bills of sale, civil legal proceedings, and hospital records.

Historians have offered two explanations for why native-born females were favored for manumission; sometimes both are given equal weight. On the one hand, since female slaves were more likely than males to work domestic jobs, they are assumed to have been more integrated into the families of their owners. They played important roles in raising their mistresses' children and keeping up the home, and the concomitant affection and ties this developed made their owners more conducive to partially freeing them.[26] Some historians have taken this idea of familiarity a step further to posit that girls and women who entered into sexual or amorous relations with free men could place pressure on their partners for greater benefits, while others have seen it in negative terms, believing that manumission was a sort of "social control" given to cultivate a sense of gratitude in slaves, which could translate into lifelong service. The gratitude, or sense of indebtedness that was fostered, might have been formed as a result of coercive or noncoercive sexual ties.[27] Keeping the sex balance of manumission letters in mind, we should consider the different types of letters and the strategies slaves might have employed for each. Excluding the paid manumission letters, males and females were fairly evenly divided. Thus, it seems more reasonable to consider the sex differences in terms

of different economic opportunities and goals, rather than affectional or sexual motivations.

As we can see in Table 6.4, female slaves continued to dominate these letters into the second half of the nineteenth century. Since the sex ratio fell after the end of the African slave trade in 1850, enslaved women and girls lost ground to men and boys, proportionally. In terms of other demographic trends, age of manumitted slaves held steady for both males and females while the proportion of slaves born in Brazil in comparison to African-born slaves rose considerably. There are some interesting shifts when it comes to the color and race of slaves, but since these categories themselves were changing, it is hard to say whether certain slave groups according to phenotype or race were finding it easier or harder to obtain a letter. In addition, information reported on age, place of birth, and color were all under 50 percent, so these numbers are only suggestive.

During the first half of the nineteenth century more women than men manumitted slaves, but in the second half of the century this reversed

TABLE 6.4

Characteristics of Manumitted Slaves, 1800–1877 (Percent)

	Manumitted Slaves		
Years of Source	All years	1800–1850	1851–1877
Sex			
Male	47	46	47
Female	54	54	53
Expected male			39
Expected female			61
Age (years, average)	(A=22)	(A=22)	(A=21)
Children	38	39	37
Place of birth			
Location listed	28	21	41
Africa	46	493	43
Brazil	55	51	58
Santos	5	6	4
Race			
Race listed	24	14	41
Preto	34	28	39
Pardo	42	28	51
Mulatto	21	45	5
Total number	(N=551)	(N=354)	(N=197)

NOTE: "Expected male" is the expected percentage of manumitted males adjusted for the changing sex ratios (between 1825 and 1872). It assumes a counterfactual world in which sex ratios changed, but rates of manumission did not.

SOURCE: Manumission letters, 1810–1880, PCNS, SCNS, CCS, FAMS.

(see Table 6.5). In terms of civil status, there was a marked shift during the century. Before 1850, single, married, and widowed owners were fairly evenly divided; after 1850, nearly two-thirds of the owners who manumitted their slaves were married. This was partly a consequence of the steep rise in slave prices, since married men and women typically were wealthier than single and widowed individuals.[28] There may have

TABLE 6.5

Profile of Slaveholders Who Manumitted Slaves, 1800–1871 (Percent)

	1800–1850	1850–1871	1800–1871
Sex			
Men	43	58	48
Women	54	38	48
Couples or business partners	3	2	2
Commercial or religious associations	1	2	1
Age (average)	(A=55)	(A=59)	(A=56)
Civil status			
Single	36	18	30
Married	28	64	41
Widowed	36	18	30
Race			
White	78	nd	80
Of color	22	nd	20
Birthplace			
Portugal	33	44	40
Brazil (including Santos)	67	50	56
Santos	48	24	33
Europe	0	7	4
Occupation			
Business	44	42	43
Public office	10	28	20
Church	18	6	11
Farming	15	4	8
Army	5	6	5
Liberal profession	0	8	5
Other	10	6	8
Country landowners	25	22	24
Total number of documents	(N=343)	(N=179)	(N=522)
Total number of owners	(N=238)	(N=134)	(N=372)
Total number of cross-listed individuals	(N=94)	(N=86)	(N=180)

NOTES: "Documents" are both manumission letters and baptisms. "Total number of owners" may have included repeating individuals. "Total number of cross-listed individuals" included those who were found in other historical sources (see Introduction for a description and discussion of those sources).

SOURCE: Manumission letters, 1800–1871, PCNS, SCNS, CCS, FAMS.

been a connection between the higher number of married and male owners. Enidelce Bertin, who found a similar phenomenon for manumission letters in São Paulo (city) after 1850, suggests that some married couples who manumitted were represented solely by the husband.[29] All in all, the majority of these owners were quite old and manumitted their slaves when they expected to live for only a short time more. The average age of owners increased over the century as life expectancies lengthened slightly and slaves became more expensive (and thus less affordable to younger individuals). In fact, owners who manumitted slaves tended to be about five to ten years older than those who bought and sold slaves, but both groups would have been considered fairly advanced in age for their day.

Beyond sex differences, racial or color diversity is another clue that owners with the most money manumitted less frequently.[30] This idea is supported in several ways. First, while owners who manumitted were mostly white, there were a surprisingly high number of "*pardo*" or black owners, indicating lower levels of wealth in a society in which the wealthiest groups were generally not people of color. Bills of sale and tax records present a sharp contrast: only a handful of slave buyers and sellers were listed in other documents as mixed or black. Another hint is the birthplace of those manumitting: during a period of time when only 16 percent of slave buyers declared Santos as their birthplace, nearly half of the manumission owners were Santista. Brazilian manumitters also greatly outnumbered Portuguese, but Portuguese were the majority among buyers and sellers.

Connected to the finding that higher wealth among owners lowered manumission rates, businessmen were more likely to buy or sell a slave than to manumit one. This group, after all, included town elite who often made their livelihood off the labor of their bondspeople. Among other occupation groups, there were proportionally more church officials and slaveholders in the "liberal professions" (such as law, education, and medicine) among owners who manumitted than among the buyers and sellers. Coffee merchants and men who ran import and export businesses during the coffee boom of the second half of the century rarely manumitted their slaves, preferring instead to buy and sell them. These were the wealthiest groups in town. Nearly 5 percent of the 331 individuals who appeared in the slave market records and for whom we have occupational data were involved in the lucrative business of coffee or general imports and exports.[31] In contrast, less than 2 percent of the 211 men found in the manumission records were involved in these occupations. Mid- to large-sized merchants bought and sold fifty-five slaves but manumitted only five. These businessmen, on average, were of higher status and wealth than the men or women who ran small shops or who worked as vendors or peddlers. Finally, fewer men in the manumitting group had high-status symbols such as titles of nobility, educational degrees, or prestigious club associations.[32]

Clearly, the chances of a manumission letter rested not only on the slaves' earning power and market price but also on the demographic and occupation background of the owners. The evidence presented here shows that those who typically manumitted slaves had somewhat less wealth and more diverse jobs and were far less involved with coffee, the port's signature trade after 1850.[33] We should not go too far with this point, however, since men and women of a wide spectrum of wealth, status, and occupation bought, sold, and manumitted slaves.

Regardless of owner background and status, certain slaves had more privileges than other slaves when it came to receiving manumission letters. Brazilian-born infants and children, for example, were in a particularly strong position to receive a letter of manumission because their price was low. Certain groups of slaves, which included an even number of males and females, earned enough money (or found someone who was willing to pay) for their manumission. Buying oneself or finding a buyer were certainly "onerous," as this category was properly called, but these slaves were in a better position compared to those who could not earn money or knew no one who would sponsor them. The letters also reveal the active role that slaves played in the manumission process and the fact that some were much better situated than others in this unequal society.

ESCAPE THROUGH FLIGHT

When manumission was not an option, slaves may have considered flight. Running away carried enormous risks of punishment and often permanently separated slaves from the communities within which they lived and worked.[34] In the nineteenth century and perhaps even before, runaways mostly sought nonisolated places where they could live under the guise of being legally free. Or they looked for other runaways who had banded together in *quilombos* (maroon communities), places where former slaves scraped by on the fringes of society. In the eyes of the law, slaves were "stealing" themselves, taking property that could be worth more than a year's wages for most owners. Punishment for such acts was often severe: violence meted out in the form of whippings or beatings, or confinement to prison for weeks or months while shackled to the wall with iron chains. Owners occasionally mandated that slaves who had run away permanently wear iron collars, chains, and heavy weights as a measure to prevent future flight.[35] An unknown number of slaves were killed during punishment or through their attempts to escape capture.

Despite the risks, some slaves attempted to flee more than once. The jail registers carried notices to owners of unknown slaves who were found without papers but with the marks of previous whippings or the scars of iron shackles and chains. When slaves ran away and were not immediately caught, some owners placed a notice in the newspapers that carried a description of the slave, his or her clothing, mannerisms, and occupations or skills. Some notices are filled with minute details about the shape of a slave's scar or length of their beards; others are brief and general. When these notices are collected they begin to give a portrait of the slaves who took considerable chances to escape slavery.[36] Those who chose to escape slavery illegally differed from the typical slave who bargained for his or her legal escape through manumission. These differences reflect the stratified world of slavery and the opportunities available for slaves and owners based on their position within a hierarchy of wealth and status.

Between 1851 and 1871, there were 110 notices for 139 individuals who, in groups or on their own, had escaped from plantations, small farms, or urban homes.[37] Only a small number of these slaves were from Santos; the others worked and lived in towns and rural areas scattered throughout the state of São Paulo. Santos was a common destination for many slaves, partly because many had passed through the city when they were transported from other provinces within the Brazilian Empire or from Africa. As the city expanded, driven by the growing business of coffee, fugitives learned that Santos had such a need for workers that some employers might turn a blind eye to the history of a stranger. This was especially true by the late 1870s and 1880s, when Santos attracted large numbers of fugitive slaves, and abolitionists battled police in order to shelter, protect, and in some cases profit from them.[38] Many owners placed notices for the same slaves in multiple town and city newspapers, with the hope of increasing their chances of recovery. A notice in Santos's *Revista Commercial* thus did not necessarily imply that the owner knew the slave was destined for the port town.

Most slaves that chose to run away had untypical characteristics. First of all, nine of every ten runaways were men, as shown in Table 6.6. Men ran away at much higher rates in other parts of Brazil during the nineteenth century.[39] Second, the runaways were on average older: about four years older than a slave who was purchased or manumitted. The average age of a fugitive was twenty-six in the 1850s, and this even increased somewhat in the 1860s. Third, a little less than two-thirds of the fugitives were native-born, but the percentage of Africans actually increased slightly, bucking the demographic trend brought about by the end of the

TABLE 6.6

Profiles of Runaways, 1851–1872 (Percent)

Sex	
Males	91
Females	9
Age (years, average)	(A=28)
Birthplace	
With information	53
Africa	32
Brazil	60
From the north or northeast (birthplace or previous home)	8
Color/race	
Notices with race information	22
Preto	33
Mulatto	23
Fulo	20
Pardo	13
Negro	7
Cabra	3
Total	(N=139)

SOURCES: "Runaway advertisements," *Revista do Commercio* (Santos), 1849–1867, *Diario de Santos*, 1872–1873, FAMS, HS.

international slave trade in 1850.[40] Fourth, more runaways were from Bahia, Pernambuco, Maranhão, or Pará (all northern or northeastern provinces) than the large group of slaves bought and sold on the local market during these two decades. Fifth, runaways were more likely to be described as having a light skin color, but dark-colored slaves may have simply received less notice because they were the largest group. In today's race-conscious world, it is surprising that only a fifth of the announcements mentioned the race or color of the slave. Far more advertisements described face shape or body size than skin color. Finally, a fugitive was also more likely to be skilled. Of the notices that gave information on jobs, most slaves worked skilled trades that included carpentry, cooperage, tailoring, or tile making. Farmers and herders were the next largest group, yet those who drove animals may have had more opportunities for escape. Other fugitives worked jobs that allowed them to travel and enjoy relative independence. Muleteers and timber men, for example, were both knowledgeable about the road system and regional geography. Three fugitive slaves likely hoped to use their sailing skills as part of a ship's crew. Compared to slaves who were sold and manumitted, men and women involved in domestic tasks such as cleaning, cooking, or sewing were noticeably absent from runaway notices. Only one domestic servant and two cooks were listed in these records. In contrast, domestic service was the largest occupation group among the many slave sales.

Slaves who worked within the home of their owner were more likely to be manumitted than to run away. We can attribute this to several reasons. First, as already discussed, the price differences between the expensive farming or skilled male workers and the lower-priced female domestic servants was a crucial element of manumission rates. Second, domestic servants faced greater surveillance of the family and neighbors and, most likely, stronger connections to a community of people who were part of the house. Related to this, domestic servants might have had a much smaller incentive to try escaping because of their limited experience in the world beyond the few blocks or few kilometers of countryside they traveled for their daily chores. Furthermore, owners were probably less likely to take a domestic servant into their house with an unknown or hidden past, making it more difficult to earn a living for escaped slaves with domestic service skills. Slaves with skills or trades that were in demand and who could work and live apart from the house probably did not need as many personal references to find employment. Owners that placed notices for missing slaves who were domestic servants may have excluded the occupational information because it did not reflect well on their own "duty" of benevolence and patriarchy within their household.

Runaway slaves were among the highest priced in the Santos slave market because of their age, sex, and skills. In 1865, an African slave carpenter in his upper twenties would have been priced between 1,500 and 2,000 *mil-réis*. In comparison, a native-born female domestic servant, in the group most likely to bargain for manumission, would have been sold for about 1,000 *mil-réis*. These are coastal prices; near the recently planted coffee plantations in the São Paulo interior, prices for working-age males were more than 30 percent higher.[41] It is no wonder, then, that owners often placed rewards in amounts between 50 and 200 *mil-réis* on top of a repayment for any expenses accrued in capture and return. On the other hand, owners did not have to offer a reward. The 10–20 *mil-réis* expense of placing notices in multiple newspapers for a week would have been a small price to pay for the recovery of a female or an older slave that had been purchased for 500 *mil-réis*.

Because of the great amount of detail in these notices, much can be learned about the men and women who fled. In *Escravos nos anuncios* (Slaves in Advertisements), Gilberto Freyre (1979) describes many of the unusual characteristics that appeared in these advertisements. He was particularly interested in finding traces of African customs such as filed teeth or tribal scarring. Beyond the particular and surprising, Freyre was less interested in general characteristics. He did observe, however, that "no one suffered more in Brazil than the slave of the poor owner."[42] He based this argument on a great range of clothing, marks and scars of punishment, illness and disabilities, and mannerisms that he attributed to the social position and resources of different slaves. Since there is little information about owners who placed these advertisements, it is difficult to tell if Freyre was right. One way to get at this is to look at the few additional bits of evidence included in the advertisements. For example, the bigger slaveholders may have been more likely to list one of the town's powerful commission houses as their local contact. Among the runaways of these owners, there were higher rewards, more groups, and only one female—all indicating that these slaves probably had worked at the larger plantations. The runaway slaves of this group did have a slightly smaller percentage of afflictions or disabilities than those of less wealthy owners, adding some credence to Freyre's argument (and to the argument of this book).

The most common description of runaways focused on their bodies. Notices often began in general terms by specifying the height or weight of a slave. Tall and fat slaves appeared more often than short and skinny slaves, and some had "good" or "regular builds" while others were "very robust" or had "proportionate bodies." Faces were the next most commonly described feature. Slaves had thin or round faces, long or short foreheads, deeply set or big eyes, sharp chins, thick or thin mouths, or wide or fine noses. Descriptions of hair, particularly of beards, took up many words as to whether runaways had or did not have facial hair and describing the beards themselves as "slight," "full," or "wild." Since teeth were often a common distinguishing feature, owners noted missing front teeth, gaps, or "good dentition." Four slaves had teeth that were filed (*dentes limados*), as was customary in some African traditions. Interestingly, only one with this distinctive feature was listed as African; the other three were from the Northeast and two were listed as native-born. Finally, legs, feet, and hands were described as possessing a variety of ailments and disabilities, but a few were simply "in good shape."[43]

Advertisements listed nearly one in every three runaways as having some sort of affliction, disability, or marks from earlier diseases or wounds.[44] If we include broken or missing teeth, the number rises to one in every two. Most of these were scars, either from smallpox or other diseases, or were marks from an injury. Eleven slaves were scarred from whippings, mostly on the back and chest, but one on the buttocks and another on the legs. Some slaves had other injuries that may or may not have been accidental. Firmino, who ran away in 1864, had his neck cut by a big hook, a wound that had healed and scarred, while another unnamed slave had an old bullet wound on his hip. Owners left their marks on slave bodies in other ways, sometimes branding them as they did their cattle. Marks and scars on the face were a common point of description, such as pockmarked noses and foreheads, eczema, small tumors, and cists. Some slaves escaped with open wounds, such as Francisco, who had a festering wound next to his left eye that "continuously discharges liquid."[45]

Owners concentrated on physical aspects of their runaway slaves but they also left us a picture of personality, manners, and habits. We might expect slaves to be depicted in mostly negative terms since, after all, owners saw their runaway slaves as thieves and bandits who (by running away) had created a significant financial and personal problem for their owners. A master, who was likely to view himself as a stern but caring father, probably felt disappointment and a sense of wounded pride when his slave broke an arrangement of "trust."[46] Slaves were described in advertisements variously as "untrustworthy," "shrewd," "unpleasant," and "rude." Several had "downcast eyes," and one "always seems frightened." Contrary to expectations, however, more notices carried fairly positive descriptions of personalities or manners. One slave had "manners that are gentle and kind"; another was "intelligent and quick." Some were "very polite" or "friendly." Owners who described quirks and habits of their slaves knew the slave better than the majority of owners who could offer only laundry lists of scars or types of facial hair. Emilio, who disappeared in 1861, "walks quickly," "shakes his arms when he walks," and often "shrugs his shoulders." One unnamed slave from Mogi das Cruzes "has the habit of kicking one foot in front of the other while talking to a white man, resting his weight on his back leg."[47]

Speech and education were also mentioned in the notices. We cannot assume that African runaways were listed with greater speech difficulties because native-born and African-born slaves were almost equally categorized by their owners as speaking well, poorly, or with an accent. The great expanse of the Brazilian Empire encompassed many regional accents and vernaculars, and the "rough" speech of a native-born Bahian might not have sounded any worse or better than an African accent. Slaves had particular accents that owners assumed newspaper readers would be familiar with, such as the Angolan accent or the speech of slaves from Matto Grosso. One slave, Emilio, spoke Portuguese so well that "he almost doesn't seem to be black."[48] Two African slaves spoke Portuguese well enough that the owner warned that they might be mistaken as native-born slaves. These were "ladino" slaves, a term used for acculturated Africans and occasionally paired with speaking ability.[49] Beyond vocabulary and language construction, some slaves spoke softly, "in a pleasing manner," or "roughly" or were characterized as stammering.

One in six slaves was noted as partly or fully literate in these notices, a remarkably high number. Historians can only guess at the literacy rates of Brazilian slaves, but the rate among the Paulista runaways studied seems to have been considerably higher than among the general population of slaves. A range of literacy level was apparent. Emilio, the slave who spoke Portuguese "as if he doesn't seem to be black" also knew some of the letters of the alphabet; Vicente, who disappeared in 1861, not only could read and write, but could help conduct mass; and although Paulino could read and write Portuguese only "poorly," he escaped carrying papers and a lesson book (*cartilha*).[50]

Slaves carried a range of other items, possessions that provide a clue to their backgrounds. Many escaped with mules or horses and the accoutrements they needed for long rides. Some carried bags or purses with weapons hidden inside. Ignacio carried a sharp knife with a bone handle inside his red goatskin bag. Two other slaves had firearms: Valeriano was armed with a Laporte Pistol while Simião tied a bundle of his clothing to the end of his rifle and slung it over his shoulder. One slave escaped with a manumission letter that had been written for a slave belonging to his master's father, while two slaves carried money or items of value. Francisco brought 600 *mil-réis* in cash, possibly his manumission savings (*peculio*). One can better imagine this hierarchical society after reading that Luis carried a new umbrella and a "fine English watch" when he made his escape.[51]

Clothing also demonstrated the range of changing styles and the ways that some slaves used their appearance to mark their positions of rank and status. Luis, the slave with the umbrella and English watch, also wore a richly colored felt hat and slightly used kerseymere pants. These were unusually fine trappings for a slave. Most other slaves wore only the few items of clothing they were given or had to buy on their plantation. This might include a pair of rough, homespun cotton pants and a thin white shirt. Two slaves were noted as having large numbers stamped onto their shirts, probably to help owners identify them in the fields. Runaways usually carried more than one change of clothing, a blanket, and a jacket or coat of some kind.[52] In some advertisements masters warned that their runaways might try to trade their extra clothing for other pants and shirts that would better conceal their identity. Fugitives faced many days in the rain, especially during the winter months in São Paulo, and they brought clothing that would protect them. Ponchos were more commonly listed during the 1850s, but they were largely replaced by overcoats by the 1860s. Clothing was fairly standard among the runaways, but slaves may have distinguished themselves and their personalities with their hats. There were a surprising variety of hats described made from a wide range of materials, including straw hats, large brimmed caps with hare-tail tassels, and "chile" hats.[53]

The clothing and possessions that slaves carried indicate that they often prepared for long journeys. If in fact they were heading to Santos, the number of kilometers that they had to travel could have been considerable. In Figure 6.2, the former homes of the runaways were placed on a regional map. Slaves escaped from farms that spread along a northwest-southeast axis that reflected the inward growth of the coffee business. The farthest town, Piraçununga, was 245 kilometers away in a straight line, but double that distance over roads. If we consider these notices to be evidence of a communication network between planters and traders, the region that it covered was larger than the network region of the buyers and sellers in the bills of sale.

I found no instance of an owner assuming that runaways had escaped by boat along the coast. For example, no owners who lived in neighboring coastal towns, even the most proximate towns such as Itanhaem or São Sebastião, had posted a runaway advertisement in a Santos newspaper. The small and medium-sized sailboats that daily took

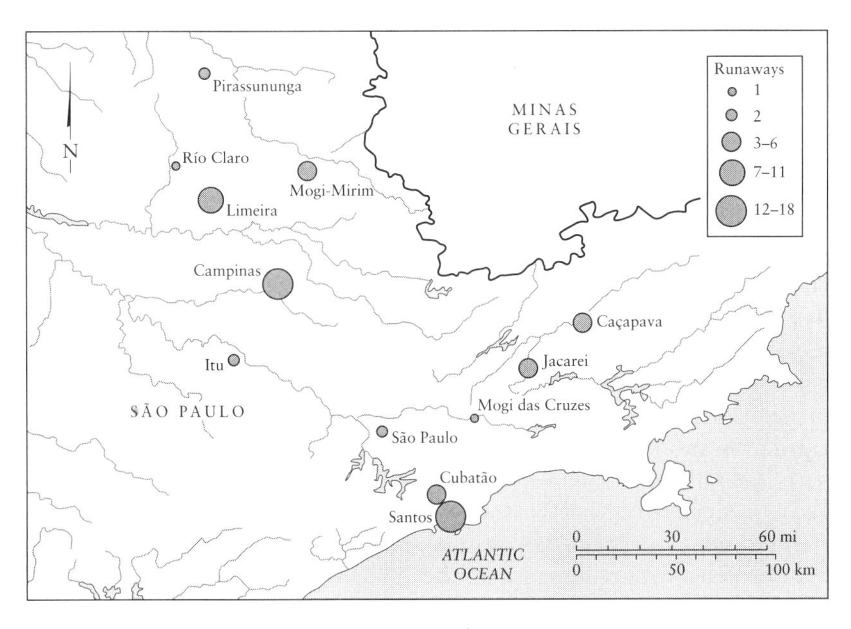

FIGURE 6.2

Number and Former Homes of Slave Runaways, 1851–1872

SOURCE: *Revista do Commercio* (Santos), 1849–1867, *Diario de Santos*, 1872–1873, FAMS, HS.

passengers to Rio de Janeiro or down to Porto Alegre probably had strict requirements for passports and papers, especially for individuals of color and with accents. Yet there was a busy network of canoes that departed Santos and traveled to neighboring communities, and the men who paddled these boats in order to sell their *aguardente* or manioc flour (many who were slaves themselves) would probably have been less inquisitive about the identity or history of passenger who were willing to pay a little more than the normal cost of passage. Moreover, several slaves escaped while aboard ships within the Santos harbor and some runaways who had been on plantations in the interior were described as having sailing skills. Why owners did not believe their slaves capable of following the same maritime routes they traveled upon arriving in Santos remains a puzzle.

This chapter has examined slaves who sought freedom from their forced and belittling servitude. These were men and women who followed different pathways to freedom: manumission (with or without conditions) and flight. The hunger for freedom may have been shared by all of these people, but the groups in these two categories were considerably different. Certain slaves had more or fewer chances either to receive a free or conditional letter or to compel an owner to "sell themselves to themselves" (via *coartação* or onerous manumissions).

In keeping with this book's principal idea that slaves were "unequally bound," I believe that manumission and flight demonstrate the ways that different groups of slaves found opportunities depending on the position of their owners. For example, as a wealthy and powerful owner, José Teixeira da Silva Braga owned slaves not commonly owned by owners with less means. This included two skilled coopers, Jacintho and Francisco, and Amelia, a woman who was being trained to run the staff and domestic chores of an elite household. Other owners could not afford either to buy a slave with guildcraft knowledge or to put them into the long training for such skills. But it was enslaved men such as these coopers who were most likely to sell their labor as fugitives in this part of Brazil. In addition, Braga felt sufficiently confident in his family's finances to grant a condition-free letter to Camelia, the enslaved toddler and daughter of Benedita. Other, poorer families would have hesitated with such a decision since Camelia's price would substantially rise as she grew, providing wealth for Braga's heirs. Yet, as we have seen, it appears that the wealthier the owner, the less likely he or she would manumit. While owners faced different options depending on their resources and positions, slaves also faced different options for attaining freedom, depending on their price, the amount they earned, or whether their owners were inclined to write conditional manumission letters.

Camelia's manumission did not occur at baptism, but as we have seen, baptismal manumission was an important part of the freedom-granting and earning process. Besides including baptism records, this chapter has also taken another unorthodox approach by discussing manumission and runaways side by side. Again, we find pressing inequalities within slavery, since only certain groups were in a position to gain partial or full freedom through manumission or to take the illegal and dangerous path to freedom through flight. Furthermore, a slave who was in a more likely position for one of these avenues of freedom was less likely to take steps that would have jeopardized that position. The men and women who attempted flight in São Paulo, for example, may have thought twice if they had not had to pay such a high price for a manumission letter. Therefore, in considering the hopes—dashed or fulfilled—for escaping bondage, I return to the theme of this book: at the edges of what the law defined as enslavement, there were hierarchies that made action toward freedom possible for some but impossible for others.

Historians have explored the system of manumission as one that sometimes gave slaves opportunities to act in strategic ways to pursue legal freedom. Manumissions were either freely given, or carried a costly burden in expected payments, or demanded servitude for long stretches of time, and the type depended on both the price of the slave and the actions he or she took. This included earning favor over many years to increase chances of the bestowal of the gift of freedom for themselves or their children, earning enough money to buy freedom, or forming a connection with a patron who might facilitate a manumission letter. As important as strategy was for slaves, it may have been equally important for owners. More research is needed, but future scholars who compare the costs and benefits of renting, buying, or manumitting a slave may discover that manumission letters, in certain situations, were the most lucrative and least risky option of these three. Up to this point, we may not have sufficiently considered the manumission process as one driven by economic motives. Nor has the idea of manumission letters as labor contracts been emphasized, even though the procedures for legitimating and recording manumissions were similar to other legal contracts. We see evidence of this in the fact that the market prices of slaves appear to have had a strong effect on rates of manumission, especially when baptism records are included. Furthermore, it seems doubtful that small-scale and less wealthy owners manumitted more than the richest Santistas because they were kinder or more humanitarian. Rather, it may have been the case that these groups of owners were more likely to find themselves in situations in which a cash payment was quickly needed to cover a short-term debt obligation. Of course, this applies only to the paid manumission letters, including those connected to indentured service contracts that were found separately in the notary office of Santos. Many others were granted without barriers or costs, but even these may have carried the price of expected loyalty and continued patronage, for better or for worse.[54]

The risks to runaways were high as they faced dangers on the road and the likelihood of severe punishment if they were captured. The few possessions slaves carried with them on their journeys and the type of clothing they wore indicate that many slaves had prepared for the trip. Preparation was simplified for those with jobs that required long periods of outdoor activities or travel. Nonetheless, these were not journeys that most slaves were willing or able to undertake. The runaways that did take the risk tended to be physically strong and of an age to have sufficient knowledge of the world to survive. Like Jacintho and Francisco, they typically had skills that could transfer to a fugitive life, they were often rudimentarily educated, and they carried items that would be useful on their journey.

Santos had long attracted runaways from the highlands because its coastal geography and climate ensured thick forests and swamps, which were highly suitable locations for maroon communities. The port also offered jobs to some runaways who forged manumission letters or convinced employers that they had been born free. In the early to mid-1880s, the numbers of runaways to the township increased enormously. As explored in the next chapter, slavery remained hierarchical and with limited opportunities for particular slaves, even in the final moments of slavery.

CHAPTER SEVEN

"Manumissionists," Abolitionists, and Emancipation

In 1850, nearly two out of every five residents in Santos was enslaved, a proportion that was higher than in the province of São Paulo and most of the wider southeastern region. By 1880, the demographic picture had changed to such a degree that Santos was exceptional in how few slave owners remained in the township. In fact, in 1886, two years before slavery was abolished nationally, the township officially declared itself a "free territory."[1] Thus, in less than two decades, the township government went from a firm commitment to slavery to vehement opposition. By exploring how Santistas "switched sides" so radically and quickly, we can touch on a broader question about the kinds of people who fought for and against abolition in Brazil. With backgrounds come motives. Additionally, within this political and biographical story of Brazilian abolition is found additional evidence that even in slavery's final moments, many of the significant life opportunities that slaves faced depended on the position of their owners.[2]

Despite the "free territory" declaration and imminent proclamation of national emancipation, a quick end to slavery was far from assured in 1886. A conservative victory in the Brazilian House of Deputies assuaged some slaveholders who had worriedly watched slave and coffee prices fall several years in a row.[3] Both the conservatives and the liberals openly supported emancipation, but the conservatives fought angry battles with their adversaries to delay the final destruction of the legal edifice that supported bondage. Conservatives controlled the Imperial government, but the liberal party maintained or recovered power in many provincial and municipal governments, including the Santos Town Council. Among some of these liberals, some were especially determined to be at the vanguard of abolitionism by supporting civil disobedience.

With the aid of local activists, the township became the endpoint of a major provincial underground railroad. A "railroad," with its spokes and hubs, may not be the best metaphor, although slaves were certainly conveyed in groups from refuge to refuge. The routes of slaves' escape better resembled an expansive river basin with slender streams reaching hundreds of miles deep into the plantations and small farms of the Paulista highlands, becoming thicker in the larger cities near the escarpment, and converging into a fast-flowing river of fugitives into Santos Township. Abolitionists coordinated over long distances in order to maintain such an expansive network. In fact, Santista abolitionists anticipated groups of hungry and exhausted fugitives arriving from the deep Paulista interior and the slave catchers who sometimes pursued them. When men such as Quintino de Lacerda received arrival notices disguised as merchandise export inventories, they would ride out into the mountains at night to intercept, guide, and protect groups of incoming fugitives.[4]

With or without help from abolitionists, thousands of slaves took the risky journey to Santos. In fact, Jabaquara held as many as ten thousand runaway slaves by 1888.[5] Even if this number is exaggerated, it still appears to have been the largest *quilombo* in Brazilian history, larger than the "Republic" of Palmares (albeit far more ephemeral). The actions that men and women took in Santos to make what some called the "slaves' Canaan" reverberated far beyond the borders of this coastal township.[6] We must also keep in mind, however, that many of the merchants and moneymakers in Santos may have turned a blind eye to the growing runaway population because of the town's strong need for labor and concerns that the economic boom would come to an end. The underlying motivator for harboring refugees was the humanitarian idea of disabling or destabilizing slavery, but many businessmen also saw opportunities for profit.

Considering the deeply entrenched nature of the institution of slavery in Santos during the 1880s, the township has been rightfully grouped with Ceará and Amazonas, two northern provinces where a flourishing abolition movement also led many to question slavery's durability.[7] While Santos was far smaller and its township politicians less powerful than the men running these provincial governments, it had a more strategic location barely a hundred miles from the large agricultural region in Brazil where enslaved men and women remained an integral part of the labor force.

THE ABOLITIONIST MOVEMENT IN SANTOS

Many Santistas today proudly believe that the abolitionist movement began in their city earlier and more profoundly than in other parts of Brazil.[8] The town's most famous native son, José Bonifácio de Andrada e Silva, was Brazil's first minister of the interior and of foreign affairs. Other members of the Andrada family became notable figures in nineteenth-century Brazilian politics, but Bonifácio particularly stands out for his role in shaping Brazil's first independent government. He also famously denounced slavery in a number of speeches and publications around the time of Brazil's independence, and in the 1820s he freed the slaves that worked on his "Outeririnhos" estate in Santos.[9] Interestingly, Bonifácio's critiques of slavery were mostly published abroad and were all but unknown in Brazil until 1880, when his actions and figure were enlisted in the cause of abolitionism.[10] Bonifácio worried that slavery impeded efforts to unify the new nation and caused moral corruption among whites, but he also criticized the brutality that slaves endured, especially while transported.[11] Today Santos pays homage to Bonifácio and the Andrada family; his antislavery attitudes have played into a durable myth that Santos was less dedicated to slavery in the nineteenth century than other parts of Brazil.

Another famous Brazilian, connected to Santos through a prominent contracting business, was Senator Nicolau Pereira de Campos Vergueiro. Vergueiro is credited today as an early opponent to slavery because he created Brazil's first society promoting European colonization and free labor.[12] Vergueiro and his sons, however, were among the biggest slave traders in town and capitalized on labor of diverse types.[13] While Nicolau Vergueiro's involvement in slavery was no secret in town, some believed nonetheless that the senator was leading Brazil on the right path. In 1855, for example, the *Revista Commercial* of Santos praised the arrival of fifty-five Portuguese colonists at the Santos harbor. The colonists were on their way to one of Vergueiro's farms and their ship passage had been paid by the Brazilian government in a program that Vergueiro had spearheaded. The newspaper wrote that "the example that Senator Vergueiro is setting will soon become a great part of our *fazendeiros*. . . . We sincerely wish that this illustrious gentleman will continue his important enterprise and the immense service he is doing for the province, introducing European colonists; for we have profound faith that this is the truest and most lethal blow given to the deep-rooted vice of the barbarous slave trade."[14]

While critics of slavery had lived alongside slave traders in Santos for decades, the town's first abolitionist societies were not founded until 1870, soon after the end of the war with Paraguay.[15] These early groups might be better called "manumission societies," since their main function was to collect money for manumission. I have found no evidence—although it may exist—that any group openly advocated the complete end of slavery in Brazil at this time.[16] The first group was organized by a number of the town's powerful matriarchs and was called "A Emancipadora" (The Emancipator). The society's founder, Ana Benvinda Bueno de Andrada had years before married José Bonifácio's great nephew.[17] The Emancipators concentrated on providing refuge to young female runaway slaves. They sheltered these women of color behind their houses, "turning their backyards and gardens into veritable *quilombos*."[18] Most likely, they purchased or forged manumission letters for these girls and placed them in neighboring houses as domestic servants. As the newspaper advertisements reveal, demand for female servants was strong and many who posted advertisements either preferred free labor or did not discriminate. The society received financial support through a monthly membership fee and counted men among their dues-paying members. The second society, Sociedade Dramática Particular Libertadora ("Private Liberation Drama Society) was a group of actors who performed in the town's single small theater and also collected money for a manumission fund. Their ambitions were fairly limited—in its first year, society members purchased manumission letters for four enslaved girls.

Francisco Xavier da Silveira, a Santos resident, was one of the first Brazilians to urge slaves to flee from plantations in a series of fiery speeches delivered before Paulista crowds. His family was from São Paulo and he appeared to have connections that allowed him to move between the coast and the *planalto*. Silveira died of natural causes in 1874, but the campaign he founded paralleled a similar endeavor by the famous São Paulo abolitionist and former slave, Luiz Gama, whom Silveira had known.[19] In fact, Gama is reputed to have said that "while Xavier da Silveira lived, a light came from Santos, because he was the flag bearer of Abolition in the Province of São Paulo and all of us listened for his word of command."[20] Residents of Santos carried on Silveira's campaign and collaborated with antislavery advocates in São Paulo and other parts of the province. Through the 1870s, this group and its networks grew in political strength, took even greater control of the local newspapers, and continued efforts to undermine slavery in the province by providing assistance to runaways. By the early 1880s they were joined by a new and more militant generation that helped create and expand several large *quilombos* on the outskirts of town. In 1882, for example, the *quilombo* of Jabaquara was estimated to hold five hundred runaway slaves and to be growing quickly. There were also fugitives in Vila Mathias, Pai Felipe, and on the neighboring island of Guarujá.[21]

The abolition movement continued to gather momentum, attract new members, and make consequential declarations. In 1882, members of the Bohêmia Abolicionista (Bohemian Abolitionist), founded by mostly local youth, were distributing stacks of pamphlets and newspapers they printed in a press on Santa Catarina Street. Included in their handouts were

"O embrião" (The Embryo), "O porvir" (The Future), and "O alvor" (The Dawn). In one of the most important achievements of the movement, a number of abolitionists, drawn mostly from the older generation, were elected to the township council. Brazil still had two years before national emancipation, but the newly elected township council of 1886 mustered enough support to declare Santos "free of slavery."[22] In this measure, Santos joined a handful of towns in the southern province of Rio Grande do Sul and the northern provinces of Ceará and Amazonas with antislavery proclamations.[23] There is no evidence that the declarations in any of these places were legally binding. For example, the legal framework for town governance rested on the *Codigo de posturas* (municipal statute), a set of laws that needed approval by the provincial assembly. Furthermore, slaves' legal status as property remained unchanged in 1886 and protected by the Brazilian constitution, regardless of any abolition declarations made below the imperial level.

The Santos declaration may not have been legally binding, but it did have symbolic importance. The liberal township council intended to convey the message that township officials would not cooperate with planters in the *planalto* who sought their runaways. Whether this message was received or not is hard to tell. The São Paulo Chamber of Deputies made no official mention of the declaration.[24] Furthermore, people remained enslaved within Santos afterwards. One abolitionist lawyer drew up lists of the remaining slaveholders and their slaves in 1887 and again in early 1888. Santos may have been "free of slavery" in name, but there were still about a hundred slaveholders, principally in the outlying regions of town.[25] Technically, any slave owner who brought his or her slaves into Santos remained their rightful master under law, but they probably would not have been able to count on the town police if their slaves fled.[26] As Maria Helena Machado found in correspondence between police in Santos and the provincial capital, security forces in the township were unwilling and unable to enforce slavery laws on several occasions in 1886.[27] Paradoxically, despite the hands-off attitude of local authorities, slaves were still counted among the city's residents in 1887 and 1888. These men and women had to have been aware of local events, yet they may have remained with owners out of dependence, inertia, or preference.

Soon after the Santos township council acted, several city residents formed a new abolitionist club called "Sociedade de 27 de Fevereiro" (27th of February Society), based on the date of the "free territory" declaration in Santos. Its members dedicated themselves to civil disobedience, often by partnering with the *caifazes*, a loosely organized group of men and women who worked in the agricultural areas in the *planalto* to attract and assist fugitive slaves, often against the law.[28] The 27th of February Society was similar to hundreds of abolitionist groups that appeared throughout Brazil. These clubs usually counted on the strong participation of women who helped put on extravagant public ceremonies that included skits, music, speakers, and a display of several former slaves who had recently been granted their freedom. For example, during the nearly four-hour initiation ceremony held in the town's main theater, the 27th of February Society presented its audience with a large throne placed center stage, covered with bright petals and green leaves. Perched on top, among the foliage, was a young girl who recited a poem on the theme of her character as "Liberty." Next to the throne, several other young girls stood as mock guards of the "freedom goddess." If similar to other abolitionist performances, the performing girls were probably of color, adding an element of race to the play's symbolism. The effect of the recitation was "profound and true," according to the broadsheet *Diario de Santos*. Rituals such as these were more than entertainment or frivolity; they drew connections between the political struggle and a moral story, thereby denying the standing legal order of legitimacy.[29]

By 1887, in part due to the help of abolitionists involved in clubs like the 27th of February, numerous enslaved men, women, and children made the difficult passage down to Santos, at times violently clashing with landowners and police.[30] Slaves also pushed the courts to gain freedom, making full use of the Rio Branco law, which often granted them the right to use even small amounts of savings to gain manumission. For the small group of African-born slaves who were still alive, some gained their freedom by successfully arguing that because they had been brought into Brazil after the official prohibition against African slave importations in 1831, they had been illegally enslaved.[31] Many such liberty suits succeeded, but there is also evidence that owners remained quite capable of defending their interests and preventing freedom.[32] Additionally, some slaves, as we will see, were freed through a government-funded program.

By February 1888, the *quilombo* of Jabaquara had expanded even further and was estimated to have thousands of fugitive slaves. Their fugitive status was soon to end because a month later, on May 13, 1888, Princess Isabel signed the "Golden Law," ending legal slavery within Brazil. The month that followed was a festive one for Brazilians across the Empire, with celebrations, ceremonies, and dedications of monuments to mark the law. During one of the largest celebrations in Santos, on May 31 a group of former slaves living in Jabaquara was invited to perform a few of their "original dances" in front of the large crowds. The *Diario de Santos* described these performances as giving "*brilho*" (splendor) to the ceremonies. This marks an important move away from the position, only four decades before, when police were by law ordered to arrest Afro-

Brazilians doing similar dances and to give twenty-five lashes from a whip to each dancer and musician involved.[33] Although the dances celebrating the emancipation proclamation were anticipated and controlled, their performance demonstrates a new acceptance and, perhaps, a changing national identity that appropriated Afro-Brazilian cultural traditions.

The emancipation of slaves in Brazil did not end strong ties of dependency between slaves and their former masters, however, and opportunities for people of color remained terribly limited. The fugitives of Jabaquara appear to have been fairly quickly displaced by "sanitary reforms," developmental projects, and new arrivals to such a degree that by the twentieth century the community had few memories or connections to its roots as a *quilombo*.[34] There were still enough former slaves to be organized in 1891 by their longtime defender and leader (and former slave) Quintino de Lacerda. That year, port workers, most of whom were Spanish and Portuguese immigrants with affiliations to anarchist, socialist, and syndicalist groups, had begun what would become one of Brazil's most significant labor movements. The port company colluded with Quintino de Lacerda to bring former male slaves of the Jabaquara community onto the ships and docks. It appears that this group took their jobs as strikebreakers willingly.[35]

THE ABOLITIONISTS' SLAVES

Historians have explored the backgrounds of abolitionists under the standard assumption that their motives were shaped by background, race, class, and occupation.[36] Some of the first who explored this topic targeted the urban middle classes as a primary catalyst for Brazilian abolitionism of the 1870s and 1880s. According to Emília Viotti da Costa and Richard Graham, this group and their ideas emerged in the middle of the wealth-holding spectrum and from a new set of economic and social conditions. The seedbed for the movement was the town and city environments in which industrialists constructed new factories, cable cars ferried passengers through busy streets, and harbors became so crowded that steamships could not find empty piers to unload crowds of anxious European immigrants. In the port cities, stevedores unloaded a growing range of products onto waiting railroad cars and loaded countless bags of coffee, sugar, and cotton destined for ports around the world. For da Costa, abolitionists came from these conditions and were drawn from the ranks of professors, lawyers, journalists, doctors, small-business owners, immigrants, students, artisans, and freed people of color. Richard Graham, in contrast, believed that military officers, engineers, and industrialists chiefly participated in the movement. Despite identifying different groups, both scholars argued that abolitionism was the ideological product of a shift away from the old agricultural and predominantly rural social and political order.[37] The men and women of these groups came from the progressive urban environment within the many growing Brazilian cities where citizens were envisioning a new liberal and republican order.

Some have questioned whether the occupations of abolitionists differed widely from those of the final slaveholders. For example, Robert Conrad argued that Graham put too much weight on the involvement of industrialists. "Although merchants and the owners of industries stood to profit from an end to slavery, as an interest group they did not back the movement" because, as Conrad saw it, they were too closely allied with landowners and slaveholders. For Conrad, abolitionists were a heterogeneous group with "representatives of every class and profession" including "slaves and the owners of slaves" as well as "laborers and landlords, actors, musicians and entertainers, capitalists and railroad workers, merchants, lawyers, teachers, soldiers and students." Similarly, Seymour Drescher argued that the most active participants of the Brazilian abolitionist movement were "the free masses," but not necessarily those in cities. Zephyr Frank has also expressed doubts about connections that are automatically drawn between urban middle groups and abolitionists because the evidence of these ties is "rarely made explicit."[38]

There is still much to be learned about the group that wished for an immediate end to a system and culture of oppression rooted in centuries of Brazilian, Portuguese, and Roman law. The evidence already gathered gives us a good place to start. Da Costa looked at the participants of an important Carioca abolitionist group, "Confederação Abolicionista" (Abolitionist Confederation), while Richard Graham cited bibliographies of André Rebouças, Luiz Tarquino, and the Visconde de Mauá. Robert Conrad examined one election and its voters in Rio de Janeiro, pulling this important case from Joaquim Nabuco's autobiography. As Conrad recounted the story, Nabuco ran on an abolitionist ticket in 1881 but suffered a large defeat. The voters who cast ballots against Nabuco included public employees, merchants, commercial employees, or those with liberal professions; groups typically included in urban "middle classes." This contrasts with research by Rebecca Bergstresser, who uncovered the occupational background of 255 abolitionists active in the Imperial capital during the 1880s. Among these, she found public employees, lawyers, shopkeepers, soldiers and officers, engineers, journalists, and students. Priests and large-scale merchants were, however, underrepresented among Rio's strongest opponents to slavery.[39] While these studies are important for stimulating questions and providing some starting points, there appears to be no strong support for any single hypothesis.

We can turn to the lists of abolitionists and slaveholders in Santos to draw more connections between backgrounds and ideology. Local historians have listed the names and described the personalities of participants of three abolitionist clubs—A Emancipadora, Bohêmia Abolicionista, and Sociedade de 27 de Fevereiro—published in commemorations and chronologies of the movement. In addition, several abolitionists recorded the names of the remaining slave owners and their slaves between 1886 and 1888 and published the lists in the *Diario de Santos*, one of the town's dailies and a mouthpiece for their cause. Some slaveholders were included in reports to the provincial government. Publicizing these men and women, these groups believed, might cause them indignity and pressure them to release their slaves from legal bondage. Since many of the abolitionist leaders and the final slaveholders are found in multiple sources, I have collected this biographical information to discover the profile of "typical" Brazilian abolitionists and final slaveholders.

Looking over the two decades of struggle against slavery in Santos, there were two generations of abolitionists. The older "initiators" were active in the 1870s, while a "youthful force" supplanted them in the 1880s.[40] Both groups had a great deal of occupational diversity, but the first group contained a more notable presence of wealthy slaveholding townspeople. This included Francisco Martins dos Santos, who lent his *chácara* (country home) for abolitionist gatherings, and who was considered the successor to Francisco Xavier da Silveira as the "head of intellectualism in Santos."[41] He was in charge of the port customs house and a property owner. Another wealthy man and abolitionist, João Octavio dos Santos, was a liberal politician and well-to-do businessman who operated a general commissioning business, an *armazen* for groceries, and a storage building for salt.[42] Octavio dos Santos was also reputed to be one of the principal financiers of the local movement. Similar to other abolitionists, both men owned slaves. Francisco dos Martins Santos's slave, named Manoel, was buried in the cemetery in 1881.[43] João Octavio dos Santos owned as many as twenty slaves during the 1870s, several of whom entered the hospital or jail or were buried in the cemetery.

The second, younger generation of Santos abolitionists came from all kinds of backgrounds, but few were as wealthy or prominent as Francisco Martins dos Santos or João Octavio dos Santos. In a historical account printed in 1937, seventy men were listed as part of the leadership of the "second wave" of the antislavery movement in Santos.[44] Of the ten abolitionists of this group whose birthplaces I found in other documents, only two were Portuguese. These abolitionists worked as journalists, career politicians and judges, small businessmen, teachers, doctors, and pharmacists. Seven were either involved with publishing or wrote for newspapers, fourteen were public officials, twelve ran businesses, five taught classes or directed schools, and three were caretakers or janitors (*zeladores*). Large commission-house owners, army officers, and church officials were noticeably underrepresented. We find some surprises in this list. For example, Scipião Ferreira Goulart Junqueira, who dominated the slave trade in the 1860s, was involved in an abolitionist club called Sociedade Emancipadora, maybe as director. Six abolitionists had been slaveholders in the 1870s, and four of these were slaveholders in the 1880s. In fact, Teófilo de Arruda Mendes, whose pharmacy was a gathering point for abolitionists, was on the abolitionists' "blacklist" of final slaveholders in Santos. The slave of the pharmacist, Rafael, was born only a few months before the Rio Branco Law was enacted. At age sixteen in 1886, the abolitionist's slave may not have known any other slaves younger than himself.[45]

The slaveholders in Santos during the last fifteen years of slavery differed less from the abolitionists than one might expect. During the 1870s three of the largest slaveholders were women (two of whom may have been sisters) who together sent more than 150 slaves to the hospital, jail, or cemetery.[46] Two important male slaveholders of that decade, Henrique Porchat and Henrique Ablas, owned tan yards and lime factories.[47] Four big slaveholders were coffee and cotton merchants, another operated a cigar factory. Two companies, Salles Oliveira & Companhia and Souza Queiroz & Vergueiro, held many slaves toward the end. These companies probably rented out their slaves or had them working in their *armazens*, loading or unloading ships. By the 1880s, the slaves of many of the big slaveholders of the previous decade, including those owned by Henrique Porchat, Henrique Ablas, and their two companies, no longer appeared in the registers of the hospital or cemetery. These men and organizations may have freed or sold their slaves, but a number of slaves still were found in town. The final slaveholders worked in a variety of occupations that included three army officers, three coffee merchants, two liquor distillery owners, two shopkeepers, a potter, a councilman, a music professor, a pharmacist, and a tailor.[48] Men were overrepresented in this group and, compared to the abolitionists, relatively more had birthplaces outside of Santos. Some of the last masters and mistresses in Santos may have been city outsiders since fewer overall were found in the marriage records.

There were 136 slaves hospitalized or buried between 1886 and 1888. This set of the last remaining slaves in Santos had a relatively high male-female sex ratio. Compared to the colored population, there were more *pretos* than *pardos*, while the color/race for a little more than half of these slaves is unknown. Most of the final enslaved men and women worked as a house or personal servant or as a field slave; only three slaves (excluding the six cooks) worked within the skilled creative trades (see Table 7.1). These final slaves may have excluded a number of slaves who were general workers or wagon drivers, since slaves with these occupations entered the hospital or were buried in the cemetery in relatively much higher numbers during the early 1880s. For example, out of the 123 slaves who entered the hospital between 1880 and 1883, 61 were general workers or day laborers (*jornaleiros*).[49] In the final years, enslaved domestic servants, especially those owned by wealthier Santos residents, were more likely to receive hospital care. "General work," however, was the most commonly listed occupation among the 201 slaves buried in the more "inclusive" cemetery between 1880 and 1886.[50] Presumably, slaves treated both privately and charitably ended up in the city cemetery if they did not recover.

In the final two years of slavery in Santos, slaveholders and abolitionists were found among people of a wide range of occupations. In this respect, the profile of these two groups of people supports Robert Conrad's argument that the abolitionists in Brazil were "representatives of every class and profession."[51] While the majority of abolitionists were not found in the records of slaveholders, many of them came from families that had long owned slaves. When this group is compared to the final slaveholders, abolitionists had more familial roots in town and fewer seem to have been Portuguese or European. In contrast, some of the last slaveholders were European, including one Italian and one Swiss man.

TABLE 7.1
Occupations of Santos's Last Slaves, 1886–1888

Occupation	Frequency
Domestic servant (*domestico*)	17
Field worker	10
Servent (*servente*)	10
Cook	6
Chambermaid (*Mucama*)	3
Carpenter	2
Washerwoman	2
Tailor	1
Waiter or butler	1
General worker (*trabalhador*)	1
Unknown	83

SOURCES: Cemetery registers, 1880–1883, FAMS; hospital patient registers, 1880–1886, ASCMS.

These slaveholders also included several prominent businessmen and commercial associations that were largely absent in the second generation of abolitionists. The slaveholding group was far less organized and rarely vocal in support of slavery, but it appears that they were wealthier on average and more connected to the coffee trade.

These descriptions show that the final slaveholders and abolitionists were more alike than different. In some cases, ideological positions also overlapped. Andre Rosemburg discusses a fascinating case in which a prominent Santos abolitionist, Joaquim Xavier Pinheiro, brought a lawsuit against another township resident for harboring his runaway slave. Pinheiro is believed to have been one of the first to have assisted in transforming a forested farm on the outskirts of town into what would become the *quilombo* of Jabaquara in the early 1880s. Pinheiro showed similar concern when he publically accused a man of forcing his former slave to serve as an indentured servant.[52] Unpaid labor contracts were legal, as discussed in the last chapter, but they had to be officially witnessed, usually in the form of notarized manumission letters. In this case, however, no such step appeared to have been taken. When it came to his own slaves, Pinheiro acted differently. In 1883, he learned that his slave, Matheus, had run away to a farm on the banks of the River Curumaú, located in the thick forests and swamps beyond the city. Pinheiro filed a lawsuit against the farm's owner, a Portuguese man named Manuel Alves Ferreira, charging him with slave stealing. Pinheiro persuaded the judge, and Ferreira was put in jail. Soon after, however, Ferreira filed a successful appeal, based on irregularities in the trial and uncertainties over the identity and age of Matheus. The defendant argued that Matheus had the right to work on his farm because he was an African illegally imported after 1831. Pinheiro's actions toward the *quilombo*, the indentured servant, and his own runaway slave seem contradictory, but the abolitionist may have found no contradiction in his loyalty to the constitutionality of "property protections" when it came to his own slaves.

THE EMANCIPATION FUND: FREEDOM FOR A SELECT FEW

In the final two decades of slavery in Brazil the number of slaves continued to fall. Officially, no one entered slavery, since importation had ended in 1850 and children born to slaves were conditionally freed according to the Rio Branco Law of 1871. V.D. Laerne estimated that in 1882 there were 194,000 fewer slaves compared to 1873. Of these, 55 percent were slaves who died, 29 percent had received privately funded or granted manumission letters, 9 percent had successfully sued to gain their freedom, and 7 percent had been freed through the government-run Emancipation Fund.[53] Since the rate of slaves freed under the fund doubled after 1883, the proportion of slaves given freedom during the full period of the program's existence probably exceeded 10 percent.[54] The Emancipation Fund was a significant part of the Rio Branco law but is less well known than the set of articles in this law that freed newborn children of enslaved mothers. The legislation mandated that money collected from provincial taxes on slaves, lottery sales, and fines would be periodically divided among townships in amounts that corresponded with their slave populations. Municipal townships were ordered to form small classification boards that were led by each township's Orphan Judge. Once the money had trickled through the bureaucratic channels, selected slaves would appear before the board and be given a letter granting their freedom.

Historians have not given the Emancipation Fund much attention, largely because it has been viewed as inadequate and ineffective by both contemporaries and historians, although recent scholarship is reconsidering this perspective.[55] We can see the fund's insignificance in the fact that the Rio Branco Law is often called the "Free Womb Law," referring to its freedom-to-newborns clause and ignoring the other half of the legislation that created and regulated the Emancipation Fund. Only a minority of slaves was freed through government funds, but using this fact as a measure of the program's success disregards the fund's potent symbolism. Once established, the Emancipation Fund became a constant reminder to Brazilians of imperial, provincial, and municipal commitments to eventual emancipation that stressed a respect to the constitution's property rights. It also may have inspired many owners to privately grant freedom as part of the larger national cause. Finally, there is evidence that the fund's effectiveness became greatly enhanced in provinces and townships that contributed additional money, increasing the number of slaves freed in those areas.[56]

The Emancipation Fund was viewed in a variety of ways by people who called themselves abolitionists. Some, like Joaquim Nabuco, supported the program because it reduced the ranks of slaves, even if it did so too slowly. Others criticized it as a smokescreen for the government's underlying commitment to protect the institution of slavery.[57] Instead of the complicated and sometimes fraudulent registration that the fund required, the bureaucratically onerous distribution of funds, and the government's shallow monetary contribution, radical abolitionists demanded immediate emancipation.[58] And until that happened, they reasoned, illegal acts and civil disobedience were justified in the moral cause, as practiced in Santos. These different views reflect a movement membership that included people from all ranks of society.

The distribution of Emancipation Funds was weighted in favor of townships with the most slaves and clearly gave preference to freeing slaves with particular demographic profiles. As a result, the manumission fund created by the national government mostly assisted wealthy slave owners and their slaves. This is an important and final substantive point for this book's larger argument. The preference system was built directly into the law. Decree 5135, passed on November 13, 1872, regulated the Rio Branco law. In Article 27, preference for manumission was given to families of slaves before individuals. The definition of "families," however, was limited to slaves married in the Catholic Church and mothers with enslaved children. Many more slaves were unquestionably within other kinds of combinations that we would today recognize as families, such as long-lasting partnerships (*amazias*) with children born and raised by one or both partners, but officially unmarried by the church, yet these families were excluded. In addition, the "individuals" category put weight on mothers and fathers who had formerly enslaved children, also a group we would today consider to be a family. We can see the detailed order of preferences that classifications were meant to follow in the text of the article: "In granting freedom of families, there will be a preference for:

I. married slaves held by different owners;

II. married slaves with children freed by law and younger than eight years old;

III. married slaves with formerly enslaved children (*libertos*) that are less than 21 years;

IV. married slaves with enslaved children;

V. mothers with enslaved children;

VI. married slaves without children.

If there were no more slave "families" that fit these categories, then classification boards could move to "individuals" in the following order:

I. mothers or fathers with formerly enslaved children;

II. slaves between 12 and 50 years, beginning first with the youngest women and oldest men within this group."[59]

The provincial government of São Paulo and the Santos township council appear to have been careful that these preferences were implemented. On June 22, 1886, the Baron of Parnahyba, writing from the provincial government palace, sent a reminder to Santos of the freedom preferences contained in article 27. In two short letters returned to the provincial government, in 1885 and 1886, the Santos township council president stated that the classification board would follow these rules when deliberating.[60]

These letters were not disingenuous; mostly special slaves were freed in Santos and elsewhere. In two short lists from 1883 and 1886, four couples and one unmarried slave were given their freedom in Santos through the Emancipation Fund. A disproportionate number of married slaves lived in the Four Corners or the two other wealthy neighborhoods in town (see Chapter Four), where they were held by slave masters with more means than average. We might remember that official church marriages were relatively expensive and difficult for most slaves, thus largely out of reach. Therefore, the owners of the few slaves freed in Santos by the Emancipation Fund were for the most part powerful and wealthy residents. Three of the six owners who received Emancipation Fund money were coffee merchants, while another two were high-ranking army officers. Francisco Martins dos Santos, an early participant of the "first-wave" abolition movement in town, was one owner who received money, while Captain Gregorio Innocencio de Freitas, one of Santos's most connected and active slave traders during the 1860s, was another.[61]

Slaves were encouraged to build a savings for their manumission, and these savings (*peculios*) also appear to have played an important role in the disbursement of Emancipation Funds.[62] As discussed in Chapter Four, slaves of wealthy owners often had multiple skills for earning money. This gave additional advantages to certain slaves in respect to the Rio Branco Law. For example, within each "class" of slaves categorized by Decree 5135, classification boards were ordered to give preference to slaves who could cover part of their manumission expense with their own savings. The order of Article 27 could not be trumped, however, by slaves with manumission savings. In 1881, when the township of Campo Largo in the province of Paraná gave preference to a slave with a manumission savings of ten *mil-réis*, but who was "out of order" according to the law, the Ministry of Agriculture revoked the manumission. The decision was printed as a reminder of the "many government orders (*avisos*) that the manumission savings can only be used to give preference for slaves within the same order and number." The Agriculture Minister, Manoel Buarque de Macedo, argued in a separate but similar decision in 1881 that giving preference to slaves with manumission savings would "stimulate the work and economy and foster the good morals (*morigeração*) of slaves." Indeed, there were penalties for breaking the law. A judge who presided over a municipal classification board in Alagoas was fined two hundred *mil-réis* for "inverting" the numerical order of article 27.[63]

In other parts of Brazil, the municipal boards created to distribute Emancipation Fund money appear to have largely followed the article.

For example, in 1877, the classification board of the Lages District (Termo de Lages), a region in the interior of the province of Santa Catarina, freed nine slaves through Emancipation Fund money. All were married. Additionally, these slaves had spouses owned by different masters. For Recife and Rio de Janeiro, Celso Castilho and Camilia Cowling recently found that women were the "principal targets" of the Emancipation Funds. Nevertheless, the classification boards in the northern province of Pará chose more men than women in 1886.[64] Since we do not yet have separate categories for these three cases (Pernambuco, Rio de Janeiro, and Pará), it is difficult to discern whether or not the law was followed. We might guess that more women would be freed because of the preference for mothers with children, but if a township had more married male slaves than unmarried mothers with children, the men would have by law received Emancipation Funds first.

If the wealthier residents were the largest beneficiaries of the limited amount of government compensation money, then even in its final stages certain slave owners had opportunities that were closed to other owners. This, of course, also held true for the slaves of these owners. In the case of the Rio Branco Law, the Imperial government acknowledged and promoted a hierarchy of slaves in which married slaves with opportunities to earn extra money, many of whom were already in advantageous positions relative to other slaves, were placed first in line for the restricted Emancipation Funds. As observed in the larger manumission system, the institution of slavery was most stratified in its ultimate "reward." Freedom was an opportunity for only a small minority of slaves throughout this period. Furthermore, there is no doubt that this hierarchy of opportunity was known to slaves and affected their view of bondage. In addition to eventual freedom, other opportunities afforded by high-status owners included effective tools for skilled slaves, medical care, special burials, and covering the cost of the jail rather than performing punishment in the home (an "opportunity" for an owner was not always seen as such for a slave).

By the 1870s and 1880s, Santos's abolitionists and final slaveholders mostly shared the same backgrounds. There were abolitionists among many groups within society, and particular occupation groups cannot be given too much credit as creating or leading the abolitionist movement. The changing and modernizing urban milieu may have made slavery appear antithetical to some, but the institution was fully functional within the new forms of technology, jobs, and financial instruments of the growing cities. By the 1880s few were mounting soap boxes to decry the sins of slavery. While it was hardly a popular position for any Brazilian to publically defend slavery, some vehemently argued that its end had to be delayed for the sake of agricultural production, the Brazilian economy, and even the well-being of the slaves. Certain groups such as coffee merchants (many of whom still used slaves as warehouse workers and stevedores), clergy, Santista army officers, and longtime foreign residents appear to have been relatively less inclined to fight for the end of slavery in Brazil, at least in the case of Santos. Nonetheless, men and women of all stripes appeared among the abolitionists.

Some of the abolitionists, especially among those of the first generation, owned slaves. Slaveholders somehow justified the contradiction between their ownership of slaves and their opposition to slavery. None of these men left recorded reasons for why they continued to own slaves while opposing slavery, but they likely saw themselves as benevolent owners. Although slavery seems so barbarous as to be beyond contemporary parallels, there are many today who protest the flaws of the roughest edges of our current social system yet feel obliged to rely on this system daily. There are also many among us who feel forced to compromise admitted ethical positions when facing a perceived economic necessity. Similarly, Joaquim Xavier Pinheiro, one of the "founders" of Jabaquara, was willing to help create a refuge for thousands of slaves owned by others, yet he pursued a lawsuit against a man who he accused of stealing his own slave.

Finally, the Emancipation Fund should be recognized as an important part of Brazil's story of abolition. It freed only a fraction of slaves, yet it served as a reminder that the government intended to dismantle slavery without disrupting the valuable investments that remained in slaves, especially as Brazil depended more and more on coffee exports produced by slaves. Metaphorically, the Emancipation Fund was a way for the government to land a plane with a malfunctioning engine; it was losing altitude but had to be brought down in a way that avoided or minimized injury. Whether the government succeeded is another question, but we do know that the fund largely targeted married slaves who had opportunities or connections to build manumission savings. Slaves married in the eyes of the Catholic Church were a minority and largely in the hands of rich owners such as those living in the Four Corners neighborhood. When slaves learned of the preference system contained in Article 27 of the amended Rio Branco Law in 1872, likely they were not surprised. After all, this was one more of many instances in which the opportunities for big decisions and action existed for certain enslaved men and women only in particular and fleeting situations. Slaves were never without the ability to act or think on their own, of course, but when we consider actions that led to improvements in their lives, the status and treatment of their masters cannot be ignored.

Conclusion

> The series of events that I am about to narrate to you occurred in the year of our Savior 1858.
>
> In that epoch, Santos was a third of its current size and possessed a character wholly different than today. It was a small town, poorly ventilated, muddy and unhealthy.
>
> I offer these opening words of the narrative so the reader comes to know the place as it once was.[1]

In this way, José Maria Lisboa began a historical account of an increasingly busy, but dreadfully unhealthy town. This article appeared in the eighth edition of the *Literary Almanak of the São Paulo Littoral*, published in 1886. Lisboa told the story of a city and township at the cusp of momentous change, which in the twenty-eight years between the year he described and his almanac's appearance had transformed from a backwater port and neglected stretch of coast into one of the Brazilian Empire's busiest and most commercially viable maritime cities. In spite of the progress, much of Lisboa's audience expected grim details. Some believed that only a few of the most intractable Santos residents could be proud of a place so muddy and malarial, that even if one survived the city or swampy countryside, life was wretched. These critics looked at the township from the outside and followed the news of its frenetic rate of development with amazement, amusement, and perhaps a touch of envy. There, in Santos, a thicket of masts towered over some of the world's largest ocean vessels and a wide horizon of uninhabitable marshland.

Lisboa wrote for residents of his own—grander and more "cultured"—city of São Paulo and those in the other coastal towns, including the Imperial capital of Rio de Janeiro. These readers sometimes held less than positive views of Santos and an unshakable image of the coastal inhabitants as "*povo caiçara*," a label often used by those living in the urban areas of the *planalto* that roughly translates as "coastal yokel" but held a different and prouder meaning among the people it targeted. *Caiçaras* wore rough rain ponchos, paddled dugout canoes, cast hand-woven fishing nets, and were an illiterate, marginal, and often mixed-blood people.[2] Lisboa did not use this term precisely, but he tailored his narrative to the unlikely causes and negative consequences of a back-water's sudden development. As he would later explain, neither was the city better off after three decades of progress, nor did Santistas deserve all the credit for the change.

Lisboa described the town's roads and the ways they connected people to one other. He lingered on a number of particular streets and referred to the collective identities held within several neighborhoods that stretched across one or more streets. He did not provide the commercial names of the handful of general stores, artisan workshops, professional offices, stables, and *armazens* that were in business in 1858 because readers would better recognize these places by the families or individuals that ran these businesses and often lived on the floor above. He thus listed the names of several men and women who had lived on corners and byways of the town's small grid of avenues, such as Dona Angelica or Domingos José Rodrigues. Paulistas or Cariocas may not have known these names, but they were accustomed to a description of towns or cities that used people and family residences as landmarks.

Interestingly, Lisboa made an even more glaring omission: he did not say a single word about the thousands of slaves who lived and worked in Santos in the mid-nineteenth century. As we have learned, these slaves participated in nearly every walk of life and served a wide range of masters and mistresses, including those with limited resources, those with enormous wealth and power, and many in between. Indeed, if Santos slaves were to have suddenly vanished in 1858, nearly all of the township's brooms, mops, hoes, wagons, ovens, picks, trowels, saws, and countless other tools would have fallen into immediate disuse.[3] At that time about one out of every three residents was an enslaved man, woman, or child, and many spoke Portuguese with difficulty. When Lisboa picked up his pen in 1886, Brazil was only two years away from emancipation. Abolitionists were making a fuss in nearly every Brazilian political forum. Lisboa certainly knew that Santos was making history as one of the few places in southern Brazil to officially declare itself "free of slavery" and for the well-noted efforts of its residents to illegally harbor hundreds or thousands of slave fugitives. He did not mention this, either.

Prior to emancipation, Santos shifted from a slave society to one with a nominal number of slaves. Before the 1850s the township had one of the highest ratios of slaves to total population in the province of São

Paulo, rivaling regions in the Brazilian Northeast where sugar-plantation slavery had reigned for centuries.[4] Around 1875, the slave population began to decline irrevocably, even with many new slaves entering the township through the inter- and intraprovincial slave trade. By the 1880s, Santos had one of the lowest concentrations of slaves in the province. Why did this transformation—equal to or more remarkable than the town's dramatic increase in size, population, and trade—escape Lisboa's attention? He was quick to talk about the shameful lack of sanitary conditions and callous degradation caused by coffee furor, but apparently the subject of slavery was either unnoteworthy or sufficiently taboo to sweep under the rug.[5]

Before it was abolished from township life and the Brazilian Empire, slavery reflected, contributed to, and fit within a hierarchical society. Depending on owner status, slaves had different choices regarding work, family, markets, healthcare, and manumission. In terms of these opportunities, slaves should not be thought to have composed only the lowest tier of society, below the poor, despite the fact that this group was seen as chattel in the eyes of the law. As this book has shown, owner characteristics such as wealth, occupation, status, and residential location can be correlated to slave profiles with sometimes unexpected results. Owners with particular social and economic characteristics meted out different forms of treatment. Similarly, slaves with particular social, economic, or demographic characteristics found that they had different chances to pursue their goals of mitigating the harsh reality of slavery.

The argument that slaves lived in greatly varying conditions and experienced different treatment is found first in the places where slaves lived. In the 1820s and 1830s, the households in the small Santos neighborhood of Four Corners and Dockside owned mostly male *pardos*, while slaves held in the poorer households of the Áurea neighborhood were almost all black women, most who worked as seamstresses. Other neighborhoods concentrated slaves who worked particular jobs. Slave masons and carpenters were more likely to be advertised for sale or rent in one of the peripheral neighborhoods, while the wealthier center neighborhoods advertised "jack-of-all-trades" slaves. Outside of town, some slaves were more fortunate than others to work with tools that were more effective. The wealthier farms, for example, owned presses and ovens that could process far more cassava with less effort, while other, poorer farms had tools that barely worked or were often broken.

Slaves were born into these circumstances or they were purchased into households of distinctive neighborhoods and regions. The market was a gateway into a world of diverse conditions and treatment, but particular demographic characteristics and skills made some slaves attractive to certain buyers. By the 1860s, the slave trade was dominated by two men who appear to have specialized in different types of slaves. Residents looking for a strong, enslaved black man to haul coffee bags turned to Captain Gregorio Innocencio de Freitas, whereas those who were in the market for younger female slaves to wash or cook for their families sought the assistance of the township vicar, Scipião Junqueira. Buyers and sellers often knew these traders socially and thus depended on the existing township networks to facilitate slave trading.

After moving into the household of a new owner slaves found themselves in situations that either permitted or impeded the formation of families and communities. The poorer neighborhoods had high levels of turnover. In fact, between 1817 and 1818, nearly half of the houses of the Áurea neighborhood had been replaced by new tenants and owners. In these conditions, a slave had a difficult time forging ties that were more than ephemeral. They also had a difficult time marrying, probably because of monetary barriers and catechistic obligations that imposed a nearly impossible barrier to this mostly illiterate group. Conversely, slaves who lived in the neighborhood of Four Corners were much more likely to marry. This wealthier neighborhood had greater stability but it did not have the lowest rates of household turnover. The poor to middling cassava-growing regions several hours north of the port were remarkably stable, even though marriage rates were low. Household stability and wealth may have influenced rates of marriage and perhaps lasting unions, but across the township slave women continued to bear children at nearly equal rates despite the enormous heterogeneity of their living conditions, occupations, and background.

As Lisboa noted, the city and township changed considerably over the century, as coffee wealth transformed Santos from a backwater town that was not so different from its colonial form into one of the nation's busiest ports. He did not mention that slaves were put to work in new jobs and frequently sent to one of the growing institutions of city life: jail. Once a slave became accustomed to a new household, he or she sometimes broke the rules. In fact, slaves were about four or five times more likely to be arrested than free residents, but different groups of slaves faced different risks. Young to mid-age slaves were arrested for "disobedience," "disorder," and violent crimes, while older slaves (over thirty) were thrown behind bars often for breaking the nightly curfew or for drinking too much. Physical features even seemed to have had an effect on perceived crimes. Tall and skinny slaves "disobeyed" more than short and stout slaves, but the latter were more likely to be arrested because they "lacked respect."

While whipping and jail time were dismal prospects, slaves faced even worse risks from their environments. Disease took the lives of many slaves, including thousands of babies barely out of their mothers' wombs. The top causes of death, however, varied less between the free and enslaved than among various slave demographic groups. Slaves and free were largely killed by the same illnesses (although tuberculosis took a slightly greater toll on slaves and yellow fever killed many more free). By the 1860s, the top three causes of death among Brazilian-born slaves killed proportionately far fewer African-born slaves. Brazilian-born slaves faced the greatest danger from tuberculosis, tetanus, and smallpox, accounting for 31 percent of deaths among their group. These same diseases killed only 9 percent of African-born slaves.[6] Unequal risks went beyond demographics. Among the slaves of the wealthier coffee merchants, smallpox was a mortal danger and syphilis frequently committed them to the hospital. This venereal disease, along with others such as colds and rheumatic disorders, brought hundreds of slaves into the hospital, but usually did not kill them. This shows that for certain slaves (adult males, mostly), masters considered symptoms and guessed maladies before deciding whether or not to send a slave to a hospital bed.

Slaves who were fortunate enough to dodge a debilitating illness or deadly disease could live to an old age. An even luckier group of slaves were able to find a way out of slavery. Two small possibilities existed for slaves who longed for freedom: manumission and flight. Historians have discovered that in other parts of Brazil during different periods, Brazilian-born females were the most likely to receive manumission. The same is true for Santos in the nineteenth century. It may have been the case that manumission letters were sometimes used as a kind of labor contract that could be more profitable and less risky than renting or selling a slave. More research needs to be done on the connection between indentured servant contracts and manumission letters to learn if this was the case. Brazilian-born females were manumitted proportionally more than other slaves, but very few ran away. In fact, the group that could least expect to receive manumission letters in Santos—African-born male slaves of working age—was the most likely to flee. These slaves must have known that their high price eliminated the common incentives of a manumission letters. They were also possibly the most capable of leading a clandestine life, with skills they could sell and knowledge of tenuous routes to safety.

By the mid-1880s, slavery was disappearing from town life, even as the number of runaway slaves was growing enormously in several "maroon" communities, or *quilombos*, in or near town, such as Jabaquara. The hundred or so slaves remaining were enumerated publicly by men intent on embarrassing and pressuring slave owners into granting them freedom. Some slaves took matters into their own hands by appearing before sympathetic judges. These "freedom suits" were commonly successful when slaves could show that they had entered into a contract for manumission (*coartação*) and had begun making or were able to make payments to buy their freedom. A slightly smaller group received their freedom through the government-financed Emancipation Fund. Some bondspeople were freed when they showed they had been illegally transported via the Middle Passage after 1831. Others received symbolic freedom in plays promoted by abolitionist clubs and performed before the public. These were the legal and creative means for slowing the gears of slavery's machinery, but Santos is more famous for the ways that its residents pursued illegal means of debilitating slavery. Many residents broke constitutionally guaranteed property rights and centuries of tradition enshrined in the *Ordenações Filipinas* by aiding slave refugees arriving from across São Paulo. In fact, this community of refugees not only formed the largest maroon community in Brazilian history, but was also instrumental in deeply undermining slavery in São Paulo, one of the last strongholds of legal bondage in Brazil. While Santos deserves its renown for helping hasten the end of slavery in the nation, this book has also shown that, like other townships across Brazil, Santos was also very good at perpetuating slavery.

Slavery in the township of Santos was a hierarchical system with largely illusory promises of internal opportunities for betterment. Indeed, when the life conditions of slaves and their treatment varied enormously due to status and demographic differences, owners and perhaps slaves may have believed there was potential for social mobility, even within slavery. Such a belief may have tempered any overall antagonism. For example, Brazilian-born slave women knew that if they were lucky and saved some money, they might free their children. Yet such an option rested upon their acquiescence to the larger structures of power. Another situation might have involved private medical care, a service that was expensive for many owners, especially for long and debilitating illnesses. How did bondspeople who received private treatment feel about their friends and neighbors who entered the terribly crowded Misericórdia Hospital, or who had to suffer illnesses with rudimentary or no medical support? Some slaves knew valuable trades such as cooperage or tinsmithing, skills they could sell on the run. What did they think of their enslaved friends who, because of the lack of skills or familiarity with the land and people beyond their neighborhood, shrugged off escape as impossible? Finally, working-age male slaves were more likely than others to be purchased by a household with a good deal of stability, where they had a greater chance for a church-sanctioned marriage. These married men and their wives also had a reasonable chance to receive Emancipation Fund money after 1871. How did they view the slaves they knew who, by laboring for a poor or lazy farmer, faced the real prospect of severe malnutrition in the event of a serious drought or other misfortune? The answer seems clear: the frustrations and helplessness slaves might have felt about bondage was deflected or tempered if they considered themselves to have gotten a few big breaks in life. The slaves that did not see themselves as the lucky ones may have been a quieted minority, were brought under the whip, or else thought that better fortunes were around the corner, even as they remained enslaved.

Research on slavery (including this book) has filled more theses, books, and articles than any other topic of Brazilian history. Most projects have been driven by the idea that such history reveals the nature of their oppression and, as expressed by Katia Mattoso, rescues "these men and women from the anonymity in which they have been kept for so long."[7] Historians working on slavery today, however, must engage with a wide and ever-expanding literature. Indeed, for the history of the nineteenth century there are more articles and books written about slaves than individuals who did the enslaving.[8] In the biggest Brazilian bookstores or research libraries are found shelves of books detailing the history of slavery. A search for books on how Brazilian elites often corrupted the political system to maintain their power and institutions they controlled (generally known as *coronelismo*) will turn up fewer books than would have been found two decades ago. Furthermore, Brazilian textbooks targeting middle or high school history classes written or revised since 2000 usually make resistance a mandatory theme of slavery.[9] Some books even discuss how slaves successfully formed families. These shifts in historiography and pedagogy reflect and reaffirm popular assumptions that are quite different from when Mattoso was writing. Fewer people today, specialists or not, believe that the most common slave was the docile slave, always submitting to his or her master's whims. Yet by replacing the "submissive" slave with an equally unrealistic potent one, are historians and educators following the same thorny path, but in an opposite direction? For example, are we as able to productively recount and engage with the forces that made slavery oppressive when nearly all interactions between slave and masters are probed for signs of "negotiation" or "resistance"? The current avoidance of the word *treatment* may be a case in point, as hard as it is to deny that owners usually treated their slaves in a way that deprived them of the ability to make major life-changing decisions. Of course, there are many good histories that get it right. These narratives describe a small minority of slaves who used acumen and luck to exploit tiny cracks in an inhumane system of domination, leading to autonomous and meaningful decisions.

In contrast, their brothers and sisters, neighbors, and workmates simply tried to survive against terrible odds.

Regarding terrible odds, poverty was as much or more of an oppressive force as slavery.[10] As we have seen in this book, while some slaves were owned by poor owners, others lived and worked in the most luxurious of homes, especially with the new wealth brought by coffee and servicing the booming port. Slavery was rooted in law, and poverty was rooted in class and condition; both slaves and poor sometimes found sufficient luck to improve their situations. Yet again, we find approximately ten books and articles on the social history of slavery for every book on the social history of the free Brazilian poor. This imbalance has much to do with the economic forces that sell books and open hiring lines in universities. Slaves—as historical figures in published books and as topics of university lectures—remain capitalized subjects. Considering the disproportionate ratio of slave studies to histories of the Brazilian poor, it is the latter historical group that remains shrouded by the kind of obscurity that Mattoso identified.

Further complicating typical depictions of the slave-master relationship is the fact that as the nineteenth century wore on, general treatment of slaves improved. Contemporaries and historians have often made this claim.[11] It is also reinforced by the fact that slaves became concentrated in the hands of wealthy owners after 1850. Such owners had more resources to spend on their slaves, even if they viewed their bondspeople as walking investments. In Santos, slaves also received slightly better treatment, but in a complicated way. Institutions such as the hospital and jail took a greater role in the lives of slaves. Private companies increasingly paid these places to do what had long been the responsibility of owners. Even within the overcrowded Misericórdia Hospital, slaves may have had a greater chance of recovering from smallpox, yet they might have faced a week in the newly expanded city jail for a mildly disrespectful offense. More work needs to be done to determine whether slavery itself became more hierarchical during the nineteenth century and, if so, what kind of impact this had on the multiple ways that slaves viewed slavery and their position within the institution. However much treatment improved, until its final day, slavery remained a system that deprived its captives of full dignity and a sense of personhood.

The fact that owners had more resources to spend on their slaves in Santos also raises intriguing questions about whether slavery would have lost legitimacy sooner if treatment had not improved.[12] By concentrating ownership, raising prices, and improving treatment, did the forcible end to the slave trade in 1850 lengthen or delay the period of abolition as slaves were viewed as increasingly better off than the poor? Of course, such speculations should not imply that people in freedom and abject poverty were worse or better off than those in slavery and material privilege. Rather, historians should continue to explore the multiple ways that class, social status, and legal condition overlapped in revealing and meaningful ways.

Reference Matter

Appendix

The sources used in this project are categorized by their thematic use:

1. Wealth, status and occupation of owners and slaves:
   a. Inheritance records[1]
   b. Census lists or reports[2]
   c. Business almanacs[3]
   d. Rural estate lists[4]
   e. Bills of sale and exchange of real estate[5]
   f. General tax lists[6]
   g. Construction permits[7]
   h. Judicial processes[8]
   i. Church marriage records[9]
2. Slave markets:
   a. Slave sales tax lists[10]
   b. Slave bills of sale[11]
   c. Newspaper advertisements[12]
3. Slave families and work:
   a. Census lists
   b. Carmelite convent records[13]
   c. Inheritance records
4. Slave crime and punishment:
   a. Municipal law codes[14]
   b. Jail registration records[15]
   c. Newspaper crime reports[16]
5. Slave health and healthcare:
   a. Hospital patient registers[17]
   b. Provincial reports[18]
6. Slave death and burial:
   a. Hospital records
   b. Municipal death certificates[19]
   c. Cemetery registers[20]

7. Manumission and flight:
   a. Manumission letters[21]
   b. Newspaper announcements of runaways
   c. Baptism records[22]
   d. Indenture contracts[23]
8. Abolition and emancipation:
   a. Newspaper reports
   b. Municipal and provincial slaveholder lists[24]

A novel method was used to find evidence that slaves were unequally bound. Diverse data were compiled on thousands of slaves, owners, and nonslaveholding free within a single database, with every entry organized around the names of a slave owner and their slaves, or nonslaveholders. Most databases of slaves used by historians in the past have not included slave names or their owners' names, nor made an attempt to match slaves using this information. For every individual found in multiple sources, a unique code was applied.[25] An excess of Marias, Josés, Antonios, and Manoels, however, made it difficult to ascertain whether one individual appeared in multiple sources or whether the data represented multiple individuals who shared a common name. On many occasions, the problem was averted by comparing other pieces of information, such as name of owner, names of slaves, family member names, birthplace, age, race, civil status, or address. But when there was room for doubt and in the absence of supporting information, the individual was not coded.

Santos was not a highly populated township; the data collection was far more manageable compared to other regions. Moreover, database programs greatly reduced the legwork of cross-referencing thousands of names. Consequentially, we were able to identify thousands of unique slave owners and hundreds slaves in two or more sources. Many enslaved men, women, and children owned by coded masters appeared in multiple sources. Some of the more prominent and active owners could be found in more than eight different sources. For example, Guilherme Bachkeuser, German-born but a long-time resident, appears in several almanacs, a rural real estate register of 1856, several different municipal property tax rolls, judicial documents, and church marriage records.[26] His slaves were recorded in hospital, cemetery, and jail records.[27] Some slaves appeared in as many as four different sources.

In other cases, it was difficult to cross-reference names; the name "Maria Victoria" (or "Maria Vitoria") appeared fourteen times in several different sources, but since Maria Victoria of Rua São Antonio (Saint Anthony Street) owned slaves who appeared in multiple years of the census record (and who could be corroborated by comparing their ages), she and her repeating slaves were each given unique codes.[28] Maria Victoria of Rua São Antonio may have owned a slave named Feliciano who was given a manumission letter in 1829. A slave by this name, formerly owned by a Maria Victoria da Silva, appeared among the notarized copies of nineteenth-century manumission letters in the Costa e Silva collection in the municipal archive of Santos.[29] Because there was a small but sufficient degree of doubt, however (both former owner and slave had relatively common names and not all of the information perfectly matched), this Feliciano was not given the code attached to the Feliciano of Maria Victoria of the census records. For thousands of other matching names, however, all evidence pointed to the similar individual in multiple sources.

Notes

INTRODUCTION

1. Schwartz, *Sugar Plantations*, 252. As a township (*municípios*, translated sometimes as "counties"), Santos was the administrative center of several hundred square kilometers of rural land. It was elevated to the position of a city in 1836. A person from Santos is a Santista.

2. "Status" of a slaveholder is defined as a combination of wealth and occupation. Status changed according to other variables as well: family position, residential location, education or training, or the bestowal of titles or honors from esteemed groups. These additional variables were less likely to appear in the available historical sources, but it is not believed this hinders the use of status as a category of analysis. An individual who took a more commanding position within his or her family, moved to a prestigious part of town, acquired a higher education, learned a valuable skill, or received an honorary title often became wealthier and took a higher-ranking job.

3. Examples include Barickman, *Bahian Counterpoint*; Karasch, *Slave Life*; Luna and Klein, *Slavery and the Economy*; Schwartz, "Patterns of Slaveholding" and *Slaves, Peasants, and Rebels*; Slenes, *Na senzala*; Bergad, *Comparative Histories*, 33–63; and Russell-Wood, "Technology and Society."

4. Tannenbaum, *Slave and Citizen*, xi; Williams, "Treatment of Negro Slaves"; Degler, *Neither Black nor White*, 70–74.

5. Genovese, "Treatment of Slaves," 202–10 and Sheridan, *Doctors and Slaves*, 130.

6. Treatment was discussed frequently when it was common to debate whether the Spanish and Portuguese slave societies were more or less cruel than the British slave societies. See Tannenbaum, *Slave and Citizen*; Elkins, *Slavery: A Problem*; and Degler, *Neither Black nor White*.

7. Ira Berlin perceptively notes, "Although the playing field was never level, the master-slave relationship was nevertheless subject to continual negotiations. The failure to recognize the ubiquity of those negotiations derives neither from an overestimation of the power of the master (which was awesome indeed), nor from an underestimation of the power of the slaves (which rarely amounted to much), but from a misconstruing of the limitations humanity placed upon both master

and slave." Berlin, *Many Thousands Gone*, 2. See also Reis and Silva, *Negociação e conflicto.*

8. Motta, "Derradeiras transações"; Machado, "Tráfico interno"; Neves, "Sampauleiros traficantes."

9. Slenes, *Na senzala*, 104–5; Florentino and Góes, *A paz das senzalas*; Teixeira, "Reprodução e familias escravas," 111–12; and Andrade, "Casamento entre escravos," 188–89.

10. Holloway, *Policing Rio*, 196; Pires, *Crime na cor*, 127–50; Machado, *Crime e escravidão*; Wissenbach, *Sonhos Africanos.*

11. More than ten recent studies of manumission show that women and children were the most favored to receive manumission letters. For a list and discussion of these studies, see Klein, "American Slavery," 115–16.

12. Out of almost 2,000 announcements of runaways collected from newspapers published in Rio de Janeiro, São Paulo, Pernambuco, and Pará between 1845 and 1875, 82 percent of the fugitives were male and many had skills that could be sold on the run. Read and Zimmerman, "Fugitive Runaways." See also Petiz, *Buscando a liberdade.*

13. Neto, "O Fundo." A preference for married slaves (and hence those most likely to be in the hands of wealthy owners) was written into the law. See Chapter Seven (this volume) for the law's preference system and its effects in Santos.

14. José Bonifácio de Andrada e Silva, Brazil's most famous founder, and his two brothers, Antonio Carlos and Martim Francisco, were all born in Santos. Two other well-known Santistas are José Ricardo da Costa Aguiar, one of Brazil's first Supreme Court judges, and Joaquim Otávio Nebias, who was São Paulo's president in the 1850s, a congressman, and the Empire's Minister of Justice in the 1870s.

15. Holloway, *Immigrants on the Land*, 50–51.

16. That is, until the railroad began carrying enough of these insects into the interior of São Paulo and Rio de Janeiro that they became a problem during the summer months. Telarolli Junior, "Imigração e epidemias," 275–79.

17. Nishida, *Slavery and Identity*, 20–21; Klein, *African Slavery*, 129–30; Pierson, *Negroes in Brazil*, 90; Martin, "Slavery and Abolition in Brazil," 165–67.

18. Barickman, *Bahian Counterpoint*, 152–53. Mary Karasch describes a number of slave groups in Rio de Janeiro that would not have existed anywhere else, such as the Emperor's slaves, or those connected with the Valongo, a short-lived and busy slave market that was unique to the Imperial capital. Karasch, *Slave Life*, 36.

19. Luna and Klein, *Slavery and the Economy*, 24–25, 108.

20. See Garcia, *Transformações econômicas* and Ressurreição, *São Sebastião*, for general histories of the region.

21. Just as Eugene Genovese looked for the "world that slaves made," Mattoso sought to "rescue these men and women from the anonymity in which they have been kept for so long." *To Be a Slave*, 86. In *Bahia, século XIX*, she pursued this goal with a wide range of sources that, in the process, showed the enormous potential of estate inventories, wills, judicial records, emancipation papers, church records, and police archive documents. For regional studies, see Stein, *Vassouras*;

Karasch, *Slave Life*; Luna and Klein, *Slavery and the Economy*; Libby, *Transformação e trabalho*; Libby, *Trabalho escravo*; Slenes, *Os múltiplos*; Bergad, *Demographic and Economic History*; and Eisenberg, *The Sugar Industry*.

22. Chalhoub, *Visões da liberdade*; Rocha, *Famílias escravas*; Silva, *Prince of the People*.

23. For analyses of inheritance records, see Frank, *Dutra's World*; Mello, *Metamorfoses da riqueza*; and Mattoso, *Bahia, século XIX*. For a discussion of inheritance laws and customs, see Lewin, *Surprise Heirs*. For analyses of census records, see Luna and Klein, *Slavery and the Economy*; Libby and Filho, "Reconstructing Freedom"; Rocha, *Famílias escravas*; and Teixeira, "Reprodução e famílias."

24. Schwartz, *Slaves, Peasants, and Rebels*; Barickman, *Bahian Counterpoint*; Marcondes, "Small and Medium Slaveholdings."

25. Barickman, "Revisiting the casa-grande"; Motta, "Historical Demography"; Faria, "História da família"; Samara, *A família brasileira*; Kuznesof, "Sexuality, Gender," 120–21.

26. Slenes, *Na senzala*, 43–53.

27. Slenes, *Os múltiplos*, 80; Libby, *Transformação e trabalho*; Bergad, *Demographic and Economic History*.

28. Luna and Klein, *Slavery and the Economy*.

29. Stein, *Vassouras*; Frank, *Dutra's World*.

30. Gilberto Freyre is a well-known example. His earliest and most popular books, *Casa grande e senzala* (*Masters and Slaves*), saw the plantation both as a unit of analysis and a metaphor for race relations, miscegenation, and family in Brazil.

31. Frank, *Dutra's World*; Karasch, *Slave Life*; Hahner, *Poverty and Politics*; and Dias, *Power and Everyday Life*. Nearly half of those buried in the Santa Casa de Misericórdia did not or could not pay the small burial fees. This confirms separate estimations made by Frank and Karasch that nearly half the population of nineteenth-century Brazil had very little wealth.

32. Beeghley, *Structure of Social Stratification*; Grusky, *Social Stratification*.

33. Hess, *Concepts of Social Stratification*, 6; Weber, Roth, and Wittich, *Economy and Society*, 305; Weber and Swedberg, *Essays in Economic Sociology*, 89.

34. For example, Stuart Schwartz has claimed the sugar mill had a division of labor and hierarchy of occupations that mirrored the larger social structures of society. *Sugar Plantations*, 156. Lockhart and Schwartz describe the body politic of the Spanish-American monarchy as one of social divisions between the nobility, clergy, artisan guilds, and commoners. *Early Latin America*, 8. On the frontier of the Brazilian province of Minas Gerais, settlers "reproduced" the "social structures" of older settled areas in Minas Gerais, according to Laird Bergad. *Demographic and Economic History*, 66–67. For Peter Bakewell, at the "pinnacle" of early Spanish-American "social structure" were the viceroys. Below them stood the untitled dons, "the artisans, agricultural workers, merchants petty and not so petty, muleteers, the odd miner or man of arms." Upon immigrating to the New World, they "jostled to find a place to live, a means of support and a niche in the

ranks of the developing society." *History of Latin America*, 163. See also Oliveira and Roberts, "Urban Social Structures."

35. Mattoso, *Bahia, século XIX*, 588–91. See also Prado Júnior, *Formação do Brasil*, 279–83.

36. Karasch, *Slave Life*, 70.

37. Sandra Lauderdale Graham argued in *House and Street* that the free and enslaved domestics who worked within the home led very different lives than women who worked mainly on the streets; each had their advantages and disadvantages that could transcend the legal category of slavery or freedom.

38. There were many words that referred to skin color, social position, and family lineage. *Pardos* and *mulattos* (along with *cabras*, *fulos*, and a number of other racial/color/social categories) appear to have signaled different things to different people at different times and places. Historians have yet to sort all this out, and much debate and ambiguity remain. *Pardo* has been translated literally as "brown," but we now know that this is an insufficient translation because *pardos* were seen and saw themselves as a social group with particular characteristics and lineage that did not always depend on phenotype. See Castro, *Cores do silĕncio*, and Libby and Filho, "Reconstructing Freedom."

39. Freyre, "Social Life," 607; Williams, "Treatment of Negro Slaves."

40. Williams "Treatment of Negro Slaves," 316–17.

41. Ibid. On this point, Karasch claims the opposite. *Slave Life*, 151.

42. Williams, "Treatment of Negro Slaves," 319.

43. Thomas Ewbank, *Life in Brazil*, 17; Horne, *Deepest South*, 104.

44. Stewart, *Brazil and La Plata*, 295.

45. Thomas Ashe, a British merchant, was more imaginative. He reported to his superiors: "The domestic negroes of the Brasils wear none but solid gold trinkets, consisting of collars, bracelets, and chains; and plates for the forehead, breast and shoulders, and crucifixes and molten images to suspend from these various articles. And the field negroes, and mertchoes [mulattos?] wear none but trinkets of pure materials." *Commercial View*, 17.

46. *Annaes do parlamento brazileiro* (1871, Tomo 4), 300; Malheiro also made this point in *A escravidão no brasil* (vol. 2), 95. See Sidney Chalhoub's discussion of Malheiro's point in the context of manumission in *Visões da liberdade*, 134.

47. Kidder and Fletcher, *Brazil and the Brazilians*, 630; Freyre, "Social Life," 606.

48. Pereira, "Práticas de curar," 4–5; Graham, "Slave Families."

49. Karasch, *Slave Life*, 191, 200, 209, 210; Costa, *Da senzala*, 191; Lauderdale Graham, *House and Street*, 110; Frank, *Dutra's World*. Of course, there is also Brazil's most famous freed slave, Xica da Silva.

50. Naro, *A Slave's Place*, 60–61. Eufrasia may have been given a privileged position relative to most slaves, but her relation to her owner was less than happy. Eufrasia was given her freedom, but then this freedom was revoked due to her "ungratefulness." She was also whipped and sexually exploited.

51. Sousa, *Os Andradas*; Stein, *Vassouras*, 137.

52. Klein, *African Slavery*, 165.

53. Stein, *Vassouras*, 140.

54. Mattoso, *Bahia, século XIX*, 542.

55. Portuguese orthography of the nineteenth century differs from that used today. The original spelling of formal names (i.e., "Gregorio Innocencio de Freitas") has been maintained.

CHAPTER ONE

1. These hills did not prevent Thomas Cavendish, the English navigator and freebooter (or "pirate," depending on one's perspective), from occupying Santos in 1591. When Cavendish and his men arrived, they burned "all of the outward part of the town" and set alight the ships in the harbor. They remained in town for about five weeks, where they rested and restored after their long journey across the Atlantic. Soon after he left, Cavendish made several tactical errors, he and his crew ran into storms, and several attacks by the Portuguese left the expedition in ruin. Cavendish died as his ship hobbled back to Europe. Edwards, *Last Voyages*. São Jerŏnimo hill became known as Mont Serrat in the twentieth century.

2. This is how Claude Lévi-Strauss described the region on his way up to the highlands to collect material for *Triste tropiques*, 90–91.

3. They were rivals mostly in town politics, but their disputes took a nasty turn on several occasions when young Quarteleiros or Valongueiros were knifed or beaten during disputes that took place during the high energy of the town festivals. Olao Rodrigues, "Valongueiros e Quartaleiros." In terms of wealth and slaveholding, both neighborhoods were similar. They were separated by a walk of about thirty minutes, but that did not diminish the fact that they at times saw their interests as irreconcilable.

4. This is according to the 1817 town census. By 1822, a few more slaves became residents. Nominal lists, 1817, 1822, AESP.

5. Streets were part of neighborhoods but did not always delineate them. Breaking the city into segments along its roads can hide homogeneous areas centered at street corners and intersections.

6. Nominal lists, 1817–1830, AESP.

7. On this street in 1817, 17 percent of the slaves were owned by *pardos*. In 1830, 27 percent of the slaves were owned by this racial/color group. The tendency and ability of people of color to emulate their white neighbors in household and slaveholding patterns during the nineteenth century is discussed in Klein and Luna, "Free Colored."

8. Nominal lists, 1817–1830, AESP.

9. For this project, a geographic information system (GIS) was used that helps place households and individuals in the map according to their address and assign variables related to wealth or demography. The program's spatial analysis tool identifies clusters of individuals with similar characteristics and aggregates data so as to find correlations between variables. In other words, a physical map is transformed into a social map. For an introduction to GIS in historical research, see Gregory and Ell, *Historical GIS*.

10. Value here is based on the tax amount that property owners paid. Since

tax collectors determined the tax amount from assessed rental values, this is not a perfect indicator of property value.

11. Frank, *Dutra's World*, 88; Mattoso, *Bahia, século XIX*; Klein and Luna, "Free Colored," 913–41.

12. In comparison, twelve *mil-réis* could purchase about sixty sacks of rice or two hundred pounds of dried meat in the 1820s.

13. Urban property tax rolls, 1834–35, AESP.

14. I do not necessarily claim that these two individuals were most representative of their larger neighborhoods. They were chosen because they appeared in multiple sources, and I could piece together a detailed bibliography of them, their slaves, and some of their neighbors.

15. The big planters had larger households and more slaves, as is evident in the census records. Of the 64 households on those two streets in 1817, 24 listed more than 10 slaves for their residences. On Rua Antonina, the street where Machado officially lived, only 2 out of 14 owners had more than 10 slaves. Clearly, Machado held more common ground with his neighbors across the street than with those farther down his block. Nominal lists, 1817, 1822, 1830, AESP.

16. Sobrinho, *Santos noutros tempos*, 474–84.

17. Ibid.; Nominal lists, 1830, AESP. This demonstrates the ambiguity of those listed as *agregados* in the census rolls. Some *agregados* appear to rely on the principal family to provide work or provisions and were in a subservient position. In other cases, as with Maria Luiza, they were close family members that held nearly identical positions of power within a family as the person listed as the "head" of the household.

18. Urban property tax rolls, 1834–1835, AESP.

19. Nominal lists, 1817, AESP.

20. Compared to Rio de Janeiro, however, this amount was not extraordinary.

21. Inheritance records, 1825, vol. 49, 51, CCS, FAMS. Gilberto Freyre described the oratory: "Practically every city house had its *oratorio* with the images in a glassed case, before which the family gathered for worship in a sweet atmosphere of incense and scent of rose." "Social Life," 616.

22. Nominal lists, 1822; Urban property tax rolls, 1834–35, AESP. There was a great range in house prices, even near the Four Corners. The highest annual earning of Travessa da Alfândega (number five) owned by Anna de Jesus Vieira was more than seventy-two times higher than the property at Beco do Inferno (number five). The neighbors on Inferno closest to the corners were better off than down the alley. But the affluence of Four Corners did not penetrate deeply. Within Machado's immediate neighborhood of twenty-one households in 1822, many were headed by men (67 percent), all but one were white, over half were or had been married (62 percent) and older (average age of forty-eight).

23. Nominal lists, 1817–1830, AESP. Of the 287 slaves listed by Machado's immediate neighbors in 1817, 38 percent were female, one percentage point less than Machado's holding. By 1825, the females made up 41 percent of the slaves. Additionally, a fairly large number of Machado's slaves and slaves owned by his neighbors were married. A little less than a quarter of slaves in the neighborhood had a spouse, but a third of Machado's were married. This finding adds evidence

that some plantation owners permitted or encouraged their slaves to marry. See Chapter Four (this volume).

24. Nominal lists, 1817–1830, AESP.

25. Defined as a radius of five houses. Nominal lists, 1817–1830, AESP.

26. Most neighborhoods in Santos still have at least one shop that employs small groups of women working side by side as seamstresses.

27. Nominal lists, 1817–1830, AESP.

28. One woman named Maria Leite was exceptional. She was a seamstress, and listed seventeen people in her household, including family members and dependents. Leite was also the largest slaveholder around, with five slaves.

29. The slave rental market in Rio de Janeiro appears to have been fairly large and active. An average of twenty-five rental notices were published each Sunday throughout 1850 in only one newspaper. Frank, *Dutra's World*, 48. In contrast, the main Santos newspaper published about ten advertisements offering slaves for rent per year, but most rental agreements were probably formed without the use of the newspaper since this was the case in slave sales. See Chapter Three (this volume).

30. Extending the analysis down Rua Áurea to get a larger sample, the pattern largely continues. Of the forty-two slaves who lived on the street, most were black, single, and young. Nominal lists, 1817–1830, AESP.

31. Ibid.

32. Inheritance records, 1838, vol. 94, CCS.

33. Lisboa, "Almanak litterario" in Lichti and Santos, *Poliantéia santista*, 167–68.

34. The networking program is called Pajek, and it is a popular tool among network theorists. It is available for free at: http://vlado.fmf.uni-lj.si/pub/networks/pajek/. For a use of this program in social scientific or historical research, see Nooy, Mrvar, and Batagelj, *Exploratory Social Network*.

35. Church marriage records, 1812–1870 (vols. 1, 3, 5), CDS, CCS, FAMS. See Kuznesof, *Household Economy*, 42–44, for a similar kinship network.

36. Klein, *African Slavery*, 170; Lauderdale Graham, *Caetana Says No*; Schwartz, *Sugar Plantations*, 73; Vasconcellos, "Casar ou não."

37. Church marriage records, 1825 (vol. 1), CCS; Sobrinho, *Santos noutros tempos*, 325, 524.

38. Inheritance records (vol. 16), CCS, FAMS.

39. Frank, *Dutra's World*, 108–13; Klein and Luna, "Free Colored."

40. Urban property tax rolls, 1874, CCS, FAMS.

41. Almanak Laemmert (1874).

42. Slave bills of sale, 1865, vol. 24, CCS, FAMS.

43. Hospital patient registers, 1881, ASCMS; Cemetery register, 1881, FAMS.

44. This general idea of societal composition is an old one for Brazil although few have looked closely at social networks. Many have connected the vertical and horizontal links or Brazilian society to politics and the political economy: Carone, "Coronelismo"; Carvalho, *A construção da Ordem*; Duarte, *A Ordem privada*; Faoro, *Os donos do poder*; Graham, *Patronage and Politics*, especially chapter one; Leal, *Coronelismo*; Lewin, *Politics and Parentela*; Pang and Secklinger, "The Mandarins."

CHAPTER TWO

1. Luna and Klein, *Slavery and the Economy*, 12, 16, 111.

2. Fausto, *História do Brasil*, 557–60. The fortunes of the port town were irrevocably connected to the state of the highway that scaled the Serra do Mar and connected the expansive *planalto* to ocean trade. The highway, however, was continuously a source of despair for provincial administrators and Santista merchants during the colony and Empire periods. In addition to the steep grade and nearly impassible terrain, the constant rain meant that, at worst, it was washed out and closed or, at best, it was treacherous, slow, and expensive. Highway administrators were closing the highway as late as 1862. The provincial government lamented that when it had been open that year, fifty or more mules, horses, or cattle had fallen to their deaths per week during the long rainy season; Costa, *Da senzala*, 204.

3. *100 anos*, 1–20; Luna and Klein, *Slavery and the Economy*, 12. Thomas Cavendish burned five sugar mills on the short road between Santos to São Vicente in 1591. Edwards, *Last Voyages*, 86.

4. *100 anos*, 6.

5. Ibid., 26; Cleto, *Dissertação a respeito*, quoted in Petrone, *A lavoura*, 25–26.

6. 1777 data is from Francisco Vidal Luna and Herbert S. Klein, "Unpublished Data from Santos Nominal Lists, 1777, 1804, 1830" (Excel database).

7. Parallels can be made between Santos and parts of the Northeast, such as Bahia, where half the population was enslaved as late as 1824. Mattoso, *Bahia, século XIX*, 747.

8. Ressurreição, *São Sebastião*, 77.

9. Schwartz, *Sugar Plantations*; Mello, *Metamorfoses da riqueza*; Stein, *Vassouras*; Frank, *Dutra's World*.

10. These are decedents who owned at least a little wealth. An unknown but larger percentage owned nothing.

11. The Santos judicial archive (containing documents from the nineteenth century) has been closed to consultations for more a decade due to a contract with a private archival company that has made its sources inaccessible (against federal law). This prevented our access to inventories and wills commonly attached to property disputes. Additional records do exist in the two private notary offices, but either these were unavailable or there was insufficient time to record them.

12. John Luccock, an English traveler, claimed somewhat flippantly that "In Brazil, the door made of plank forms the legal distinction between a house and a resting place—a permanent and a temporary abode; the latter sometimes having a door made of straw twisted round sticks, or of a hide stretched over a slight piece of framework." *Notes on Rio de Janeiro*.

13. Urban property tax rolls, 1834–1835, AESP; Inheritance records, 1800–1880, CCS, FAMS. The property tax did not count rural structures.

14. Inheritance records, 1835, CCS (vol. 81), FAMS; Nominal lists, 1817–1830, AESP.

15. Rural estate lists, 1817, CCS (vol. 19), FAMS; Inheritance records 1832, CCS (vol. 79), FAMS. The *armação* (fort) run by Tenente-Coronel João da Costa

had fifty-four slaves in 1817. In 1826, his wife, Maria Francisca da Costa, was running the operation that then included forty-six slaves. By 1830, it was only a quarter of its 1817 size, with many of the slaves probably too old to work. Nominal lists, 1817–1830, AESP.

16. Inheritance records 1832, CCS (vol. 79), FAMS.

17. Ibid.

18. Ibid., 1830, CCS (vol. 52), FAMS.

19. Some historians translate *agregado* as "dependent." I prefer "additional" because a dependent relationship is rarely explicit. Some *agregados* were capable of independently providing for themselves, but preferred to pool their resources with another family, usually one who owned a house. See Chapter One (this volume) for an example of an *agregado* who was not a dependent.

20. Nominal lists, 1817, 1822, 1830, AESP.

21. Zephyr Frank makes a similar point for slave and real estate wealth in Rio de Janeiro. See *Dutra's World*, 79.

22. Inheritance records, 1838, CCS (vol. 81), FAMS.

23. Nominal lists (Santos), 1817, 1822, AESP.

24. Instituto Histórico e Geográfico de São Paulo and others, "Carta de Morgado de Mateus ao Conde de Oeyra"; Ressurreição, *São Sebastião*, 46.

25. Nominal lists, 1830, AESP.

26. Inheritance records, 1838, CCS (vol. 81), FAMS.

27. Ibid., 1835, CCS (vol. 81), FAMS.

28. Ibid., 1826, 1849, CCS (vols. 49, 81, 89, 97), FAMS.

29. Ibid., 1826, 1828, 1831, 1832, 1838 (vols. 30, 39, 49, 50, 79), CCS, FAMS.

30. Nominal lists, 1825, AESP.

31. São Paulo and Brazil, *Discurso com . . . Almeida . . . de 1856.*

32. Ibid.

33. Duke and Allen, "Rhizophora Mangle," at www.agroforestry.net/tti/Rhizophora-AEP.pdf. Accessed 2 September 2008.

34. Nominal lists, 1818, AESP; rural estate lists, 1817, CCS, FAMS. When rural property holders of 1817 are compared to the urban census for 1818, 24 out of 120 rural title holders also held urban property. These title holders listed 460 slaves as part of their town residences, although many of these slaves must have lived and worked a long way from the port town. The slaves owned by these landowners and listed as part of the urban household made up more than 20 percent of the entire slave population for that year.

35. Church marriage records, 1812–1870 (vols. 1, 3, 5), CDS, CCS, FAMS.

36. U.S. Department of State, "Letters from Consul William T. Wright." The total world coffee trade was 2,213,000 bags, in which Rio de Janeiro was the central exporter.

37. Summerhill, *Order Against Progress*. In one particularly bad storm, several people who lived near the highway in the mountain died because of floods. *Revista Commercial* (Santos), May 21, 1850, FAMS.

38. Morse, *From Community to Metropolis*, 150. Rio de Janeiro, still the dominant coffee export, shipped 44 percent of the world's total. Wileman, *Brazilian Year Book*.

39. São Paulo and Brazil, *Discurso com . . . Almeida . . . de 1856*, 991, Mapa SN; Brazil, Directoria Geral de Estatistica, *Recenseamento da população . . . 1872*.

40. Almanak Laemmert, 1885, CSS, FAMS.

41. Inheritance records, 1850–1890, CCS, FAMS. Barickman found a different picture for planters in Bahia who "continued to buy for their slaves the very same items their grandfathers had purchased in the late eighteenth century." *Bahian Counterpoint*, 70.

42. Inheritance records, 1879, CCS (vol. 16), FAMS.

43. "Legal reasons" include the end of the African slave trade in 1850 and the Rio Branco law of 1871–72. The British forcibly ended the Atlantic slave trade in 1850, ending Brazil's ready supply of African slaves. For a discussion of the Rio Branco law, see Chapter Seven. The reasons why the slave population did not increase naturally likely have to do with the social and environmental conditions they faced (i.e., high infant mortality) and the continuing flow of manumission, mostly among female slaves, often of childbearing age.

CHAPTER THREE

1. Small parts of this chapter have been reprinted with the permission of Taylor & Francis, from "Off the Block But in the Neighborhood: Local Slave Trading in São Paulo," *Slavery and Abolition* (Fall 2011).

2. Karasch, *Slave Life*, 44; Slave bills of sale, CCS (vol. 24), 199, 205, FAMS; Azevedo and others, *Santos e seus arrabaldes*, 36. Employees of the British diplomatic corps were prohibited from owning slaves. Hayden might have hoped to avoid attention by naming his wife as the official buyer for their family.

3. Baptism records, 1865, CCS (vol. 9), FAMS; Slave bills of sale, CCS (vol. 24), 199, FAMS. The image slave owners wished to convey, especially within urban areas, is a topic richly explored in Johnson, "A Nettlesome Classic."

4. Read, "Off the Block."

5. For an overview of how slaves got to Brazil in the first place, there are several useful surveys. See: Klein, *Middle Passage*; Northrup, *Atlantic Slave Trade*; and Eltis, *Economic Growth*. For studies that focus on the economic and demographic causes and consequences of the internal slave trade of the nineteenth century, see those by Slenes: *Demography and Economics* and "Brazilian Internal Slave Trade"; or Johnson, "Grandeza ou decadência," in *Chattel Principle*. Another study on this topic is by Klein, "Internal Slave Trade." Robert Conrad and Richard Graham approached the internal slave trade as it related to abolitionist movement: Conrad, *Destruction of Brazilian Slavery*, 47–65, 172–73; and Richard Graham, "Another Middle Passage?" in Johnson, *Chattel Principle*, 291–324. For the slave market in Rio de Janeiro, see Karasch, *Slave Life*, 29–53. For New Orleans, see Johnson, *Soul by Soul*. For a traveler's description of the Rio market, see Debret, *Viagem Pitoresca*. Slenes estimated that 95,000 slaves were transferred to the southeast between 1872 and 1881. "Brazilian Internal Slave Trade," 331.

6. *Procuradores* (agents or proctors) were men employed to manage the affairs of another. The scripted protocol is evident in the legal form that buyers and

sellers used in contracting their transactions. The bills of sale often ran for four or five pages, but followed a single form in the language used and information included. It is assumed that beyond the written contract, traders who bought and sold a number of slaves followed a standard, legal procedure that, ideally, minimized their effort, maximized their profit, yet maintained the social bonds necessary for a good business.

7. The editors of the first newspaper in Santos, the *Revista Commercial*, printed their newspaper four times per week in 1848, and it remained the primary regional newspaper until the late 1860s when a rival publication, *O diario de Santos,* was founded. *Revista Commercial*, *Diario de Santos*, CCS (vols. 103–10, 115, 118, 144–46), FAMS; *Revista Commercial*, 1850–1872, HS. Potential customers had the additional inconvenience of going to the journal to find the slave owner's address, but the profits to these publicly veiled sellers were worth the trouble. Private advertisers were not alone in hiding contact information when it came to slave trading. When the first detailed almanac of the city was published in 1865, not one owner of a commission or auction house listed slaves among their traded goods. Slave-trading agencies may have received less acrimony a decade earlier, and the concealed contact information within the slave trading advertisements of the Santos newspaper may have simply reflected custom. Sandra Lauderdale Graham points to growing disapproval toward businesses that sold and rented slaves in Rio de Janeiro during the 1870s. Lauderdale Graham, *House and Street*, 19.

8. Karasch, *Slave Life*, 36–54. One foreign visitor to the Valongo wrote: "When a person is desirous of making a purchase, he visits the different depots, going from one house to another, until he sees such as please him, who, upon being called out, undergo the operations of being felt and handled in various parts of the body and limbs, precisely after the manner of cattle in a market. They are made to walk, to run, to stretch their arms and legs [. . .] and to show their tongue and teeth; which latter are considered as the surest marks whereby to discover their age and judge of their health." Chamberlain and Borba de Moraes, *Vistas e costumes da cidade*, 161. Signs of punishment (or torture, depending on one's perspective) were often mentioned in newspaper notices describing runaways and stolen slaves. I assume that most buyers also knew to look for these signs during the sales.

9. More than ten sources are used to investigate slave transactions and slave buyer and seller backgrounds and social position, but three sources provide the bulk of the information. The tax records run with a few interruptions from 1832 to 1859, and the bills of sale follow with a fairly steady series of records between 1861 and 1870. Slave advertisements cover a series of years that overlap the first two sources, beginning in 1849 and ending in 1873. Neither the tax nor the bill of sale was expensive. Relative to the population of slaves in the township, it appears these records cover a relatively high number of slaves sold in and out of Santos. Even though the cost of the bill of sale was relatively small, between 0.3 percent and 3.0 percent of the cost of the slave (2–6 *mil-réis*).

10. Slave bills of sale (vols. 24–33, 135), PCNS, CCS, FAMS.

11. Ibid.

12. Ibid. Jarbas Vargas Nascimento and Izilda Maria Nardocci analyzed the

language used in one bill of sale from Mogi das Cruzes. "Compra e venda de homens negros."

13. Motta, "Derradeiras transações"; Machado, "Tráfico interno"; Neves, "Sampauleiros traficantes"; Read, "Off the Block." In total, the customs house noted 289 tax payments covering the sale of 396 slaves for various years between 1832 and 1858. Multiple slaves were traded in single transactions, with an annual average of 10 tax payments for every 13 slaves sold. The bills of sale follow a similar pattern. Officials of the First Notary Office of Santos noted 197 bills of sale that covered the sale of 241 slaves. The annual average per year, 25 bills for 30 slaves, is lower overall than the tax records, but the ratio of slaves per payment is nearly the same.

14. Several foreign visitors to the Valongo depicted the slave traders as "gypsies," including Robert Walsh and Jean Baptiste Debret, and this depiction has been carried on by historians even though next to nothing is known about the ethnicities of the Valongo dealers. For these travelers' references, see Karasch, *Slave Life*, 36–54. Gypsies are also discussed in relation to slavery in Soares, *O "povo de cam*," 60–62. "Comboieiros," a deprecating term meaning "conveyers" also appears in the literature on the slave trade. See Moura, *Dicionário da escravidão*; Stein, *Vassouras*, 73–74; and Furtado, *Homens de negócio*, 266, 270.

15. Judicial processes, 1827 (vol. 49), CCS, FAMS.

16. Slave sales tax lists, 1842 (October) and 1843 (August), AESP; Judicial processes, 1835, 1843 CCS (vols. 81, 87), FAMS.

17. The dominance of Portuguese-born residents in the commercial life of town comes from a sample of 319 trials that included 1,706 witnesses (although many individuals repeated). Witnesses were normally required to state their birthplace. Judicial processes, 1820–1880 (vols. 13, 16, 48–52, 79–94), CCS, FAMS. Sousa, *Os Andradas*, 145. For the numerical movement of Portuguese into Brazil during the nineteenth century, see Fundação Instituto Brasileiro de Geografia e Estatística, *Estatísticas históricas do Brasil* (vol. 3), 273–74.

18. Slave sales tax lists, Santos, 1832–1859, AESP; Slave bills of sale, 1861–1873, PCNS and SCNS. More rural slaves may have been sold into Belem than were sold out during the 1860s and 1870s. Neto, "Mercado, conflitos e controle," 272–73.

19. There were also a small number who had been born in the Azores and had probably accompanied Portuguese immigrants. Slave sales tax lists, Santos, 1832–1859, AESP.

20. See Introduction (this volume), footnote 38, for a discussion of these racial/color/social categories.

21. Libby and Filho, "Reconstructing Freedom"; Castro, *Das cores do silĕncio*, 426; *Revista Commercial*, 1850–1873, HS. Antonio de Morais Silva defined *fulo* as "That said of the negro and the mulatto who do not have a firm color, but one that drifts toward a yellowish or pale hue." ("*Diz-se do preto, e do mulato, que não tem a sua cór bem fixa, mas tirante a amarello, ou pallido*"). *Diccionario da lingua portugueza*, 898. Perhaps in consultation with Morais Silva's dictionary, Julius Cornet translated the racial term in 1891 as "yellowish black, sallow black (negro, mulatto); pale; furious." *Novo diccionario*, 374.

22. Johnson, *Soul by Soul*, 102, 208.
23. Hospital patient registers, 1869 (patient num. 9825), ASCM. Slave sales tax lists, Santos, 1840, AESP.
24. Slave bills of sale, CCS (vol. 24), 146, 197, 202, 205; *Revista Commercial*, 1865 (September), HS.
25. *Revista Commercial*, 1863 (October), HS; Slave bills of sale, 1863, 1864, CCS (vol. 24), FAMS.
26. Hospital patient registers, 1873 (patient No. 12,059), 1881 (patient No. 526), ASCM.
27. Slave bills of sale, 1869 (June), PCNS. Prison registers, June 1868, MPCSP. Bento's price is compared to the average price of the nine male slaves, aged forty to sixty, sold between 1866 and 1872. Slave bills of sale, 1866–1872, PCNS, CCS, FAMS.
28. Slave bills of sale, 1867 (March), PCNS; CCS (vol. 24, pg. 198), Manumission letters, 1875, CCS, FAMS.
29. Dean, *Rio Claro*, 55.
30. Slave sales tax lists, Santos, 1832–1859, AESP; Slave bills of sale, 1861–1873, PCNS and SCNS.
31. Johnson, *Soul by Soul*, 155.
32. *Revista Commercial*, 1850–1873, HS.
33. Slave sales tax lists, Santos, 1832–1859, AESP; Slave bills of sale, 1861–1873, PCNS.
34. Pajek was used to create networks for this project; it is available at http://pajek.imfm.si/doku.php.
35. Except for individuals connected by lines representing their slave trades, the points are arbitrarily positioned. For example, the slave Luisa, her owner Maria do Carmo, and the two postmen (no. 1 in the diagram) are located near Gregorio Freitas's network, but that does not necessarily indicate a relationship between the two groups.
36. Considering Iguape's small size and unimportance, slaves from this town very likely were contraband.
37. Slave bills of sale, 1864–1865 (vol. 24, 29), CCS; Almanak Laemmert (1865, 1870, 1875); Inheritance records, 1867, 1879, CCS (vols. 16, 99); Judicial processes, 1868, CCS (vol. 99), FAMS.
38. Judicial processes, 1820–1880, CCS, FAMS.
39. Slave bills of sale, 1864–1866, CCS (vols. 24), FAMS, PCNS.
40. It was not uncommon for slaves born in Africa and shipped to the Northeast to later be exported south via Rio de Janeiro. It is surprising, however, that only two slaves out of the group sold by residents in Rio de Janeiro were born in the Northeast. This indicates that a more common route for this large, interprovincial, and southern transfer was inland along the Paraíba Valley.
41. Slenes, "Demography and Economics," 595–99.
42. Slave sales tax lists, 1832–1855, AESP.
43. Slave bills of sale, 1862–1872, CCS, PCNS, SCNS.
44. *Diario de Santos*, Feb. 1873, FAMS, HS; *Revista Commercial*, 1849–1867, FAMS, HS; Frank, *Dutra's World*. Sellers commonly advertised a slave who could

perform "all services" (*todos os serviços*). This referred to slaves who might be destined for households without other domestic servants, for they could do a variety of tasks.

45. *Revista Commercial*, 1869–1872, FAMS, HS.

46. Almanak Luna, 1871, CCS, FAMS; *Revista Commercial*, 1862–1865, FAMS, HS; Slave bills of sale, CCS (vols. 24), FAMS; *Almanak administrativo . . . do Rio de Janeiro* [1860, 1865, 1870]; Costa e Silva, *Santos noutros tempos* (São Paulo, 1953).

47. This included five cooks, one painter, one chambermaid, and one steamship engine operator.

48. *Revista Commercial*, 1852–1872, FAMS, HS.

49. This figure covers a slightly larger area than Figure 3.5. Comparing the numbers of advertisements on the longer stretch of buildings of Rua Áurea to the shorter Rua Direita, the relative frequency of advertisement postings in two different neighborhoods can be observed. Maps produced using ArcGIS.

50. Frank, "Slave Market in Rio de Janeiro," 1–30. As for the impact on interprovincial slave trading, slaves in Minas Gerais have received attention in a debate over the scale of movement of bondspeople within the province. Some have argued that slaves were transferred from the "decadent" mining region of Minas Gerais to the coffee-producing region of the province in the nineteenth century. Others have argued against such a transfer. See Furtado, *Formação econǒmica do Brasil*, 122–23; Mattoso, *Ser escravo no Brasil*, 59; Martins, "Growing in Silence"; and Slenes, "Os múltiplos," 452. Robert Slenes writes that "the fact that slave prices in Pernambuco and Bahia responded primarily to sugar prices, not to labor and commodity prices in the Center-South, suggests that the major component of slave demand in these north-eastern provinces was that of the sugar sector." In other words, it appears that in the Northeast, supply and demand of slaves (and hence price levels) was as connected to the regional economy as the national one. Slenes, "Brazilian Internal Slave Trade," 337.

CHAPTER FOUR

1. Marcondes, *Diverso e desigual*, 14, 49. In 1870, Recife and Santos were nearly equal in their percentage of national exports.

2. For a discussion in this volume of that stigma, as evident in the town almanac and newspaper commentary, see Chapter Three. For a discussion of the efforts of abolitionists, see Chapter Seven.

3. Florentino and Góes, *A paz das senzalas*; Slenes, *Na senzala*; Motta, *Corpos escravos*; Reis, *Histórias de vida familiar*. Many other studies have touched on the subject. See Barickman, *Bahian Counterpoint*, 161; Klein, *African Slavery*, 170–71; Bergad, *Demographic and Economic History*, 154; Dean, *Rio Claro*, 77–79; Lauderdale Graham, *House and Street*, 10–12; Mattoso, *Bahia, século XIX*, 212; and Nishida, *Slavery and Identity*, 53–54, 130. For the United States, see Gutman, *Black Family in Slavery*; Dunaway, *African-American Family in Slavery*; and Fleischner, *Mastering Slavery*. *More than Chattel*, an edited volume

by Gaspar and Hine, discusses similarities and differences in family formation in the Americas.

4. For the view of slave families as social control, see Florentino and Góes, *A paz das senzalas*, 250. For the view of slave families' independent social space, see Slenes, *Na senzala*, 299.

5. For example, see Luna: *Minas Gerais, escravos e senhores* and "Observações sobre casamento"; Luna and Costa: "Posse de escravos" and "Vila Rica"; Graham, "A família escrava"; Costa and Gutierez, "Nota sobre o casamento"; Gutierez, "A harmonia dos sexos"; Fragoso and Florentino, "Marcelino, filho"; Costa, Slenes, and Schwartz, "A família escrava em Lorena"; Metcalf: "Vida familiar dos escravos," "Searching for the Slave Family," and *Family and Frontier*; Motta: "A família escrava" *Corpos escravos*, and "Contribuições da demografia histórica"; Motta and Marcondes, "A família escrava em Lorena"; and Slenes: "Demography and Economics" and "Escravidão e família." Many of the studies that focus on slavery and slave families are available online. See the conference proceedings for the Associação Brasileira de Estudos Populacionais (ABEP) at http://www.abep.org.br/usuario/GerenciaNavegacao.php, the Centro de Desenvolvimento e Planejamento Regional (CEDEPLAR) at http://www.cedeplar.ufmg.br/pesquisas/apresentacao/index.php, and the Associação Brasileira de Pesquisadores em História Econômica (ABPHE) at http://ideas.repec.org/s/abp/he2003.html.

6. Florentino and Góes: *A paz das senzalas* and "Tráfico, parentesco e esterilização"; Luna, *Observações sobre casamento*; Luna, *Minas Gerais, escravos e senhores*; Luna and Costa, *Posse de escravos*; Motta and Valentim, "A família escrava"; Fragoso and Florentino, "Marcelino, filho"; Costa and Gutierez, *Nota sobre o casamento*; Costa, Slenes, and Schwartz, "A família escrava em Lorena"; Garavazo, "Relações familiares"; Vasconcellos: "Estrutura de posse" and "Casar ou não"; Brügger, "Legitimidade, casamento e relações"; Freire, "Compadrio em uma freguesia"; and Teixeira, "Reprodução e famílias escravas."

7. Luna, *Observações sobre casamento*; Garavazo, *Relações familiares*; Florentino and Góes, *Tráfico, parentesco e esterilização*; Teixeira, *Reprodução e famílias escravas*; Slenes, *Na senzala*.

8. I use "infant" to refer to any child five years old or younger.

9. Nominal lists (Santos), 1817–1830, AESP.

10. Ibid.

11. Ibid.

12. Ibid.

13. Ibid.

14. Luna: *Observações sobre casamento*, 4 and *Recenseamento do Brasil em 1872, São Paulo*. "Marriage rates" includes slaves that were married or had been married previously.

15. Some slave infants may have been purchased or adopted without their mothers, but there is little evidence that this practice was common. Rarely were children five years or under bought or sold unaccompanied by their mothers. In the bills of sale and slave tax records, mothers and infants were often treated legally as one individual (with the children called *crias de peito* or *filhos de braço* ["children of the breast" or "children in arms"], with a single price leading to one

entry in these registers. On the other hand, children in the vulnerable and formative ages of twelve to eighteen were commonly traded locally in Santos and Rio de Janeiro. See Frank, "Slave Market in Rio de Janeiro."

16. Barickman, *Bahian Counterpoint*, 161.

17. Inheritance records, 1835, CCS (vol. 81), FAMS; Nominal lists (Santos), 1817–1830, AESP.

18. Among the 4,750 slaves listed in three years of the Santos census (1817, 1822, and 1830), the ratio of unmarried black slaves to unmarried *pardo* slaves was about five to one. Among the married slaves, however, the ratio was higher: eight to one. There were fifty-two widowed slaves in the census records of these three years, and darker-skinned widowed slaves were relatively more numerous (with four black widowed slaves for every widowed *pardo* slave). Many of these slaves are likely to have been double or triple counted. In 1871, *pretos* continued their slight advantage over *pardos* in marriage rates: 7.7 percent of *pretos* were married, compared to 6.9 percent of *pardos*. Church marriage records, 1837–1875, CDS; nominal lists (Santos), 1817, AESP; *Recenseamento do Brasil em 1872, São Paulo.*

19. This was Decree 1695 of 15 September 1869, *Coleção leis do Império do Brasil 1869*, 129–30.

20. Luna, *Observações sobre casamento*, 215–236; Luna and Klein, *Slavery and the Economy*, 273.

21. Inheritance records, 1810–1880, CCS, FAMS.

22. Carmelite convent records, 1865, ANB.

23. Almanak Laemmert, 1880, 1885; Almanak Thorton, 1871, CCS, FAMS; Church marriage records, CCS, 1837–1875; Rural estate lists, 1818, CCS, FAMS. The regular Catholic parish maintained books in which officials conducted and registered marriages of both free and slave couples. Officiating priests included the names of the couple and the date, time, and place of the ceremony. Sometimes they included their birthplaces, names of parents (of free individuals) or masters (of slaves), and the names of two or three witnesses. Slave marriages were usually placed into their own register, a book that recorded 22 marriages between 1837 and 1875. Twenty other slave couples were recorded among the hundreds of free unions in another set of much thicker parish registers.

24. Before 1850, more weddings of free or enslaved couples took place in the evening. After 1850, more Santos free and slave married in the morning and late afternoon, but the evening also remained popular for weddings. In the first period, the most popular hours to be married in Santos were 7 p.m. (60 weddings) and 9 p.m. (46 weddings). In the second, the hours of 7 a.m. (73 weddings) and 5 p.m. (78 weddings) were the desired or available hours.

25. Church marriage records, CCS, 1837–1875. Birthplace may have been excluded more frequently for native-born slaves than African slaves.

26. Municipal death certificates, 1857–1880, FAMS; Teixeira, "Reprodução e famílias," 106; for marriage rates for four regions of Rio de Janeiro, see Slenes, *Na senzala*, 86.

27. Within slaveholdings of 11–20 slaves in Mariana, 34 percent of slave families were fully united after 5–9 years and 25 percent were united after 10–14

years. In the largest slaveholdings (20+), 24 percent of slave families were united after 5–9 years and 15 percent were united after 10–14 years. Teixeira employed a similar method of comprehensive cross-listing of sources. She recorded the individual names of the slaves and then tracked them in estate inventories, church records, bills of sale, and slave registration lists, creating stories of changing slave families over time. Teixeira also presents a compelling case that historians will profit more in the future with studies that examine slaveholding stability in addition to size.

28. This idea accepted especially among the specialized jobs of a sugar mill. See Schwartz, *Tropical Babylons*, 185–86. For the United States, see Genovese, *Roll, Jordan, Roll.*

29. Karasch, *Slave Life*; Rock, *New York City Artisan.* Maria José de Souza Andrade examined hundreds of property assessment lists in inheritance records from Salvador and found 82 occupations listed for male slaves and 16 listed for female slaves. *A mão de obra escrava*, 129–30.

30. Sources used for collecting data on slave occupation in Santos are: Slave sales tax lists, 1833–1845, AESP; Slave bills of sale, 1863–1870, CCS in FAMS, PCNS, SCNS; Manumission letters, 1844–1875, CCS in FAMS, PCNS, SCNS; Inheritance records, 1830–1872, CCS in FAMS, *Revista Commercial*, *Diario de Santos*, 1850–1873, CCS in FAMS, HS; Cemetery registers and municipal death certificates, FAMS. The nominal list (1844) from São Sebastião was included for a discussion of slaves in the county to the immediate north. The Santos sources give occupation data and other types of information such as race, age, birthplace, and owner for 1,040 slaves. The São Sebastião "mappas" gives similar information for 2,067 slaves who worked in that township. The cemetery registers and death certificates are in FAMS.

31. "Important" occupations are defined as those with more that 2.5 percent of slaves of the total sample.

32. A third of all slaves during these two decades were declared to be *sem officio* (without a trade).

33. Other sellers appeared to be trying to avoid outdoor work for their slaves. A popular variant of these generic occupation categories was "good for any house service" ("*presitmoso para todo o serviço interno de casa de famila*" or "*proprio para serviço de casa de familia*").

34. Of the 2,226 slaves in an unusually detailed census from São Sebastião census in 1844, 2,067 were listed with occupation information. This is an extraordinary document since there are few detailed censuses of its type in the province after 1840. Furthermore, the census takers listed occupations of individual slaves. The three most common jobs of male slaves were farming (931), carpentry (33), and masonry (23). Farming also dominated the activities of female slaves. There were many more female farmers (784) than any other occupation. Female cooks (88) and seamstresses (48) took distant second and third places.

35. Three-quarters of working slaves in the total sample for Santos were black.

36. São Sebastião had no black slave tailors. There were only two out of twelve in Santos. Two-thirds of the carpenters in both São Sebastião and Santos were mulatto. In São Sebastião, however, relatively more *pardos* were cooks.

37. The area defined as "Bertioga" in the 1817, 1822, and 1830 nominal lists had an average of 127 *negros* and 131 *pardos*. The proportion of blacks to *pardos* changed over the sampled years but this may have been because the boundaries of this community slightly shifted in each year the census was tabulated. Of the 489 São Sebastião slaves who lived in small slaveholding households (defined as five or fewer slaves) in 1844, 66 percent were black. Among the 817 slaves of large households (20 or more slaves), 75 percent were black. Farming slaves (with *roça* or *lavoura* occupations) were also more numerous in the large households. Among slaves in the large slaveholding households, 82 percent tended the fields. In small slaveholding households, 64 percent of enslaved men and women were farmers.

38. Excluded slave jobs include butchers, clerks, railroad workers, vegetable vendors, warehouse workers, washerwomen, and wet nurses. The "domestic servant" category includes cooks, servants, and butlers while "general workers" include both those "without a trade" and "workers."

39. The coffee merchants were not too different from the larger set of owners identified in multiple sources. Evidence comes from the kinds of jobs worked by slaves of the "identified" men and women. These were individuals who owned a business in the city or were involved in local politics, clubs, or religious groups and thus appeared more than once in the more than twenty sources related to slaveholding in the Santos archives. It is no surprise that on average the identified owners were wealthier and more active in the town's social and commercial life than those not indentified.

40. Almanak Lemmert (1850, 1865, 1870, 1875, 1880).

41. Technological changes of the late nineteenth century also decreased the division of labor of some occupations, especially in transportation. The railroad eventually made muleteers obsolete, with their vast knowledge of how to move tons of merchandise on the backs of animals. The steamship eliminated a large range of sailing occupations, some of which were highly specialized and took a lifetime to master.

42. The changing environment of jobs in the town can be seen in the lives of several slaves. A slave named Laurinda, who was a domestic servant, entered the hospital in 1881. Three years later she appeared in the cemetery rolls, identified as a "washerwoman." Feliciano and Roque worked as farmers in the 1860s for two different masters. When Feliciano appeared again in 1874 and Roque in 1882, they were classified as "workers," which probably meant they were hauling goods or working in town warehouses. *Jornaleiro* (day wage worker) and *trabalhador* (worker) were often used interchangeably.

43. For similar efforts in Rio de Janeiro, see Holloway, *Policing Rio de Janeiro*, 35, 223, 275.

44. Municipal law code, 1847, FAMS.

45. Municipal law code, 1852, FAMS; Holloway, *Policing Rio de Janeiro*. José Justiano Bittencourt was also one of the first local slave traders to rely on the newspaper advertisements (see Chapter 3, this volume).

46. Unlike many other towns and cities in Brazil that had an area for clothes washing directly connected to the fountain, Santista slaves had to fill buckets or tubs and wash at a distance from the fountain.

47. Municipal law code, 1847, 1852, 1890, FAMS.
48. Jail registration records, 1860–1880, MPCSP. This estimate is based on the following data: of 197 arrests between January and October 1878, 29 percent were of slaves, the rest of free persons. Of the 139 arrested free men and women, 60 were European or American, almost all mariners. Slaves made up around 15 percent of the town population at this time. In total, the police registers include 461 slaves, and the newspaper listed 138 names of arrested slaves.
49. *Revista Commercial*, 1866–1867, HS.
50. Jail registration records, 1860–1880, MPCSP; *Revista Commercial*, 1866–1867, HS.
51. Jail registration records, 1860–1880, MPCSP; *Revista Commercial*, 1866–1867, HS. "Lighter-skinned slaves" included *pardos*, *mulattos*, *fulos*, and *cabras*.
52. More than two-thirds of 599 register entries for arrested slaves included physical descriptions. Eighty six slaves were described as "tall" and 54 as "short." Fifty seven were described as "stout" and 55 as "skinny."
53. Jail registration records, 1860–1880, MPCSP; *Revista Commercial* (Santos), 1866–1867, HS.
54. Costa e Silva, *Santos noutros tempos*, 99–101.
55. This description is taken from a diagram of the jail, reproduced in Costa e Silva, *Santos noutros tempos*, 543. The jail building was restored several decades ago and can be visited, although it no longer operates as a jail.
56. Jail registration records, 1860–1880, MPCSP; *Revista Commercial*, 1866–1867, HS.
57. Jail registration records, May 1870, Nov. 1871, Sept. 1878, MPCSP. Most of the suspects brought into the jail "under investigation" were taken in by *paisanos*.
58. Jail registration records, 1860–1880, MPCSP; *Revista Commercial*, 1866–1867, HS.
59. Jail registration records, Sept. 1878 and Feb. 1879, MPCSP.
60. Jail registration records, 1860–1880, MPCSP; *Revista Commercial*, 1866–1867, HS.
61. Four slaves were interned with unknown charges.
62. Jail registration records, 1860–1880, MPCSP; *Revista Commercial*, 1866–1867, HS.
63. Jail registration records, 1860–1880, MPCSP; *Revista Commercial*, 1866–1867, HS; *Livro de pacientes, 1861–1883*, ASCMS; Cemetery registers, 1857–1888, FAMS.
64. Jail registration records, 1860–1880, MPCSP; *Revista Commercial*, 1866–1867, HS. English and Portuguese mariners were most frequently arrested. Yet while the English consul brought charges against nine of his countrymen, the Portuguese consul did not charge anyone. Of the 16 Italians arrested, five were brought to jail with their consul's request. Four Americans spent a night among slaves and free in the Santos jail, all charged by William T. Wright, a slaveholding American consul from Long Island, New York.
65. Jail registration records, 1860–1880, MPCSP; *Revista Commercial*, 1866–1867, HS.
66. These were common or limited liability partnerships.

67. Jail registration records, 1860–1880, MPCSP; *Revista Commercial*, 1866–1867, HS.
68. Ibid.
69. "Identified" meant that an individual was found in one of the many cross-listed sources used for this study. See the Appendix for more details on methodology. Of 7,000 names of free individuals (townspeople or visitors) found in various sources during the 1860s and 1870s, 3,300 were found in more than one source.
70. Jail registration records, 1860–1880, MPCSP; *Revista Commercial*, 1866–1867, HS.
71. Jail registration records, Apr. 1879, MPCSP.

CHAPTER FIVE

1. Hospital patient registers (May 1869, March 1874), ASCMS; Almanak Luna (1871), CCS, FAMS; Jail registers (December 1870), MPCSP.
2. Merck Manual, "Hypertrophic Cardiomyopathy," http://www.merck.com/mmhe/sec03/ch026/ch026c.html (accessed August 18, 2010); McCance and Huether, *Pathophysiology*, 1061.
3. Hospital patient registers (May 1874), ASCMS.
4. Hospital patient registers, 1861–1883, ASCMS. This claim is based on a comparison of the number of patients released from the hospital compared to the number of patients who died. Between 4 and 5 percent of slave patients returned to the hospital, but only a few due to causes related to their first visit. Since so few patients returned, I believe that most slaves left the hospital feeling better than they did when they entered.
5. Tannenbaum, *Slave and Citizen*, 3–5.
6. Some of the new work done on this subject is the result of a Portuguese translation edition of a pioneering work by Mary Karasch, who analyzed hospital and cemetery records to examine the top afflictions of slaves in Rio de Janeiro during the first half of the nineteenth century in *Slave Life*, 147–84. The medical history of Brazilian slaves has also been supported by research grants supplied by the Fundação Oswaldo Cruz. New studies include Amantino, "As condições físicas e de saúde dos escravos fugitivos; Assis, "Tráfico atlăntico"; Barbosa, "Escravidão, mortalidade e doenças"; Chambouleyron, "Escravos do atlăntico equatorial"; Guimarães, "Os manuais de medicina popular"; Pereira, "Práticas de curar e doenças"; Reis, "Doença e escravidão"; and the collection of conference papers organized by Ăngela Porto and published by the Casa de Oswaldo Cruz as "Doenças e escravidão." Among older studies, Robin Anderson used cemetery records reprinted in a São Paulo newspaper to explore the leading causes of death in that city during the late 1800s, but perhaps because of the limitations of her source, Anderson did not discuss the health of slaves. See Anderson, "Public Health and Public Healthiness." Others have looked at the health of slaves indirectly. Sidney Chalhoub argued that yellow fever epidemics altered the political response toward slavery and race in "Politics of Disease Control." For informa-

tion on yellow fever in Brazil, see Cooper, "Death by the Sea." Yellow fever in Rio de Janeiro is discussed in Chalhoub, *Cidade febril*; Graden, "An Act 'Even of Public Security'; and Lauderdale Graham, *House and Street*; and Needell, *The Party of Order*. For readings on the history of health and disease for nineteenth-century Brazil, see Alden and Miller, "Out of Africa"; Benchimol, *Febre amarela: A doença; Dos micróbios aos mosquitos*; and *Pereira Passos*; Cooper, "New 'Black Death'"; Peard, *Race, Place, and Medicine*. A more comprehensive bibliography is available through the Brazilian Association of Historians of Disease and Health (GT História da Saúde e das Doenças) at http://www.ideiad.com.br/gt/ (accessed July 31, 2010).

7. For the argument that the Imperial government altered its policy and laws on several important issues because of the impact of yellow fever, see Chalhoub, "Politics of Disease Control."

8. Variance is important. Tuberculosis, for example, varied between 5 and 10 percent of slave deaths, while smallpox could fluctuate between 5 and 47 percent. Cemetery registers, 1865–1875, FAMS.

9. Lamberg, *O Brazil*.

10. Read, "Hemispheric Movement." Epidemics were certainly not unknown during the colonial period, but little has been written about them. In one of the few sources detailing an epidemic during this period, A.J.R. Russell-Wood describes the spread of yellow fever in 1668 from Pernambuco to Bahia. In both provinces, hundreds of people died. The Bahian Misericórdia Hospital buried 288 people in May 1668, more than 1 percent of the city's population. Russell-Wood, *Fidalgos and Philanthropists*, 226, 288, 429. Smallpox played a strong role in decimating the indigenous populations in colonial Brazil. The disease was known to kill thousands in 1621 (Maranhão), 1642 (Pernambuco), 1663 (littoral, from Paraíba to Rio de Janeiro), 1666 (Pernambuco, Bahia, Espirito Santo, Rio de Janeiro), and 1743 (Pará), 1749 (Brazilian Northeast). Nava, *Capítulos da história*, 102.

11. Spix and others, *Viagem pelo Brasil*, 154–55, cited in Blount, "Public Health Movement," 27. John Mawe had specifically observed that the port of Santos was free of epidemic because of a successful vaccination program. Mawe, *Viagens ao interior do Brasil*, 69, 79, cited in Blount, "Public Health Movement," 27; São Paulo and Brazil, *Discurso recitado . . . de 1847*, 1845–1849; Siguad, *Do clima e das doenças*.

12. Karasch, *Slave Life*, 149. In all, Karasch identified 148 specific types of diseases and afflictions, but two-thirds of these illnesses were rare and appeared in fewer than ten cases at the hospital. Karasch also gives figures from Soares, who lists pulmonary tuberculosis, tetanus, diarrhea, convulsions, and elephantitis as the causes of death of slaves buried by the Misericórdia Hospital between 1695 and 1839. Soares, *A escravatura na Misericórdia*, 156. Of the 22,474 slaves buried in Rio during this period, 4,071 were recorded with a cause of death. Yellow fever and cholera are not listed and, surprisingly, neither is smallpox, despite recorded epidemics in the 1830s. Siguad, *Do clima e das doenças*, 150–51; Rĕgo, *Esboço histórico*.

13. Donald Cooper nearly stands alone in studying the impact of epidemics

in Brazil during the nineteenth century. See "Brazil's Long Fight," "New 'Black Death,'" "Death by the Sea," and "Yellow Fever and the Modernization."

14. Siguad, *Do clima e das doenças*; Horner, *Medical Topography of Brazil*; Egbert, "Yellow Fever of Brazil" in Kidder and Fletcher, *Brazil and the Brazilians*, 609–13.

15. Congresso Brasileiro de Hygiene.

16. "The Fever Ship," in Masefield, *Poems and Plays*, 11.

17. Cooper, "New 'Black Death'."

18. Provincial Presidential Report (São Paulo), 1856, 1–12.

19. Echenberg, *Plague Ports*; Britto, *Oswaldo Cruz*, 71.

20. Hospital San Nicolás de Bari was the first hospital founded in the Americas, built in Santo Domingo between 1503 and 1508. The oldest hospital to be providing service without interruption is the Hospital de Jesus in Mexico City, built in 1523, with funds given by Hernán Cortés.

21. Novomilenio, "Historias e lendas de Santos," http://www.novomilenio.inf.br/santos/ho260d.htm (accessed August 18, 2010).

22. Santos, *Historia de Santos*; Cemetery registers, 1857–1888, FAMS.

23. Provincial Presidential Report (São Paulo): 1855, 14; 1856, 53; 1858, 12; 1862, 26; 1866, 26; 1883, 26. Sobrinho, *Santos noutros tempos*, 241–43. The expansion of hospitals occurred in other parts of Brazil as well. Hospital Nossa Senhora da Saúde and Hospital Nossa Senhora do Socorro both opened in the city of Rio de Janeiro as a result of a decree by Dom Pedro II to assist with the cholera epidemics. In 1855, another hospital opened in Vassouros, a coffee town in the interior of Rio de Janeiro province. Stein, *Vassouras*, 194.

24. Patient movements, 1878–1885, ASCMS. Almanak Laemmert, 1881. When a few cases of cholera appeared in the city in 1856, the township worked with the Convent of Saint Anthony to create a special infirmary. Cholera never became a serious threat, thus the infirmary may not have been used. "Provincial Report" (São Paulo), 1856, 43.

25. Hospital patient registers, 1861–1883, ASCMS.

26. Ibid. John Luccock, writing about the Rio de Janeiro Misericórdia Hospital, said "it would appear matter of regret that there is no ward in the hospital for females, nor nurses of that description allowed, if the vicious dispositions and habits of the people were not taken into due consideration." Luccock, *Notes on Rio de Janeiro*.

27. Hospital patient registers, 1861–1883, ASCMS.

28. Ibid.

29. Ibid.

30. Judicial trials (Vol. 86, p. 29a), 1842, CSS, FAMS. In 1828, when the military hospital was providing temporary services for the Misericórdia Hospital, the daily rate was 640 *réis* (.64 *mil-réis*). Casas de Saude, private clinics that competed with hospitals, advertised the prices of their services in newspapers and almanacs. Dr. Fairbank's private homeopathic clinic in Salvador, Bahia, offered a daily fee of 1 *mil-réis* for slaves in 1849. All patients were required to pay for ten days, however, limiting the kinds of afflictions treated to those that were most debilitating. A. J. Peixoto's clinic in Rio de Janeiro charged the owners or rent-

ers of slaves two *mil-réis* in 1855. *Correio Mercantil* (Bahia), 8 Oct. 1849; and Almanak Laemmert (1855).

31. Hospital patient registers, 1861–1883, ASCMS.

32. Ibid.; cemetery registers, 1857–1886, FAMS.

33. Hospital patient registers, 1850, 1865, 1885, ASCMS.

34. Laird Bergad found that about 10 percent of slaves in Minas Gerais had some sort of illness or injury. *Demographic and Economic History*, 155–58. Sergio Buarque de Holanda thought the "normal" percentage of incapacitated slaves was a little higher, between 10 and 25 percent. Holanda and Campos, *História geral da civilização brasileira* (Tomo II, vol. 5), 178. Some chronic illnesses and bad injuries might have required repeated medical care.

35. Hospital patient registers, 1871–1872, ASCMS. Yellow fever became epidemic in 1872, elevating the hospital admission rate. In 1871, a nonepidemic year, 54 slaves were admitted into the Misericórdia Hospital.

36. Chalhoub, *Artes e ofícios de curar*, 331–54.

37. Porter, *Greatest Benefit to Mankind*, 304–96. In 1845, 135 slaves and 1,433 free people entered the Misericórdia Hospital of Porto Alegre. Twenty-two percent of the enslaved patients and 17 percent of the free patients died during the year. Hospital patient registers, 1845, Santa Casa de Misericórdia, Centro Histórico-Cultural Santa Casa, Porto Alegre. In Recife's Hospital Pedro II in 1878, 47 enslaved patients (21 percent) died out of 224 who were treated. This death rate was about three percentage points higher than the death rate of free patients. Provincial Presidential Report (São Paulo), 1878, 6. Stein reports that "over a twenty-eight year period, roughly one out of seven patients" died in the Santa Casa de Misericórdia of Vassouras, Rio de Janeiro. He writes that these death rates "seemed to bear out the fear" that was commonly held among people toward the hospital. Mortality rate was 5 percent at twenty English county infirmaries in 1877. The Royal Bath Hospital in Harrogate, North Yorkshire, had the worst rates, but, at 8 percent, this was still much better than any Brazilian hospital. Tait, *Essay on Hospital Mortality*, 68.

38. Porter, *Greatest Benefit to Mankind*, 390–91.

39. A more detailed analysis of the most common afflictions that sent slaves and free people to the hospital or the cemetery can be found in Read, "Sickness, Recovery and Death," 63–76.

40. Ibid., 73.

41. Karasch, *Slave Life*, 169; cemetery registers, 1878–1886, FAMS.

42. Swedish authorities greatly lowered the threat of smallpox as early as 1810. There were continued smaller outbreaks until the 1880s, but the incidence of smallpox in Sweden was much lower in the nineteenth century compared to the preceding century due to an effective compulsory vaccination program administered by the state. See Sköld, "From Innoculation to Vaccination."

43. Merck Manual, "Yellow Fever," http://www.merck.com/mmhe/sec17/ch198/ch198k.html (accessed September 7, 2010). Kiple: *African Exchange*, 280, and *Blacks in Colonial Cuba*, 115; Kiple and King, *Another Dimension to the Black Diaspora*.

44. Carrigan, *Saffron Scourge*, 255–56; Kiple, *Caribbean Slave*.

45. Read, "Sickness, Recovery and Death," 67–69.
46. Hospital patient registers, 1861–1883, ASCMS; Almanak Luna (1871), FAMS.
47. Hospital patient registers, 1861–1883, ASCMS.
48. McCance and Huether, *Pathophysiology*, 820.
49. Hospital patient registers, 1861–1883, ASCMS.
50. Hospital patient registers, October 1872, September 1873, November 1874, ASCMS.
51. Hospital patient registers, 1861–1883, ASCMS.
52. Sobrinho, *Santos noutros tempos*; Reis, *Death Is a Festival*, 13.
53. Nishida, *Slavery and Identity*; Viana, *O idioma da mestiçagem*; Tavares, *Irmandades, igreja e devoção.*
54. Novomilenio, "Histórias e lendas de Santos—Cemetério de Paquetá," http://www.novomilenio.inf.br/santos/h0260d.htm (accessed August 18, 2010).
55. The cost of the public cemetery for the second trimester of 1866, for example, was 134 *mil-réis*, while its income was 204 *mil-réis*. *Revista Commercial*, January 20, 1866, HS.
56. Municipal law codes, 1847, 1852, FAMS.
57. Municipal law codes, 1890, FAMS.
58. Reis, *Death Is a Festival*, 41.
59. Ibid., 47.
60. Cemetery registers, 1857–1886, FAMS.
61. Cemetery registers, 1874, FAMS; Reis, *Death Is a Festival*, 47. St. Benedict was a black saint popular among slaves and people of color. The first line of a common contemporary prayer dedicated to him reads: "St. Benedict, son of slaves, who found true freedom serving God and your brothers, independent of race or color, you free me from all of life's slavery and help me take discrimination from my heart so I can recognize all men as my brothers."
62. Cemetery registers, 1857–1886, FAMS.
63. Ibid.

CHAPTER SIX

1. *Revista Commercial*, June 1858, HS. Of course, it may have been raining as it often does during the winter months on the Paulista coast.
2. This is the same man who played a central role in the social network of Cypriano da Silva Proost and the freed slave Thereza de Jesus Januaria (see Chapter One, this volume). Since the owner of these two slaves neighbored Januaria, they probably knew each other.
3. Jacintho entered the hospital suffering from hepatitis in 1864, with Braga listed as his owner. Hospital patient registers, November 1864, ASCMS.
4. The manumission letter was a judicial act in which the owner conferred freedom (partial or full) upon one or more slaves. The letter was usually written, notarized, and filed at a notary office. Manumissions also were written into baptism records, wills, and final testaments, all binding documents that supplied suf-

ficient legal proof of the owner's intent regarding his or her slave. "Conditional" manumissions carried a labor obligation, and "unconditional" (or freely given) manumissions bestowed freedom without such obligations. Paid manumissions could be either conditional or unconditional, in which the conditions referred to expected labor instead of cash payments.

5. Municipal death certificates, 1875, FAMS; Manumission letters, 1871, CCS, FAMS; jail registration records, 1878, MPCSP.

6. The word *freedom*, so often used in the literature of manumissions, is not always the appropriate description of the lives of most ex-slaves after manumission. Since many could not leave the work of their owner and had to continue to act in specific and limiting ways toward the person who had owned them, their lives were far from free. For different views on the meaning of *liberty* in Brazilian slave society, see Carvalho, "Liberdade, liberdades, alforria," in *Liberdade: Retinas e ruptura*; Castro, *Das cores do silêncio*; and Chalhoub, *Visões da liberdade*, 23.

7. Chalhoub, *Visões da liberdade*, 137. Sidney Chalhoub argues, however, that revoked manumissions were common enough to be a threat.

8. Manumission letters, 1844, CS, FAMS; Frank, *Dutra's World*, 106; Inheritance records, 1800–1880, CCS, FAMS.

9. Malheiro, *A escravidão no Brasil* (vol. I), 53. See also Conrad, *Children of God's Fire*, 242. Unlike the Spanish-American slave systems, Brazil does not seem to have developed a legal tradition that allowed slaves access to self-purchase. In Cuba, for example, *coartação* (the process of gradual self-purchase) was based on the Roman *Siete Partidos* tradition. Thus, until 1871, Cuban slaves likely had a better chance than Brazilian slaves of compelling their owners to accept money in exchange for their eventual freedom, as long as the money and terms were deemed legally sufficient. See Bergad, *Comparative Histories*, 196–99.

10. Grinberg, "Reescravização, direitos," in Lara and Nunes Mendonça, *Direitos e justiças no Brasil*, 101–28.

11. Kiernan, "Manumission of Slaves."

12. This total comes from the subtraction of the 85 baptismal letters from the total set of 379 letters.

13. Another 7 percent were unknown. Of the purchased letters, most do not list who paid.

14. Ressurreição appears to have included paid manumissions in the category of "conditional," making it difficult to compare the different kinds of obligations that slaves faced. See Ressurreição, *São Sebastião*, 200.

15. Eisenberg, "Ficando livre," 175–216.

16. Other studies can be categorized by place and time. For Paraty (RJ) between 1789 and 1822, see Kiernan, "Manumission of Slaves." For Bahia between 1680 and 1850, see Schwartz, "Manumission of Slaves," and Mattoso, "A propósito de cartas." Both Schwartz and Mattoso, however, found that paid manumission letters surpassed unpaid letters for several decades in the eighteenth century. Schwartz explains this in terms of changing economic climates. For Salvador between 1808 and 1850, see Nishida, "Manumission and Ethnicity." For Rio de Janeiro between 1840 and 1850, see Florentino, "Do que Nabuco já sabia." For Juiz

do Fora (SP) between 1844 and 1888, see Lacerda, "Economia cafeeira," available online: http://ideas.repec.org/s/cdp/diamo2.html (accessed August 20, 2009).

17. Antônio Henrique Duarte Lacerda discusses the use of *contratos de locação* in the manumission process in "Economia cafeeira," 18. He does not mention how many of the indenture contracts he used were written separately from their corresponding manumission letters. Evidence of a set of separate (yet closely connected) historical sources may indicate that previous studies of manumission may have undercounted conditional letters.

18. Manumission letters, 1864, CCS, FAMS; and indenture contracts, 1864, CCS, FAMS.

19. Manumission letters, 1863, CCS, FAMS; and indenture contracts, 1865, CCS, FAMS.

20. Manumission letters, 1810–1871, PCNS, SCNS, CCS, FAMS. Most studies of manumission in Brazilian cities or regions in the colonial or postcolonial period have found that paid and indenture manumissions, taken together, exceeded free manumissions. There are two exceptions to this rule. Katia Mattoso found that free manumissions (*alforrias gratuitas*) surpassed payment manumissions (*alforrias pagas*) for many years between 1779 and 1850 in Salvador, but she does not clarify whether she placed indenture manumissions in the "free" or "payment" category. See "A propósito de cartas," 23–52. Eisenberg found that free manumissions in Campinas, São Paulo, exceeded paid and indenture manumissions after 1885. He attributes this decline to the 50 percent drop in prices that also occurred at the midpoint of the 1880s. See "Ficando livre," 200.

21. Manumission letters, 1811, 1813 and 1847, CCS, FAMS; and nominal lists, 1817, AESP.

22. Manumission letters, 1810–1871, PCNS, SCNS, CCS, FAMS. Lacerda found that the largest group who received the indenture service contracts (*contratos de locação*) in Juiz de Fora were children. See "Economic cafeeira," 18.

23. For a discussion of the *coartação*, see Paiva, *Escravos e libertos*, 21–22; Kittleson, *Practice of Politics*, 86–87; and Lacerda, "Economic cafeeira."

24. According to Keila Ginberg, the masters or former masters who argued for reenslavement in courts relied on several laws. For example, article 179 of the constitution protected private property. Two parts of the *Ordenações filipinas* also gave legal ammunition for slave owners. Title 11 (book 4) listed stipulations that favored or did not favor freedom, while Title 63 outlined when a manumission letter could be annulled. See "Reescravização, direitos," in Lara and Nunes Mendonça, *Direitos e justiças no Brasil*, 108–11.

25. Klein and Luna, *Slavery in Brazil*, 257.

26. This might work in an opposite direction. According to Karasch, "living in close quarters also bred enmity, however, and some women had no compunction about forcing aged slaves into the streets." Karasch, *Slave Life*, 346.

27. Higgins gives a few examples of men who placed pressure on female slaves to enter into relationships with the promise of manumission. See *Licentious Liberty*, 145–74.

28. Manumission letters, 1810–1871, PCNS, SCNS, CCS, FAMS. Among slave buyers and sellers, married couples predominated.

29. Bertin, "Alforrias em São Paulo."

30. Others have found a correspondence between rates of manumission and size of slaveholdings: the smaller the holding, the higher the rate of manumission. Klein, "American Slavery," 116.

31. "Slave market records" include the slave tax, bills of sale, and the advertisement records. Occupations for these men were found in the town almanacs or among the civil judicial witnesses.

32. Manumission letters, 1810–1871, PCNS, SCNS, CCS, FAMS.

33. Karasch noticed a great range of occupations among those who manumitted slaves, and suspected that "a majority of them came from middle-income groups in society." Karasch, *Slave Life*, 344.

34. Alternatively, it could reunite them, if only temporarily. Slaves sometimes ran away to reunite with family members. For example, the motivation of a slave named Isidoro who fled from his owners in Rio de Janeiro may have been to reunite with family near the "cloth factory in Andarahy." *Revista Commercial*, 10 June 1865. One slave owner who lived in rural Pernambuco believed his slave Feliciano had escaped to Recife in 1875 because he had relatives there. *Diario de Pernambuco*, 4 January 1875. See also Santos, "Resistência escrava," 35–39.

35. See descriptions of shackles and iron collars in Ewbank, *Life in Brazil*, 116, 164, 438, 442. Mary Karasch discusses the physical abuse and torture that slaves had to endure in *Slave Life*, 113–17.

36. There have been few studies of fugitive slaves using the runaway notices of newspapers, despite the wealth of information these provide. Gilberto Freyre's study is best known, and he was the first to point out the enormous diversity of slaves who attempted flight. See *O escravo nos anúncios*. See also Petiz, *Buscando a liberdade*. Ana Josefina Ferrari analyzed the language used in Brazilian slave advertisements in *A voz do dono*. In the United States, more attention has been given to runaways, including works by Frazier, *Runaways and Freed Missouri Slaves*; Johnson, "Runaway Slaves"; Lehner, *Reaction to Abuse*; Parker, *Stealing a Little Freedom*; Schafer, "New Orleans Slavery"; and Whitman, *The Price of Freedom*.

37. "Runaway advertisements," *Revista Commercial*, 1850–1855, 1860–1867, *Diario de Santos*, 1872; CCS, FAMS, HS.

38. Machado: *O plano e o pănico* and "De rebeldes a fura-greves," in Cunha and Gomes, *Quase-cidadão*; Rosemberg, *Ordem e burla*.

39. A slightly higher percent of females fled in the 1860s than the 1850s. "Runaway advertisements," *Revista Commercial*, 1850–1855, 1860–1867; *Diario de Santos*, 1872; CCS, FAMS, HS. The slaves described in the Santos advertisements can be compared to those in numerous advertisements from Rio de Janeiro's *Revista Commercial*. This newspaper posted 363 advertisements in January and June of 1865. Of those who ran away (or were kidnapped) 87 percent were male, similar to the Santos average. "Slave runaways," *Jornal do Commercio*, Rio de Janeiro, 1865, dataset courtesy of Kari Zimmerman. According to Silmei de Sant'Ana Petiz, of 944 slaves recorded by police in Rio Grande do Sul as fugitives in 1850, only 5 percent were female. See Petiz, *Buscando a liberdade*, 110. Of the 132 runaways in or near São João del Rei, Minas Gerais, 99 percent were male. Santos, "Resistência escrava," 35–39.

40. Fugitives in Rio de Janeiro were also similar when it came to place of birth: 64 percent of slaves listed in Rio were native-born (although there is no birthplace information for 122 of the runaways).

41. Read, "Off the Block," 19–22. A more detailed analysis of slave prices in Santos and the province is available at http://eraofepidemics.squarespace.com/storage/Ian%20Read%20Slave%20Trading%20Brazil%20Working%20Draft.doc.pdf, 19–22.

42. Freyre, *O escravo nos anuncios*, 28.

43. Runaway advertisements, *Revista Commercial*, 1850–1855, 1860–1867; *Diario de Santos*, 1872; CCS, FAMS, HS.

44. Marks and changes brought to the body by the jobs the slaves performed were not included. An owner of a slave tailor noted that "the conditions of his hands indicate his profession." Runaway advertisements, *Revista Commercial*, April, 1863, HS. A handful of other slaves rode mules and horses from an early age, indicated by being bow-legged (*zaimbro das pernas* or *pernas arcadas*).

45. *Revista Commercial*, February 1863, July 1863, HS.

46. Owners sometimes seemed unwilling or unable to believe that the slave was to blame. Some saw the work of slave robbers and accomplices. It was common among runaway advertisements to state a protest, such as "protesta-se por percas e danos contra quem o tiver acoutado" (I protest against the losses and damages caused by whomever was involved). *Revista Commercial*, February 1862, HS.

47. *Revista Commercial*, April 1861, February 1862, HS.

48. *Revista Commercial*, April 1861, HS.

49. Karasch, *Slave Life*; Klein, *African Slavery*, 18.

50. *Revista Commercial*, February 1861, April 1861, March 1864, HS.

51. *Revista Commercial*, June 1852, March 1863, October 1863, November 1864, January 1867, May 1867, HS.

52. The print patterns of pants and shirts may have changed in style during these two decades. During the 1850s, more were printed with stripes, but a decade later checkered patterns were more common.

53. The clothing that slave runaways in the United States wore appear to have taken on a distinctiveness that their Brazilian counterparts did not have. For example, U.S. runaways displayed a deliberate clash of bright colors that historians have attributed to West African traditions. For an analysis of clothing worn by runaways in the United States, see White and White, "Slave Clothing."

54. Chalhoub, *Visões da liberdade*, 102–8.

CHAPTER SEVEN

1. Some have claimed that this was a "law," but Lúcia Duarte Lanna is correct in stating that this was an official declaration that Santos would not respect slave laws. See *Uma cidade na transição*, 190–91. The township could write laws only into the municipal law code (*Codigo de posturas*).

2. For an overview of abolitionism in Santos, see Santos, *History of Santos*,

213–40; Machado, *O plano e o pănico*, 143–67; Lanna, *Uma cidade na transição*, 182–97; Rosemberg, *Ordem e burla*, 187–241.

3. Slenes, "Brazilian Internal Slave Trade."

4. Machado, *O plano e o pănico*, 96; "Inquérito histórico sobre a Abolição entre os abolicionistas vivos," in *O Estado de S. Paulo* (Coleção de 1926), reprinted in "Histórias e lendas de Santos—Quilombos: Depoimentos de quem viveu os fatos de 1888, os momentos finais da escravidão negra no País, pelas testemunhas" at http://www.novomilenio.inf.br/santos/h0222h.htm#64.

5. Francisco Martins dos Santos was probably the first to give this number, and it has been frequently cited since. See Santos, *Historia de Santos*, 40. Machado claimed that ten thousand is exaggerated, see "De rebeldes a fura-greves" in Cunha and Gomes, *Quase-cidadão*, 249. Laird Bergad claimed that twenty thousand slaves in total escaped to Santos, but Jabaquara was one of many destinations. See *Comparative Histories*, 287.

6. Conrad, *Destruction of Brazilian Slavery*, 240–41; Baronov, *Abolition of Slavery*, 154–55; Toplin, *Abolition of Slavery in Brazil*, 209–10; Bergad, *Comparative Histories*, 287; Costa, *Da senzala à colŏnia*, 377. For Santos as the "slave's Canaan," see "Inquérito histórico sobre a Abolição entre os abolicionistas vivos," in *O Estado de S. Paulo* (Coleção de 1926), reprinted in "Histórias e lendas de Santos—Quilombos: Depoimentos de quem viveu os fatos de 1888, os momentos finais da escravidão negra no País, pelas testemunhas" at http://www.novomilenio.inf.br/santos/h0222h.htm#64.

7. Klein, *African Slavery*, 256.

8. For example, in an article titled "Abolitionist Santos," a local newspaper reported in 2003 that "even in the first years of the nineteenth century, a large part of the [Santos] population became favorable to freeing the slaves and even several famous Santistas had joined this fight." *Diário Oficial de Santos*, June 13, 2003, HS. Another newspaper claimed that "Santos was never a slave society." "Santos abolicionista," *A Tribuna*, May 11, 2003, HS.

9. Bonifácio's most famous speech on the subject of slavery, made in front of the Imperial Constitutional Assembly in 1823, was "Representação sobre a escravatura" (A Representation of Slavery's Effects). Andrada e Silva and Barbosa, *Discursos parlamentares* (vol. 13), 327. See also Lichti and Santos, *Poliantéia Santista*, 217.

10. Conrad, *Destruction of Brazilian Slavery*, 18. In 1887, the Parliament of São Paulo approved a bill to pay six *contos* to erect a monument dedicated to Jose Bonifácio de Andrada e Silva, stating that in the forty-eight years since his death he had not been forgotten by Paulistas. The monument, to be built in Santos, would be dedicated to his contributions to science, poetry, and *liberdade de nossa patria* (freedom of our fatherland). While no direct mention of his involvement in abolitionism was mentioned, the timing of this monument was likely seen as symbolic support for abolitionism. *Annaes da Assembléa Legislativa de São Paulo* (1887), 36.

11. Lichti and Santos, *Poliantéia santista*, 217; Bonifácio and Caldeira, *José Bonifácio de Andrada e Silva*.

12. Vergueiro was a liberal politician who served as one of three regents for

the young Dom Pedro II (1831–1840). For his involvement in the *parceria* system, see Costa, *Da senzala à colŏnia*, 110–30. A study of his plantation in Rio Claro is found in Warren Dean, *Rio Claro*, 88–103.

13. For example, the Santos branch of the Vergueiro Company made the largest purchase of slaves registered in any of the surviving books. In 1865, the company bought twenty slaves from a seller in São Paulo who had connections to Rio Claro. Slave bills of sale (vol. 24), 1865, FAMS, CCS. Vergueiro made much of his fortune from a slave-importing business in Santos during the 1830s and 1840s. Bethell, *Brazil: Empire and Republic*, 126. Vergueiro's two sons lived in Santos for many years and were both involved in politics and local commerce.

14. Notice that it is the international slave trade that is attacked here, not the institution of slavery or an internal trade of slaves. *Revista Commercial*, November 11, 1851, CCS, Vol. 118, 112.

15. Santos, *Historia de Santos*, 5. For the view that the war with Paraguay prompted abolition, see Richard Graham, *Causes for the Abolition*, 123–37. For the view that the war strengthened the pro-slavery conservative party, see Conrad, *Destruction of Brazilian Slavery*, 87.

16. Cristiano Benedito, a senator representing Minas Gerais, argued that a distinction should be drawn between "emancipationists" who "desire the actual liberation of the slaves on a large scale, [and the] owners to be indemnified by the state" and the "abolitionists" who "demand that the slave have his freedom immediately without indemnification." Laërne, *Brazil and Java*, 108.

17. Santos, *Historia de Santos*, 5; Sobrinho, *Santos noutros tempos*, 361. Ana de Andrada had been a widow for many years by the time she became the society's president.

18. Santos, *Historia de Santos*, 5.

19. Ibid., 5–6; Judicial processes, 1836, CCS, vol. 101, 1858, CCS, vol. 96.

20. Lichti and Santos, *Poliantéia santista* (vol. 2), 219.

21. Santos, *Historia de Santos,* 10–12. The other two *quilombos* were Vila Mathias and Pai Felipe. See Machado, "De rebeldes," in Cunha and Gomes, *Quase-cidadão*, 243–49.

22. Lichti and Santos, *Poliantéia santista*, 225.

23. Conrad, *Destruction of Brazilian Slavery*, 199–209. Conrad writes that the town Pelŏtas in Rio Grande do Sul was said to have been "freed of slaves," but there were still advertisements for "the rental of black cooks and childless wet nurses" after that declaration. Pŏrto Alegre still had at least fifty-eight slaves in 1888, four years after the city had proclaimed that it no longer had slaves. Ibid., 209.

24. *Annaes da Assembléa . . . de São Paulo*, 1886.

25. Pacheco e Chavas, *Relatorio apresentado*. See also Graham, *Causes for the Abolition*, 123–37.

26. In the Chamber of Deputies, Andrade Figueira declared "there is no law to decree the emancipation in Ceará, that it is not true that slavery is abolished there" because "the president of the province could neither proclaim this law nor prevent the entrance of slaves." Quoted in Nabuco, *The Life of Joaquim Nabuco*, 115.

27. Machado: *Plano e pănico* 150 and "De rebeldes," in Cunha and Gomes, *Quase-cidadão*, 273; Rosemberg, *Ordem e burla*, 195.
28. Santos, *Historia de Santos*, 223–25.
29. Castilho and Cowling, "Funding Freedom"; Drescher, "Brazilian Abolition," 450–54.
30. Toplin, "Upheaval, Violence," 226.
31. The Brazilian General Assembly, controlled by the liberal party, passed legislation in 1831 that automatically freed any slaves imported into Brazil after that time. Additionally, enslavement or reenslavement were made crimes under most circumstances. The Brazilian government did not have the will and may not have had the means to enforce these laws, thus thousands of slaves continued to be imported, albeit largely at clandestine locations. In fact, more slaves were imported during the 1840s, when such activity was officially illegal, than during any other decade. Conrad, "Contraband Slave Trade," 618.
32. Rosemberg, *Ordem e burla*, 185–94.
33. "Os grandes festejos," *Diario de Santos*, 31 March, 1888, reprinted in CSS, vol. 103, p 22; municipal law code, 1847, FAMS.
34. Lanna gives evidence that the township government evicted many former slaves from their homes in Jabaquara on the grounds of sanitation reform. Anna Lúcia Duarte Lanna, *Uma cidade na transição*, 214.
35. Ibid., 196; Machado, "De rebeldes," in Cunha and Gomes, *Quase-cidadão*, 278.
36. For a discussion of the historiography on this question up to 1973, see Bergstresser, "Movement for the Abolition of Slavery."
37. Costa: *Da senzala à colŏnia*, 295, 404, 429 and *Brazilian Empire*, 161; Graham: "Causes for the Abolition," 123–28 and *Britain and the Onset*, 161–62.
38. Conrad, *Destruction of Brazilian Slavery*, 144–45; Drescher, "Brazilian Abolition"; Frank, *Dutra's World*, 3.
39. Costa, *Da senzala à colŏnia*, 40. Costa may have used other evidence, but he does not cite other sources. Conrad, *Destruction of Brazilian Slavery*, 145; Bergstresser, "Movement for the Abolition of Slavery," 21–60.
40. Santos, *Historia de Santos*, 223–25.
41. This is according to his nephew, also named Francisco Martins dos Santos, who wrote a history of the Santos abolitionist movement in 1937. Lichti and Santos, *Poliantéia santista* (vol. 2), 219, and (vol. 3), 204.
42. Alamanack Laemmert (1880).
43. Cemetery registers, 1881, FAMS.
44. This list was taken from Francisco Martins dos Santos's (the nephew's) history of the local movement. Lichti and Santos, *Poliantéia santista*, 220–27.
45. "Santos abolicionista," *A Tribuna*, 11 May 2003; Lichti and Santos, *Poliantéia santista*, 224; Pacheco e Chavas, *Relatorio apresentado*.
46. They were Antonia Maria de Jezus, Emilia de Jezus Cortez, and Maria Angelica Cortez. Little is known about these three women. Antonia Maria de Jezus may have moved from São Sebastião, because a woman with the same name lived there in 1844. Nominal lists (São Sebastião), 1844. Emilia de Jezus Cortez had a daughter who was born in Vila Bela da Princesa, on the island across from São

Sebastião. Church marriage records, 1865 (vol. 1), CCS, FAMS. Since "Cortez" was not a common name in Santos, Emilia and Maria were likely related.

47. Henrique Porchat was one of the first men in Brazil to install a steam-powered factory. Zaluar, *Peregrinação pela província*, 323. Historians of abolition have confused the older slaveholding industrialist with his younger abolitionist son, Henrique Porchat de Assis. For example, see Costa, *senzala à colŏnia*, 431 and Morais, *A campanha abolicionista*, 225.

48. Bergstresser argues that the motivation of professional groups to become involved in abolitionist causes may have been personal rather than humanitarian reasons. Engineers and urban businessmen, for example, could "complement their desire for economic reform which [. . .] might improve their personal prospects." Bergstresser, "Movement for the Abolition of Slavery," 97.

49. Cemetery registers," 1880–1883, FAMS.

50. Hospital patient registers, 1880–1886, ASCMS.

51. Conrad, *Destruction of Brazilian Slavery*, 146.

52. Rosemberg writes that Pinheiro was a *delegado* (similar to a police chief), but he is listed as a town councilman in the *Almanak Laemmert* of 1880 and *Alamanac Thorton* of 1885, CSS, FAMS.

53. Laërne, *Brazil and Java*, 114–15. Other authors have given estimates that are not too different. Monteiro estimated that 5.7 percent of the decline was attributable to the Emancipation Fund. Toplin, *Abolition of Slavery in Brazil*, 95. Christopher Columbus Andrews guessed between 6.3 and 6.7 percent. See *Brazil; Its Conditions*, 312.

54. The number of slaves freed in the five years between 1884 and 1888 was nearly equal to the number freed in the eleven years between 1873 and 1883. Toplin, *Abolition of Slavery in Brazil*, 95.

55. Robert Conrad titled one section of a chapter "The Failure of the Emancipation Fund" in *Destruction of Brazilian Slavery*, 110–16. See also Toplin, *Abolition of Brazilian Slavery*, 81, 95. For the perspective that the Emancipation Fund succeeded in some ways, see Celso Castilho and Camilia Cowling, "Funding Freedom."

56. Hastings Charles Dent wrote that "every day one reads in the papers of some slaves liberated by this [emancipation] fund." See A *Year in Brazil*, 283. Dent also claimed that in Ceará, a large provincial tax "made slaveholding impossible, the value of the slave being less than the tax." Ibid., 287.

57. Nabuco, C. *Life of Joaquim Nabuco*. 68; Nabuco, J. *Abolitionism*, 30; Toplin, *Abolition of Slavery*, 95.

58. Conservatives also directed their mirth at the implementation of Rio Branco Law. One newspaper wrote in 1884, "There has never been an honest registration of slaves, nor a strict observance of the provision guaranteeing liberty to the children of slave mothers . . . No man can justly claim the protection of laws which he habitually and openly violates. If a law is worth enforcing, it is worth obeying." *Rio News*, July 5, 1884; quoted in Dent, *A Year in Brazil*, 283.

59. The full text of Law 2,040 (1871), or the Rio Branco Law, and Decree 5135 (1872), which regulated the Emancipation Fund, among other things, is reprinted in Freitas, *Escravidão de índios e negros*, 59–93.

60. "Circular da. P. da província de repasse de verba do Fundo de Emancipação (1886)"; and "Ofício da P. da Província de regulamentação sobre classificação de escravos (Fundo de Emancipação) (1886)," FAMS.

61. *Escravos libertados por conta do fundo da emancipação*, 1883, 1886, AESP. See Chapter Three (this volume) for a description of Freitas's trading activities.

62. Dent wrote that the slaves who saved manumission funds were "preferred as recipients from the Emancipation Fund." Dent, *A Year in Brazil*, 284.

63. "N. 91" *Coleção das leis* (V. 1983), 79. "N. 101" *Coleção das leis* (V. 1983), 87. "N. 116" *Coleção das leis* (V. 1983), 99.

64. Neto, "O Fundo de Emancipação," 11; Castilho and Cowling, "Funding Freedom"; Salles, *O negro no Pará*, 318.

CONCLUSION

1. "Almanach litterário de São Paulo" (1877–1885), in Lichti and Santos, *Poliantéia santista*, 167.

2. Megale, *Folclore brasileiro*; Ressurreição, *São Sebastião*; Araújo and Lanzellotti, *Brasil: Histórias*.

3. As Richard Wade described slavery in the U.S. urban south, "In short, slave labor could be found nearly anywhere there was a task to perform." See *Slavery in the Cities*, 38.

4. For population figures, see Chapter One (this volume).

5. Borges, "Intellectuals and the Forgetting of Slavery."

6. In another example, parasitic worms were the top killer among Brazilian-born slaves between 1860 and 1870, responsible for the deaths of 10 percent of those buried in the town's only cemetery. In sharp contrast, worms killed less than 1 percent of African-born slaves.

7. Mattoso, *To Be a Slave*, 86. Genevese was influenced by Kenneth Stamp, who was among the first to frame slaves' culture in terms of "resistance." See Genovese, *Roll, Jordan, Roll* and Stampp, *Peculiar Institution*. Dylan Penningroth has a good discussion of this historiography in *Claims of Kinfolk*. For a compelling critique of Genovese, see Johnson, "A Nettlesome Classic."

8. A search on Worldcat for works within the subject of Brazilian history with titles containing "escravidão," "slavery," "escravos" (plural and singular), or "slaves" produces a list of 114 books. Searching within this same subject for the terms "elite," "oligarquia," "oligarchy," "monarquia," "monarchy," or "coronelismo" produces 83 books.

9. See, for example, Pinsky, *Escravidão no Brasil*; Neves, *Documentos sobre a escravidão*; or Maestri, *O escravismo no Brasil*.

10. I am not, of course, the first person to point this out. See, for example, Franco, *Homens livres*; Hahner, *Poverty and politics*; Castro, *Ao sul da história*; Dias, *Power and Everyday Life*; Faria, *A colônia em movimento*; Klein and Luna, "Free Colored in a Slave Society."

11. Cristiano Benedito Ottoni, senator of Minas Gerais, declared in 1884: "I, Mr. President, have completed my seventy-third year; for more than half a century

I have had the full use of my faculties. I see, I hear, I observe, and I can bear witness that the treatment of slaves in Brazil has gone on steadily improving." Translated and quoted in Andrews, *Brazil: Its Conditions and Prospects*. Agostinho Marques Perdigão Malheiro saw evidence of an improvement in general treatment of slaves in the disappearance of iron face masks and foot shackles. He also took note of many more slaves well-dressed and shod. See *A escravidão no Brasil*, 114–15. Emília Viotti da Costa agreed with these contemporary assessments in *Da senzala à colŏnia*, 324.

12. As explored in Chapter Five, the proportion of slaves committed to the hospital increased in the final two decades of slavery. Senator Cristiano Benedito Ottoni also drew a connection between the increasing price of slaves and the ability of owners to pay for medical services. He believed that this reduced infant mortality among slaves, although he recognized that it remained terribly high. See Ottoni, *A emancipação dos escravos*, 65–68, translated and quoted in Conrad, *Children of God's Fire*, 100. Toplin claimed a connection between improved treatment and a reduction in overall mortality rates; see *Abolition of Slavery in Brazil*, 19.

APPENDIX

1. 1810–1880; CCS-FAMS.
2. 1817–1830, 1854, 1872, 1890; AESP, BN.
3. 1865, 1870, 1871, 1875, 1880, 1885; CCS-FAMS, http://www.crl.edu/content/almanak2.htm.
4. 1817, 1856; CCS-FAMS.
5. 1820–1880; CCS-FAMS.
6. 1874, 1878, 1885; CCS-FAMS.
7. 1803–1835; CCS-FAMS.
8. 1820–1890; CCS-FAMS.
9. 1812–1872; CCS-FAMS, CDS.
10. 1832–1859; AESP.
11. 1863–1870; PCNS, SCNS.
12. *Revista Commercial*, (1849–1866); *Diario de Santos* (1872–1889); CCS-FAMS, HS.
13. 1860–1880; Archivo do Convento do Carmo de Santos, ANRJ.
14. 1847–1890, FAMS.
15. 1860–1880, MPCSP.
16. *Revista Commercial* (1866–67); HS.
17. 1861–1888; ASCMS.
18. 1849–1880; http://www.crl.edu/content/provincial.htm.
19. 1857–1859, 1863, 1866, 1874–1879, 1888; FAMS.
20. 1857–1858, 1865–1875, 1878–1888; FAMS.
21. 1800–1871; CCS-FAMS, PCNS, SCNS.
22. 1832–1850, 1858–1872; CCS-FAMS, CDS.
23. 1800–1871; CCS-FAMS.

24. 1886–1888; CCS-FAMS, HS.

25. Searching was facilitated by the ordering and filtering tools available in the Microsoft Excel database program. Individuals were distinguished with three-letter codes such as AAA, AAB, or AAC. We avoided codes that replicated common letter patterns found in names or other source data so that these individuals could be electronically located or sorted easily.

26. "Guilherme Backheuser," "Almanak administrativo, mercantil e industrial da corte e provincia do Rio de Janeiro" (1848–1871). [1865, 1870, 1875]; Almanak Luna, 1871; rural estate lists, 1856; impostos diversos, 1878; *Testamunhas judiciais*, 1843, 1850, 1859, 1866; CCS-FAMS, FAMS.

27. "America (slave of Guilherme Backheuser)," *meia-sizas*, 1858; "Tibirça (former slave of Guilherme Backheuser)," cartas de alforrias, 1863; "Leandra (former slave of Guilherme Backheuser)," cartas de alforrias, 1864; "Jacob (slave of Guilherme Backheuser)," registros de presos, 1867, 1868; "Ezequiel (slave of Guilherme Backheuser)," registros de pressos, 1868, 1869; "Vicente (slave of Guilherme Backheuser)," cemetery registers, 1869; "João (slave of Guilherme Backheuser)," cemetery registers, 1870; "Miguel (slave of Guilherme Backheuser)," livros de pacientes, 1871; "Jacob (slave of Guilherme Backheuser)," cemetery registers, 1878; "Miguel (slave of Guilherme Backheuser)," cemetery registers, 1878, CCS-FAMS, FAMS.

28. "Gertrudes (slave of Maria Victoria [or Victoriana] of Rua Santo Antonio)," nominal lists, 1817, 1830; AESP.

29. "Feliciano" (slave of Maria Victoria da Silva), "manumission letters," 1829; CCS-FAMS.

Bibliography

"Almanak administrativo, mercantil e industrial da corte e provincia do Rio de Janeiro" [Almanak Laemmert]. Rio de Janeiro: Eduardo e Henrique Laemmert, 1848–1889.

100 Anos: Porto de Santos, 1892–1992 (Port of Santos, Brazil: 100 Years). Brasil, CODESP: Banco Nacional, 1992.

Amantino, Márcia. "As condições físicas e de saúde dos escravos fugitivos anunciados no Jornal do Commercio (RJ) em 1850." *História, ciências, saúde—Manguinhos*. 14 (2007), 1377–99.

Anderson, Robin L. "Public Health and Public Healthiness, São Paulo, Brazil, 1876–1893." *Journal of the History of Medicine and Allied Sciences* 41, no. 3 (1986), 293–307.

Andrade, Maria José de Souza. *A mão de obra escrava em Salvador, 1811–1860*. Baianada. Vol. 8. SP i.e. São Paulo: Corrupio, 1988.

Andrade, Rŏmulo. "Casamento entre escravos na região cafeeira de Minas Gerais." *Revista Universidade Rural, Série Ciências Humanas* 22 (2000), 188–89

Andrews, Christopher Columbus. *Brazil: Its Conditions and Prospects*. New York: D. Appleton and Co., 1889.

Annaes do Parlamento Brazileiro. Camara dos Srs. Deputados, terceiro anno da decima-quarta legislatura. Rio de Janeiro: Typographia Imperial E Constitucional de J. Villeneuve & C., 1871.

Araújo, Alceu Maynard, and José Lanzellotti. *Brasil: Histórias*. São Paulo: Editora Três, 1972.

Ashe, Thomas. *A Commercial View, and Geographical Sketch, of the Brasils*. London: Allen & Co., 1812.

Assis, Marcelo Ferreira, "Tráfico atlăntico, impacto microbiano e mortalidades escrava, Rio de Janeiro, c.1790–c.1830." Masters diss., Universidade Federal do Rio de Janeiro, 2002.

Azevedo, Militão Augusto de, Gino Caldatto Barbosa, Marjorie de Carvalho F. de Medeiros, Solange Ferraz de Lima, and Vănia Carneiro de Carvalho. *Santos e seus arrabaldes: Álbum de Militão Augusto de Azevedo*. São Paulo: Magma, 2004.

Bakewell, P. J. *A History of Latin America: c. 1450 to the Present*. Malden, MA: Blackwell, 2004.
Barbosa, Keith. "Escravidão, mortalidade e doenças: Notas para o estudo das dimensões da diáspora africana no Brasil." São Paulo, Brazil, Anais do XIX Encontro Regional de História: Poder, Violência e Exclusão. ANPUH/SP-USP. 8–12 September, 2008.
Barickman, B. J. *A Bahian Counterpoint: Sugar, Tobacco, Cassava, and Slavery in the Recôncavo, 1780–1860*. Stanford, CA: Stanford University Press, 1998.
———. "Revisiting the Casa-Grande: Plantation and Cane-Farming Households in Early Nineteenth century Bahia." *Hispanic American Historical Review* 84, no. 4 (2004), 619–59.
Barman, R. J. *Brazil: The Forging of a Nation, 1798–1852*. Stanford, CA: Stanford University Press, 1994.
Baronov, David. *The Abolition of Slavery in Brazil: The "Liberation" of Africans through the Emancipation of Capital*. Westport, CT: Greenwood Press, 2000.
Beeghley, Leonard. *The Structure of Social Stratification in the United States*. 3rd ed. Boston: Allyn and Bacon, 2000.
Benchimol, Jaime Larry. *Dos micróbios aos mosquitos: Febre amarela e a revolução pasteuriana no Brasil*. Rio de Janeiro: Editora Fiocruz, 1999.
———. *Febre amarela: A doença e a vacina, uma história inacabada*. Rio de Janeiro: Ed. Fiocruz, 2001.
———. *Pereira Passos: Um Haussmann tropical: A renovação urbana da cidade do Rio de Janeiro no início do século XX*. Rio de Janeiro: Prefeitura da Cidade do Rio de Janeiro, Secretaria Municipal de Cultura, Turismo e Esportes, Departamento Geral de Documentação e Informação Cultural, 1990.
Bergad, Laird W. *The Comparative Histories of Slavery in Brazil, Cuba, and the United States*. Cambridge, UK; New York: Cambridge University Press, 2007.
———. *Slavery and the Demographic and Economic History of Minas Gerais, Brazil, 1720–1888*. New York: Cambridge University Press, 1999.
Bergstresser, Rebecca Baird. 1973. "The Movement for the Abolition of Slavery in Rio de Janeiro, Brazil, 1880–1889." PhD diss., Stanford University, 1973.
Berlin, Ira. *Many Thousands Gone: The First Two Centuries of Slavery in North America*. Cambridge, MA: Belknap Press of Harvard University Press, 1998.
Bertin, Enidelce. *Alforrias em São Paulo do século XIX: Liberdade e dominacão*. São Paulo: Humanitas, 2004.
Bethell, Leslie. *The Abolition of the Brazilian Slave Trade; Britain, Brazil and the Slave Trade Question, 1807–1869*. Cambridge: Cambridge University Press, 1970.
———. *Brazil: Empire and Republic, 1822–1930*. New York: Cambridge University Press, 1989.
Blount, John Allen. "The Public Health Movement in São Paulo, Brazil: A History of the Sanitary Service, 1892–1918." PhD diss., Tulane University, 1971.
Bonifácio, José, and Jorge Caldeira. *José Bonifácio de Andrada e Silva: Coleção Formadores do Brasil*. 1st ed. São Paulo: Editora 34, 2002.
Borges, Dain. "Intellectuals and the Forgetting of Slavery in Brazil." *Annals of Scholarship* 11 (1996).

Brazil. *Recenseamento da população do Imperio do Brazil a que se procedeu no dia 10. de Agosto de 1872*. Rio de Janeiro: Typ. Dous de Dezembro, 1877.
Britto, Nara. *Oswaldo Cruz: A construção de um mito na ciência brasileira*. Rio de Janeiro: Editora Fiocruz, 1995.
Brügger, S.M.J. "Legitimidade, casamento e relações ditas ilícitas em São João del Rei (1730–1850)." Diamantina, IX Seminário sobre a Economia Mineira, CODEPLAR, 29 August 2000.
Carone, Edgard. "Coronelismo: Definição, história, e bibliografia." *Revista de Administração de Empresas* 11, no. 3 (July–Sept. 1971), 85–92.
Carrigan, J. A. *The Saffron Scourge: A History of Yellow Fever in Louisiana, 1796–1905*. Lafayette: Center for Louisiana Studies, 1994.
Carvalho, José Murilo de. *A constução da ordem: A elite política imperial*. Contribuições em Ciências Sociais no. 8. Rio de Janeiro, 1980.
———. *Liberdade: rotinas e rupturas do escravismo no Recife, 1822–1850*. Recife: Editora Universitária UFPE, 1998.
Castilho, C., and C. Cowling. "Funding Freedom, Popularizing Politics: Abolitionism and Local Emancipation Funds in 1880s Brazil." *Luso-Brazilian Review* 47 (2010), 89–120.
Castro, Hebe Maria Mattos de. *Ao sul da história*. São Paulo: Editora Brasiliense, 1987.
———. *Das cores do silěncio: Os significados da liberdade no sudeste escravista, Brasil século XIX*. Prěmio Arquivo Nacional de Pesquisa. Rio de Janeiro: Arquivo Nacional, 1995.
Chalhoub, Sidney. *Artes e ofícios de curar no Brasil: Capítulos de história social*. Coleção Várias Histórias. Vol. 15. Campinas, SP: Editora UNICAMP, 2003.
———. *Cidade febril*. São Paulo: Companhia das Letras, 2006.
———. "The Politics of Disease Control: Yellow Fever and Race in Nineteenth Century Rio de Janeiro." *Journal of Latin American Studies* 25, no. 3 (1993), 441–63.
———. *Visões da liberdade: Uma história das últimas décadas da escravidão na corte*. São Paulo: Companhia das Letras, 1990.
Chamberlain, Henry, and Rubens Borba de Moraes. *Vistas e costumes da cidade e arredores do Rio de Janeiro em 1819–1820*. Rio de Janeiro: Livraria Kosmos Editora, E. Eichner & Cia. Ltda., 1943.
Chambouleyron, Rafael. "Escravos do atlăntico equatorial: Tráfico negreiro para o Estado do Maranhão e Pará (século XVII e início do século XVIII)." *Revista Brasileira de História* 26, no. 52 (2006), 79–114.
Cleto, Marc Pereira. *Dissertação a respeito da Capitania de S. Paulo, sua decadência e modo de restabelecê-la la Escripta em 25 de Outubro de 1782*. Annaes da Bibliotheca Nacional do Rio de Janeiro; Dl, 21. Rio de Janeiro, 1900.
Congresso Brasileiro de Hygiene. *Annaes do Segundo Congresso Brasileiro de Hygiene: realizado em Bello Horizonte em dezembro de 1924*. Rio de Janeiro: Livraria, Papelaria e Litho-Typographia Pimenta de Mello, 1928.
Conrad, Robert Edgar. *Children of God's Fire: A Documentary History of Black Slavery in Brazil*. Princeton, NJ: Princeton University Press, 1983.

———. "The Contraband Slave Trade to Brazil, 1831–1845." *Hispanic American Historical Review* 49, no. 4 (1969), 617–38.

———. *The Destruction of Brazilian Slavery, 1850–1888*. Berkeley: University of California Press, 1972.

Cooper, D. B. "Brazil's Long Fight against Epidemic Disease, 1849–1917, with Special Emphasis on Yellow Fever." *Bulletin of the New York Academy of Medicine* 51 (1975), 672–96.

———. "'Death by the Sea.' The Yellow Fever Epidemics of Brazil, 1849–1853." *New World* 3, no. 1 (1988), 51–74.

———. "The New 'Black Death': Cholera in Brazil, 1855–1856." *Social Science History* 10, no. 4 (1986), 467–88.

Cornet, Julias, and H. Michaelis. *Novo diccionario da lingua portugueza e ingleza*. Leipzig: F. A. Brockhaus, 1893.

Costa, Emília Viotti da. *The Brazilian Empire: Myths and Histories*. Chapel Hill: University of North Carolina Press, 2000.

———. *Da senzala à colônia*. 3rd ed. São Paulo: Editora Brasiliense, 1989.

Costa, I. del N. da, and H. Gutierez. "Nota sobre o casamento de escravos em São Paulo e no Paraná." *História: Questões e debates* 5, no. 9 (1984), 313–21.

Costa, I. del N. da, Robert W. Slenes, and Stuart B. Schwartz. "A família escrava em Lorena (1801)." *Estudos econômicos* 17, no. 2 (May–Aug. 1987), 245–95.

Cunha, Olivia Maria Gomes da, and Flávio dos Santos Gomes. *Quase-cidadão: Histórias e antropologias da pós-emancipação no Brasil*. Rio de Janeiro: Editora FGV, 2007.

Dean, Warren. *Rio Claro: A Brazilian Plantation System, 1820–1920*. Stanford, CA: Stanford University Press, 1976.

Debret, Jean Baptiste. *Voyage pittoresque et historique au Brésil, ou séjour d'un artiste français au Brésil, depuis 1816 jusqu'en 1831 inclusivement*. Paris: Firmin Didot frères, 1834.

———. *Viagem pitoresca e historica ao Brasil. Biblioteca Histórica Brasileira*. Vol. 4. São Paulo: Livraria Martins, 1940.

Degler, Carl N. *Neither Black nor White: Slavery and Race Relations in Brazil and the United States*. Madison: University of Wisconsin Press, 1986.

Dent, Hastings Charles, *A Year in Brazil, with Notes on the Abolition of Slavery, the Finances of the Empire, Religion, Meteorology, Natural History, etc*. London: K. Paul, Trench and Co., 1886.

Dias, Maria Odila Leite da Silva. *Power and Everyday Life: The Lives of Working Women in Nineteenth Century Brazil*. Cambridge, UK: Policy Press, 1995.

Drescher, Seymour. "Brazilian Abolition in Comparative Perspective." *Hispanic American Historical Review* 68, no. 3 (Aug. 1988), 429–60.

Duarte, Nestor. *A ordem privada e a organização politica nacional*. Brasiliana no. 172. São Paulo, 1939.

Duke, Norman C., and James A. Allen, "Rhizophora mangle, R. samoensis, R. racemosa, R. × harrisonii." http://www.agroforestry.net/tti/Rhizophora-AEP.pdf. Accessed September 7, 2010.

Dunaway, Wilma A. *The African-American Family in Slavery and Emancipation:*

Studies in Modern Capitalism. New York: Maison des sciences de l'homme/ Cambridge University Press, 2003.
Echenberg, Myron J. *Plague Ports: The Global Urban Impact of Bubonic Plague, 1894–1901*. New York: New York University Press, 2007.
Edwards, Philip. *Last Voyages: Cavendish, Hudson, Ralegh: The Original Narratives*. Oxford: Clarendon Press, 1988.
Eisenberg, Peter L. "Ficando Livre: As alforrias em Campinas no século XIX," *Estudos Econŏmicos* 17, no. 2 (May–August 1987), 175–216.
———. *The Sugar Industry in Pernambuco: Modernization without Change, 1840–1910*. Berkeley: University of California Press, 1974.
Elkins, Stanley M. *Slavery: A Problem in American Institutional and Intellectual Life*. Chicago: University of Chicago Press, 1976.
Eltis, David. *Economic Growth and the Ending of the Transatlantic Slave Trade*. New York: Oxford University Press, 1987.
Ewbank, Thomas. *Life in Brazil*. New York: Harper & Brothers, 1856.
Faoro, Raymundo. *Os donos do poder: Formação do patronato politico brasileiro*. 2nd ed. 2 vols. Pŏrto Alegre: Editora Globo, 1975.
Faria, Sheila de Castro. *A colŏnia em movimento: fortuna e família no cotidiano colonial*. Rio de Janeiro: Editora Nova Fronteira, 1998.
———. "História da família e demografia histórica." In *Domínios da história: Ensaios de teoria e metodologia*. Edited by Ciro Flamarion Cardoso and Ronaldo Vainfas. Rio de Janeiro: Campus, 1997.
Fausto, Boris. *História do Brasil*. Didática. Vol. 1. São Paulo: EDUSP: Fundação para o Desenvolvimento da Educação, 1994.
Ferrari, Ana Josefina. *A voz do dono: Uma análise das descrições feitas nos anúncios de jornal dos escravos fugidos*. Campinas, SP, Brasil: Pontes, (2006).
Fleischner, Jennifer. *Mastering Slavery: Memory, Family, and Identity in Women's Slave Narratives*. New York: New York University Press, 1996.
Florentino, Manolo, and José Roberto Góes. *A paz das senzalas: Famílias escravas e tráfico atlăntico, Rio de Janeiro, c. 1790–c. 1850*. Rio de Janeiro: Civilização Brasileira, 1997.
———. "Do que Nabuco já sabia: Mobilidade e miscigenação racial no Brasil escravista." Congresso Internacional Brasil-Portugal ano 2000—Sessão de História. Rio de Janeiro, September 2000.
———. "Tráfico, parentesco e esterilização de fortunas entre os escravos do Agro Fluminense, séculos XVIII e XIX." Caxambu, Brazil, *Anais do X Encontro de Estudos Populacionais*, ABEP, 1996.
Fogel, Robert William. *Without Consent or Contract: The Rise and Fall of American Slavery*. 1st ed. New York: Norton, 1989.
Fragoso, J.L.R., and M. G. Florentino. "Marcelino, filho de Inocência Crioula, neto de Joana Cabinda: Um estudo sobre famílias escravas em Paraíba do Sul (1835–1872)." *Estudos Econŏmicos* 17, no. 2 (May–August, 1987), 151–73.
Franco, Maria Sylvia de Carvalho. *Homens livres na ordem escravocrata*. São Paulo: Fundacão Editora da UNESP, 1997.
Frank, Zephyr L. *Dutra's World: Wealth and Family in Nineteenth Century Rio de Janeiro*. Diálogos. Albuquerque: University of New Mexico Press, 2004.

———. "Slave Market in Rio de Janeiro circa 1869: Context, Movement, and Social Experience." Preprint, 2010.

———. "Wealth Holding in Southeastern Brazil, 1815–60." *Hispanic American Historical Review* 85, 223–58. 2005.

Frazier, Harriet C. *Runaways and Freed Missouri Slaves and Those Who Helped Them, 1763–1865*. Jefferson, NC: McFarland & Co, 2004.

Freire, Jonis. "Compadrio em uma freguesia escravista: Senhor Bom Jesus do Rio Pardo (MG) (1838–1888)." Caxambú, Minas Gerais, Brazil, XIV Encontro Nacional de Estudos Populacionais, ABEP, September 20–24, 2004.

Freitas, Décio. *Escravidão de índios e negros no Brasil*. Porto Alegre, RS: Escola Superior de Teologia São Lourenço de Brindes, 1980.

Freyre, Gilberto. *Brazil: An Interpretation*. New York: A. A. Knopf, 1945.

———. *O escravo nos anúncios de jornais brasileiros do século XIX*. São Paulo; Recife: Companhia Editora Nacional; Instituto Joaquim Nabuco de Pesquisas Sociais, 1979.

———. *The Masters and the Slaves: A Study in the Development of Brazilian Civilization*. Berkeley: University of California Press, 1986.

———. "Social Life in Brazil in the Middle of the Nineteenth Century." *Hispanic American Historical Review* 5, no. 4 (Nov. 1922), 597–630.

Fundação Instituto Brasileiro de Geografia e Estatística. *Estatísticas históricas do Brasil. Séries estatísticas retrospectivas*. Rio de Janeiro: IBGE, 1987.

Furtado, Celso. *Formação econômica do Brasil*. São Paulo: Cia. Editora Nacional, 1979.

Furtado, Júnia Ferreira. *Homens de negócio: A interiorização da metrópole e do comércio nas Minas setecentistas*. São Paulo: Editora Hucitec, 1999.

Garavazo, J. "Relações familiares e estabilidade da família escrava: Batatais (1850–88)." Caxambú, Minas Gerais, Brazil, XIV Encontro Nacional de Estudos Populacionais, ABEP, 20–24 September 2004.

Garcia, Ramón Vicente. *Transformações econômicas no litoral norte paulista (1778–1836)*. São Paulo: FEA; USP, 1992.

Gaspar, David Barry, and Darlene Clark Hine. *More than Chattel: Black Women and Slavery in the Americas*. Bloomington: Indiana University Press, 1996.

Genovese, Eugene D. *Roll, Jordan, Roll: The World the Slaves Made*. 1st Vintage Books ed. New York: Vintage Books, 1976.

———. "The Treatment of Slaves in Different Countries: Problems in the Application of the Comparative Method." In *Slavery in the New World: A Reader in Comparative History*, ed. Laura Foner and Eugene D. Genovese. Englewood Cliffs, NJ, 1969.

Graden, Dale T. "An Act 'Even of Public Security': Slave Resistance, Social Tensions, and the End of the International Slave Trade to Brazil, 1835–1856." *Hispanic American Historical Review* 76, no. 2 (May 1996), 249–82.

Graham, Richard. *Britain and the Onset of Modernization in Brazil 1850–1914*. Cambridge Latin American Studies. Vol. 4. London: Cambridge University Press, 1968.

———. "Causes for the Abolition of Negro Slavery in Brazil: An Interpretive Essay." *Hispanic American Historical Review* 46, no. 2 (May, 1966), 123–37.

———. "A família escrava no Brasil colonial." In *Escravidão, reforma e imperialismo*. São Paulo: Perspectiva, 1979.

———. *Patronage and Politics in Nineteenth-century Brazil*. Stanford, CA: Stanford University Press, 1990.

———. "Slave Families on a Rural Estate in Colonial Brazil." *Journal of Social History* 9 (1976, 382–402.

Gregory, Ian, and Paul S. Ell. *Historical GIS: Technologies, Methodologies, and Scholarship*. Cambridge Studies in Historical Geography, 39. Cambridge: Cambridge University Press, 2007.

Grusky, David B. *Social Stratification: Class, Race, and Gender in Sociological Perspective*. 2nd ed. Boulder, CO: Westview, 2001.

Guimarães, Maria Regina Cotrim. "Chernoviz e os manuais de medicina popular no Império." *História, Ciências, Saúde—Manguinhos* 12 (2005), 501–14.

Gutierez, H. "A harmonia dos sexos: Elementos da estrutura demográfica da população escrava do Paraná, 1800/1830." Águas de São Pedro, Brazil, *Anais do IV Encontro de Estudos Populacionais*, ABEP, 1986.

Gutman, Herbert George. *The Black Family in Slavery and Freedom, 1750–1925*. 1st ed. New York: Pantheon Books, 1976.

Hahner, June Edith. *Poverty and Politics: The Urban Poor in Brazil, 1870–1920*. 1st ed. Albuquerque: University of New Mexico Press, 1986.

Hess, Andreas. *Concepts of Social Stratification: European and American Models*. New York: Palgrave, 2001.

Higgins, Kathleen J. *"Licentious Liberty" in a Brazilian Gold-Mining Region: Slavery, Gender, and Social Control in Eighteenth Century Sabará, Minas Gerais*. University Park: Pennsylvania State University Press, 1999.

Holanda, Sérgio Buarque de, and Pedro Moacyr Campos. *História geral da civilizaça brasileira*. São Paulo: Difel [Difeusão Editorial S.A.], 1976.

Holloway, Thomas H. *Immigrants on the Land: Coffee and Society in São Paulo, 1886–1934*. Chapel Hill: University of North Carolina Press, 1980.

———. *Policing Rio de Janeiro: Repression and Resistance in a 19th century City*. Stanford, CA: Stanford University Press, 1993.

Horne, Gerald. *The Deepest South: The United States, Brazil, and the African Slave Trade*. New York: New York University Press, 2007.

Instituto Estadual do Patrimônio Cultural. "Casa de Farinha." http://www.inepac.rj.gov.br/arquivos/CasadeFarinha10.10.05.pdf. Accessed May 5, 2011.

Horner, Gustavus R. B. *Medical Topography of Brazil and Uruguay, with Incidental Remarks by G.R.B. Horner*. Philadelphia: Lindsay and Blakiston, 1845.

Instituto Histórico e Geográfico de São Paulo, Arquivo do Estado de São Paulo, São Paulo. "Carta de Morgado de Mateus ao Conde de Oeyra. São Paulo, 13 de Dezembro de 1786." In *Documentos interessantes para a historia e costumes de São Paulo*. Vol. 73. São Paulo: Instituto Historico e Geografico de S. Paulo, 1937.

Johnson, Michael P. "Runaway Slaves and the Slave Communities in South Carolina, 1799 to 1830." *The William and Mary Quarterly: A Magazine of Early American History* 38, no. 3 (1981), 418–41.

Johnson, Walter. *The Chattel Principle: Internal Slave Trades in the Americas.* New Haven, CT: Yale University Press, 2004.

———. "A Nettlesome Classic Turns Twenty-Five." *Common-Place* 1, no. 4 (2001).

———. *Soul by Soul: Life Inside the Antebellum Slave Market.* Cambridge, MA: Harvard University Press, 1999.

Karasch, Mary C. *Slave Life in Rio de Janeiro, 1808–1850.* Princeton, NJ: Princeton University Press, 1987.

Kidder, Daniel Parish, and James Cooley Fletcher. *Brazil and the Brazilians.* Philadelphia: Childs & Peterson, 1857.

Kiernan, James Patrick, "The Manumission of Slaves in Colonial Brazil: 1789–1822." PhD diss., New York University, 1976.

Kiple, Kenneth F. *The African Exchange: Toward a Biological History of Black People.* Durham, NC: Duke University Press, 1987.

———. *Blacks in Colonial Cuba, 1774–1899.* Latin American Monographs. Vol. 2, ser. 17. Gainesville: University Presses of Florida, 1976.

———. *The Caribbean Slave: A Biological History. Studies in Environment and History.* Cambridge Cambridgeshire; New York: Cambridge University Press, 1984.

——— and Virginia Himmelsteib King. *Another Dimension to the Black Diaspora: Diet, Disease, and Racism.* Cambridge; New York: Cambridge University Press, 1981.

Kittleson, Roger Alan. *The Practice of Politics in Postcolonial Brazil: Porto Alegre, 1845–1895.* Pittsburgh: University of Pittsburgh Press, 2006.

Klein, Herbert S. *African Slavery in Latin America and the Caribbean.* New York: Oxford University Press, 1986.

———. "American Slavery in Recent Brazilian Scholarship, with Emphasis on Quantitative Socio-economic Studies." *Slavery & Abolition* 30 (2009), 111–33.

———. "The Internal Slave Trade in Nineteenth-Century Brazil: A Study of Slave Importations into Rio de Janeiro in 1852." *Hispanic American Historical Review* 51, no. 4 (1971), 567–85.

———. *The Middle Passage: Comparative Studies in the Atlantic Slave Trade.* Princeton, NJ: Princeton University Press, 1978.

———, and Francisco Vidal Luna. "Free Colored in a Slave Society: São Paulo and Minas Gerais in the Early Nineteenth century." *Hispanic American Historical Review* 80, no. 4. Special Issue: Colonial Brazil: Foundations, Crises, and Legacies (Nov. 2000), 913–41.

———. *Slavery in Brazil.* Cambridge, UK; New York: Cambridge University Press, 2010.

Kuznesof, Elizabeth Anne. *Household Economy and Urban Development: São Paulo, 1765 to 1836.* Dellplain Latin American Studies. Vol. 18. Boulder, CO: Westview Press, 1986.

———. "Sexuality, Gender, and the Family in Colonial Brazil." *Luso-Brazilian Review* 30, no. 1 (1993), 120–21.

Lacerda, Antônio Henrique Duarte. "Economia cafeeira, crescimento populacional e manumissões onerosas e gratuitas condicionais em Juiz de Fora na segunda metade do século XIXÆ." Diamantina, Brazil. Anais do X Seminário sobre a Economia Mineira, 19–22 June 2002.

Laerne, C. F. Van Delden. *Brazil and Java: Report on Coffee-Culture in America, Asia and Africa, to H.E. the Minister of the Colonies*. London: W.H. Allen & Co., 1885.

Lamberg, Mauricio, and Luiz de Castro. *O Brazil, illustrado com gravuras*. Rio de Janeiro: Edietor Lombaerts, 1896.

Lanna, Anna Lúcia Duarte. *Uma cidade na transição*. São Paulo-Santos: Editora Hucitec, Prefeitura de Municipal de Santos, 1996.

Lara, Silvia Hunold. *Campos da violência: Escravos e senhores na Capitania do Rio de Janeiro, 1750–1808*. Coleção Oficinas da história. Rio de Janeiro: Paz e Terra, 1988.

———, and Joseli Maria Nunes Mendonça. 2006. *Direitos e justiças no Brasil: Ensaios de história social*. Coleção Várias Histórias, 22. Campinas, SP: Editora UNICAMP, 2006.

Lauderdale Graham, Sandra. *Caetana Says No: Women's Stories from a Brazilian Slave Society*. Cambridge, UK; New York: Cambridge University Press, 2002.

———. *House and Street: The Domestic World of Servants and Masters in Nineteenth century Rio de Janeiro*. Cambridge Latin American Studies. Vol. 68. Cambridge Cambridgeshire; New York: Cambridge University Press, 1988.

Leal, Victor Nunes. *Coronelismo: The Municipality and Representative Government in Brazil*, trans. June Henfrey. Cambridge Latin American Studies no. 28. Cambridge, UK; New York: Cambridge University Press, 1977.

Lehner, J. Christopher. *Reaction to Abuse: Maryland Slave Runaways, 1750–1775*. Thesis—Morgan State University, 1978.

Lévi-Strauss, Claude. *Triste tropiques*. New York: Atheneum, 1974.

Lewin, Linda. *Politics and Parentela in Paraíba: A Case Study of Family-Based Oligarchy in Brazil*. Princeton, NJ: Princeton University Press, 1987.

———. *Surprise Heirs*. Stanford, CA: Stanford University Press, 2003.

Libby, Douglas Cole. *Trabalho escravo e capital estrangeiro no Brasil: O caso de Morro Velho*. Biblioteca de Estudos Brasileiros. Vol. l.1. Belo Horizonte: Editora Itatiaia, 1984.

———. *Transformação e trabalho: Em uma economia escravista: Minas Gerais no século XIX*. São Paulo: Editora Brasiliense, 1988.

———, and Afonso de Alencastro Graça Filho. "Reconstructing Freedom: Manumission and Freedmen in the Parish of São José (Brazil), 1750–1850" (unpublished manuscript, Universidade Federal de Minas Gerais and Universidade Federal de São João Del Rei, Minas Gerais).

Lichti, Fernando Martins, and Francisco Martins dos Santos. *Poliantéia santista*. 1st ed. São Vicente, SP: Editora Caudex Ltda., 1996.

Lockhart, James, and Stuart B. Schwartz. *Early Latin America: A History of Colonial Spanish America and Brazil*. Cambridge Latin American Studies. Vol. 46. Cambridge Cambridgeshire; New York: Cambridge University Press, 1983.

Luccock, John. *Notes on Rio de Janeiro, and the Southern Parts of Brazil; Taken during a Residence of Ten Years in that Country, from 1808 to 1818*. London: S. Leigh, 1820.

Luna, Francisco Vidal. "Observações sobre casamento de escravos em São Paulo (1825)." Olinda, Brazil, *Anais do VI Encontro de Estudos Populacionais*, 1988.

———. *Minas Gerais, escravos e senhores: Análise da estrutura populacional e econŏmica de alguns centros mineratórios (1718–1804)*. Instituto de Pesquisas Econŏmicas, 1981.

———, and Costa, I. del N. da. "Posse de escravos em São Paulo no início do século XIX." *Estudos Econŏmicos* 13, no. 1 (1983), 211–21.

———. "Vila Rica: Nota sobre casamentos de escravos (1727–1826). Africa." *Revista do Centro de Estudos Africanos da USP* (São Paulo) 4, (1981), 3–7.

Luna, Francisco Vidal, and Herbert S. Klein. *Slavery and the Economy of São Paulo, 1750–1850*. Social Science History. Stanford, CA: Stanford University Press, 2003.

———. "Unpublished Data from Santos Nominal Lists, 1777, 1804, 1830." Excel database (2005).

Machado, Maria Helena Pereira Toledo. *Crime e escravidão: Trabalho, luta e resistẽncia nas lavouras Paulistas, 1830–1888*. São Paulo: Editora Brasiliense, 1987.

———. *O plano e o pănico: Os movimentos sociais na década da abolição*. Rio de Janeiro: Editora UFRJ, 1994.

———. "Tráfico interno e concentração de população escrava no principal município cafeeiro da Zona da Mata de Minas Gerais: Juiz de Fora (segunda metade do século XIX)." Diamantina, Brazil, Anais do X Seminário sobre a Economia Mineira, 19–22 June 2002.

Maestri, Mário, Maria Helena Rolim Capelato, and Maria Ligia Coelho Prado. *O escravismo no Brasil*. São Paulo: Atual Ed., 1996.

Malheiro, Perdigão. *A escravidão no Brasil: Ensaio historico-juridico-social*. Rio de Janeiro: Typographia Nacional, 1866.

Marcondes, Renato Leite. *Diverso e desigual: O Brasil escravista na década de 1870*. São Paulo: FUNPEC-Editora, 2009.

———. "A família escrava em Lorena e Cruzeiro (1874)." Caxambu, Brazil, *Anais do XII Encontro Nacional de Estudos populacionais da ABEP*, 2000.

———. "Small and Medium Slaveholdings in the Coffee Economy of the Vale do Paraíba, Province of Sao Paulo." *Hispanic American Historical Review* 85 (2005), 259–82.

Martin, Percy Alvin. "Slavery and Abolition in Brazil." *Hispanic American Historical Review* 13 (May 1933), 151–96.

Martins, Roberto Borges. 1982. "Growing in Silence: The Slave Economy of Nineteenth-Century Minas Gerais, Brazil." PhD diss., Vanderbilt University, 1980.

Masefield, John. *The Poems and Plays of John Masefield*. New York: Macmillan & Co., 1918.

Mattoso, Kátia M. de Queirós, "A propósito de cartas de alforria na Bahia, 1779–1850," *Anais de História* 4 (1972), 23–52.

———. *Bahia, Século XIX: Uma Província no Império*. Rio de Janeiro: Editora Nova Fronteira, 1992.

———. *Ser escravo no Brasil*. São Paulo: Ed. Brasiliense, 1982.

———. *To Be a Slave in Brazil, 1550–1888*. New Brunswick, NJ: Rutgers University Press, 1986.

Mawe, John, Solena Benevides Viana, and Clado Ribeiro de Lessa. *Viagens ao interior do Brasil, principalmente aos distritos do ouro e dos diamantes*. Rio de Janeiro: Z. Valverde, 1944.

McCance, Kathryn L., and Sue E. Huether. *Pathophysiology: The Biologic Basis for Disease in Adults and Children*. 3rd ed. St. Louis: Mosby, 1998.

Megale, Nilza Botelho. *Folclore brasileiro*. Petrópolis: Editora Vozes, 1999.

Mello, Zélia Maria Cardoso de. *Metamorfoses da riqueza, São Paulo, 1845–1895: Contribuição ao estudo da passagem da economia mercantil escravista à economia exportadora capitalista*. Estudos Históricos. São Paulo: Editora Hucitec; Prefeitura do Município de São Paulo, Secretaria Municipal de Cultura, 1985.

Merck Manual. "Hypertrophic Cardiomyopathy." http://www.merck.com/mmhe/sec03/ch026/ch026c.html. Accessed September 7, 2010.

———. "Yellow Fever." http://www.merck.com/mmhe/sec17/ch198/ch198k.html#sec17-ch198-ch198j-919. Accessed September 7, 2010.

Metcalf, Alida C. *Family and Frontier in Colonial Brazil: Santana de Parnaíba, 1580–1822*. Austin: University of Texas Press, 2005.

———. "Searching for the Slave Family in Colonial Brazil: A Reconstruction from São Paulo." *Journal of Family History* 16, no. 3 (1991), 283–97.

———. "Vida familiar dos escravos em São Paulo no século dezoito: O caso de santana de Parnaíba." *Estudos Econômicos* 17, no. 2 (May–Aug., 1987), 229–43.

Morais, Evaristo de. *A campanha abolicionista (1879–1888)*. Rio de Janeiro: Leite Ribeiro, Freitas Bastos, Spicer & Cia., 1924.

Morais Silva, António de. *Diccionario da lingua portugueza, recopilado de todos os impressos até o presente*. Lisboa: Na typ. de M.P. de Lacerda, 1823.

Morse, Richard M. *From Community to Metropolis: A Biography of Sao Paulo, Brazil*. New and enl. ed. New York: Octagon Books, 1974.

Motta, José Flávio. "A família escrava e a penetração do café em Bananal, 1801–1829." *Revista Brasileira de Estudos de População* 5, no. 1 (Jan.–June 1988), 71–101.

———. "Contribuições da demografia histórica à historiografia brasileira." Caxambu, *Anais do IX Encontro de Estudos Populacionais*, ABEP, October 1994.

———. *Corpos escravos, vontades livres: Posse de cativos e família escrava em Bananal, 1801–1829*. 1a. ed. São Paulo: FAPESP: Annablume, 1999.

———. "Derradeiras Transações. O comércio de escravos nos anos de 1880 (Areias, Piracicaba, e Casa Branca, Província de São Paulo)." *Almanack Braziliense* 10 (2009), 147–63.

———. "The Historical Demography of Brazil at the V Centenary of Its Discovery." *Ciência e cultura* 51, no. 5–6 (1999), 454–56.

Motta, José Flávio, and Agnaldo Valentim. "A família escrava e a partilha de bens: um estudo de caso." Ouro Preto, *Anais do XIII Encontro Nacional de Estudos Populacionais*, ADEP, 4–6 November 2002.

Moura, Clóvis. *Dicionário da escravidão negra no Brasil*. São Paulo: EDUSP, 2004.

Nabuco, Carolina. *The life of Joaquim Nabuco*. Stanford, CA: Stanford University Press, 1950.

Nabuco, Joaquim. *Abolitionism: The Brazilian Antislavery Struggle*. Urbana: University of Illinois Press, 1977.

Naro, Nancy Priscilla. *A Slave's Place, a Master's World: Fashioning Dependency in Rural Brazil*. The Black Atlantic. London; New York: Continuum, 2000.

Nascimento, Jarbas Vargas, and Izilda Maria Nardocci. "Compra e venda de homens negros: Uma prática cartorial no século XIX." *Academos, Revista Electrŏnica da FIA* 2, no. 2 (2006), 1–11.

Nava, Pedro. *Capítulos da história da medicina no Brasil*. Cotia, São Paulo: Ateliê Editorial, 2004.

Needell, Jeffrey D. *The Party of Order: The Conservatives, the State, and Slavery in the Brazilian Monarchy, 1831–1871*. Stanford, CA: Stanford University Press, 2006.

Neto Álvaro de Souza Gomes, "O Fundo de Emancipação de Escravos: Funcionamento e *A Slave's Place, a Master's World: Fashioning Dependency in Rural Brazil*. Resultados no Termo de Lages, Santa Catarina." Porto Alegre, Brazil, Segunda Encontro Escravidão e Liberdade no Brasil Meridional, October 26–28, 2005.

Neto, José Maia Bezerra. "Mercado, conflitos e controle Social." *História & Perspectivas, Uberlăndia* 41 (2009), 267–98.

Neves, Erivaldo Fagundes. "Sampauleiros traficantes: Comércio de escravos do Alto Sertão da Bahia para o Oeste Cafeeiro Paulista." *Afro-Asia* 24 (2000), 97–128.

Neves, Maria de Fátima Rodrigues das. *Documentos sobre a escravidão no Brasil*. São Paulo: Editora Contexto, 1996.

Nishida, Mieko. "Manumission and Ethnicity in Urban Slavery: Salvador, Brazil, 1808–1888." *Hispanic American Historical Review* 73, no. 3 (1993), 361–91.

———. *Slavery and Identity: Ethnicity, Gender, and Race in Salvador, Brazil, 1808–1888*. Blacks in the Diaspora. Bloomington: Indiana University Press, 2003.

Nooy, Wouter de, Andrej Mrvar, and Vladimir Batagelj. *Exploratory social network analysis with Pajek*. Structural analysis in the social sciences. New York: Cambridge University Press, 2005.

Northrup, David. *The Atlantic Slave Trade*. Boston: Houghton Mifflin, 2002.

Novomilenio. "Histórias e lendas de Santos—Medicina, Santa Casa de Misericórdia." http://www.novomilenio.inf.br/santos/h0260d.htm. Accessed September 7, 2010.

Oliveira, Orlandina de. "Urban Social Structures in Latin America, 1930–1990." In *Latin America: Economy and Society since 1930*. Edited by Leslie Bethell. Cambridge, UK; New York: Cambridge University Press, 1998.

Ottoni, Christiano Benedicto. *A emancipação dos escravos*. Rio de Janeiro: Typ. Perseverança, 1871.

Pacheco e Chavas, Elias Antŏnio, ed. *Relatório apresentado ao Exm. Sr. Presidente da Provincia de S. Paulo pela Comissão Central de Estatistica*. São Paulo: n.p., 1888.

Paiva, Eduardo Franca. *Escravos e libertos em Minas Gerais do século XVIII: Estratégias de resistência através dos testamentos*. São Paulo: Annablume, 1995.
Pang, Eul-Soo, and Ron L. Secklinger. "The Mandarins of Imperial Brazil." *Comparative Studies in Society and History* 14, no. 2 (Mar. 1972), 215–44.
Parker, Freddie L. *Stealing a Little Freedom: Advertisements for Slave Runaways in North Carolina, 1791–1840*. New York: Garland Pub, 1994.
Peard, Julyan G. *Race, Place, and Medicine: The Idea of the Tropics in Nineteenth Century Brazilian Medicine*. Durham, NC: Duke University Press, 1999.
Penningroth, Dylan C. *The Claims of Kinfolk: African American Property and Community in the Nineteenth century South*. John Hope Franklin Series in African American History and Culture. Chapel Hill: University of North Carolina Press, 2003.
Pereira, Júlio César Medeiros da Silva. "Práticas de curar e doenças na comunidade escrava da Imperial Fazenda de Santa Cruz, na segunda metade do século XIX." Rio de Janeiro, XIII Encontro de Historia Anpuh-Rio, 4–7 August, 2008.
Petrone, Maria Thereza Schorer. *A Lavoura Canavieira em São Paulo*. São Paulo: Difusão Européia do Livro, 1968.
Petiz, Silmei de Sant'Ana. *Buscando a liberdade: As fugas de escravos da província de São Pedro para o além-fronteira, 1815–1851*. Passo Fundo, RS: Universidade de Passo Fundo, UPF Editora, 2006.
Pierson, Donald. *Negroes in Brazil: A Study of Race Contact at Bahia*. Chicago: University of Chicago Press, 1942.
Pinsky, Jaime. *A escravidão no Brasil*. São Paulo: Editora Contexto, 1988.
Pires, Maria de Fátima Novaes. *Crime na cor: Escravos e forros no alto sertão da Bahia (1830–1898)*. São Paulo: Annablume, 2003.
Porto, Ăngela. "Doenças e escravidão: Sistema de saúde e práticas terapêuticas." Rio de Janeiro: Casa de Oswaldo Cruz, 2007. CD.
Porter, Roy. *The Greatest Benefit to Mankind: A Medical History of Humanity*. New York: Norton, 1997.
Prado Júnior, Caio. *Formação do Brasil contemporăneo*. São Paulo: Livraria Martins Editora, 1942.
Read, Ian. "The Hemispheric Movement of Yellow Fever." Paper presented at the Tenth International Congress of the Brazilian Studies Association, Brasília, July 22–24, 2010.
———. "Off the Block But in the Neighborhood: Local Slave Trading in São Paulo." *Slavery and Abolition* (fall 2011).
———. "Sickness, Recovery, and Death among the Enslaved and Free People of Santos, Brazil, 1860–1888." *The Americas* 66, no. 1 (2009), 57–80.
———. "Unequally Bound: The Conditions of Slave Life and Treatment in Santos County, Brazil, 1822–1888." PhD diss., Stanford University, 2006.
———, and Kari Zimmerman. "Fugitive Slaves of the Brazilian Empire." Paper presented at the Fifteenth Annual Southern California Brazilian Studies Conference, Irvine, California, May 22, 2010.
Rĕgo, José Pereira. *Esboço histórico das epidemias que tem grassado na cidade*

do Rio de Janeiro desde 1830 a 1870. Rio de Janeiro: Typographia Nacional, 1872.

Reis, Isabel Cristina Ferreira dos. *Histórias de vida familiar e afetiva de escravos na Bahia do século XIX*. Centro de Estudos Baianos. Vol. 149. Salvador: Centro de Estudos Baianos; EDUFBA, 2001.

Reis, João José. *Death Is a Festival: Funeral Rites and Rebellion in Nineteenth century Brazil*. Latin America in Translation/en Traducción/em Tradução [Morte É uma Festa]. Chapel Hill: University of North Carolina Press, 2003.

———, and Eduardo Silva. *Negociação e conflicto*. Sõ Paulo: Companhia das Letras, 2005.

Reis, Thiago de Souza dos. "Doença e escravidão: Vassouras, 1865–1888." Rio de Janeiro, XIII Encontro de Historia Anpuh-Rio, 4–7 August 2008.

Ressurreição, Rosangela Dias da. *São Sebastião: Transformações de um povo caiçara*. São Paulo: Humanitas, 2002.

Rocha, Cristiany Miranda. *Histórias de famílias escravas: Campinas, século XIX*. Coleção Tempo e Memória. Vol. 1. Campinas, SP: Editora UNICAMP, 2004.

Rock, Howard B. *The New York City Artisan 1789–1825: A Documentary History*. SUNY Series in American Labor History. Albany: State University of New York Press, 1989.

Rodrigues, Olao. "Valongueiros e Quartaleiros." In *Cartilha da história de Santos, de Olao Rodrigues*. Santos, SP: n.p., 1980.

Rosemberg, André. *Ordem e Burla: Processos sociais, escravidão e justiça, Santos, década de 1880*. São Paulo: Alameda, 2006.

Russell-Wood, A.J.R. *Fidalgos and Philanthropists; the Santa Casa da Misericórdia of Bahia, 1550–1755*. Berkeley: University of California Press, 1968.

———. "Technology and Society: The Impact of Gold Mining on the Institution of Slavery in Portuguese America." *Journal of Economic History* 37 (1977), 59–83.

Salles, Vicente. *O negro no Pará: Sob o regime da escravidão*. Belém: Instituto de Artes do Pará, Programa Raízes, 2005.

Samara, Eni de Mesquita. *A família brasileira: Tudo é história*. São Paulo: Brasiliense, 1983.

Santos, Elizabeth Márcia dos. "Resistência escrava: As fugas de escravos em São João del Rei." http://www.ufsj.edu.br/portal2-repositorio/File/pghis/monografias/resistencia.pdf. Accessed September 7, 2010.

Santos, Francisco Martins dos. *Historia de Santos, 1532–1936*. São Paulo: Empreza Graphica da "Revista dos Tribunaes," 1937.

Schafer, Judith Kelleher. "New Orleans Slavery in 1850 as Seen in Advertisements." *Journal of Southern History* 47, no. 1 (1981), 33–56.

Schwartz, Stuart B. "The Manumission of Slaves in Colonial Brazil: Bahia, 1684–1745," *HAHR* 54, no. 4 (Nov. 1974).

———. "Patterns of Slaveholding in the Americas: New Evidence from Brazil." *The American Historical Review* 87, no. 1 (Feb. 1982), 55–86.

———. *Slaves, Peasants, and Rebels: Reconsidering Brazilian Slavery*. Blacks in the New World. Urbana: University of Illinois Press, 1992.

———. *Sugar Plantations in the Formation of Brazilian Society: Bahia, 1550–*

1835. Cambridge Latin American Studies. Vol. 52. Cambridge Cambridgeshire; New York: Cambridge University Press, 1985.

———. *Tropical Babylons: Sugar and the Making of the Atlantic World, 1450–1680*. Chapel Hill: University of North Carolina Press, 2004.

Sheridan, Richard B. *Doctors and Slaves: A Medical and Demographic History of Slavery in the British West Indies, 1680–1834*. Cambridge Cambridgeshire; New York: Cambridge University Press, 1985.

Siguad, J.F.X. *Do clima e das doenças do Brasil ou estatística médica deste império*. Rio de Janeiro: Editora Fiocruz, 2009.

Silva, Eduardo da. *Prince of the People: The Life and Times of a Brazilian Free Man of Colour*. London; New York: Verso, 1993.

Silva, José Bonifácio de Andrada, and Francisco de Assis Barbosa. *Discursos parlamentares*. Perfis Parlamentares. Vol. 13. Brasília: Cămara dos Deputados, 1978.

Silva, Marilene Rosa Nogueira da. *Negro na rua: A nova face da escravidão*. São Paulo: Editora Hucitec, 1988.

Sköld, Peter. "From Innoculation to Vaccination: Smallpox in Sweden in the Eighteenth and Nineteenth Centuries." *Population Studies* 50 (1996), 247–62.

Slenes, Robert W. "The Brazilian Internal Slave Trade, 1850–1888: Regional Economies, Slave Experience, and the Politics of the Peculiar Market." In *The Chattel Principle: Internal Slave Trades in the Americas*, edited by Walter Johnson. New Haven, CT: Yale University Press, 2004.

———. "The Demography and Economics of Brazilian Slavery, 1850–1888." PhD diss., Stanford University, 1975.

———. "Escravidão e família: Padrões de casamento e estabilidade familiar numa comunidade escrava (Campinas, Século XIX)." *Estudos Econŏmicos* 17, no. 2 (1987), 217–27.

———. *Na senzala, uma flor: Esperanças e recordações na formação da família escrava: Brasil sudeste, século XIX*. Coleção Histórias do Brasil. Rio de Janeiro: Editora Nova Fronteira, 1999.

———. *Os Múltiplos de Porcos e Diamantes: A Economia Escravista de Minas Gerais no Século XIX*. Cadernos IFCH UNICAMP. Vol. 17. Campinas: Comissão de Pós-graduação-IFCH-UNICAMP, 1985.

Soares, Luís Carlos. *O "povo de cam" na capital do Brasil: A escravidão urbana no Rio de Janeiro do século XIX*. Rio de Janeiro: 7 Letras, 2005.

Soares, Ubaldo. *A escravatura na Misericórdia*. Subsídios. Rio de Janero: Arquivista da Santa Casa, 1958.

Sobrinho, Costa e Silva. *Santos noutros tempos*. São Paulo, 1953.

Sousa, Alberto. *Os Andradas; Obra comemorativa do 1. centenário da independência do Brasil, mandada executar pela cămara municipal da cidade de Santos*. São Paulo: Typographia Piratininga, 1922.

Spix, Johann Baptist von, Karl Friedrich Philipp von Martius, Ernst Winkler, and Johann Baptist von Spix. *Viagem pelo Brasil: 1817–1820*. São Paulo: Edições Melhoramentos, 1976.

Stampp, Kenneth M. *The Peculiar Institution: Slavery in the Ante-Bellum South*. 1st ed. New York: Knopf, 1956.

Stein, Stanley J. *Vassouras, a Brazilian Coffee County, 1850–1900: The Roles of Planter and Slave in a Plantation Society*. Princeton, NJ: Princeton University Press, 1985.

Stewart, C. S. *Brazil and La Plata: The Personal Record of a Cruise*. New York: G.P. Putnam & Co, 1856.

Summerhill III, William R. *Order Against Progress: Government, Foreign Investment, and Railroads in Brazil, 1854–1913*. Stanford, CA: Stanford University Press, 2003.

Tait, Robert Lawson. *An Essay on Hospital Mortality, Based upon the Statistics of the Hospitals of Great Britain for Fifteen Years*. London: Churchill, 1877.

Tannenbaum, Frank. *Slave and Citizen*. Boston: Beacan Press, 1992.

Tavares, Mauro Dillmann. *Irmandades, igreja e devoção no sul no Império do Brasil*. São Leopoldo, RS: Editora Oikos, 2008.

Teixeira, Helenal Maria. "Reprodução e famílias escravas em Mariana (1880–1888)." Diamantina, Minas Gerais, Brazil, X Seminário sobre a Economia Mineira, COLDEPLAR, 18–22 June 2002.

Telarolli Junior, Rodolpho. "Immigração e epidemias no estado de São Paulo." *Manginhos* 3, no. 2 (1996), 265–83.

Toplin, Robert Brent. *The Abolition of Slavery in Brazil*. New York: Atheneum, 1972.

———. "Upheaval, Violence, and the Abolition of Slavery in Brazil: The Case of Sao Paulo." *Hispanic American Historical Review* 49, no. 4 (1969), 639–55,

United States Department of State. "Letters from Consul William T. Wright in Santos to the Assistant Secretary of State, 29 September 1882 and 12 July 1883." In *Dispatches from United States Consuls in Santos, 1831–1906*. Washington, DC: National Archives, National Archives and Records Service, General Services Administration.

Vasconcellos, Márcia Cristina de. "Casar ou não, Eis a questão. Os casais e as mães solteiras escravas no litoral sul-fluminense, 1830–1881." *Estudos Afro-Asiáticos* 24, no. 2 (2002).

———. "Estrutura de posse de escravos em Angra dos Reis, século XIX." Caxambu, Minas Gerais, Brazil," *Anais do V Congresso Brasileiro de História Econômica e 6ª Conferência Internacional de História*, ABPHE, September 7–10, 2003.

Viana, Larissa. *O idioma da mestiçagem: As irmandades de pardos na América portuguesa*. Campinas, SP: Editora Unicamp, 2007.

Wade, Richard C. *Slavery in the Cities: The South, 1820–1860*. New York: Oxford University Press, 1964.

Weber, Max, and Richard Swedberg. *Essays in Economic Sociology*. Princeton, NJ: Princeton University Press, 1999.

———, Guenther Roth, and Claus Wittich. *Economy and Society: An Outline of Interpretive Sociology*. Berkeley: University of California Press, 1978.

White, S., and G. White. "Slave Clothing and African-American Culture in the Eighteenth and Nineteenth Centuries." *Past and Present* 148 (1995), 149–86.

Whitman, T. Stephen. *The Price of Freedom: Slavery and Manumission in Balti-*

more and Early National Maryland. Lexington: University Press of Kentucky, 1997.

Wileman, J. P. "*The Brazilian Year Book; Issued under the Patronage of the Brazilian Government. 1st–2nd Issue; 1908–1909.*" Rio de Janeiro: Offices of the Brazilian Year Book, 1909, 1908.

Williams, Mary Wilhelmine. "The Treatment of Negro Slaves in the Brazilian Empire: A Comparison with the United States of America." *Journal of Negro History* 15, no. 3 (July 1930), 315–36.

Wissenbach, Maria Cristina Cortez. *Sonhos africanos, vivěncias ladinas: Escravos e forros em São Paulo, 1850–1880*. São Paulo: Editora Hucitec, 1998.

Zaluar, Augusto Emílio. *Peregrinação pela província de S. Paulo (1860–1861)*. São Paulo: Livraria Martins Editora, 1953.

Index

Page numbers followed by *f*, *n*, or *t* indicate figures, notes, or tables, respectively.